Psychological Perspectives *on*

Understanding *and* Addressing

Violence Against Children

Psychological Perspectives *on* Understanding *and* Addressing Violence Against Children

Towards Building Cultures of Peace

EDITED BY

SCOTT L. MOESCHBERGER &

LAURA E. MILLER-GRAFF

OXFORD
UNIVERSITY PRESS

OXFORD
UNIVERSITY PRESS

Oxford University Press is a department of the University of Oxford. It furthers the University's objective of excellence in research, scholarship, and education by publishing worldwide. Oxford is a registered trade mark of Oxford University Press in the UK and certain other countries.

Published in the United States of America by Oxford University Press
198 Madison Avenue, New York, NY 10016, United States of America.

Library of Congress Cataloging-in-Publication Data
Names: Moeschberger, Scott L., editor. | Miller-Graff, Laura E., editor.
Title: Psychological perspectives on understanding and addressing violence against children : towards building cultures of peace / Scott L. Moeschberger, Laura E. Miller-Graff.
Description: New York, NY : Oxford University Press, [2023] | Includes bibliographical references and index.
Identifiers: LCCN 2022019640 (print) | LCCN 2022019641 (ebook) | ISBN 9780197649510 (paperback) | ISBN 9780197649534 (epub) | ISBN 9780197649541
Subjects: LCSH: Children—Crimes against. | Children and violence. | Abused children—Psychology.
Classification: LCC HV6250.4.C48 P78 2022 (print) | LCC HV6250.4.C48 (ebook) | DDC 362.88083—dc23/eng/20220706
LC record available at https://lccn.loc.gov/2022019640
LC ebook record available at https://lccn.loc.gov/2022019641

DOI: 10.1093/med-psych/9780197649510.001.0001

9 8 7 6 5 4 3 2 1

Printed by Marquis, Canada

CONTENTS

Violence is one of the most destructive and significant challenges to the development, growth, well-being, and survival of children, youth, and adults in every nation. In the prepandemic era, the magnitude and consequences of such violence were already shocking. For example, worldwide data confirmed that one of every two children under age 18 experiences serious sexual, physical, or emotional abuse every year; such violence increases the lifelong risk of death from every major cause of death across nations, cultures, and contexts.

The pandemic exacerbated the threats of the already-ubiquitous violence by increasing both their frequency and intensity. At the time of this writing, the COVID-19 pandemic has led to nearly 7 million deaths and over 7 million children facing COVID-19–associated orphanhood and caregiver death. These deaths, along with extensive social, economic, political, and public health upheaval, have thrown the public and private sectors, as well as community and faith support sectors, into far-reaching disarray. Specifically, the pandemic has accelerated the synergistic convergence of destructive, pervasive, enduring, and escalating threats of social macrosystems and microsystems of violence, as addressed by the authors in this volume. The pandemic has further thrown into the level of emergency the need to rapidly accelerate successful policies and programs that build peace within both macrosystems and microsystems.

Yet, there is hope. Heads of state from every nation agreed, in the 2030 Sustainable Development Goals, to promote peaceful and inclusive societies for sustainable development, the provision of access to justice for all, and building accountable institutions at all levels. Because of the pandemic's rampant destruction across systems, stakeholders, sectors, and society, the urgency of promoting peace has never been greater. The authors of this volume have made a welcome contribution that helps link the urgent global challenges to the converging hope of multiplying peace through multisystemic transformation.

As a welcome surprise, the coauthors paint a new picture—for a pandemic of peace.

Susan Hillis, PhD, MS
Senior Research Fellow, University of Oxford
Former CDC Senior Technical Advisor, Global Health
Lead Coauthor of *INSPIRE: Seven Strategies for Ending Violence Against Children*

Alhassan Abdullah, BA, Doctoral Student, Social Work and Social Administration, University of Hong Kong

Donte L. Bernard, PhD, Assistant Professor of Clinical Psychology, University of Missouri

Neil Boothby, EdD, Professor and Director, Global Center for the Development of the Whole Child; University of Notre Dame

E. Mark Cummings, PhD, Professor of Psychology, University of Notre Dame

Clifton R. Emery, PhD, Associate Professor of Social Work and Social Administration, University of Hong Kong, SAR

Fundación para la Reconciliación, Colombia

Cynthia García Coll, PhD, Charles Pitts Robinson and John Palmer Barstow Professor Emerita, Brown University

Sadiyya Haffejee, PhD, Senior Researcher, Centre for Social Development in Africa, University of Johannesburg

Mahmoud Hammoud, MS, Monitoring, Evaluation, Accountability, and Learning Officer, Syrian American Medical Society Foundation

Tobias Hecker, PhD, Assistant Professor of Developmental and Clinical Psychology, Bielefeld University

Katharin Hermenau, PhD, Senior Researcher, Clinic for Child and Adolescent Psychiatry and Psychotherapy, University Hospital OWL of Bielefeld University

Kathryn H. Howell, PhD, Associate Professor of Psychology, The University of Memphis

Fabio Idrobo, PhD, Investigador Asociado, Salud Poblacional, Fundación Santa Fe de Bogotá

Savannah L. Johnson, MA, Psychology and Neuroscience, Duke Global Health Institute, Duke University

Åsa Källström, PhD, Professor of Social Work, Örebro University

Kelly Kinnish, PhD, Director of the National Center on Child Trafficking, School of Public Health, Georgia State University

Kathleen Kostelny, PhD, Senior Research Associate, Child Resilience Alliance

Michelle Lee, BA, Undergraduate Research Assistant, University of Notre Dame

Rose E. Luehrs, MA, Doctoral Student, Psychology, Suffolk University

Catherine Maloney, MSc, Doctoral Student, Psychology and Peace Studies, University of Notre Dame

Amy K. Marks, PhD, Professor of Psychology, Suffolk University

Cecilia Martinez-Torteya, PhD, Associate Professor of Education, Universidad de Monterrey

Faustine Bwire Masath, MA, Doctoral Student in Psychology and Scholar of Deutscher Akademischer Austauschdienst (DAAD), Bielefeld University

Laura E. Miller-Graff, PhD, Associate Professor of Psychology and Peace Studies, University of Notre Dame

Abigail L. Mills, PhD, Postdoctoral Fellow in Child Development, Global Center Development of the Whole Child, University of Notre Dame

Scott L. Moeschberger, PhD, Professor of Global Studies, Taylor University

Taylor R. Napier, MS, Doctoral Student, Psychology, The University of Memphis

Mabula Nkuba, PhD, Lecturer in Educational Psychology, Dar es Salaam University College of Education (DUCE), University of Dar es Salaam

Kathryn O'Hara, BS, Graduate Student, Public Health, Georgia State University

Ken Ondoro, MA, Research Associate, Child Resilience Alliance

Elizabeth Perry, MPH, Doctoral Student, Public Health, Georgia State University Programa Nacional de Educación para la paz—Educapaz, Colombia

Eve S. Puffer, PhD, Assistant Professor, Psychology and Neuroscience, Duke Global Health Institute, Duke University

Solfrid Raknes, PhD, Project Leader and Clinical Psychologist, Innovation Norway

Katherine Reuben, MPH, Graduate, Public Health, Georgia State University

Regina Roberg, MS, Doctoral Student, Psychology, Suffolk University

Shukrani Salvatory, BA, Research Associate, Child Resilience Alliance

Shannon Self-Brown, PhD, Professor of Public Health, Co-Director of National SafeCare Training and Research Center, Georgia State University

Ygal Sharon, BSc, Research Associate, Child Resilience Alliance

Amanda L. Sim, DPhil, Assistant Professor, Department of Psychiatry and Behavioural Neurosciences, McMaster University

Effua E. Sosoo, PhD, Postdoctoral Fellow, Durham Veterans Affairs Health Care System, University of North Carolina at Chapel Hill

Joseph Ssenyonga, PhD, Senior Lecturer, Department of Educational Foundations and Psychology, Mbarara University of Science and Technology (MUST)

Linda Theron, DEd, Full Professor, Department of Educational Psychology, University of Pretoria

Kari N. Thomsen, BS, Doctoral Student, Psychology, The University of Memphis

Dana Townsend, PhD, Mental Health and Psychosocial Support Specialist, Syrian American Medical Society Foundation

Michael Ungar, PhD, Canada Research Chair in Child, Family, and Community Resilience; Director, Resilience Research Centre; Scientific Director, Child and Youth Refugee Research Coalition, Dalhousie University

Gabriel Velez, PhD, Assistant Professor of Educational Policy and Leadership, Marquette University

Bethany Wentz, MA, Doctoral Student, Psychology, University of Notre Dame

Michael G. Wessells, PhD, Professor of Clinical Population and Family Health, Columbia University

BreeAnna White, BA, Graduate, Department of Global Studies, Taylor University

Henry A. Willis, PhD, Postdoctoral Research Scientist, Columbia University School of Social Work

Building Peace From the Ground Up

Global Efforts to Understand and Address Violence Against Children

LAURA E. MILLER-GRAFF, SCOTT L. MOESCHBERGER, AND
CATHERINE A. MALONEY ■

AUTHOR NOTE

The development of this work was supported by the Kroc Institute for International Peace Studies via the Visiting Fellows program. Dr. Moeschberger was in residence as a visiting fellow during fall 2019.

Violence against children (VAC) is one of the most significant, widespread, and preventable threats to human development in our world today. Not only does VAC have direct consequences for children in myriad domains, including physical health, mental health, educational outcomes, and social relationships (e.g., Fry et al., 2018; Hughes et al., 2017; Noonan & Pilkington, 2020; Norman et al., 2012), but emerging research also suggests that the incredible stress induced by VAC may result in the intergenerational transmission of negative outcomes, conferred through a variety of pathways. For example, children impacted by VAC may view violence as an acceptable method of conflict resolution and be more likely to engage in violent behaviors as they grow into adulthood, thus modeling violence for future generations (Affolter & Valente, 2019; Britto et al., 2014; Donaldson et al., 2018; Yale University & Mother Child Education Foundation [AÇEV] Partnership, 2012). Although VAC has been extensively studied in psychology, an approach that incorporates frameworks from peace studies is useful for understanding VAC in its broader social context, articulating the complex, compounding, and intersecting forms of violence and oppression experienced by children and placing research within its sociohistorical setting (Christie, 2021;

Wessells & Kostelny, 2021). Further, the integration of peace studies frameworks in research on VAC presses scholars to consider prevention of multiple types of violence, including direct, structural, and cultural forms of violence. Peace psychology perspectives thus advance the importance of multisectoral supports that facilitate a just and sustainable peace for children, promoting multigenerational health and well-being. While these approaches may directly benefit the development and flourishing of children, they also inherently stand to benefit society as a whole (Leckman et al., 2014).

DEFINING VIOLENCE AGAINST CHILDREN

Historically, psychological research defined violence as "behavior that is (a) intentional, (b) unwanted, (c) nonessential, and (d) harmful" (Hamby, 2017, p. 167). Such definitions readily capture direct forms of violence that are clearly observable, are measurable, and occur at the individual level. These definitions also effectively capture a broad range of VAC and generally reflect categories of analysis that are fairly well studied (e.g., child maltreatment). In the past decade, psychological research on direct violence increasingly employed a polyvictimization framework (Hamby & Grych, 2013). Development of this framework has sought to combat the "siloing" of studies on violence into distinct domains, which masks the extent to which different types of violence are interrelated. Research has also demonstrated that understanding co-occurrence of violence has important implications for better describing variations in developmental outcomes and trajectories of risk, as the effects of violence are both additive and compounding over the lifespan (Ford & Delker, 2018).

The empirical work on polyvictimization has been viewed by many psychologists as having a parallel resonance with intersectionality (de Oliveira Ramos et al., 2021), or the ways in which intersecting matrices of individual sameness and difference interact with the dynamic, compounding forces of power and oppression (Cho et al., 2013). Though polyvictimization stems from a different epistemological framework than much of intersectional theory and its applications, psychologists have nonetheless taken seriously the ways in which violence, oppression, and injustice interact, further expanding polyvictimization frameworks to include identity-based experiences of victimization and discrimination (e.g., Garcini et al., 2018; Sugarman et al., 2018). Further, researchers have documented that polyvictimization itself occurs disproportionately: historic marginalization and legacies of colonialism not only affect identity-based forms of victimization (e.g., experiences of discrimination) but also increase risks of other types of victimization (de Oliveira Ramos et al., 2021).

Thus, the integration of peace studies frameworks advances understandings of VAC in psychological research and practice, acknowledging that VAC can occur in many systems, that these systems are dynamically interrelated, and that they can coproduce and reproduce various forms of violence (Wessells & Kostelny, 2021). This approach recognizes that direct forms of VAC do not arise "in a vacuum" but interrelate with ongoing forms of structural and cultural violence. *Structural violence* typically refers to "violence that is 'built into' the structure and shows up as unequal power and consequently as unequal life chances" (Galtung, 1969, p. 171; Weigert, 2008), while *cultural violence* refers to "aspects of culture . . . that can be used to justify or legitimize direct or structural violence" (Galtung, 1996, p. 196). To effectively integrate structural and cultural forms of violence into psychological theory and practice, psychologists move toward contextualizing psychological research within a sophisticated structural analysis of the broader systems individuals inhabit. This lens is important because, as contemporary peace theorists note,

in many cases, the power of structural violence consists precisely in its capacity to hold exploitative, repressive, and dehumanizing conditions in place without producing direct or deadly violence. In fact, frequently, it is in virtue of not leading to direct violence or deadly conflict that structural violence avoids drawing attention to itself in ways that direct forms of violence typically do, thereby attracting the recognition and intervention of those concerned to understand and combat direct violence (or structural violence identifiably related to direct violence). (Springs, 2015, p. 157)

Thus, this volume highlights not only the direct forms of VAC that are present around the world but also structural and cultural forms of VAC that are situated within legacies of collective and historical trauma. This volume thus shares Wessells and Kostelny's (2021) understanding of VAC as inclusive of direct, structural, and cultural forms of violence that unfold across time throughout diverse social-ecological systems. Further, and consistent with polyvictimization and intersectional frameworks (Hamby & Grych, 2013; Cho et al., 2013), this volume frames forms of VAC as intersecting, coproducing, and compounding. Chapters in this volume also reflect the use of diverse methods, including both quantitative and qualitative forms of inquiry. In an intentional effort to emphasize local voices and perspectives, the incorporated methods highlight not only ways in which children's experiences of violence can be assessed quantitatively but also ways in which ethnographic and qualitative modes of inquiry can highlight "silent" forms of structural violence that undergird and quietly promulgate harm against children.

NAVIGATING THIS VOLUME

In addition to the consideration of a multiplicity of forms of violence against children from family violence (Chapter 8, Howell et al.) to trafficking (Chapter 7, Kinnish et al.), this volume also includes analyses of ways in which direct, structural, and cultural forms of violence interact to produce unique manifestations of violence particular to specific contexts, such as during migration (Chapter 4, Marks et al.) or in refugee camps (Chapter 15, Townsend et al.; Chapter 12, Boothby et al.). This volume also addresses pressing questions about the intersection of different forms of violence as they pertain to practice and policy. For example, Puffer and colleagues note that interventions for VAC must acknowledge and address the incredible burden of poverty (Chapter 13), and Theron and colleagues describe the ways in which youths' access to key resources may be depleted through historic and intergenerational structural violence (Chapter 5).

It is important to recognize that this volume is best understood as a Gestalt: although each chapter takes up a particular form of violence as a focal point and is often grounded in a specific local context, the intersecting and mutually reinforcing nature of different forms of violence as well as transnational norms and processes that perpetuate violence are clearly evident. Wessells and colleagues (Chapter 10), for example, highlight the intersection of structural and episodic forms of violence in girls' experiences of sexual violence in Kenya. Bernard and colleagues (Chapter 6) highlight how common understandings of "adverse childhood experiences," or ACEs, in the United States are woefully incomplete without understanding and identifying the ways in which these experiences are inextricably linked to how racism is embedded across social-ecological systems. Together, these chapters provide a robust mapping of the complex interplay of violence within and across children's lives and provide insights into how supports for families and children can better address this reality to prevent violence and promote well-being.

SECTION I: VIOLENCE AGAINST CHILDREN IN SOCIAL MACROSYSTEMS

The first section of this volume focuses on violence in social macrosystems. In social-ecological models, macrosystems are defined as

> the overarching institutional patterns of the culture or subculture, such as the economic, social, educational, legal, and political systems. . . . Macrosystems are conceived and examined not only in structural terms but as carriers of information and ideology that, both explicitly and implicitly, endow meaning and motivation to particular agencies, social networks, roles, activities, and their interrelations. (Bronfenbrenner, 1977, p. 515)

Thus, in this section we include chapters that take up (as a primary focus) ways in which broader political or social infrastructures exert violence on children.

In Chapter 2, Cummings and colleagues provide an overview of the literature on the developmental effects of exposure to political violence and armed conflict, with a particular focus on research conducted in the context of Northern Ireland. Their work provides a strong example of how social-ecological perspectives can be meaningfully put to purpose to understand how violence in social macrosystems interacts with and is modified by relationships in other social-ecological systems (e.g., peer relationships, family relationships). Further, the longitudinal nature of this team's work highlights the ways in which violence—and particularly ideologically motivated violence—promulgates cascading negative effects across systems over time. Chapter 3, by Velez and colleagues, provides an overview of the literature on youth combatants, including motivations for joining armed groups, youth needs during demobilization, and mental health and psychosocial support. Grounding their broader analysis in the specific context of Colombia, Velez and colleagues highlight the ways in which the structures put into place for youth demobilization and reintegration have failed to fully address underlying forms of structural violence that motivated youth engagement in armed conflict, thereby weakening the extent to which youths' postconflict psychosocial needs can be effectively met. They describe programs working to address these "silent" forms of violence and inequity, denaturalizing violence and promoting positive peace through education, advocacy, and community social rebuilding.

Chapter 4, by Marks and colleagues, brings to the fore another key global impact of sociopolitical violence: migration. Consistent with polyvictimization and intersectionality, their research review highlights the multiple forms of VAC and severe hardship experienced in the context of forced migration. Taking a developmental perspective that considers how VAC unfolds across the migration experience, Mark and colleagues' work underscores not only the prevalence and harmful effects of direct violence throughout children's migration experiences but also the ways in which dehumanizing migration infrastructures and policies further perpetuate harm. They conclude that national and international legal and social norms that actively seek to eliminate oppression, xenophobia, and discrimination provide a critical foundation for psychosocial supports for children and families.

Theron and colleagues (Chapter 5) also poignantly highlight the intersection of structural and direct violence in the lives of youth, describing findings from a qualitative, community-based participatory research study in South Africa. Notably, participating youth described ways in which structural violence not only produces inequity but also serves to repress hope for a better future. Theron and colleagues also contextualize these data within the broader social context, noting the intersecting forces of capitalism and the historical legacy of apartheid and its contemporary social manifestations. Nonetheless, many youth underscored the importance of not only personal agency but also the structural supports that enabled that agency to effect meaningful change; thus, Theron and colleagues highlight ways in which work to combat structural VAC must necessarily be integrated into multisectoral efforts pursuing justice.

Turning to the United States and bridging our sections on violence in macrosystems and microsystems, Bernard and colleagues (Chapter 6) highlight the ways in which racism in the United States pervades Black children's social environments, appearing across systems (e.g., schools, neighborhoods, media) and appearing in a multiplicity of forms, including in direct, structural, and cultural forms of violence. As do many of the chapters in this volume, their work underscores the importance of measuring, understanding, and redressing violence as a complex construct. By articulating the multisystemic and multifaceted nature of racism, Bernard and colleagues advance a compelling foundation for the integration of psychological supports with "systemic and policy-based approaches [that] are needed to reduce the adverse societal conditions that undergird the etiology of violence among marginalized communities both domestically and globally."

SECTION II: VIOLENCE AGAINST CHILDREN
IN SOCIAL MICROSYSTEMS

The second section of this volume focuses on violence in social microsystems. According to Bronfenbrenner, social microsystems are understood as "the complex relations between the developing person and environment in an immediate setting containing that person (e.g., home, school, workplace, etc.)" (Bronfenbrenner, 1977, p. 514). For children, immediate social-relational settings include their families, schools, and neighborhoods. Unfortunately, many of these social environments, which are supposed to be places of safety and security for children, are also threatened by ongoing violence. As many of our authors in this section highlight, legal provisions for the protection of children in these settings are necessary but insufficient to prevent violence. Thus, the successful prevention and amelioration of interpersonal forms of violence necessitates a comprehensive agenda that considers variations in understandings of how violence is defined, ways in which attitudes and beliefs promulgate VAC, the structural elements that contribute to direct forms of violence, and ways in which families and communities can be effectively engaged in the development and implementation of evidence-based interventions.

Chapter 7, by Kinnish and colleagues, focuses on the convergence of these multiple, intersecting forms of risk in the context of child trafficking. Specifically, they highlight ways in which violence in children's social microsystems—including maltreatment, family violence, foster care, and sexual assault—compounds with forms of structural violence (e.g., poverty, gender-based violence) and cultural violence (e.g., marginalization), all of which converge to increase children's vulnerability to trafficking. They emphasize that the key to reintegration is not only evidence-based interventions to address the psychological effects of trafficking but also work oriented toward rebuilding healthy and robust social microsystems that can support and protect children from being retrafficked.

Similarly, the chapter by Howell and colleagues (Chapter 8) examines the convergence of various forms of family violence (i.e., maltreatment and exposure to intimate partner violence). Using two contextually focused literature reviews in Sweden and Mexico, Howell and colleagues demonstrate how structural forms of violence and cultural norms uniquely intersect to foment family violence or to create "blind" spots in research, practice, and policy. As do many of the chapters in this volume, the work by Howell and colleagues not only highlights the universal harms caused by VAC in family settings but also advances the importance of a contextually grounded and particularistic analysis of the unique sociocultural manifestation of violence in context. Together, this chapter underscores the importance of contextually grounded prevention and intervention programs that take into account the sociocultural dynamics of family violence.

Building on the complex, intersecting forces that contribute to VAC in children's microsystems, Moeschberger and White (Chapter 9) examine the global literature on children who enter institutional care—due to either familial loss, violence, or dissolution of the family unit. Their work highlights the pattern of compounding risks for children living in institutional settings, underscoring the importance of structural supports that enable children who have experienced familial loss to have access to stable, family-like settings that include supportive, ongoing care.

In Chapter 10, Wessells and colleagues examine ways in which direct and structural forms of violence interact in the context of urban slums in Kenya, highlighting the contributing roles of unequal power relations and patriarchal influences in sexual exploitation of teenage girls. Importantly, they note that the relationship between direct and structural forms of violence is not linear, but *circular*, with direct forms of violence reinforcing the power structures that enable them. They urge researchers, practitioners, and policy makers not to let the complexity of violence to inaction—rather, they reinforce the possibility that "deep" change, even on complex social issues, is imminently possible.

SECTION III: PRACTICE AND POLICY TO REDRESS VIOLENCE AGAINST CHILDREN

Many psychologists are trained at the nexus of research and practice and, as such, are uniquely equipped to navigate questions about translational work. The closing section of this volume focuses on approaches to redressing VAC, all of which are rooted in the reflexive relationship between research and practice, and like the first two sections of the volume, situates programmatic evaluations in the broader social context of VAC.

Schools represent a key social environment for young children. In Chapter 11, Hecker and colleagues highlight the high prevalence of VAC in school settings, detailing the adverse consequences on children's health and development. They review several evidence-based intervention strategies that hold promise of effectiveness, underscoring the importance of brief, teacher-focused, and school-based interventions that can address the diverse drivers of VAC in school settings.

In addition to violence in school settings, children's educational contexts may also be disrupted by large-scale conflict and migration. In Chapter 12, Boothby and colleagues examine the experiences of children whose education had been disrupted by conflict and/or displacement and who were enrolled in accelerated education programs (AEPs) in Tanzania and the Democratic Republic of Congo. Findings from their study highlight the potential promise of AEPs for children's educational outcomes but also underscores key challenges for children related to intersecting social and environmental risks, including separation from caregivers, poverty, and differential school dropout for children highly exposed to violence.

They conclude that multisectoral approaches to education that address not only educational needs but also social and emotional ones are warranted.

Together, these two chapters highlight ways in which school-based prevention and intervention may be effectively combined to create wraparound programmatic supports for children in order to both prevent violence and address the diverse needs of at-risk populations. What is not reviewed in this volume but is also important to note is that school settings may be a promising context for the delivery of other mental health and psychosocial support services that contribute to children's holistic well-being. This is an important area for continued work. Although social and emotional learning programs have an established evidence basis in Western contexts (Durlak et al., 2011), they have had greater difficulty establishing consistent and long-term effectiveness in conflict-affected settings (Aber et al., 2021). Similarly, delivering trauma-focused services in school settings has had mixed support, with some evidence of effectiveness, but also concerns about potential iatrogenic effects (Ertl & Neuner, 2014; Tol et al., 2012). Yet school settings are an important system for children, and if effective interventions and delivery mechanisms for psychosocial care in school settings can be further developed, such interventions would be a significant contribution to the network of supportive care for violence-exposed children (Miller-Graff, 2021).

Moving to family systems, Chapter 13 by Puffer and colleagues examines how interventions in low- and middle-income (LMIC) and conflict-affected settings can flexibly address the integrated goals of violence prevention, violence reduction, promotion of protective factors, and remediation of the adverse consequences of violence (e.g., psychological distress). Their model for family- and community-level approaches to care highlights the importance of integrated models that reflect the simultaneous pursuit of both negative and positive forms of peace at multiple levels. Importantly, they highlight a number of critical implementation strategies that promote sustainable and relevant interventions, including task sharing and community engagement.

Emery and Abdullah (Chapter 14) advance understandings of how formal and informal social controls can be used to prevent and address family violence. They review the literature on the effectiveness of policy approaches to reduce family violence and consider how turning from punitive approaches toward protective and restorative approaches may further advance the sustainable protection of children and promotion of familial health. They emphasize not only the importance of understanding the social context in which violence occurs but also how practice and policy can better respond to family heterogeneity within context.

Townsend and colleagues' (Chapter 15) chapter advances research on sustainable forms of psychosocial care, reviewing and evaluating a digital psychosocial support program, *Helping Hand*, with Syrian youth living in refugee camps in Lebanon. The *Helping Hand* intervention, which seeks to promote emotional awareness and well-being as well as interpersonal functioning, demonstrated promising initial evidence of effectiveness. Importantly, Townsend and colleagues attribute the effectiveness of the approach to a participatory method of program development, which enhanced the extent to which the program reflected youth's specific needs as well as values and social norms.

CONCLUSIONS

Together, this volume provides an overview of the global literature on VAC, with each chapter situated in a particular, specific context. Researchers will benefit from the diverse methodological insights of our authors—a wide variety of rigorous approaches are used, and together, it is clear how methodological plurality contributes to a more integrative, complete understanding of VAC. In each chapter, practitioners will find insights into evidence-based methods of intervention and prevention, as well as future directions for program development. Policymakers will find the broad framing of VAC—in particular, the ways in which each chapter elaborates how it is fomented by other, co-occurring forms of violence and injustice—useful for more deeply considering how local and global policies can better address the complex systems that underlie VAC in pursuit of policies that create just and sustainable change. A full explication of the implications of the work of this volume for research, practice, and policy can be found in Chapter 16. It is also important to recognize that this volume, while comprehensive, is not exhaustive. We therefore encourage researchers, practitioners, and policymakers to seek out additional, context-specific resources that support a holistic understanding and analysis of the dynamic and multisystemic processes at play relative to VAC in their setting .

REFERENCES

Aber, J. L., Dolan, C. T., Kim, H. Y., & Brown, L. (2021). Children's learning and development in conflict-and crisis-affected countries: Building a science for action. *Development and Psychopathology, 33*(2), 506–521. https://doi.org/10.1017/S09545 79420001789

Affolter, F. W., & Valente, A. A. (2019). Learning for peace: Lessons learned from UNICEF's peacebuilding, education, and advocacy in conflict-affected context programme. In N. Balvin & D. J. Christie (Eds.), *Children and peace: From research to action* (pp. 219–239). Springer. https://doi.org/10.1007/978-3-030-22176-8_14

Britto, P. R., Gordon, I., Hodges, W., Sunar, D., Kagitcibasi, C., & Leckman, J. F. (2014). Ecology of peace. In J. F. Leckman, C. Panter-Brick, & R. Salah (Eds.), *Pathway to peace: The transformative power of children and families* (pp. 27–39). MIT Press. http://doi.org/10.7551/mitpress/9780262027984.001.0001

Bronfenbrenner, U. (1977). Toward an experimental ecology of human development. *American Psychologist, 32*(7), 513–531. https://doi.org/10.1037/0003-066X.32.7.513

Cho, S., Crenshaw, K. W., & McCall, L. (2013). Toward a field of intersectionality studies: Theory, applications, and praxis. *Signs: Journal of Women in Culture and Society, 38*(4), 785–810. https://doi.org/10.1086/669608

Christie, D. J. (2021). The moonshot and ending violence against children. *Peace and Conflict: Journal of Peace Psychology, 27*(1), 39–41. https://doi.org/10.1037/pac 0000514

de Oliveira Ramos, D., Goes, E. F., & Ferreira, A. J. F. (2021). Intersection of race and gender in self-reports of violent experiences and polyvictimization by young girls in Brazil. *Journal of Racial and Ethnic Health Disparities, 9*, 1–11. https://doi.org/ 10.1007/s40615-021-01089-2

Donaldson, C. K., Affolter, F. W., Ponguta, L. A., Salah, R., Britto, P. R., Leckman, J., Connolly, P., Fitzpatrick, S., & Walmsley, P. (2018). *Contributions of early childhood development programming to sustainable peace and development.* Early Childhood Peace Consortium. https://ecdpeace.org/sites/default/files/files/background_paper _ecpc_issues_brief_2018.pdf

Durlak, J. A., Weissberg, R. P., Dymnicki, A. B., Taylor, R. D., & Schellinger, K. B. (2011). The impact of enhancing students' social and emotional learning: A meta-analysis of school-based universal interventions. *Child Development, 82*(1), 405–432. https:// doi.org/10.1111/j.1467-8624.2010.01564.x

Ertl, V., & Neuner, F. (2014). Are school-based mental health interventions for war-affected children effective and harmless? *BMC Medicine, 12*(1), 1–4. https://doi.org/ 10.1186/1741-7015-12-84

Ford, J. D., & Delker, B. C. (2018). Polyvictimization in childhood and its adverse impacts across the lifespan: Introduction to the special issue. *Journal of Trauma & Dissociation, 3*, 275–288. https://doi.org/10.1080/15299732.2018.1440479

Fry, D., Fang, X., Elliott, S., Casey, T., Zheng, X., Li, J., . . . McCluskey, G. (2018). The relationships between violence in childhood and educational outcomes: A global systematic review and meta-analysis. *Child Abuse & Neglect, 75,* 6–28. https://doi. org/10.1016/j.chiabu.2017.06.021

Galtung, J. (1969). Violence, peace, and peace research. *Journal of Peace Research, 6*(3), 167–191. https://doi.org/10.1177/002234336900600301

Galtung, J. (1996). *Peace by peaceful means: Peace and conflict, development and civiliza-tion.* SAGE Publications Ltd. http://dx.doi.org/10.4135/9781446221631

Garcini, L. M., Chen, M. A., Brown, R. L., Galvan, T., Saucedo, L., Berger Cardoso, J. A., & Fagundes, C. P. (2018). Kicks hurt less: Discrimination predicts distress beyond trauma among undocumented Mexican immigrants. *Psychology of Violence, 8*(6), 692–701. https://doi.org/10.1037/vio0000205

Hamby, S. (2017). On defining violence, and why it matters [Editorial]. *Psychology of Violence, 7*(2), 167–180. https://doi.org/10.1037/vio0000117

Hamby, S., & Grych, J. H. (2013). *The web of violence: Exploring connections among dif-ferent forms of interpersonal violence and abuse.* Springer.

Hughes, K., Bellis, M. A., Hardcastle, K. A., Sethi, D., Butchart, A., Mikton, C., . . . Dunne, M. P. (2017). The effect of multiple adverse childhood experiences on health: A sys-tematic review and meta-analysis. *Lancet Public Health, 2*(8), e356–e366. https:// doi.org/10.1016/S2468-2667(17)30118-4

Leckman, J., Panter-Brick, C., & Salah, R. (2014). Peace is a lifelong process: The impor-tance of partnerships. In J. Leckman, C. Panter-Brick, & R. Salah (Eds.), *Pathways to peace: The transformative power of children and families* (pp. 3–17). Strüngman Forum Reports.

Miller-Graff, L. (2021). Supporting mental health in conflict-affected settings: Effectiveness, innovation, and contemporary challenges. In J. G. Kestenbaum, C. O. Mahoney, A. E. Meade & A. F. Fuller (Eds.), *Public health, mental health, and mass atrocity prevention* (pp. 32–49). Routledge.

Noonan, C. B., & Pilkington, P. D. (2020). Intimate partner violence and child attachment: A systematic review and meta-analysis. *Child Abuse & Neglect, 109*, 104765. https://doi.org/10.1016/j.chiabu.2020.104765

Norman, R. E., Byambaa, M., De, R., Butchart, A., Scott, J., & Vos, T. (2012). The long-term health consequences of child physical abuse, emotional abuse, and neglect: A systematic review and meta-analysis. *PLoS Medicine, 9*(11), e1001349. https://doi.org/10.1371/journal.pmed.1001349

Springs, J. A. (2015). Structural and cultural violence in religion and peacebuilding. In A. Omer, R. S. Appleby, & D. Little (Eds.), *The Oxford handbook of religion, conflict, and peacebuilding* (pp. 146–179). Oxford University Press.

Sugarman, D. B., Nation, M., Yuan, N. P., Kuperminc, G. P., Hassoun Ayoub, L., & Hamby, S. (2018). Hate and violence: Addressing discrimination based on race, ethnicity, religion, sexual orientation, and gender identity. *Psychology of Violence, 8*(6), 649–656. http://dx.doi.org/10.1037/vio0000222

Tol, W. A., Komproe, I. H., Jordans, M. J., Vallipuram, A., Sipsma, H., Sivayokan, S., . . . De Jong, J. T. (2012). Outcomes and moderators of a preventive school-based mental health intervention for children affected by war in Sri Lanka: A cluster randomized trial. *World Psychiatry, 11*(2), 114–122. https://doi.org/10.1016/j.wpsyc.2012.05.008

Weigert, K. M. (2008). Structural violence. In L. Kurtz (Ed.), *Encyclopedia of violence, peace, and conflict* (2nd ed., pp. 2004–2011). Academic Press. https://doi.org/10.1016/B978-012373985-8.00169-0

Wessells, M. G., & Kostelny, K. (2021). Understanding and ending violence against children: A holistic approach. *Peace and Conflict: Journal of Peace Psychology, 27*(1), 3. https://doi.org/10.1037/pac0000475

Yale University & Mother Child Education Foundation (AÇEV) Partnership. (2012). *The ecology of peace: Formative childhoods and peace building. A brief note.* https://ecdpeace.org/sites/default/files/files/BriefNote.pdf

Violence Against Children in Social Macrosystems

Sociopolitical Violence and Child Development

New Directions Informed by Longitudinal, Process-Oriented Research in Northern Ireland

E. MARK CUMMINGS, BETHANY WENTZ, AND
MICHELLE LEE ■

More than 1 in 10 children worldwide are affected by armed conflict (UNICEF, 2015). From the lingering tensions of the Troubles of Northern Ireland, to the wars in the Middle East and Africa, to the crises in Ukraine and Russia, there is a diverse range of circumstances and adversities youth face. Through the loss of security in their homes, schools, and communities, children's social ecologies are broken, and yet, they must learn to adapt and continue navigating development. Much of the current body of literature points to the substantial risks and challenges these violent contexts pose to child development, and this compels the need for increased study and intervention for the youth in these contexts.

In this chapter, we will use the terms *political violence* and *armed conflict* to refer broadly to context involving sectarian or politically, ethnically, or religiously motivated acts of violence. This definition is in line with Dubow and colleagues' (2009) definition of *ethnic-political violence* as "violence sanctioned by different influential political and social bodies based on a history of conflict between . . . groups" (p. 114). Acts of political violence and armed conflict are different from other forms of interpersonal violence that lack group-based motivations, such as murder or domestic abuse; however, these interpersonal forms of violence can be affected and influenced by political violence and armed conflict (Boxer et al., 2013). Throughout this chapter, we will use the terms *political violence* and *armed conflict* interchangeably.

The link between exposure to political violence and increased risk of numerous negative outcomes has been well established by previous research. Many studies have documented the risk for negative outcomes, including externalizing problems, such as aggression; internalizing disorders, such as depression; and posttraumatic stress symptoms, due to exposure to political violence (Cummings et al., 2017a). However, individual outcomes also vary widely; some youth exhibit resilience in the face of threats and challenges (Barber, 2013). Given this wide range of outcomes, more research is needed to broaden the understanding of the processes accounting for relations between political violence and child development, including identifying the risk factors that relate to risk for maladjustment or protective factors that foster positive outcomes (Cummings et al., 2009).

A large proportion of past research consists of cross-sectional studies. Currently, conclusions are qualified by limited longitudinal research from a process-oriented, social-ecological perspective. What is greatly needed is process-oriented, longitudinal work that illuminates the mechanisms of action that lead to both positive and negative outcomes, as well as evidence-based intervention work designed to protect youth from the negative outcomes associated with exposure to political violence (Cummings et al., 2017b; Miller-Graff & Cummings, 2017). An advanced understanding of the causal processes related to exposure to violence, the significance of the many levels of youths' social ecologies that are affected by armed conflict, and the impact of evidence-based prevention and intervention programs aimed at quelling the negative outcomes associated with violence exposure and bolstering protective factors are all needed (Cummings et al., 2017b).

In this chapter, process-oriented, longitudinal work from Northern Ireland will be showcased to serve as an example of the type of scientific inquiry needed to further advance the understanding of youth development in contexts of armed conflict. A developmental psychopathology perspective is employed to integrate the current empirical literature on this topic. Developmental psychopathology integrates developmental and clinical sciences to illuminate explanatory models of both typical and atypical development to inform prevention efforts and treatment. A key goal is to articulate the dynamic developmental processes that underpin maladaptive outcomes as well as adaptive or resilient outcomes (Cummings et al., 2000). To that end, research will be organized to highlight exemplary longitudinal, process-oriented work and to examine cutting-edge prevention and intervention research. Additionally, work that underscores both maladaptive and adaptive outcomes associated with exposure to ethnopolitical violence will be presented. Common to many of the studies that will be presented in this chapter is the use of multilevel modeling and between- and within-person analyses, which allow researchers to assess the impact of developmental processes across time. First, between-person analyses allow scientists to make comparisons across the sample. In contrast, within-person analyses allow for the examination of how change occurs relative to an individual's own baseline measures. Statistical approaches that model within-person (or in other words, individual) changes over time inform person-oriented conceptualizations of change (Nesselroade & Molenaar, 2010; Sterba & Bauer, 2010). Finally, multilevel modeling applied to longitudinal work supports insights into these different processes by allowing researchers to examine these effects across time.

While researchers have made remarkable progress, there are considerable challenges related to conducting research in contexts marred by violence, and significant gaps in knowledge remain. This chapter will highlight such remaining questions. Furthermore, while much work has been conducted in specific geopolitical contexts, such as Northern Ireland, Sierra Leone, and Israel and Palestine, limited English-language documentation exists from Latin America. Cultural and other societal variations may significantly affect relations between political violence and child development, and thus, research across diverse contexts of political violence is an important goal for future research. The chapter will be concluded through an illumination of the path forward for future research to advance greater empirical and theoretical understanding and more efficacious and effective interventions from a developmental psychopathology perspective.

A FRAMEWORK FOR RESEARCH ON YOUTH AND POLITICAL VIOLENCE

Children and adolescents constitute a large portion of the global population affected by political violence, and yet, they receive relatively little attention from scientists and public policymakers in comparison to adults affected by political violence. Moreover, young people are not only targeted as victims of violence but also recruited as actors in conflicts (Betancourt, Borisova, et al., 2013). Exposure to ethnopolitical violence during childhood has the capacity to be especially harmful in comparison to exposure in adulthood. Early childhood exposure to violence may initiate lasting detrimental developmental trajectories (Cummings et al., 2012; Cummings et al., 2013; Davies et al., 2014; Merrilees et al., 2013; Taylor et al., 2016). Additionally, youth are frequently exposed to several risk factors during and after periods of active violence, including bodily danger, poverty, displacement, and disruptions of their education and relationships. These experiences can have a long-term negative impact on several areas of functioning (such as cognitive functioning, socioemotional functioning, etc.) that are still developing throughout childhood (Betancourt, Newnham, et al., 2013; Shaw, 2003). Furthermore, youth exposed to violence will ultimately grow up to be adults, parents, community leaders, or perhaps combatants, and may potentially contribute to the intergenerational transmission of violent conflict. Hence, resilience must be leveraged and psychopathology remediated through proper and timely identification, which may also potentially increase peacebuilding engagement.

In order to develop programming to afford such opportunities for youth, researchers must engage in research that (a) documents the risks for maladaptation and factors for adaptation for youth exposed to violence, (b) identifies processes related to risk and protection through cross-sectional work, (c) illuminates these processes underlying risk and protection through longitudinal work, and (d) translates research findings into prevention and intervention development and evaluates program efficacy, including the process-oriented examination of why programs and their key elements do or do not work (Cummings et al., 2017a,

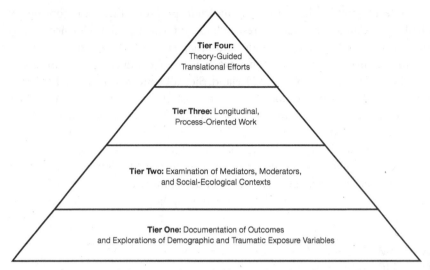

Figure 2.1 A Framework for Research on Children, Political Violence, and Armed Conflict: A Developmental Psychopathology Perspective.

2017b). Cummings et al. (2017a) conceptualized a four-tiered pyramid based on the tenets of developmental psychopathology to organize the published research on the topic of political violence and youth development (Figure 2.1).

Each tier lays the foundation for subsequent tiers, highlighting the increased theoretical and methodological rigor necessary for higher tiers of research. Without the first three tiers of basic research as support, Tier 4 translational work could, at best, be risky and unnecessarily costly and, at worst, be inadvertently harmful to youth. Thus, in the long run, investing in substantial and rigorous research in Tiers 1 through 3 will pay dividends later in the form of efficacious, cost-effective intervention and prevention Tier 4 research.

Globally, exposure to political violence has been linked to increased rates of general psychological problems in youth. There are several current trends in Tier 1 research, including the identification of strong linkages between violence exposure and psychopathology symptoms, especially posttraumatic stress disorder (PTSD); variability in the rates and severities of such psychopathology symptoms; exploration of the relations between demographic variables, traumatic exposure type, and adjustment; and emerging academic interest in the study of resilience processes among youth affected by political violence (Cummings et al., 2017a). As an example of Tier 1 research, Klasen et al. (2010) conducted basic cross-sectional research in Uganda during a period of ongoing conflict to determine if there are associations among traumatic war experiences and exposure to domestic and community violence and psychological problems including PTSD, depression, and behavioral and emotional problems. Among 330 former Ugandan child soldiers attending a special needs school for war-traumatized youth, the researchers found that traumatic war experiences and domestic violence exposure were both positively associated with PTSD symptoms, depression symptoms, and behavioral and emotional problems (Klasen et al., 2010). More specifically, 33% of study participants exhibited PTSD symptoms, 36% exhibited depressive symptoms, and 61% exhibited behavioral and emotional problems (Klasen et al., 2010). In this study, the researchers documented the link between exposure to violent conflict and youth adjustment, which is an important first step in paving the way for more advanced research. However, the cross-sectional nature of the data collection methods and analyses limits the ability of this type of work to assess the direction of effects or test mediators and process-oriented moderators (Cummings et al., 2017a). Tier 1 research establishes the risks for youth exposed to violence and serves as the solid base of the research pyramid, laying the groundwork to inform process-oriented longitudinal work and ultimately translational intervention efforts (Cummings et al., 2017a).

Tier 2 research provides a stronger foundation for later work by exploring factors that moderate and mediate the effects of armed conflict on youth adjustment across multiple socioecological domains (Cummings et al., 2017a). For example, Newnham et al. (2015) examined the effects of exposure to war events and daily stressors on youth adjustment in Sierra Leone. Participants were youth who reported at least one exposure to traumatic war events, including former child soldiers who received postwar disarmament, demobilization, and reintegration services; former child soldiers who did not receive postwar services; and a community sample of war-affected youth (Newnham et al., 2015). Findings indicate that the level of war exposure was positively associated with PTSD symptoms, and a significant proportion of this relationship was explained by indirect pathways through daily stressors as a mediator (Newnham et al., 2015). Additionally, the relationship between the war exposure and depression symptoms was completely explained by indirect pathways through daily stressors (Newnham et al., 2015). Tier 2 research begins to bring clarity to the adjustment of youth exposed to political violence by providing cross-sectional evidence for moderating and mediating processes in several socioecological contexts (Cummings et al., 2017a). However, due to the cross-sectional design of studies at this level, this type of research cannot advance our knowledge of long-term youth adjustment in contexts of violence (Cummings et al., 2017a, 2017b).

Tier 3 research utilizes longitudinal methods to explore factors that mediate and moderate the effects of exposure to armed conflict on youth adjustment in multiple contexts (Cummings et al., 2017a). In other words, this type of research illustrates the dynamic processes through which violence exposure impacts youth adjustment over time. As an example, Panter-Brick et al. (2011) conducted a longitudinal study in Afghanistan amidst ongoing political violence and armed conflict to explore linkages among youth exposure to traumatic events; youth psychological symptoms, including youth PTSD; caregiver psychological symptoms; stressors; and protective factors. They surveyed 234 child-caregiver dyads who completed repeated measures of a larger school-based mental health survey at two assessment points spaced 1 year apart (Panter-Brick et al., 2011). Results showed that youth psychological symptoms (except PTSD) improved significantly between assessment points and that greater cumulative life trauma was associated with higher levels of PTSD symptoms (Panter-Brick et al., 2011). Additionally, higher levels of family violence prospectively predicted worsening symptoms of other disorders between assessments, higher levels of major family conflict predicted worsening depressive symptoms, and improvements in family life between assessment points were associated with better youth mental health outcomes at the final assessment (Panter-Brick et al., 2011). Through longitudinal Tier 3 work, researchers are able to tease apart contextual influences, processes, and outcomes. However, relatively few researchers are engaging in this type of work, highlighting the need for exploration of dynamic processes through which violence exposure leads to a variety of different youth adjustment outcomes. In the next section, we provide a detailed example of the type of longitudinal research needed globally in order to inform future translational work.

THE NORTHERN IRELAND PROJECT

Toward providing concrete examples for how longitudinal, process-oriented research may be approached, we will consider the research design and findings from a 6-year longitudinal survey of mother-adolescent dyads in Belfast, Northern Ireland, conducted from 2006 to 2012, with mothers and one adolescent from each family surveyed annually. There were 656 dyads surveyed at Time 1 of data collection, and a supplemental sample was added at Time 3 so that the total number of unique family dyads across the 6 years totaled 999. Mothers were selected instead of fathers, given that the majority of households in working-class Belfast are headed by single mothers, and mothers are more likely to be available for in-home surveys. Consistent with the Northern Irish population of ethnic Catholics and Protestants, the sample was exclusively White. At Time 1, the age of adolescents ranged from 8 to 17 ($M = 12.18$, $SD = 1.82$). The youngest child eligible for participation was selected for households with more than one child, as this permitted the maximum time families could be followed prior to a child leaving home. The total adolescent sample gender distribution was 48% males and 52% females.

An expert demographer on Belfast's ethnic composition provided analyses of representative neighborhoods and family structures, which informed the selection process of neighborhoods. Across 18 socially deprived areas of Belfast, stratified random sampling was employed to select families. This process secured proportional sampling of families within Protestant and Catholic areas alike regarding socioeconomic status and at risk for sectarian violence due to closeness to the opposing community. The sample was representative of Belfast's overall population (43% Catholic, 57% Protestant; Darby, 2001), and around 35 families were randomly selected from specific Belfast wards (i.e., neighborhoods) with homogeneous ethnic groupings (over 90% Protestant or over 90% Catholic). Furthermore, the spatial location of interface "peace" walls was examined by the demographer, as families residing in communities adjacent to an interface are likely to experience greater levels of violence compared to families in communities separated by buffer zones. At least one boundary was present between each study area and a community of the other ethnicity, and moreover, the demographer chose neighborhoods in the survey with the aim of reducing socioeconomic status differences. All of the selected neighborhoods were in the bottom 20th percentile in a social deprivation measure calculated by neighborhood in Northern Ireland, along with all being in regions associated with the Troubles in Northern Ireland (Cummings et al., 2010).

Families were surveyed in the late spring of each year. An established survey company based in Northern Ireland, with great experience working in the Belfast community, conducted data collection through in-home interviews. Families in the study were provided monetary compensation for their time; they received £20 for participation at Times 1 and 2, £40 at Times 3 and 4, and £50 at Times 5 and 6. The surveys included a wide range of measures to capture data regarding relevant demographic information, general well-being, family dynamics, and participants' experience with and perceptions of sectarian and nonsectarian violence.

The next two sections will highlight exemplary research from the Northern Ireland data set that examines development gone awry as well as development gone right through a process-oriented lens. Maladaptive outcomes associated with childhood exposure to violence appear first, with an outline of three noteworthy studies that make use of advanced statistical methods to trace the process through which various maladaptive outcomes occur. The following section covers research that highlights how youth exposed to political violence can achieve positive outcomes, raising hopes that youth can serve as agents of change in their communities.

Maladaptive Outcomes

The link between an array of maladaptive developmental outcomes for youth and exposure to sectarian violence has been well established by decades of research. In particular, researchers have set out to illuminate the pathways through which political violence leads to such outcomes through robust statistical analyses using data from Northern Ireland.

Youth Aggression and Delinquency. Taylor et al. (2016) sought to understand more about the developmental factors underlying the correlation between intergroup violence and youth aggression, including between-person differences in within-person change in aggression across adolescence. To explore this developmental influence related to risk for youth aggression, the researchers employed multilevel modeling. It was found that experience with sectarian (i.e., intergroup) antisocial behavior predicted greater youth aggression. However, this effect declined as participants aged, and a cohesive family environment served as a buffer to this risk. The trajectory of aggression was related to more youth engagement in sectarian antisocial behavior, but girls and those with more cohesive families were associated with lower levels of youth participation in sectarian-motivated antisocial behavior. These findings are relevant to the broader understanding of the intersection of family environment, violence exposure, and adolescent aggression in contexts of chronic sectarian conflict and have important implications for future intervention work. In particular, the results lend support to a more integrated intervention approach that includes strengthening families to help children and adolescents cope with stressors such as exposure to sectarian violence and to reduce adolescent aggression, which in turn may prolong intergroup conflict.

In a similar vein, Cummings et al. (2016) examined the impact of children's emotional insecurity about both the family and community on youth delinquency. Results indicated that intraindividual trajectories of emotional insecurity about the family were related to children's delinquency. Moreover, greater emotional insecurity about the community worsened the impact of family conflict on youth's insecurity about the family. This finding is consistent with the notion that youth's insecurity about the community leads to sensitization of youth to family conflict in the home. Overall, the results suggest that reducing children's insecurity about their family and community in contexts of sectarian violence is a crucial step toward improving adolescent outcomes, including reducing the risk for delinquency (Cummings et al., 2016).

Mental Illness. Luningham et al. (2021) tested whether family conflict in the context of father presence or absence is associated with adolescents' internalizing or externalizing problems. This study examined between-person effects to assess whether youth experiencing father absence or higher levels of family conflict are more likely to develop adjustment problems than youth experiencing father presence or lower levels of family conflict, thereby making comparisons across the sample. In contrast, the researchers also explored within-person effects to detect how change occurs relative to that individual's own baseline measures. The multilevel modeling approach using all six waves of data supports insights into these different processes. Over the many waves of data collection, family structure varied; thus, father presence was included as a time-varying predictor to account for the impact of father presence even as some families underwent transitions. It was hypothesized that father presence would be associated with reduced adjustment problems and that family conflict would be linked to both elevated internalizing and externalizing problems. Results indicated that father presence in the home was indeed linked with reduced internalizing symptoms (but not externalizing symptoms), whereas family conflict was related to elevated internalizing and externalizing problems. Furthermore, family conflict predicted higher symptoms of both internalizing and externalizing problems. Results also indicated that father presence did not moderate the effects of family conflict on either internalizing or externalizing symptoms. Thus, these findings indicated that the presence of the father in the home did not mitigate or exacerbate the effects of family conflict. The findings also show that father presence enhances adolescents' emotional security in the family, perhaps especially in contexts of social deprivation in the family or political violence, in turn reducing the likelihood of adolescent internalizing problems (Luningham et al., 2021).

Adaptive Outcomes

As explored in this chapter thus far, literature citing maladaptive impacts of both direct exposure to and perceptions of political violence and protracted intergroup conflict is well established (Cummings et al., 2014). While a majority of literature focuses on maladaptive youth outcomes, including internalizing and externalizing problems, a risk and resilience approach opens up exploration into the diverse ways in which youth respond to adversity (Barber, 2013). Through this framework, research into prosocial behaviors, defined as voluntary acts that benefit others without personal profits or external awards, have been developed (Bar-Tal, 1976). Contradicting the narrative of youth as "helpless victims or ruthless perpetrators," a new flux of research in settings of protracted conflict examines youth's peacebuilding potential, including constructs such as prosocial behaviors and civic engagement (Taylor et al., 2018). This section showcases several examples of work from the Northern Ireland data set that highlights the potential for adaptive outcomes among youth exposed to violence.

Prosocial Outcomes. In response to mixed results concluding both positive and negative links of the impact of political violence on prosocial outcomes, Taylor et al. (2018) set out to disentangle such effects over time. The study prospectively surveys the trajectories of adolescent prosocial behaviors over 6 consecutive years in Belfast. An early shallow decrease in prosocial behaviors that fell more sharply in later adolescence was discovered through a dual change model, which combines the strengths of autoregressive and latent growth curve approaches. While exposure to sectarianism related to an expedited decrease in prosocial behaviors, trajectories of prosocial behaviors related positively to later social and political engagement (Taylor et al., 2018). Researchers concluded that provided civic life participation is a strong indicator of youth agency and relates to beneficial societal implications, more research is compelled in this area.

Important steps have been made to understand the role of the family in promoting prosocial behaviors at the interpersonal level. However, less is known about the processes leading to other potentially constructive youth outcomes in settings of protracted conflict. Developing upon growing research on political violence and youth adaptive outcomes (Kereteš, 2006; Macksoud & Aber, 1996; Taylor et al., 2014), Taylor et al. (2017) examined the role of the family in promoting constructive youth outcomes in response to perceived conflict in Northern Ireland. Exploratory factor analysis pointed toward two related forms of civic engagement among youth in Belfast: volunteerism and political participation. Structural equation modeling (SEM) was employed, and it was concluded that female adolescents reported more volunteerism in comparison to males. Older adolescents reported higher political participation, such as boycotting products, whereas younger adolescents reported greater volunteerism, such as helping at school (Taylor et al., 2017). Furthermore, SEM with multiple reporters across three time points demonstrated family cohesion as a significant partial mediator between perceived political conflict and youth volunteerism and political engagement (Taylor et al., 2017). In other words, perceiving political conflict related to greater support and togetherness among youth and their families, which consequently related to more youth political engagement and volunteerism in communities and schools. Holding implications for both individuals and civic and political spheres, the findings from this study indicate that within prolonged political conflict contexts, the family may be a key factor underlying adolescents' contributions to postaccord peacebuilding (Taylor et al., 2017).

Prejudice Reduction. In examining other potential factors that promote peacebuilding and youth civic engagement efforts, Merrilees et al. (2017) explored the critical role intergroup contact plays in the reduction of prejudice. The researchers examined individual- and context-level effects of intergroup contact on change in intergroup bias through adolescence using hierarchical linear modeling. Results indicated that bias in youth increases with age, and that bias in adolescents with more frequent intergroup contact increases more quickly, and those who report higher quality of contact increase in bias more slowly. Additionally, it was found that both frequency and quality of contact at the neighborhood level predicted slower increases in bias across time. The results bolster scientists' understanding of how intergroup processes impact youth development of intergroup bias (Merrilees et al., 2017).

INTERVENTION AND POLICY IMPLICATIONS

The research highlighted previously has critical implications for future policy and intervention work. There is a critical need to more deeply understand how youth growing up in political conflict contexts can engage in civic and political life, along with how the family plays a role in fostering such prosocial behaviors (Barber, 2013). The importance of examining civic engagement outcomes is that civic engagement during adolescence may have long-term implications for societal involvement and participation (Finlay et al., 2010; Zaff et al., 2008). For instance, behaviors related to volunteerism as a form of civic engagement, such as participation in school, community service, and charity events, may be antecedents of peacebuilding (Paffenholz & Spurk, 2006; Taylor, 2015). Additionally, the political forms of civic engagement in this study are foundational for democratic participation and nonviolent means to resolve intergroup differences (Bužinkić, 2013; Checkoway & Aldana, 2013).

Through a competence-based approach that recognizes youth agency, Taylor et al. (2019) found that youth may be the drivers of positive social change, and not merely the beneficiaries. School initiatives in Northern Ireland have promoted school-community partnerships through the voluntary sector that have larger community impacts (Kinlen et al., 2013). However, as the studies discussed in this chapter conclude, agencies and institutions must also include factors outside of the school, including families, in order to promote greater youth participation (Diemer, 2012; Zaff et al., 2008). Additionally, programs that encourage volunteerism among older adolescents and those outside formal schooling should be developed (Henn & Foard, 2014). With the potentially divisive nature of Northern Ireland's politics, these programs should be critically evaluated in their promotions of constructive and nonviolent forms of civic engagement for increasing the peacebuilding potential of youth (McKeown & Cairns, 2012).

Another policy implication is the need for more collaboration between policymakers and practitioners with youth, in order to promote intergenerational research and intervention projects. The UN Convention on the Rights of the Child has supported this direction through its establishment of the youth's right to partake in decision-making that impacts their lives, to express their views and be heard, to create and join associations, to assemble peacefully, and to engage in change processes (United Nations Convention on the Rights of the Child, 1989). Specific to Northern Ireland, Taylor et al. (2019) outline a set of policy recommendations for postaccord Belfast's youth, and since 2007, school's citizenship curricula have fostered youth's civic attitudes and behaviors (O'Connor et al., 2009). Ultimately, continued development in this area of research should employ a developmental psychopathology framework to uncover further specific trajectories and underlying processes that steer youth away from violence and toward peacemaking.

FUTURE DIRECTIONS AND METHODOLOGICAL RECOMMENDATIONS

The current body of work tends to focus quite narrowly on individual processes or outcomes, ignoring the multiple socioecological levels in which violent conflicts develop. In order to manage the time and participant limitations many researchers face, planned missing designs allow researchers to assess more constructs with fewer items by randomly assigning participants to complete a subset of items on a given test or measure (Enders, 2010; Graham et al., 1996). Additionally, planned missing designs may allow researchers to balance cultural sensitivity with generalization across contexts (Cummings et al., 2017a). For example, in international settings, researchers could use locally developed measures in concert with established measures of psychopathology and other outcomes, which allows the researchers to assess potential overlap in relevant constructs across contexts while also identifying differences. This more inclusive data could help to adapt existing interventions developed in Western culture in culturally relevant ways, with implications for intervention programs. Future translational research programs would be strengthened by greater engagement with basic research on the impact of armed conflict on children and should consider targeting multiple levels of the social ecology and should keep in mind that prevention and intervention research holds particular promise for informing conceptual models and future basic research (Cummings et al., 2017a).

CONCLUSION

Decades of work have elucidated the basic effects of ethnopolitical violence on youth development. Yet, many questions on developmental pathways have yet to be examined. In this chapter, we illuminated the way forward through process-oriented, longitudinal work, with a notable project in Northern Ireland serving as an example of the type of studies needed globally. So far, researchers have engaged in exemplary work in specific geopolitical contexts in not only Northern Ireland but also Sierra Leone and Israel and Palestine (Miller-Graff & Cummings, 2017). However, the academic community has yet to engage in such empirically rigorous longitudinal work in other geopolitical contexts marred by political violence, and hardly any scientific work at even a basic level has been done in Latin America. Thus, from a global perspective, reflecting themes developed in this chapter, many directions need to be advanced in the future in order to determine the process through which violence exposure leads to maladjustment in youth and to develop empirically supported interventions to steer children exposed to violence toward resilience.

REFERENCES

Barber, B. K. (2013). Annual research review: The experience of youth with political conflict—Challenging notions of resilience and encouraging research refinement. *Journal of Child Psychology and Psychiatry, 54*(4), 461–473. https://doi.org/10.1111/jcpp.12056

Bar-Tal, D. (1976). *Prosocial behavior: Theory and research.* Hemisphere Publishing.

Betancourt, T. S., Borisova, I., Williams, T. P., Meyers-Ohki, S. E., Rubin-Smith, J. E., Annan, J., & Kohrt, B.A. (2013). Research review: Psychosocial adjustment and mental health in former child soldiers—A systematic review of the literature and recommendations for future research. *Journal of Child Psychology and Psychiatry, 54*(1), 17–36. https://doi.org/10.1111/j.1469-7610.2012.02620.x

Betancourt, T. S., Newnham, E. A., McBain, R., & Brennan, R. T. (2013). Post-traumatic stress symptoms among former child soldiers in Sierra Leone: Follow-up study. *British Journal of Psychiatry, 203*(1), 196–202. https://doi.org/10.1192/bjp.bp.112.113514

Boxer, P., Rowell, L., Dubow, E. F., Landau, S. F., Gvirsman, S. D., Shikaki, K., & Ginges, J. (2013). Exposure to violence across the social ecosystem and the development of aggression: A test of ecological theory in the Israeli-Palestinian conflict. *Child Development, 84*, 163–177.

Bužinkić, E. (2013). Croatian youth corner: Youth participation and civic education from practitioners' eyes. In R. V. Roholt, M. Baizerman, & R. W. Hildreth (Eds.), *Civic youth work: Cocreating democratic youth spaces* (pp. 139–147). Lyceum Books.

Checkoway, B., & Aldana, A. (2013). Four forms of youth civic engagement for diverse democracy. *Children and Youth Services Review, 35*(11), 1894–1899. https://doi.org/10.1016/j.childyouth.2013.09.005

Cummings, E. M., Davies, P. T., & Campbell, S. B. (2000). *Developmental psychopathology and family process: Theory, research, and clinical implications*. Guilford Publications.

Cummings, E., George, M., McCoy, K., & Davies, P. (2012). Interparental conflict in kindergarten and adolescent adjustment: Prospective investigation of emotional security as an explanatory mechanism. *Child Development, 83*(5), 1703–1715. https://doi.org/10.1111/j.1467-8624.2012.01807.x

Cummings, E. M., Goeke-Morey, M. C., Merrilees, C. E., Taylor, L. K., & Shirlow, P. (2014). A social-ecological, process-oriented perspective on political violence and child development. *Child Development Perspectives, 8*, 82–89.

Cummings, E. M., Goeke-Morey, M. C., Schermerhorn, A. C., Merrilees, C. E., & Cairns, E. (2009). Children and political violence from a social ecological perspective: Implications from research on children and families in Northern Ireland. *Clinical Child and Family Psychology Review, 12*, 16–38. https://doi.org/10.1007/s10567-009-0041-8

Cummings, E. M., Merrilees, C. E., Taylor, L. K., & Mondi, C. (2017a). *Political violence, armed conflict, and youth adjustment*. Springer.

Cummings, E., M., Merrilees, C. E., Taylor, L. K., & Mondi, C. F. (2017b). Developmental and social-ecological perspectives on children, political violence, and armed conflict. *Development and Psychopathology, 29*(1), 1–10.

Cummings, E. M., Schermerhorn, A. C., Merrilees, C. E., Goeke-Morey, M. C., Shirlow, P., & Cairns, E. (2010). Political violence and child adjustment in Northern Ireland: Testing pathways in a social-ecological model including single- and two-parent families. *Developmental Psychology, 46*, 827–841.

Cummings, E. M., Taylor, L. K., Merrilees, C. E., Goeke-Morey, M. C., & Shirlow, P. (2016). Emotional insecurity in the family and community and youth delinquency in Northern Ireland: A person-oriented analysis across five waves. *Journal of Child Psychology and Psychiatry, 57*(1), 47–54. https://doi.org/10.1111/jcpp.12427

Cummings, E. M., Taylor, L. K., Merrilees, C. E., Goeke-Morey, M. C., Shirlow, P., & Cairns, E. (2013). Relations between political violence and child adjustment: A four-wave test of the role of emotional insecurity about community. *Developmental Psychology, 49*(12), 2212–2224. https://doi.org/10.1037/a0032309

Darby J. (2001). *The effects of violence on peace processes*. United States Institute of Peace Press.

Davies, P. T., Sturge-Apple, M., Boscoe, S. M., & Cummings, E. M. (2014). The legacy of early insecurity histories in shaping adolescent adaptation to interparental conflict. *Child Development, 85*(1), 338–352. https://doi.org/10.1111/cdev.12119

Diemer, M. A. (2012). Fostering marginalized youths' political participation: Longitudinal roles of parental political socialization and youth sociopolitical development. *American Journal of Community Psychology, 50*, 246–256.

Dubow, E. F., Huesmann, L. R., & Boxer, P. (2009). A social-cognitive-ecological framework for understanding the impact of exposure to persistent ethnic-political violence on children's psychological adjustment. *Clinical Child and Family Psychology Review, 12*(2), 113–126. https://doi.org/10.1007/s10567-009-0050-7

Enders, C. K. (2010). *Applied missing data analysis*. Guilford Press.

Finlay, A., Wray-Lake, L., & Flanagan, C. (2010). Civic engagement during the transition to adulthood: Developmental opportunities and social policies at a critical juncture.

In L. R. Sherrod, J. Torney-Purta, & C. Flanagan (Eds.), *Handbook of research on civic engagement in youth* (pp. 277–305). John Wiley & Sons.

Graham, J. W., Hofer, S. M., & MacKinnon, D. P. (1996). Maximizing the usefulness of data obtained with planned missing value patterns: An application of maximum likelihood procedures. *Multivariate Behavioral Research, 31*(2), 197–218. https://doi.org/10.1207/s15327906mbr3102_3

Henn, M., & Foard, N. (2014). Social differentiation in young people's political participation: The impact of social and educational factors on youth political engagement in Britain. *Journal of Youth Studies, 17*, 360–380.

Kereteš, G. (2006). Children's aggressive and prosocial behavior in relation to war exposure: Testing the role of perceived parenting and child's gender. *International Journal of Behavioral Development, 30*, 227–239.

Kinlen, L., Hansson, U., Keenaghan, C., Canavan, J., & O'Connor, U. (2013). Education for civic engagement in post-primary schools in Ireland and Northern Ireland: A rights perspective. The Children and Youth Programme. https://www.ulster.ac.uk/__data/assets/pdf_file/0003/224256/5-Full-Report.pdf

Klasen, F., Oettingen, G., Daniels, J., & Adams, H. (2010). Multiple trauma and mental health in former Ugandan child soldiers. *Journal of Traumatic Stress, 23*(5), 573–581. https://doi.org/10.1002/jts.20557

Luningham, J. M., Merrilees, C. E., Taylor, L. K., Goeke-Morey, M., Shirlow, P., Wentz, B., & Cummings, E. M. (2021). Relations among father's presence, family conflict, and adolescent adjustment in Northern Ireland. *Child Development, 92*(3), 904–918. https://doi.org/10.1111/cdev.13446

Macksoud, M. S., & Aber, J. L. (1996). The war experiences and psychosocial development of children in Lebanon. *Child Development, 67*, 70–88.

McKeown, S., & Cairns, E. (2012). Peace-programmes in Northern Ireland. *Journal of Aggression, Conflict and Peace Research, 4*, 69–75.

Merrilees, C. E., Cairns, E., Taylor, L. K., Goeke-Morey, M. C., Shirlow, P., & Cummings, E. M. (2013). Social identity and youth aggressive and delinquent behaviors in a context of political violence. *Political Psychology, 34*(5), 695–711. https://doi.org/10.1111/pops.12030

Merrilees, C. E., Taylor, L. K., Baird, R., Goeke-Morey, M. C., Shirlow, P., & Cummings, E. M. (2017). Neighborhood effects of intergroup contact on change in youth intergroup bias. *Journal of Youth and Adolescence, 47*, 77–87. https://doi.org/10.1007/s10964-017-0684-6

Miller-Graff, L., & Cummings, E. M. (2017). The Israeli-Palestinian conflict: Effects on youth, available interventions, and future research directions. *Developmental Review, 43*, 147.

Nesselroade, J. R., & Molenaar, P. C. M. (2010). *Emphasizing intraindividual variability in the study of development over the life span: Concepts and issues.* John Wiley & Sons.

Newnham, E. A., Pearson, R. M., Stein, A., & Betancourt, T. S. (2015). Youth mental health after civil war: The importance of daily stressors. *British Journal of Psychiatry, 206*, 116–121.

O'Connor, U., Beattie, K., & Niens, U. (2009). *An evaluation of the introduction of local and global citizenship to the Northern Ireland curriculum.* Council for the Curriculum, Examinations and Assessment.

Paffenholz, T., & Spurk, C. (2006). Civil society, civic engagement, and peacebuilding. *Social Development Papers: Conflict Prevention & Reconstruction*, Paper No. 36. https://www.researchgate.net/publication/228658197_Civil_Society_Civic_Engagement_and_Peacebuil

Panter-Brick, C., Goodman, A., Tol, W., & Eggerman, M. (2011). Mental health and childhood adversities: A longitudinal study in Kabul, Afghanistan. *Journal of the American Academy of Child and Adolescent Psychiatry*, *50*(4), 349–363. https://doi.org/10.1016/j.jaac.2010.12.001

Shaw, J. A. (2003). Children exposed to war/terrorism. *Clinical Child and Family Psychology Review*, *6*(4), 237–246. https://doi.org/10.1023/B:CCFP.0000006291.10180.bd

Sterba, S. K., & Bauer, D. J. (2010). Statistically evaluating person-oriented principles revisited. *Development and Psychopathology, 22*, 287–294.

Taylor, L. K. (2015). Impact of political violence, social trust, and depression on civic participation in Colombia. *Peace & Conflict: Journal of Peace Psychology, 22*, 145–152.

Taylor, L. K, Merrilees, C. E., Baird, R., Goeke-Morey, M. C., Shirlow, P., & Cummings, E. M. (2018). Impact of political conflict on trajectories of adolescent prosocial behavior: Implications for civic engagement. *Developmental Psychology, 54*(9), 1785–1793. https://doi:10.1037/dev0000552.supp

Taylor, L. K., Merrilees, C. E., Goeke-Morey, M. C., Shirlow, P., Cairns, E., & Cummings, E. M. (2014). Political violence and adolescent outgroup attitudes and prosocial behaviours: Implications for positive intergroup relations. *Social Development, 23*, 840–859.

Taylor, L. K., Merrilees, C. E., Goeke-Morey, M. C., Shirlow, P., & Cummings, E. M. (2016). Trajectories of adolescent aggression and family cohesion: The potential to perpetuate or ameliorate political conflict. *Journal of Clinical Child & Adolescent Psychology, 45*(2), 114–128. https://doi.org/10.1080/15374416.2014.945213

Taylor, L. K., Townsend, D., Merrilees, C. E., Goeke-Morey, M. C., Shirlow, P., & Cummings. E. M. (2017). Adolescent civic engagement and perceived political conflict: The role of family cohesion. *Youth & Society, 51*(6), 616–637. https://doi.org/10.1177/0044118X17697236

Taylor, L. K., Townsend, D., Merrilees, C. E., Goeke-Morey, M. C., Shirlow, P., & Cummings, E. M. (2019). Adolescent civic engagement and perceived political conflict: The role of family cohesion. *Youth & Society, 51*(5), 616–637. https://doi.org/10.1177/0044118X17697236

UNICEF. (2015, January 29). *More Than 1 in 10 Children Living in Countries and Areas Affected by Armed Conflict.* Retrieved May 8, 2019, from https://www.unicefusa.org/press/releases/unicef-more-1-10-children-living-countries-and-areas-affected-armed-conflict/21551

United Nations Convention on the Rights of the Child. (1989). United Nations Office of the High Commissioner for Human Rights. http://www.ohchr.org/EN/ProfessionalInterest/Pages/CRC.aspx

Zaff, J. F., Malanchuk, O., & Eccles, J. S. (2008). Predicting positive citizenship from adolescence to young adulthood: The effects of a civic context. *Applied Development Science, 12*, 38–53.

3

The Psychosocial and Political Dynamics of Children and Youth Entering and Exiting Armed Groups

GABRIEL VELEZ, FABIO IDROBO, ELIZABETH PERRY, AND
CLIFTON R. EMERY ■

The involvement of children and youth in armed conflict is a significant global challenge. In 2018, over 13,000 children demobilized (i.e., left armed groups), and in 2019, almost 8,000 minors were recruited as armed actors (UNICEF, 2020). These numbers—some of the highest on record—come 15 years after the United Nations' (UN) Optional Protocol to the Convention on the Rights of the Child on the Involvement of Children in Armed Conflict (OPAC). The data are troubling both as statistical trends and as a representation of widespread disruption, risk, and harm to the lives of developing minors across the world. Understanding underage combatants' experiences, how these experiences intersect with other forms of structural inequity, and ways in which children and adolescents can be supported throughout demobilization are pressing global concerns. In this chapter, we begin by defining child and youth combatants as we address the complexity of this topic. We then review current literature on what motivates these young people to join armed actors and their reintegration processes. Each section focuses on psychosocial well-being and development, as well as programmatic interventions. We end with a case study describing work by governmental and nongovernment organizations with demobilized minors in Colombia to illustrate the complexity and opportunities for linking these efforts into constructing peaceful, just, and sustainable societies.

DEFINING CHILDREN AND YOUTH COMBATANTS

Defining who is included in the term *child and youth combatants* is complicated by heterogeneity of engagement and experiences. The rapidly shifting landscape of conflicts often makes it difficult to clearly define what it means to be a "soldier" or "combatant" (Wessells, 2016). Further, children and adolescents' pathways are varied (e.g., forced recruitment, choice of last resort, open engagement with a liberating struggle), as is the extent to which youths' activities throughout conflict are subject to legal ramifications. As one example, political motivations and the nature of conflict may necessitate different interventions and judicial processes; semiorganized groups of Palestinian youth using low levels of violence to protest Israeli occupation cannot be treated the same as young gang members using handguns to exact revenge on the streets of Chicago. Second, while the UN defines "child" as anyone under 18 years old, cognitive and psychosocial processes differ considerably for prepubescent adolescents versus those nearer to age 18 (e.g., Wessells, 1998). Even then, the use of 18 as a boundary may not be coherent with the complexity of individuals' developmental trajectories (Steinberg, 2007). In this chapter, we recognize these complexities while using the definition from the UN's OPAC: individuals under the age of 18 who, through forced recruitment or of their own volition, "participate actively in hostilities in . . . armed conflict."

MOBILIZING AND DEMOBILIZING: A REVIEW OF THE LITERATURE

Across varied political, social, and geographic circumstances, a rich body of literature has emerged on the psychosocial dynamics at play as children enter and exit armed groups as well as when they attempt to reintegrate into society. Understanding these psychosocial dynamics is critical for building effective interventions targeting youth ex-combatants' healthy development and participation in building inclusive, peaceful societies (e.g., Schauer & Elbert, 2010).

Why Young People Mobilize

Children and adolescents engage with armed groups for a variety of reasons. These may include forced recruitment; desire for revenge or power; lack of economic, political, or educational opportunities; and ideological socialization (Wessells, 2005). While not always the case, some of these pathways may involve or be motivated by traumatic experiences (Gates, 2011). There has been a growing movement to extend individualized models of trauma and resilience to address contextual and collective dynamics in considering the impacts of conflict on children. Drawing on developmental psychology, scholars argue that socio-ecological frameworks are particularly well suited for effectively modeling youth engagement in armed conflict and demobilization (e.g., Garbarino et al., 2020; Kohrt et al., 2015; Wessells, 2016). Systems theories highlight the dynamic and interrelated forces across levels that influence psychosocial development. Various contextual and individual factors interact to explain both engagement in armed conflict and the consequential psychosocial effects on child and youth combatants (Garbarino et al., 2020; Tol et al., 2013a). The individual and their development are situated within a complex network of risk and protective factors at the level of the social macrosystem, such as chronic poverty, discrimination, or weak governance (Wessells, 2016). These social macrosystems often drive the very existence of war and violent groups (such as drug cartels and gangs), who then recruit underage combatants because they are cheaper, more fearless, and easier to retain than are adults (Schauer & Elbert, 2010). Broader systemic forces may also make armed groups appealing to children and youth. Armed groups may be attractive options for financial security, safety, or status given the poverty, ethnic/political persecution, and marginalization that youth may face in the context of armed conflict (Dumas, 2003; Garbarino et al., 2020). Furthermore, high rates of orphancy—driven by conflict, poverty, inadequate educational opportunities, and lack of health care—increase vulnerability to recruitment (Amnesty International, 2000). Many underage combatants come from low-socioeconomic-status (SES) backgrounds, come from marginalized groups, or lack basic rights like food and education (Machel, 1996).

Individual factors including genetics, personality, and physical maturity interact with these contextual dynamics. Gender is a paradigmatic example, as it is linked to both exposure to risk and social expectations, producing varied pathways for enlistment. In one study of former Nepalese child combatants, reasons for joining varied by gender: Boys were often motivated by economic circumstances, whereas girls reported personal connections to the armed group or agreement with its philosophical orientation (Kohrt et al., 2010). Still, even in this work on Nepalese child soldiers, the findings have often been mixed as to systemic and individual-level factors involved in engagement. For example, the primary motivator expressed by the former soldiers in these studies was escaping difficult life situations (which the authors described as rooted in poverty, inequality, and minimal educational opportunities), including almost a fourth of the males noting poor economic conditions specifically (Kohrt et al., 2016).

Together, these data demonstrate the utility of systems thinking to conceptualize psychosocial processes of children and adolescents joining these groups; a systems-oriented analysis can provide a critical framework for understanding and intervening to uphold children's rights. Namely, inequality, economic deprivation, and inadequate educational opportunities can be understood as points of intervention to prevent youth engagement (Garbarino et al., 2020). There is a need for systemic intervention and change above and beyond targeted programs addressing the individual needs of specific high-risk groups or individual children.

The Psychosocial Needs of Former Child and Youth Combatants

Prior to joining armed groups, many underage combatants lived in conditions marked by instability, extreme poverty, oppression, inadequate education, and adverse childhood experiences (Faulkner & Doctor, 2021; Gates, 2011). In addition, underage combatants often face extended exposure to violence, possible participation in violent acts, and physical and sexual abuse before becoming involved in armed groups (e.g., Schauer & Elbert, 2010). Such experiences are broadly associated with trauma and physical and mental health concerns (e.g., Betancourt et al., 2013; Johnson et al., 2008; Kohrt et al., 2010).

Research has also demonstrated similar challenges for underage combatants from the experiences they have as members of armed groups. The most extensive review of the mental health impacts of being a child soldier was conducted by Betancourt and her colleagues (2013). Their work highlights the scarcity of this research in general—they found only eight studies of high quality—as well as the common limitations such as the lack of validated mental health measures and the inability to draw conclusions across samples. Even similar designs led to very different rates of mental health concerns. For example, two studies with youth in northern Uganda found that 99% (Amone P'Olak et al., 2007) and 27% respectively (Okello et al., 2007) would be diagnosed with posttraumatic stress disorder (PTSD) using measures developed on Western populations. In some studies, similar levels of PTSD were found in former child soldiers and control groups, possibly due to high levels of violence exposure even for those who did not engage in armed groups. Finally, in one of the few longitudinal studies following participants for years after demobilization, former child soldiers in Sierra Leone were found to have elevated levels of anxiety and depression as adults (Betancourt, Brennan, et al., 2010).

Following demobilization, former underage combatants often continue to face structural and systemic conditions that feed into the reasons they participated. There may be a lack of educational and employment opportunities, and the ones that do exist may be occluded by social stigma faced by ex-combatants (e.g., Betancourt, Borisova, et al., 2010; Betancourt et al., 2013; Miller & Rasmussen, 2010; Williamson, 2006). These stereotypes may feed into a cycle of isolation as mental health struggles and stress tied to past traumatic experiences lead to negative social behaviors that further feed into discrimination and alienation (Betancourt, Borisova, et al., 2010; Miller & Rasmussen, 2010).

Risk and Protective Factors. Identifying risk and protective factors for psychosocial well-being can help draw attention to the ways that individuals and communities manage the lasting impacts of children's experiences as combatants, and to what is needed to support their well-being (Vindevogel et al., 2014). While some risk and protective factors are based in actual experiences during the conflict, others are linked to societal conditions upon re-entry.

For risk factors, research has highlighted two main areas: the context and explicit experiences of entry and participation in armed groups and the social support upon demobilization. First, there are correlations between mental health issues and whether the child was abducted or forcibly recruited, their age of involvement, the extent to which they perpetrated violence, and whether or not they experienced violence themselves (Betancourt et al., 2013). Those who experienced sexual violence have demonstrated higher rates of anxiety, depression, and PTSD (Betancourt, Borisova, et al., 2010; "The Hidden Health Trauma of Child Soldiers," 2004), while similar connections have been made with child soldiers who engage at younger ages (Kohrt et al., 2010). Second, in the demobilization process and beyond, community and family stigma and instability have been identified as primary risk factors for poorer mental health. Importantly, individual studies have demonstrated that some of these associations may differ across contexts. For example, while female former child combatants have generally been found to be more at risk for mental health challenges (Betancourt et al., 2013), a longitudinal study of 300 former child soldiers in Nepal found no impact of gender (Adhikari et al., 2014).

Protective factors group around the opposite: social support and connected opportunities for engaging productively in society (Betancourt et al., 2013). A critical element is being reaccepted into family or community contexts, which may entail rituals or processes of healing (e.g., Boothby et al., 2006). While these social networks can provide key psychosocial supports for former child soldiers, structural considerations such as the availability of educational and economic opportunities may also contribute to positive developmental outcomes and coping with the past experiences. These types of resources may be driven by political dynamics and priorities, such as the state's ability to provide such supports and the lack of funding for demobilization programming (e.g., Baare, 2006; Blattman & Annan, 2008).

INTERVENTIONS TO SUPPORT DEMOBILIZED YOUTH

These physical and psychosocial impacts on former child soldiers not only are internal and individual but also manifest as ex-combatants may struggle to trust others, maintain relationships, and engage in school (Betancourt & Khan, 2008). Their reintegration and psychosocial well-being require attention to individual psychosocial needs, as well as challenges across socioecological levels. The UN has highlighted the fact that human rights of demobilized minors are often violated, particularly when the communities to which they return lack adequate social programming and support (Gamba de Potgieter, 2018). Other international frameworks more explicitly map out cross-system supports for demobilized children and youth, including education, inclusion in community life, and economic opportunity. For example, in line with ecological systems theories, the World Health Organization's Guidelines on Mental Health and Psychosocial Support in Emergency Settings (2007) frames support for children in conflict settings as

multitiered and multisectoral. The foundation of the guidelines' four-level pyramid entails basic services and security, including food, water, health care, and
peace. Right above these fundamental rights are community and family supports,
building a foundation upon which more targeted and specialized services can be
provided. As this conceptualization highlights, the needs of demobilized minors
involve more than psychosocial services to deal with trauma. Attention to systems
can bolster individual and collective resilience by a dual approach promoting
self-regulation, efficacy, and other cognitive conditions in addition to providing
needed material and societal resources (Vindevogel, 2017; Wessells, 2016). This
framing requires fostering inclusive communities with equitable and plentiful
opportunities to grow, learn, earn a living, and contribute to society.

An often-overlooked need for demobilized minors is *agency* in reintegration processes (Wessells, 2016). Interventions frequently give minimal voice to
participants themselves and further alienate them by prioritizing Western models
of mental health, such as assessments not developed and validated in the local
context or treatment approaches that are unattuned to local methods of healing
(e.g., Wessells, 2016). When formal interventions are disconnected from local culture and community, it may be harder for individuals to benefit, thus diminishing
collective resilience and resources and hindering reintegration (Vindevogel et al.,
2014). For example, during a war in Angola, an intervention to support children exposed to violence was found to be more efficacious in supporting these
individuals by combining Western models and tools around trauma (e.g., PTSD
and clinical treatments and talk-oriented therapies) with traditional healers'
work on spiritual distress (Wessells & Monteiro, 2004). The extent to which
children's agency is valued is culturally mediated and should be considered in
a contextualized approach to supporting their resilience (i.e., positive and productive functioning despite significant experiences of trauma as armed actors;
Vindevogel, 2017). Still, there is evidence that not integrating their voices within
demobilization processes can inhibit healing processes and development. In a
review of 95 studies on adolescents and political violence, for example, Barber
and Schluterman (2009) found that youths' differential experiences of conflict were often related to negative functioning outcomes but not attended to in
their disengagement processes. As a few examples of the gaps between programs
and individuals' experiences, other work has demonstrated that international
programs to support former child soldiers in Sierra Leone and Liberia neglected
the mental health struggles of the youth themselves (Medeiros, 2007) and that
the themes emerging from participatory action research with young mothers in
Sierra Leone, Liberia, and northern Uganda did not match the social reintegration supports they were receiving (Veale et al., 2017). Adding further complexity,
the actual experiences of underage combatants may vary across individuals and
contexts, while international programs often apply frameworks across settings
(MacMullin & Loughry, 2004).

Many scholars argue for interventions to support reintegration and well-
being through a strengths-based focus on resilience and community resources.
They maintain that the current focus on psychopathology and victimization is

detrimental and ignores the complexity of risk and protective factors across levels of socioecological context (e.g., Wessells, 2017). A critical component is attention to what is required for social healing and communal resilience; that is, in addition to psychosocial support for trauma, interventions must develop inclusive and welcoming spaces and provide for education, employment, and social engagement through equitable and ecologically attuned opportunities (Garbarino et al., 2020). These intervention frameworks focused on resilience have been framed using an ecological perspective in line with the one laid out earlier (e.g., Betancourt & Khan, 2008; Tol et al., 2013a). Importantly, emerging evidence is mixed on this approach and may speak to the complexity and nuance of ecological systems (Tol et al., 2013b). As an example, a randomized control trial of a school-based intervention in Indonesia found mixed results for a program developed with a participatory approach to focus on bolstering ecological resilience (e.g., increased hope, better scoping, play- and peer-based social supports). Girls demonstrated lower PTSD rates and the targeted resilience variables were higher in the treatment group but did not moderate changes in PTSD symptoms (whereas social support beyond the family did; Tol et al., 2010).

SUMMARY AND CONNECTIONS TO HUMAN RIGHTS AND SUSTAINABLE DEVELOPMENT GOALS

In sum, participation in armed groups can be driven by a variety of factors that may include individual choices, while also being motivated by dynamics within broader levels of the socioecological system (such as lack of economic and educational opportunity and the destabilizing nature of conflict). Psychosocial well-being and positive developmental outcomes through and beyond the demobilization process are similarly influenced by social and political factors. Still, many programs and efforts to support these youth are not responsive to context (Wessells, 2016). Furthermore, in line with the UN's Sustainable Development Goals (SDGs), further work can be done to address educational opportunities, inclusion, equity, and peace to facilitate resilience and thriving.

Children and youth combatants are included as a specific focus within SDG 8, which focuses on sustained and inclusive economic growth. Youth demobilization and reintegration, however, are also integrally interwoven with international efforts to ensure equitable education (SDG 4); reduce inequality (SDG 10); make communities inclusive, safe, and resilient (SDG 11); and promote peaceful and just societies (SDG 16).

Effectively preventing the entry of minors into armed groups is an element of peaceful and safe communities (SDGs 11 and 16). The Convention on the Rights of the Child explicitly identifies children's rights to be protected from engagement in armed conflict and to be reintegrated into society (Articles 38 and 39). Children's involvement in armed conflict is also driven by inequality and injustice (linked to SDGs 10 and 16). These dynamics can create sociocultural pressures to join armed groups, such as through limited opportunities for fulfilling legal employment and the normalization of violence (Gates, 2011; Wessells, 2016). Thus, preventing children's engagement in armed groups must address the structural inequities at play in youth mobilization. Finally, supporting young ex-combatants' well-being involves reintegration into society, including educational and economic opportunities to lead flourishing lives. To follow, we review understandings of the psychosocial processes in enlistment and demobilization as a frame for connections between child combatants and the SDGs focused on building inclusive, peaceful societies with equitable educational systems.

A CASE STUDY OF COLOMBIA

In this section, we detail Colombian programs as examples of applied, holistic frameworks in working with demobilized underage combatants. This case study is intended to demonstrate the complexity of psychosocial processes through a lens of institutions and organizations striving to serve them and the conflict-affected communities to which they belong.

CONTEXT

Colombia experienced two prolonged episodes of political violence in its recent history: *la Violencia* (1948–1958) and *el Conflicto Armado* (1964–2016). The latter is considered to have ended with the signing of the 2016 peace agreement between the Revolutionary Armed Forces of Colombia-Popular Army (FARC-EP) and the Colombian government. The conflict has resulted in no less than 260,000 deaths, over 80,000 to 160,000 forced disappearances, and more than 8 million internally displaced persons. As monitored by the National Center for Historic Memory (Centro Nacional de Memoria Histórica [CNMH] in Spanish), the consequences of the conflict have continued to unfold in the wake of the peace agreement, and there have been many social leaders and human rights defenders killed since its signing (CNMH, 2017). The Unidad de Atención y Reparación Integral a las Víctimas (UARIV) lists over 9 million victims of the armed conflict. Over 2 million—or around a quarter—of recognized victims are younger than 17 years old (UARIV, 2020).

Another legacy of the conflict is forced recruitment of children and adolescents, mostly from rural and indigenous communities (Few et al., 2021). This practice is a breach of the UN's Human Rights charter and Colombian law. Armed actors continue to dispute territories and routes for drug trafficking and fight for territorial control over natural, economic, and social resources. These fights perpetuate the need for more people and soldiers, like children and teens (Fundación Ideas para la Paz [FIP], 2020; Kroc Institute, 2020). Efforts to put local programs into place in rural areas to prevent forced recruitment can cause organizations and individuals to become targets of violence, including threats, murders, and forced displacement (CNMH, 2017). Social leaders, parents, teachers, and school principals who try to protect children and young people in their territories from the armed actors have been targets of threats from these groups (CNMH, 2017).

The Colombian Attorney General's Office has reported that 11,556 boys and girls were forced to join the FARC-EP between 1975 and 2016, with estimates reaching over 18,000 when recruitment by other armed groups is added (Villanueva O'Driscoll et al., 2017). The recruitment of minors has worsened in recent years. The Office of the Ombudsman has stated that the number of un- derage people involved in the armed groups is at the highest level since peace negotiations began in 2012 (Insight Crime, 2021). In 2020, with the pandemic, periods of lockdown, and closed schools, the risk of illicit recruitment was higher (Semana, 2021). Rural territories of the country were more exposed; the persisting socioeconomic gaps and institutional weakness represent huge challenges for the prevention of the illicit recruitment and use of children and teens for war and criminal activities (Insight Crime, 2021). In April 2021, the Colombian People's Defense Bureau acknowledged that recruitment of minors persists in 30 of the 32 departments, while unofficial numbers indicate a twofold increase in underage combatants since 2019 (Defensoria del Pueblo, 2021).

OFFICIAL PROGRAMS AND PROCESSES FOR DEMOBILIZATION AND PREVENTION

Recruiting children or adolescents is considered a war crime, violates interna- tional humanitarian law, and carries prison sentences and loss of any prescribed judicial benefits (Muñoz & Serralvo, 2019). As framed in the Colombian constitu- tion and victims' law, former child combatants are victims of the conflict and have the right to truth, justice, and reparations to re-establish their rights (Summers, 2012). In 2012, special programs were created for the protection and assistance in the reintegration of those who were forced to take part in the political violence. The Colombian Institute for Family Welfare (Instituto Colombiano de Bienestar Familiar [ICBF]) was mandated to take custody of all desvinculados (former child combatants) to re-establish their rights and provide educational and economic benefits. The ICBF registers, assists, assumes legal responsibility, and creates spe- cialized intervention programs for this population. In line with the literature described earlier, an overarching goal of the ICBF in creating a positive climate for reintegration has been to foster a return to youths' original nuclear families, to restore their basic rights, and to fight the social stigma associated with being a former combatant, as desvinculados are often considered delinquents by their communities (ICBF, 2016).

To achieve these goals, the ICBF designed a specialized psychosocial program with four paths. First, a minor's placement is determined by a team of case workers using an initial assessment that considers both the individual's age and home situ- ation. A preferred option is reuniting underage ex-combatants with their biolog- ical family. Some older children, as a secondary option, may be placed with foster families. A third option, for adolescents between ages 13 and 18, is placement in "Centers of Specialized Attention" that serve as substitute homes and provide schooling, vocational training, and registration to all the national health and social services. For ages 17 to 18, a fourth option is "Juvenile Homes" that offer more autonomy with the goal of preparing youth for their transition to adulthood. The latter of these two options for demobilized youth are run by private nonprofit organizations contracted by the government. The goal of these diverse options is to provide maximal flexibility to state agencies in attending to individual needs, local resources, and varying family and community situations.

ICBF records show that from 1999 to 2018, 6,499 youth combatants joined either the foster family or institutional programs, with numbers growing since 2017 following the 2016 peace agreement. In the two decades of ICBF records, almost three-quarters were male, and in total, these participants came from at least seven different armed groups. Initially, a large number came to ICBF programs because of an agreement with the paramilitary group *Autodefensas Unidas de Colombia*. About 60% of all participants came from the FARC-EP, 19% from the ELN, 15% from paramilitary groups, and about 5% from drug trafficking criminal organizations. Approximately 30% are girls with an average age of 13 years. Twelve percent of these girls belonged to Indigenous groups; the total Indigenous population of the country is 3.4% (ICBF, n.d.). Other ethnic minorities were also disproportionately recruited, particularly Afro-Colombians from high-conflict areas (Faulkner & Doctor, 2021).

A detailed description of a sample of children in the ICBF programs shows a glimpse of their lives before, during, and after recruitment (Defensoria del Pueblo, 2021). Prior to recruitment, they came mostly from single-mother homes or were living with unrelated, substitute parents. Before joining the armed group, 37.3% had at least one family member murdered; 25.2% of the girls and 15% of the boys reported physical abuse as a reason they left their families to join the armed group. At the time of joining an armed group, more than 90% of the child soldiers reported working in some capacity. Over 80% of youth reported joining voluntarily and cited a range of reasons, including being attracted by the weapons and uniforms (19%). Girls were more likely than boys to say they saw armed groups as a viable way of life or reported wanting to join because they had a desire for adventure (Carmona Parra et al., 2012). However, the authors concluded that all did not know the implications of joining. During their time as armed combatants, both boys and girls cooked (88.3%), engaged in active combat (84.3%) and ambushes (74.8%), and cared for the sick and wounded (49.7%). Some acted as couriers for drug-related activities or conducted mandated executions. Nearly 20% reported giving birth or becoming fathers, most around age 15. When allowed to keep their children, both parent and child were placed in substitute homes. In terms of their thinking about their futures, many of these youth reported aspirations to find work (60%) and/or return to school (58%). The adolescents enrolled in governmental institutions expressed a desire to work in agriculture (16%) or a bakery (11%), while those in foster homes expressed a desire to do secretarial work (11%) or nursing (11%), among other work possibilities.

The ICBF demobilization program uses a "social constructionist systemic approach" to guide nonprofit institutions in implementing the process. All reinsertion agencies are guided in implementing six modules designed for institutional staff to individually work with participants on gaining self-knowledge and creating new meanings of their past traumatic experiences. The goal is to construct personal narratives that enable a return to life outside an armed group on participants' terms. In practice, these modules are implemented in either one-on-one counseling sessions or in group sessions and do not follow a strict sequence. Their experience, in great measure, may be characterized by violence, negative emotions, and traumatic memories that require reframing or meaning making. The supportive staff may use any of the modules as determined by their perception of the participant's needs. A constructive dialogue is built around Gergen's (1994) views of emotions and social relations to build a new narrative of their past emotional life that enables existence in a disarmed context.

A recent qualitative study of the ICBF reintegration of child combatants yielded mixed results (Hudecovská & Schawanhaeuser, 2020). Interviews conducted with participants, staff, and foster families showed large gaps in addressing psychosocial needs. The program failed to endow child soldiers with self-sufficiency and did not prepare them well for future life; most participants in the study came from Indigenous communities or rural areas and were declared by the ICBF to not be prepared to return to rural life. They were thus provided education and resources with a focus on urban living. Though the protocol for psychosocial guidance instructed staff members to encourage the child soldiers to reimagine their futures through reflective activities and resignifying of past experiences, this practice was found to be actively discouraged by foster mothers and educators. The adolescents expressed feeling they were encouraged to forget the past or were not given supports to engage with the pain of remembering when they were asked to discuss the past. Often institutional practices like this one are not linked, or require fidelity, to the protocols established and the implementation of the protocols.

In addition to supports for demobilized minors, the Colombian government has also engaged in efforts aimed at early prevention of forced recruitment. The Colombian Agency for Reincorporation and Normalization has delivered 171 interventions to 8,141 participants under a strategy labeled "Mambru did not go to war—This is another story," a take on a popular children's song. The program is implemented in locations where early reports indicate recruiting activities are increasing. It incorporates a holistic focus—including an initial assessment of the risks faced by children in the community and the identification of their community leaders. With the children and the community, a series of activities are planned and culturally adapted to a given region. The program's aims are to generate and strengthen protective environments with family participation, community, and governmental agencies. This program has been in existence since 2003 and has aided more than 76,000 former combatants, including child combatants once they leave the ICBF programs. Currently, as with all Colombian governmental agencies, they are required to submit annual reports of the degree to which they meet their set goals, but little other empirical research has been conducted.

Despite the significant numbers of former child combatants who have received this programming, its implementation and impact have been impeded by structural factors feeding into violence, including continued unemployment, lack of housing, gender inequities, and poor mental health services (Agencia nacional para la reintegración y normalización, 2017).

EDUCATION AS PREVENTION AND DEMOBILIZATION SUPPORT

Despite these efforts oriented toward community strengthening, the Colombian state has failed to maintain a robust presence and build trust in remote areas deeply touched by violence (e.g., Richani, 2013). Nongovernment actors have helped fill this gap with efforts focused on education as a holistic prevention and reincorporation strategy, based on previous empirical work showing that people with educational options are less susceptible to recruitment to an insurgent or armed group (e.g., Andvig & Gates, 2010; Gates, 2011). In contrast, unjust and inadequate educational systems perpetuate the inequities that motivate individuals to join armed groups (Díez & Quinn, 2015). Education is also a central link between participation and demobilization of minors in armed conflict and the SDGs. Equitable education is a foundation for prevention and effective reintegration, partly by serving to make societies more inclusive (e.g., offering fulfilling options and roles in society), promoting peace (e.g., teaching interpersonal skills like conflict resolution), and providing opportunities to address inequalities that feed into violence (e.g., Perilla, 2020).

In Colombia, one effort addressing these interconnected goals is the National Program for Peace Education (Educapaz), a union of civil society organizations focused on education and peace construction through work with individuals, communities, and regional and national government. Educapaz argues that improving education is critical to closing historical gaps between urban and rural territories, while emphasizing that doing so must involve attentiveness to what matters most to these communities. Its work involves collecting voices of minors and using local teams to build trust with community members. Programmatic aims include developing effective rural education in three areas: fostering active citizenship, providing psychosocial support to encourage reconciliation (at an interpersonal level), and developing socioemotional skills. The initiative serves 25,000 students across almost 300 sites, while engaging in efforts related to regional action, advocacy, and academic research (Educapaz, 2021).

While Educapaz does not specifically target child and youth combatants, its work intersects with the rising concerns for these minors and holistic prevention and intervention strategies. In 2021, Educapaz conducted research about the effects of the pandemic in educational communities to better understand the evolving risks of recruitment and violence that children and adolescents faced, especially in rural territories of Colombia, because of dynamics created by the pandemic. A main finding was increased violence against young people and family instability (Educapaz, 2021). Education alone cannot fight all inequalities and structural conditions that favor violence and illicit recruitment of children and teens, but Educapaz's initiatives involving reconciliation and social-emotional education—as well as its advocacy for the reform of national school curricula—are conceptualized as key pillars to preventing recruitment and serving the needs of demobilized minors (Educapaz, 2021).

Educapaz is one example of organizations in Colombian civil society that work for peace and focus on children and youth, including young people at risk of being recruited by armed criminal groups. In Colombia, it is difficult for nongovernmental entities to identify and target individual demobilized children and youth due to anonymity, individual rights, community stigma, and lack of motivation of these youth to engage with reintegration programs. Broadly, during a postconflict phase, it is necessary to generate sustainable educational, employment, and cultural opportunities, especially for former combatants and the population with high risk of being recruited (Garbarino et al., 2020). Educapaz's work to improve education is a key piece—in addition to social development in rural territories and jobs for former combatants—to addressing issues of recruitment and demobilization through a holistic lens.

It is also necessary, however, to provide psychosocial supports for former combatants, especially for children and adolescents. Civil society organizations, like Educapaz, can serve as vehicles for such programming and be powerful advocates for political action (Díez & Quinn, 2015). Through their "Word Schools" program, for example, Educapaz is working in rural schools to engage students in learning the reasons for the conflict and the truth about what happened in the war. This effort aims to address mental health through a dual approach: reassuring young people about the possibility of sustainable peace via the peace accords and building their resilience to solve past and future disputes that may surface in their daily lives. Such psychosocial support is complemented by promoting advocacy, such as by creating "dynamizing teams" in schools with the intent to guarantee sustainability and provide consistent local voice within political processes at the municipal and departmental level.

Another example of a civil society organization offering peace pedagogies as psychosocial support to former combatants is the Foundation for Reconciliation (FPR). Since 2003, the FPR's mission has been to contribute to the construction of peace in Colombia through generating, developing, and promoting pedagogy to re-establish coexistence, relationships, and communal ties in diverse populations affected by violence. FPR aims to reach rural areas and foster psychosocial tools, optimism, and self-efficacy in students and teachers to create a foundation for other peacebuilding efforts. This work involves generating awareness about the need for denaturalizing violence and relinquishing historically based intergroup hatred. To this end, programming promotes conceptualizing children and adolescents (including ex-combatants) as integral, multidimensional, autonomous, and diverse subjects (see description of ESPERE program later). In areas where children and youth are vulnerable to recruitment, FPR has focused on strengthening social networks as a strategy to mitigate the impacts of violence.

This is done through community reparation projects, reconciliation rituals with offended communities and individuals, training trainers, and building national networks for political advocacy.

Finally, minors who have been involved in armed groups also need support in making sense of these experiences, their identities, and their future trajectories with a focus on dignity and psychosocial well-being. FPR's School of Forgiveness and Reconciliation (ESPERE) is a 40-hour educational intervention focused on processing "unwelcome" emotions from experiences of violence and managing resentment and trauma. ESPERE targets emotional intelligence and skills to counteract the effects of stigmatization and polarization affecting minors as they reintegrate. It aims to foster personal and collective resources promoting care. It also generates opportunities for productive processing of the thoughts and feelings that feed into hatred, resentment, and revenge, including those fed by ideologies, politics, and/or religion. Likewise, its pedagogical strategies are intended to generate welcoming and safe environments that give young people the opportunity to share feelings, take risks, and feel that they are part of a community. Participants are encouraged to be creative, express their justifications when faced with decision-making, and enjoy themselves during the process. The main goal is to process their traumatic memories, including their sense of guilt, and instead of remaining stuck in their past, project future life trajectories. The program's theory of change hypothesizes that in order to overcome the urge for revenge that a war environment foster, individuals must recuperate a sense of the sacredness of life. This process entails developing compassion and a greater respect for human dignity. While systematic evaluation of the ESPERE program is currently underway, it has been recently recognized by UNESCO's Institute for Lifelong Learning as a valuable case study of effective psychosocial support (Chatzigianni, 2019).

These short summaries of the work of ICBF, Educapaz, and FPR provide examples of how various interventions across sectors conceptualize supporting at-risk or demobilized children and youth. We describe multiple efforts that are part of a broader ecosystem. Together, they demonstrate how commitments to equitable education, inclusive and peaceful societies, and addressing structural inequality can address the psychosocial needs of children and youth at collective and individual levels.

CONCLUSION AND FUTURE DIRECTIONS

In this chapter, we have sought to highlight current understandings of the psychosocial processes for minors engaging in and demobilizing from armed groups and multilevel responses to support their reintegration. While the SDG 8.7 specifically calls for eliminating child soldiers, several other goals address issues that are integral to a systems approach to understanding and intervening in the psychosocial dynamics of minors in armed conflict. A core of this work is building equitable education systems, as these offer a foundation upon which economic opportunity and inclusion (tied to SDGs 10 and 11) can feed into peaceful societies (SDG 16), address motivators for recruitment, and create productive community contexts for reintegration.

These questions are not just theoretical or academic; rising numbers of minors engaged in armed conflict and instability created by COVID-19 make them more salient and urgent. We offer details about Colombian governmental and non-governmental organization programs to address the growing crisis of underage recruitment there. The evidence from ICBF suggests that economic concerns, family factors and violence, and social dynamics create motivators for children and youth engagement in armed groups. Emerging evidence, such as from Educapaz, indicates recruitment is growing as the COVID-19 pandemic has brought greater instability, disruption in education, and financial needs. At the same time, programs like Educapaz and ICBF demonstrate broader approaches beyond targeted psychological therapy and individualized support. These different framings, along with cultural and political contexts of the work, drive the metrics used by these organizations, such as, for ICBF, the number of citizens reached with programming targeting specific rights under Colombian law. More extensive work on the impact of these initiatives is currently taking place.

Addressing systems that former underage combatants return to—for example, robust educational opportunities, fulfilling and stable employment opportunities, inclusive and safe communities—is difficult and multifaceted, but this work is being done. Psychologists have played integral roles in demonstrating the need for systemic approaches, while providing valuable empirical evidence and evaluation of programming. These efforts are integral as numerous societies face deepening challenges related to armed conflict, violence, and cross-sector crises inflamed by the pandemic. Conceptualizing the work within the context of the UN's SDGs offers an opportunity to coordinate psychosocial theory and intervention for underage combatants with the international community's efforts to build sustainable cultures of peace based in equity and human rights.

REFERENCES

Adhikari, R. P., Kohrt, B. A., Luitel, N. P., Upadhaya, N., Gurung, D., & Jordans, M. D. (2014). Protective and risk factors of psychosocial wellbeing related to the reintegration of former child soldiers in Nepal. *Intervention, 12*(3), 367–378.

Agencia nacional para la reintegracion y normalizacion (ARN). (2017). *Estrategia nacional: Mambrú no va a la guerra. Este es otro cuento.*

Amnesty International. (2000). *Child soldiers: Criminals or victims?* https://www.amnesty.org/en/documents/IOR50/002/2000/en/

Amone P'Olak, K., Garnefski, N., & Kraaij, V. (2007). The impact of war experiences and physical abuse on formerly abducted boys in northern Uganda. *South African Psychiatry Review, 10*, 76–82.

Andvig, J. C., & Gates, S. (2010). Recruiting children for armed conflict. In S. Gates & S. Reich (Eds.), *Child soldiers in the age of fractured states* (pp. 77–92). University of Pittsburgh Press.

Baare, Anton K. G. 2006. *An analysis of transitional economic reintegration.* Sweden: Swedish Initiative for Disarmament, Demobilisation and Reintegration (SIDDR), Ministry of Foreign Affairs.

Barber, B. K., & Schluterman, J. M. (2009). An overview of the empirical literature on adolescents and political violence. In B. K. Barber (Ed.), *Adolescents and war: How youth deal with political violence* (pp. 35–61). Oxford University Press.

Betancourt, T. S., Borisova, I. I., Williams, T. P., Brennan, R. T., Whitfield, T. H., De La Soudiere, M., . . . Gilman, S. E. (2010). Sierra Leone's former child soldiers: A follow-up study of psychosocial adjustment and community reintegration. *Child Development, 81*(4), 1077–1095.

Betancourt, T. S., Brennan, R. T., Rubin-Smith, J., Fitzmaurice, G. M., & Gilman, S. E. (2010). Sierra Leone's former child soldiers: A longitudinal study of risk, protective factors, and mental health. *Journal of the American Academy of Child and Adolescent Psychiatry, 49,* 606–615.

Betancourt, T. S., Borisova, I., Williams, T. P., Meyers-Ohki, S. E., Rubin-Smith, J. E., Annan, J., & Kohrt, B. A. (2013). Research review: Psychosocial adjustment and mental health in former child soldiers—a systematic review of the literature and recommendations for future research. *Journal of Child Psychology and Psychiatry, 54*(1), 17–36.

Betancourt, T. S., & Khan, K. T. (2008). The mental health of children affected by armed conflict: Protective processes and pathways to resilience. *International Review of Psychiatry, 20*(3), 317–328.

Blattman, C., & Annan, J. (2008). Child combatants in northern Uganda: Reintegration myths and realities. In R. Muggah (Ed.), *Security and post-conflict reconstruction* (pp. 103–126). Routledge.

Boothby, N., Crawford, J., & Halperin, J. (2006). Mozambique child soldier life outcome study: Lessons learned in rehabilitation and reintegration efforts. *Global Public Health, 1*(1), 87–107.

Carmona Parra, J. A., Moreno Martín, F., & Tobón Hoyos, J. F. (2012). Child soldiers in Colombia: Five views. *Universitas Psychologica, 11*(3), 755–768.

Centro Nacional de Memoria Histórica (CNMH). (2017). *Informe del Centro Nacional de Memoria histórica. Una guerra sin edad. Informe nacional de reclutamiento y utilización de niños, niñas y adolescentes en el conflicto armado colombiano.*

Chatzigianni, S. (2019). *ESPERE: Schools of Forgiveness and Reconciliation, Colombia.* UNESCO Institute for Lifelong Learning. https://uil.unesco.org/case-study/effect ive-practices-database-litbase-0/espere-schools-forgiveness-and-reconciliation

Defensoria del Pueblo. (2021). *Reclutamiento forzado, uso y utilización de niños, niñas y adolescentes en Colombia.*

Díez, F., & Quinn, J. (2015). *Reformas educativas en los acuerdos de paz. Red de Educación para la paz y los Derechos Humanos.* Editorial Torreblanca.

Dumas, L. (2003). *Wounded childhood: The use of child soldiers in armed conflict in Central Africa.* International Labor Office.

Educapaz. (2021). *EDUCAPAZ: Programa Nacional de Educación para la Paz.* https:// educapaz.co/

Faulkner, C. M., & Doctor, A. C. (2021). Rebel fragmentation and the recruitment of child soldiers. *International Studies Quarterly, 65*(3), 647–659.

Few, R., Ramírez, V., Armijos, M. T., Hernández, L. A. Z., & Marsh, H. (2021). Moving with risk: Forced displacement and vulnerability to hazards in Colombia. *World Development, 144*, 105482.

Fundación Ideas para la Paz. (2020) *El problema del reclutamiento y la utilización de niños, niñas y adolescentes. Desafíos y respuestas urgentes.*

Gamba de Potgieter, V. (2018). *Children and armed conflict* (A/HRC/40/49). United Nations General Assembly, Human Rights Council. https://undocs.org/s/2018/465

Garbarino, J., Governale, A., & Nesi, D. (2020). Vulnerable children: Protection and social reintegration of child soldiers and youth members of gangs. *Child Abuse & Neglect, 110*, 104415.

Gates, S. (2011). Why do children fight? Motivations and the mode of recruitment. In A. Ozerdem & S. Podder (Eds.), *Child soldiers: From recruitment to reintegration* (pp. 29–49). Palgrave Macmillan.

Gergen, K. J. (1994). *Realities and relationships.* Harvard University Press.

Hudcovská, J., & Schwanhaeuser, K. (2020). Institutional and family-based models of attention for Colombian child soldiers from a psychosocial perspective. *International Journal of Psychology & Psychological Therapy, 20*(2), 188–200.

InSight Crime. (2021, April 15). *La continúa la crisis del reclutamiento de menores en Colombia.* https://es.insightcrime.org/investigaciones/continua-crisis-reclutamiento-menores-colombia/

Instituto Colombiano de Bienestar Familiar (ICBF). (2016). *Lineamiento técnico para el restablecimiento de derechos y contribución a la reparación integral de niños, niñas y adolescentes huérfanos como consecuencia del conflicto armado.*

Instituto Colombiano de Bienestar Familiar (ICBF). (n.d.). *Tablero Desvinculados.* https://www.icbf.gov.co/bienestar/observatoriobienestar-ninez/tablero-desvinculados

Johnson, K., Asher, J., Rosborough, S., Raja, A., Panjabi, R., Beadling, C., & Lawry, L. (2008). Association of combatant status and sexual violence with health and mental health outcomes in postconflict Liberia. *Jama, 300*(6), 676–690.

Kohrt, B. A., Jordans, M. J., Koirala, S., & Worthman, C. M. (2015). Designing mental health interventions informed by child development and human biology theory: A social ecology intervention for child soldiers in Nepal. *American Journal of Human Biology, 27*(1), 27–40.

Kohrt, B. A., Jordans, M. J., Tol, W. A., Perera, E., Karki, R., Koirala, S., & Upadhaya, N. (2010). Social ecology of child soldiers: Child, family, and community determinants of mental health, psychosocial well-being, and reintegration in Nepal. *Transcultural Psychiatry, 47*(5), 727–753.

Kohrt, B. A., Yang, M., Rai, S., Bhardwaj, A., Tol, W. A., & Jordans, M. J. (2016). Recruitment of child soldiers in Nepal: Mental health status and risk factors for voluntary participation of youth in armed groups. *Peace and Conflict: Journal of Peace Psychology, 22*(3), 208.

Kroc Institute. (2020). *Tres años después de la implementación de la firma del Acuerdo Final de Colombia.* Notre Dame University.

The hidden health trauma of child soldiers. (2004). *The Lancet, 363*, 831.

Machel, G. (1996). *Impact of armed conflict on children* (Report of the Expert of the Secretary-General of the United Nations). United Nations.

MacMullin, C., & Loughry, M. (2004). Investigating psychosocial adjustment of former child soldiers in Sierra Leone and Uganda. *Journal of Refugee Studies, 17*(4), 460–472.

Medeiros, E. (2007). Integrating mental health into post-conflict rehabilitation: The case of Sierra Leonean and Liberian "Child Soldiers." *Journal of Health Psychology, 12*(3), 498–504.

Miller, K. E., & Rasmussen, A. (2010). War exposure, daily stressors, and mental health in conflict and post-conflict settings: Bridging the divide between trauma-focused and psychosocial frameworks. *Social Science & Medicine, 70*(1), 7–16.

Muñoz, M. G., & Serralvo, J. (2019). International humanitarian law in Colombia: Going a step beyond. *International Review of the Red Cross, 101*(912), 1117–1147.

Okello, J., Onen, T., & Musisi, S. (2007). Psychiatric disorders among war-abducted and non-abducted adolescents in Gulu district, Uganda: A comparative study. *African Journal of Psychiatry, 20*, 225–231.

Perilla, D. (2020). Towards the construction of pedagogies and plural memories: Exploring learnings in a transitional and normalization area (Guaviare, Colombia). *Revista Colombiana de Antropología, 56*(1), 115–141.

Richani, N. (2013). *Systems of violence: The political economy of war and peace in Colombia*. SUNY Press.

Schauer, E., & Elbert, T. (2010). The psychological impact of child soldiering. In E. Martz (Ed.), *Trauma rehabilitation after war and conflict* (pp. 311–360). Springer.

Semana. (2021, April 20). Las escalofriantes cifras de reclutamiento forzado de menores durante la pandemia, que identificó la Defensoría del Pueblo. https://www.semana.com/nacion/articulo/las-escalofriantes-cifras-de-reclutamiento-forzado-de-menores-durante-la-pandemia-que-identifico-la-defensoria-del-pueblo/202151/

Steinberg, L. (2007). Risk taking in adolescence: New perspectives from brain and behavioral science. *Current Directions in Psychological Science, 16*(2), 55–59.

Summers, N. (2012). Colombia's victims' law: transitional justice in a time of violent conflict. *Harvard Human Rights Journal, 25*(1), 219–235.

Tol, W. A., Jordans, M. J., Kohrt, B. A., Betancourt, T. S., & Komproe, I. H. (2013a). Promoting mental health and psychosocial well-being in children affected by political violence: Part I—Current evidence for an ecological resilience approach. In C. Fernando & M. Ferrari (Eds.), *Handbook of resilience in children of war* (pp. 11–27). Springer.

Tol, W. A., Jordans, M. J., Kohrt, B. A., Betancourt, T. S., & Komproe, I. H. (2013b). Promoting mental health and psychosocial well-being in children affected by political violence: Part II—Expanding the evidence base. In C. Fernando & M. Ferrari (Eds.), *Handbook of resilience in children of war* (pp. 29–38). Springer.

Tol, W. A., Komproe, I. H., Jordans, M. J. D., Gross, A. L., Susanty, D., Macy, R. D., & De Jong, J. T. (2010). Mediators and moderators of a psychosocial intervention for children affected by political violence. *Journal of Consulting and Clinical Psychology, 78*(6), 818–828.

UNICEF. (2020, September 3). *Children recruited by armed forces*. https://www.unicef.org/protection/children-recruited-by-armed-forces

Unidad para la atención y reparación integral a las Víctimas (UARIV). (2020). *Cifras. Infografía*. https://cifras.unidadvictimas.gov.co/Cifras/#!/infografia

Veale, A., Worthen, M., & McKay, S. (2017). Transformative spaces in the social re-integration of former child soldier young mothers in Sierra Leone, Liberia, and Northern Uganda. *Peace and Conflict: Journal of Peace Psychology, 23*(1), 58.

Villanueva O'Driscoll, J., Loots, G., Losantos Velasco, M., Exeni Ballivián, S., Berckmans, I., & Derluyn, I. (2017). Procesos de reinserción de niños, niñas y adolescentes desvinculados de grupos armados en Colombia. *Eleuthera, 16,* 85–100.

Vindevogel, S. (2017). Resilience in the context of war: A critical analysis of contemporary conceptions and interventions to promote resilience among war-affected children and their surroundings. *Peace and Conflict: Journal of Peace Psychology, 23*(1), 76–84.

Vindevogel, S., Wessells, M., De Schryver, M., Broekaert, E., & Derluyn, I. (2014). Dealing with the consequences of war: Resources of formerly recruited and non-recruited youth in northern Uganda. *Journal of Adolescent Health, 55*(1), 134–140.

Wessells, M. G. (1998). Children, armed conflict, and peace. *Journal of Peace Research, 5,* 635.

Wessells, M. (2005). Child soldiers, peace education, and postconflict reconstruction for peace. *Theory Into Practice, 44*(4), 363–369.

Wessells, M. G. (2016). Children and armed conflict: Introduction and overview. *Peace and Conflict: Journal of Peace Psychology, 22*(3), 198.

Wessells, M. G. (2017). Children and armed conflict: Interventions for supporting war-affected children. *Peace and Conflict: Journal of Peace Psychology, 23*(1), 4.

Wessells, M. G., & Monteiro, C. (2004). Healing the wounds following protracted conflict in Angola: A community-based approach to assisting war-affected children. In U. P. Gielen, J. Fish, & J. G. Draguns (Eds.), *Handbook of culture, therapy, and healing* (pp. 321–341). Erlbaum.

Williamson, J. (2006). The disarmament, demobilization and reintegration of child soldiers: Social and psychological transformation in Sierra Leone. *Intervention, 4*(3), 185–205.

4

Promoting Peace Across Cultures

Understanding Children's Traumatic Migration Experiences and Pathways of Healing

AMY K. MARKS, REGINA ROBERG, ROSE E. LUEHRS, AND
CYNTHIA GARCÍA COLL ■

In the past two decades there has been a rapid surge in migration across the globe, with large numbers of people fleeing war and poverty-stricken countries for safety and security in a new country. Over half of today's global migrants[1] are children and adolescents, with an estimated 33 million migrant youth who have left their country of origin, oftentimes forcibly displaced from their home due to conflict and violence, poverty, or natural disasters (UNICEF, 2019). Migrant-origin children and youth (MOCY) leave their country of origin in search of safety, security, and protection from exploitation and abuse. They might also seek improved standards of living, better education, economic opportunities, family reunification, or a combination of these factors. MOCY may travel independently, with their immediate family member(s), or with an extended family or nonfamily member (Council of Europe, 2016).

MOCY can experience a number of significant stressors premigration (e.g., war, gang violence), perimigration (e.g., parental separations, child trafficking), and postmigration (e.g., racism, discrimination, oppression or exploitation). For many MOCY, this means experiencing extreme hardship, including the potential for several traumatic events across the full migration experience. The psychological experience of such traumatic events, coupled with the task of acculturating to a new country and culture, may complicate normative developmental processes and have a powerful and enduring impact on child and youth mental health and well-being (Bäärnhielm et al., 2017). At the same time, the remarkable resilience

---

1. In keeping with published literature in this area, the term *migrant* is an umbrella term that encompasses both refugees and immigrants.

of MOCY is well documented, with psychosocial factors such as family and peer social support and school connectedness functioning as protective factors that promote mental well-being and foster resilience (Curtis et al., 2018; Marks et al., 2014).

To help frame our review of migration-related trauma in childhood and youth, this chapter draws on several ecological-based theories of child and adolescent development. In our review and discussion of MOCY's well-being and postmigration adaptation, we draw from Suárez-Orozco and colleagues' (2018) integrative risk and resilience model of immigrant-origin children and youth adaptation. This recent theoretical contribution to our understanding of MOCY adaptation and resilience after trauma was built from the foundations of Bronfenbrenner's bioecological model of human development (Bronfenbrenner & Morris, 2006) and García Coll and colleagues' (1996) integrative model for the study of developmental competencies in minority children. Taken together, these perspectives posit that developmental outcomes and adaptations of MOCY in the context of the hardships of migration are shaped and influenced by the settings and social relationships in a young person's life. For example, neighborhood characteristics can have profound implications for MOCY development and well-being as this context can be a source of risk or resilience. Burgeoning evidence indicates that MOCY residing in low-income neighborhoods are at heightened risk of experiencing postmigration trauma, including exposure to gang violence (Gudiño et al., 2011), increased immigration raids in the community (Chaudry et al., 2010), and xenophobia (Marks et al., 2021; Marks et al., 2018).

Masten's (2014) risk and resilience developmental framework and Motti-Stefanidi and colleagues' (2012) integrative framework for the study of immigrant-origin children and youth adaptation also influence this work. Drawing from a resilience developmental perspective, these models help us to examine adaptation to migration using a multilevel approach, incorporating strengths-based perspectives on children's growth after hardship. These models help place contexts and social relationships as essential elements in both the postmigration adaptation and posttraumatic growth processes for youth. For example, there is strong research support that the school environment plays an important role in providing newly arrived migrant children and youth an opportunity to shape positive acculturation experiences (i.e., how quickly new cultural practices/languages/identities are formed), build healthy and supportive social connections, and foster social capital outside of the family (Suárez-Orozco et al., 2018). These school resilience-building processes may in turn reduce mental health problems and increase prosocial behaviors (e.g., Suarez-Morales & Lopez, 2009; Suárez-Orozco et al., 2010).

Importantly, the Suárez-Orozco et al. 2018 framework also incorporates *global forces* (i.e., global economic, geopolitical, and social dynamics) and unique contextual characteristics specifically related to legally vulnerable immigrants and refugee youth into our understanding of the adaptation of MOCY (Suárez-Orozco et al., 2018). These global forces, which include many of the "push" factors that initiate migration, as well as the policies that determine the receptivity character- istics of the receiving countries, are of paramount importance to consider when supporting MOCY postmigratory healing and well-being (Marks et al., 2019). For example, receiving countries with national-level policies that promote multicul- tural values and provide adequate social supports for youth in general are more likely to have physically and emotionally healthier MOCY and native-born youth alike (Marks et al., 2018).

Through the remainder of this chapter, we review recent research examining the effects of exposure to pre-, peri-, and postmigration trauma and violence. Next, we present research on posttraumatic growth in childhood, paying particular at- tention to the role of context in promoting healing. We then end our chapter with clinical care and program/policy considerations specific to supporting the well- being and development of MOCY.

MENTAL HEALTH EFFECTS OF MIGRATION TRAUMA AND VIOLENCE ON MOCY

Experiencing significant hardship and trauma before, during, and after migration can lead to MOCY being at increased risk of psychological distress and/or devel- oping psychiatric disorders such as anxiety, depression, and posttraumatic stress disorder (PTSD). In a systematic review of 46 studies of children and youth who have migrated within or into Europe, the prevalence of PTSD in young asylum- seeker and refugee migrants was reported between 20% and 84%, with unaccom- panied children being at greater risk than those who were accompanied (Curtis et al., 2018). This difference in psychiatric disorder rates for unaccompanied youth is a compelling marker of the importance of maintaining and protecting family connectedness during and after migration. Ample research has documented the challenges to youth's well-being when families are forced to separate and reunite (if possible); unfortunately for many youth, such separations can be numerous and long lasting (see Suárez-Orozco, 2015).

There is mounting evidence that trauma experienced at different stages of the migration journey may be associated with distinct mental health outcomes. A study conducted by Cleary and colleagues (2017) examined associations be- tween trauma experience pre-, peri-, and postmigration among Latinx youth aged 12 to 17 years old living in the United States. The authors found that there was a significant correlation between exposure to trauma during migration (the most common being experiencing and/or witnessing physical assault) and postmigration (the most common being witnessing violence or experiencing a serious accident or injury) with developing PTSD and depression. Premigration trauma, the most commonly reported being experiencing natural disaster, serious injury/accident, and witnessing violence, was significantly related to developing an anxiety disorder (Cleary et al., 2017).

Premigration Factors Influencing Mental Health

Premigration trauma, which oftentimes is part of the catalyzing experience or events that cause migrant children and youth to leave their homes, can have an enduring impact on youths' mental health long after they have sought refuge in a new homeland. Thibeault et al. (2017) examined the relationship between premigration trauma exposure and postmigration acculturative stress on internalizing symptoms in newly arrived migrant-origin youth from Latin America, the Caribbean, Asia, and Africa living in the United States. The results of this study found that the relationship between cumulative premigration trauma and internalizing symptoms, such as anxiety and depression symptoms, was fully mediated by acculturative stress. This indicates that a larger number of premigration traumatic events may negatively affect some youths' abilities to effectively navigate new social contexts and interpersonal relationships embedded within a new culture's environment, which in turn was related to greater internalizing symptoms later (Thibeault et al., 2017). Notably, while school-related factors, such as sense of belonging, did not moderate the relationship between acculturative stress and internalizing symptoms, most students in the sample endorsed high levels of school belonging irrespective of trauma exposure and degree of acculturation difficulties. This study's results emphasize the deep and often disruptive impact of the individual's premigration trauma history on postmigration mental health and well-being while highlighting the importance of migrant youth's postmigration environment, especially the school environment, for supporting migrant youth as they navigate through acculturative and mental health challenges.

It is also critical to acknowledge the importance of understanding—and alleviating—parents' and caregivers' own trauma and mental health challenges as part of the contextual approach to alleviating the effects of MOCY trauma and hardship. Many migrant children fleeing countries wrought with long histories of violence and instability may inherit intergenerational trauma from their parents. Studies of intergenerational trauma have found that PTSD in parents who experienced traumatic events such as wars or genocide had a significant impact on the psychological health of their offspring (Lehrner & Yehuda, 2018). In a systematic review of intergenerational migration-related trauma research, Cardeña and colleagues (2021) identified 44 studies published between 1994 and 2020 with strong evidence of intergenerational trauma experienced by Latinx individuals migrating to the United States and Canada stemming from structural vulnerability and violence, as well as specific traumatic events. Though research studies directly investigating the intergenerational effects of parent, caregiver, or grandparent trauma on MOCY are not as common as those examining direct youth effects, this is a burgeoning area of research that deserves robust future attention and support.

Perimigration Factors Influencing Mental Health

Perimigration—or the migratory journey itself prior to more permanent resettlement—can take many years to accomplish. Multiple stops through resettlement and refugee camps, as well as multiple homes prior to arrival at a final destination, are common for many MOCY. Beiser and Hou (2016) examined the role of trauma experienced at different stages of migration in immigrant and refugee mental health and found that time spent in refugee camps predicted emotional problems in youth. In addition to time spent in refugee camps, MOCY refugees are also at risk of being detained while migrating. A meta-analysis of 22 studies of the mental health consequences of detained children and families in Australia, Hong Kong, the Netherlands, the United States, and Canada found overwhelming data that showed that experiences of detention were associated with higher rates of emotional distress and psychiatric symptoms, in which a majority of the studies' samples resembled clinical cohorts (Mares, 2020). In addition, a thematic qualitative analysis of children's drawings, play, and narratives in seven of the studies identified three broad themes in detained MOCY's experiences: "confinement and surveillance," which included fences, barriers, and stories of being captured, confined, and separated; "loss and protection," which included images of threat and danger in the form of humans, animals, and police and authority figures; and "human violence," both imagined and autobiographical (Mares, 2020). Notably, developmentally normative themes commonly seen in children's play and narratives, such as schooling, peers, and "magical protective forces," were generally absent, highlighting the restrictive and dehumanizing daily life experiences of MOCY in detention centers and the potential for long-lasting effects of these governmental, macro-level practices.

In addition to refugee children and youth experiencing trauma and adversity during the migration journey, young people with low socioeconomic status who migrate to a country without authorization also frequently experience significant trauma during migration. In one study of 281 foreign-born Latinx adolescent-parent dyads who migrated to the United States, 29% of adolescents experienced trauma during the migration process and 9% were at risk for developing PTSD, which was defined by either meeting *Diagnostic and Statistical Manual of Mental Disorders*, fourth edition (DSM-IV), criteria for PTSD or meeting the frequency score threshold (Perreira & Ornelas, 2013). In this specific sample, Perreira and Ornelas (2013) also found that youth exposed to extreme poverty prior to migration were 4.4 times more likely to experience trauma during and after migration, which highlights the role of socioeconomic status as a risk factor for migration-related trauma in MOCY.

In sum, migration-related traumatic experiences include experiencing extreme physical hardships (e.g., months-long journeys on foot, dehydration, wild animal encounters; DeLuca et al., 2010), violence during migration (e.g., threats, verbal abuse, physical and sexual assault; Infante et al., 2012), detainment in immigrant detention centers with inhumane living conditions (Joung, 2021; Silove et al., 2007), and family border separations—such as those at the U.S. border (Domonoske & Gonzales, 2018). Notably, children who are unaccompanied and/or migrating at younger ages are particularly vulnerable to victimization during the migration journey, as they may have less access to social support and resiliency resources to prevent or buffer against the negative effects of trauma during migration (Perreira & Ornelas, 2013; DeLuca et al., 2010).

Postmigration Factors Influencing Mental Health

After MOCY have resettled into a more permanent residence, postmigration adaptations and acculturation processes are paramount to children's healthy development and mental well-being. Learning a new language, forming new ethnic/cultural/racial identities, and learning a host of new social customs are just some of the many social tasks young MOCY may undertake. Family dynamics and relationships shift and change as well while caregivers are acclimating to new jobs and roles in the community. Children and caregivers alike must learn how to interact with new school systems while attending to everyday family needs (Suárez-Orozco et al., 2015). For many families, these new acculturative practices and tasks take shape while also maintaining familial obligations and ties with loved ones from their culture of origin. And in many cases, caregivers and their children will experience differing rates of acculturation, with children typically acculturating more quickly than adults. This differing rate, in turn, presents opportunities for new family practices and adaptations, as well as the potential for intergenerational stress or conflict (Zhou, 1997; Marks et al., 2011).

Unfortunately for many MOCY, the context of reception in a new community may be fraught with hostility, xenophobia, and other challenging environmental experiences. Perceived discrimination is associated with a wide range of negative health behaviors and outcomes, including smoking, alcohol use, breast cancer, depression, and anxiety (Szaflarski & Bauldry, 2019). Post-resettlement factors, particularly discrimination, social marginalization, and exclusion, are the factors most highly associated with mental health challenges (Bäärnhielm et al., 2017). Szaflarski and Bauldry (2019) examined the impact of perceived discrimination and acculturation on health among immigrants and refugees, finding a negative association between perceived discrimination and mental health among first-generation immigrants, whereas acculturation had no direct association. Further, Beiser and Hou (2016) found that postmigration trauma had a significant effect on both emotional problems and aggressive behavior in refugee and immigrant youth living in Canada. In fact, postmigration experiences of discrimination had a significant predictive effect on youth's internalizing and externalizing symptoms, even when controlling for visible minority status, suggesting that there may be two sources of discrimination: one based on visible indicators (e.g., skin tone) and the other based on immigrant/refugee status.

Additional postmigration factors that can negatively impact the mental health of refugee children and youth include lack of citizenship status, which is often-times tied to limited access to educational and occupational opportunities and health services, financial and legal insecurity, lack of social capital, loneliness and boredom, and cultural dissonance (Curtis et al., 2018; Yoshikawa, 2011). The role of age and gender as potential mediating or moderating factors for these migration-related mental health experiences also remains an area in need of fur-ther research. Several studies have noted that older unaccompanied children showed greater PTSD symptoms than younger unaccompanied children (e.g., Hodes et al., 2008), whereas another study found no age-associated differences in PTSD symptoms (Jensen et al., 2015). Data regarding gender differences appears to be clearer, with some studies finding that migrant girls may be at higher risk of endorsing internalizing symptoms (e.g., anxiety, depression), while migrant boys may be more likely to exhibit externalizing symptoms, such as aggression—a pat-tern that may be related to differential parental punishment (Barajas-Gonzalez et al., 2018; Beiser & Hou, 2016).

In sum, many contextual factors—including those related to caregiver opportunities and well-being, school supports, community resources, and national policies—shape the pre-, peri-, and postmigration mental health experiences of MOCY. While there is a notable dearth of research directly studying migration-related resilience in MOCY populations, existing research identifies factors that promote mental health, such as having a positive school experience with opportunities to build social capital and develop a sense of belonging within the host country. In addition, having a secure and stable home has been found in mul-tiple studies to be a protective factor for migrant youth well-being (e.g., Groark et al., 2010). The pathways to healing for MOCY are the emphasis in our next sec-tion as we turn attention to understanding how resilience factors and resources can combine to promote healing, health, transformation, and well-being after migration-related trauma and hardship.

POSTTRAUMATIC GROWTH: CONTEXTUAL CONSIDERATIONS

Within the literature, there are varying terms used to describe positive outcomes following coping with a traumatic event. For our purposes we will touch on the two most common terms and provide a brief distinction between them. One term used widely is *posttraumatic growth* (PTG), which is believed to occur when an individual who experienced a traumatic event goes on to experience positive per-sonal gains including an improved perception of oneself, improved relationships, and/or an improved outlook on life (Tedeschi & Calhoun, 1996). Thus, PTG can be thought of as both a process and a potential outcome (Tedeschi et al., 1998).

Resilience is another commonly used term when discussing positive outcomes following trauma. Luthar and colleagues' (2000) widely used defini-tion of resilience suggests it is a process of adapting positively in the presence of adversity. It is important to note that while PTG and resilience are both associated with positive outcomes, they are distinct constructs. Resilience differs from PTG in that resilience lacks the transformative component embedded in PTG (Acquaye et al., 2018); however, the notion that resilience promotes PTG has been documented in the literature (Cengiz et al., 2019). For the purposes of this section, we focus on PTG, as the transformations occurring in oneself and in one's environment (e.g., familial, social, and religious contexts) are our main areas of focus.

Over time, the concept of PTG has been challenged for a couple of reasons. First, some have suggested that PTG does not reflect true positive change following trauma. Second, critics have questioned the validity of PTG measures (Frazier et al., 2009). In response to such criticisms, PTG researchers published work outlining the more concrete personality changes that can be observed in individuals who experience PTG (Jayawickreme et al., 2021), and others have sought to improve the psychometric properties of PTG measures, making them more valid (e.g., Boals & Schuler, 2018).

The Influence of Contextual Factors on PTG

A review of the literature on PTG in refugees conducted by K. J. Chan and colleagues (2016) highlighted several contextual factors that have been linked to higher PTG in young migrants. Specifically, findings revealed that demographic characteristics, the level of trauma experienced (e.g., experienced vs. learned about), the presence of social supports, youths' coping styles, and hope/optimism were all influential in determining self-reported PTG.

Findings on demographic characteristics suggest that younger individuals experience more PTG than older individuals, and women experience higher rates of PTG than men (Helgeson et al., 2006). Also potentially influential is the level of trauma experienced (i.e., experiencing a trauma directly vs. learning about it happening to a loved one), although findings on this are mixed (K. J. Chan et al., 2016). For example, some research has found that experiencing a trauma directly is more often associated with PTG when compared to PTG in those who learned about a traumatic event happening to a loved one (Bhat & Rangaiah, 2015; Blix et al., 2013; K. J. Chan et al., 2016). As J. K. Chan and colleagues (2016) highlighted in their review, other scholars have found that this is not the case (e.g., Teodorescu et al., 2012), indicating further research needs to be conducted in this area.

As mentioned previously, positive social support provided by both family members and peers is highly important for postmigration adjustment and also appears to be consistently predictive of PTG (J. K. Chan et al., 2016; Curtis et al., 2018). Research has found that immigrant children may broadly experience more frequent challenges with classmates and family members compared to nonimmigrant children (Caqueo-Urízar et al., 2021), and that social support disparities postmigration may contribute to the development of PTSD and depression in children (E. Y. Y. Chan et al., 2009).

Religious or Spiritual Identity and PTG

Children and adolescents who endorse a strong religious or spiritual identity seem to cope with traumatic experiences more favorably and experience more PTG (Helgeson et al., 2006). In fact, Shah and Mishra (2021) found that youth from an Eastern, religious cultural background who were exposed to armed conflict endorsed PTG significantly more than their Western, less religious counterparts. Another study focused on Liberian refugees who had been exposed to war-related trauma found that commitment to religion moderated the relationship between trauma and posttraumatic growth, such that those who were more committed to their religion had greater PTG (Acquaye et al., 2018). Taken together, these findings may have important implications for integrating religion into practice.

The Role of Rumination in PTG

Over the years many scholars have investigated positive and negative adaptations following trauma with a focus on PTSD and, more recently, PTG. Rumination, or recurrent negative thoughts about negative past experiences or feelings, has been documented in the literature as a strong predictor of PTSD (Michael et al., 2007). Research in this area often includes measures of rumination as a variable of interest when testing hypotheses of the trauma–PTSD/trauma–PTG pathways.

One study on children and adolescents who experienced a natural disaster in Chile found that rumination mediated the relationships between trauma severity and posttraumatic stress (PTS) and PTG (Andrades et al., 2018). Specifically, path analysis revealed that intrusive rumination mediated the relationship between trauma severity and PTS, whereas deliberate rumination mediated the relationship between trauma severity and intrusive rumination with PTG (Andrades et al., 2018). Another study with Japanese youth exposed to trauma found that deliberate rumination was a meaningful cognitive process associated with experiencing PTG (Taku et al., 2012). These findings on rumination are notable as previous research has suggested that the cognitive processes occurring during deliberate and intrusive rumination play a meaningful role in meaning making, which is related to adjustment to life following trauma (Stockton et al., 2011). In addition, rumination can have an effect on the way an individual is engaging with their environment following trauma. Garcia and Wlodarczyk (2017) conducted a study on rumination and PTG with women who experienced the 2010 earthquake in Chile. Their findings indicated that PTG was influenced by communal coping and rumination, which further supports the important role of one's social context in experiencing PTG.

CLINICAL, PROGRAMMATIC, AND POLICY IMPLICATIONS

In considering any type of intervention that would promote well-being and posttraumatic growth among MOCY, the many forces that lay outside of youths' control must be taken directly into account. Foremost, deep political reform is needed for many countries that do not embrace multicultural ideals and values in their resettlement practices or general public rhetoric. In many countries around the world, xenophobic violence has continued to increase and cause devastation among migrant communities. According to Human Rights Watch (2019), hundreds of people were killed in 2019 because of rising nationalism and xenophobia in South Africa. In 2020, the same organization documented the steep rises in xenophobia, racism, racial violence, and other forms of anti-migrant hate in the European Union. And in the United States, recent violence against Asian-origin youth and families has increased sharply since the COVID-19 pandemic and anti-Asian hate were linked by national political rhetoric (see Zhang et al., 2020).

Legislation that protects youth and their families from oppression, xenophobia, and other forms of discrimination are essential for supporting MOCY health and positive migration-related adaptations (Marks et al., 2018). National attitudes toward migrant youth and families, including perceptions of social similarity or compatibility, are also foundational to promoting MOCY mental and physical health (Marks et al., 2018). Moreover, developing strong national and international standards for protecting youth and families from perimigration trauma needs prioritization, and resettlement systems need to be held accountable for MOCY well-being. Such efforts may include promoting universal access to health care and its financial coverage, strengthening the monitoring of international health and resettlement systems, improving and countering global xenophobia, and attending deeply to the social determinants of health unique to migrant communities around the world (see World Health Organization report by Cheng et al., 2018).

In addition to policy, direct mental health services are clearly an important part of any comprehensive approach to supporting MOCY youth and family well-being. Given the myriad traumatic stressors a large proportion of migrant children and youth commonly encounter pre-, peri-, and postmigration, many would greatly benefit from additional sources of support such as clinical interventions to support healing post-resettlement. Therapy, holistic health care approaches, and practitioner training are all essential to promoting MOCY well-being. Whatever the intervention may be, it is essential that clinicians working with migrant children and adolescents provide culturally sensitive, developmentally appropriate trauma-focused and evidence-based interventions (Isakson et al., 2015). In taking this approach, it is necessary to adopt a socioecological framework (such as those noted earlier) that integrates individual, family, peer, school, community, cultural, and societal-level contextual factors when conceptualizing a young person's treatment plan (Betancourt et al., 2013). Innovations in delivering care to migrant communities should include language/cultural interpretive services and interdisciplinary care while prioritizing immigrant community engagement and collaboration (Pottie et al., 2014).

Using a strengths-based or resiliency approach to care, research findings repeatedly emphasize the importance of gathering relevant information about migrant spiritual and religious identities to incorporate these predictive PTG factors into therapy and other supports appropriately (Acquaye et al., 2018). Those in positions of providing support to migrant youth could benefit from taking the time to gather information about religious practices premigration, as well as how those practices may have been impacted during migration and postmigration. Further, a recent study of both migrant and nonmigrant youth found that migrant youth—though experiencing more trauma than nonmigrant youth—reported greater resilience resources and experienced better mental health outcomes after trauma than nonmigrant youth (Gatt et al., 2020). In sum, MOCY and their families are an extremely diverse population with myriad cultural and personal strengths and resources that can protect them from long-term mental health challenges and promote profound posttraumatic growth. Supports integrated into school and community practices that celebrate MOCY's unique resilience along pathways to healing and posttraumatic growth are therefore both warranted and essential.

REFERENCES

Acquaye, H. E., Sivo, S. A., & Jones, K. D. (2018). Religious commitment's moderating effect on refugee trauma and growth. *Counseling & Values, 63*, 57–75. https://doi-org.ezproxysuf.flo.org/10.1002/cvj.12073

Andrades, M., García, F. E., Calonge, I., & Martínez-Arias, R. (2018). Posttraumatic growth in children and adolescents exposed to the 2010 earthquake in Chile and its relationship with rumination and posttraumatic stress symptoms. *Journal of Happiness Studies, 19*, 1505–1517. https://doi-org.ezproxysuf.flo.org/10.1007/s10 902-017-9885-7

Bäärnhielm, S., Laban, K., Schouler-Ocak, M., Rousseau, C., & Kirmayer, L. J. (2017). Mental health for refugees, asylum seekers and displaced persons: A call for a humanitarian agenda. *Transcultural Psychiatry, 54*(5–6), 565–574. https://doi.org/10.1177/1363461517747095

Barajas-Gonzalez, R. G., Calzada, E., Huang, K., Covas, M., Castillo, C. M., & Brotman, L. M. (2018). Parent spanking and verbal punishment, and young child internalizing and externalizing behaviors in Latino immigrant families: Test of moderation by context and culture. *Parenting, Science & Practice, 18*, 219–242. https://doi-org.ezp-prod1.hul.harvard.edu/10.1080/15295192.2018.1524242

Beiser, M., & Hou, F. (2016). Mental health effects of premigration trauma and postmigration discrimination on refugee youth in Canada. *Journal of Nervous and Mental Disease, 204*(6), 464–470. https://doi.org/10.1097/NMD.0000000000000516

Betancourt, T. S., Meyers-Ohki, S. E., Charrow, A. P., & Tol, W. A. (2013). Interventions for children affected by war. *Harvard Review of Psychiatry, 21*(2), 70–91. https://doi.org/10.1097/hrp.0b013e318283bf8f

Bhat, R. M., & Rangaiah, B. (2015). The impact of conflict exposure and social support on posttraumatic growth among the young adults in Kashmir. *Cogent Psychology, 2*, 1–11.

Blix, I., Hansen, M. B., Birkeland, M. S., Nissen, A., & Heir, T. (2013). Posttraumatic growth, posttraumatic stress and psychological adjustment in the aftermath of the 2011 Oslo bombing attack. *Health and Quality of Life Outcomes, 11*, 160. https://doi.org/10.1186/1477-7525-11-160

Boals, A., & Schuler, K. L. (2018). Reducing reports of illusory posttraumatic growth: A revised version of the Stress-Related Growth Scale (SRGS-R). *Psychological Trauma: Theory, Research, Practice, and Policy, 10*, 190–198. http://dx.doi.org/10.1037/tra0000267

Bronfenbrenner, U., & Morris, P. (2006). The bioecological model of human development. In R. M. Lerner & W. Damon (Eds.), *Handbook of child psychology: Theoretical models of human development* (6th ed., Vol. 1, pp. 793–828). Wiley.

Caqueo-Urízar, A., Atencio, D., Flores, J., Narea, M., Urzua, A., & Irarrazava, M. (2021). Mental health in immigrant children and adolescents in northern Chile mental health in immigrant children and adolescents. *Journal of Immigrant and Minority Health, 23*, 280–288. https://doi-org.ezp-prod1.hul.harvard.edu/10.1007/s10903-020-01101-7

Cardeña, J. P., Rivera, L. M., & Spak, J. M. (2021). Intergenerational trauma in Latinxs: A scoping review. *Social Science & Medicine, 270*, 113662. doi:10.1016/j.socscimed.2020.113662

Cengiz, I., Ergün, D., & Çakici, E. (2019). Posttraumatic stress disorder, posttraumatic growth and psychological resilience in Syrian refugees: Hatay, Turkey. *Anatolian Journal of Psychiatry/Anadolu Psikiyatri Dergisi, 20*(3), 269–276. https://doi-org.ezproxysuf.flo.org/10.5455/apd.4862

Chan, E. Y. Y., Mercer, S. W., Yue, C., Wong, S., & Griffiths, S. M. (2009). Mental health of migrant children: An overview of the literature. *International Journal of Mental Health, 38*(3), 44–52. http://www.jstor.org/stable/41345292

Chan, K. J., Young, M. Y., & Sharif, N. (2016). Well-being after trauma: A review of posttraumatic growth among refugees. *Canadian Psychology/Psychologie Canadienne, 57*(4), 291–299. https://doi-org.ezproxysuf.flo.org/10.1037/cap.0000065

Chaudry, A., Capps, R., Pedroza, J., Castañeda, R. M., Santos, R., & Scott, M. M. (2010). *Facing our future: Children in the aftermath of immigration enforcement.* http://www.urban.org/publications/ 412020.html

Cheng, I., Advocat, J., Vasi, S., Enticott, J. C., Willey, S., Wahidi, S., Crock, B., Raghavan, A., Vandenberg, B. E., Gunatillaka, N., Wong, V. H., Girdwood, A., Rottler, A., Blackmore, R., Gibson-Helm, M., & Boyle, J. A.(2018, April). *A rapid review of evidence-based information, best practices and lessons learned in addressing the health needs of refugees and migrants.* World Health Organization report. https://www.who.int/publications/i/item/a-rapid-review-of-evidence-based-information-best-practices-and-lessons-learned-in-addressing-the-health-needs-of-refugees-and-migrants

Cleary, S. D., Snead, R., Dietz-Chavez, D., Rivera, I., & Edberg, M. C. (2017). Immigrant trauma and mental health outcomes among Latino youth. *Journal of Immigrant and Minority Health, 20*(5), 1053–1059. https://doi.org/10.1007/s10903-017-0673-6

Council of Europe. (2016, July 10). *Speech at the 10th European Forum on the Rights of the Child* [Press release]. https://www.coe.int/en/web/special-representative-secretary-general-migration-refugees/-/speech-at-the-10th-european-forum-on-the-rights-of-the-child

Curtis, P., Thompson, J., & Fairbrother, H. (2018). Migrant children within Europe: A systematic review of children's perspectives on their health experiences. *Public Health, 158*, 71–85. https://doi.org/10.1016/j.puhe.2018.01.038

DeLuca, L. A., McEwen, M. M., & Keim, S. M. (2010). United States-Mexico border crossing: experiences and risk perceptions of undocumented male immigrants. *Journal of Immigrant and Minority Health, 12*(1), 113–123. https://doi.org/10.1007/s10903-008-9197-4

Domonoske, C., & Gonzales, R. (2018, June 19). What we know: Family separation and "zero tolerance" at the border. *National Public Radio.* https://choice.npr.org/index.html?origin=https://www.npr.org/2018/06/19/621065383/what-we-know-family-separation-and-zero-tolerance-at-the-border

Frazier, P., Tennen, H., Gavian, M., Park, C., Tomich, P., & Tashiro, T. (2009). Does self-reported posttraumatic growth reflect genuine positive change? *Psychological Science, 7*, 912–919. https://doi-org.ezproxysuf.flo.org/10.1111/j.1467-9280.2009.02381.x

Garcia, F. E., & Wlodarczyk, A. (2018). Communal coping and rumination in the aftermath of Chile earthquake: Multiple mediation analysis of the relationship between subjective severity and posttraumatic growth. *Journal of Community & Applied Social Psychology, 28*, 191–199. https://doi-org.ezp-prod1.hul.harvard.edu/10.1002/casp.2350

García Coll, C., Lamberty, G., Jenkins, R., McAdoo, H. P., Crnic, K., Wasik, B. H., & Vázquez García, H. (1996). An integrative model for the study of developmental competencies in minority children. *Child Development, 67*, 1891–1914. http://dx.doi.org/10.2307/1131600

Gatt, J. M., Alexander, R., Emond, A., Foster, K., Hadfield, K., Mason-Jones, A., Reid, S., Theron, L., Ungar, M., Wouldes, T. A., & Wu, Q.(2020). Trauma, resilience, and mental health in migrant and non-migrant youth: An international cross-sectional study across six countries. *Frontiers in Psychiatry, 10*, 1–15. https://doi.org/10.3389/fpsyt.2019.00997

Groark, C., Sclare, I., & Raval, H. (2010). Understanding the experiences and emotional needs of unaccompanied asylum-seeking adolescents in the UK. *Clinical Child Psychology Psychiatry, 16*(3), 421e42.

Gudiño, O. G., Nadeem, E., Kataoka, S. H., & Lau, A. S. (2011). Relative impact of violence exposure and immigrant stressors on Latino youth psychopathology. *Journal of Community Psychology, 39*(3), 316–335. https://doi.org/10.1002/jcop.20435

Helgeson, V. S., Reynolds, K. A., & Tomich, P. L. (2006). A meta-analytic review of benefit finding and growth. *Journal of Consulting and Clinical Psychology, 74*, 797–816. https://doi-org.ezproxysuf.flo.org/10.1037/0022-006X.74.5.797

Hodes, M., Jagdev, D., Chandra, N., & Cunniff, A. (2008). Risk and resilience for psychological distress amongst unaccompanied asylum seeking adolescents. *Journal of Child Psychology and Psychiatry, 49*(7), 723–732. http://dx.doi.org/10.1111/j.1469-7610.2008.01912.x

Human Rights Watch. (2019). *South Africa: Events of 2019.* https://www.hrw.org/world-report/2020/country-chapters/south-africa#

Infante, C., Idrovo, A. J., Sánchez-Domínguez, M. S., Vinhas, S., & González-Vázquez, T. (2012). Violence committed against migrants in transit: Experiences on the Northern Mexican border. *Journal of Immigrant and Minority Health, 14*(3), 449–459. https://doi.org/10.1007/s10903-011-9489-y

Isakson, B. L., Legerski, J.-P., & Layne, C. M. (2015). Adapting and implementing evidence-based interventions for trauma-exposed refugee youth and families. *Journal of Contemporary Psychotherapy: On the Cutting Edge of Modern Developments in Psychotherapy, 45*(4), 245–253. https://doi.org/10.1007/s10879-015-9304-5

Jayawickreme, E., Infurna, F. J., Alajak, K., Blackie, L. E. R., Chopik, W. J., Chung, J. M., Dorfman, A., Fleeson, W., Forgeard, M. J. C., Frazier, P., Furr, R. M., Grossmann, I., Heller, A. S., Laceulle, O. M., Lucas, R. E., Luhmann, M., Luong, G., Meijer, L., McLean, K. C., . . . Zonneveld, R. (2021). Post-traumatic growth as positive personality change: Challenges, opportunities, and recommendations. *Journal of Personality, 89*, 145–165. https://doi.org/10.1111/jopy.12591

Jensen, T. K., Fjermestad, K. W., Granly, L., & Wilhelmsen, N. H. (2015). Stressful life experiences and mental health problems among unaccompanied asylum-seeking children. *Clinical Child Psychology and Psychiatry, 20*, 106–116. doi:10.1177/1359104513499356

Joung, M. (2021, April 30). What is happening at migrant detention centers? Here's what to know. *Time.* https://time.com/5623148/migrant-detention-centers-conditions/

Lehrner, A., & Yehuda, R. (2018). Trauma across generations and paths to adaptation and resilience. *Psychological Trauma: Theory, Research, Practice, and Policy, 10*(1), 22–29. https://doi.org/10.1037/tra0000302

Luthar, S. S., Cicchetti, D., & Becker, B. (2000). The construct of resilience: A critical evaluation and guidelines for future work. *Child Development, 71*, 543–562.

Mares, S. (2020). Mental health consequences of detaining children and families who seek asylum: A scoping review. *European Child & Adolescent Psychiatry, 30*(10), 1615–1639. https://doi.org/10.1007/s00787-020-01629-x

Marks, A. K., Ejesi, K., & Garcia Coll, C. (2014). The U.S. immigrant paradox in childhood and adolescence. *Child Development Perspectives, 8*(2), 59–64. doi:10.1111/cdep.12071

Marks, A. K., McKenna, J., & Garcia Coll, C. (2018). National receiving contexts: A critical aspect of native-born, immigrant, and refugee youth well-being. *European Psychologist, 23*(1), 6–20. doi:10.1027/1016-9040/a000311

Marks, A. K., Patton, F., & Coyne, L.C. (2011). Acculturation-related conflict across generations in immigrant families. In R. Moreno & S. S. Chuang (Eds.), *Immigrant Cchildren: Change, adaptation and cultural transformation.* (pp. 255–270). New York, NY: Rowman & Littlefield Publishers.

Marks, A. K., Woolverton, G. A., & Garcia Coll, C. (2019). Children's migratory paths between cultures: The effects of immigration patterns on the adaptation of children and families. In R. D. Parke & G. H. Elder (Eds.), *Children in changing worlds: Sociocultural and temporal perspectives* (pp. 112–130). Cambridge University Press.

Marks, A. K., Woolverton, G. A., & Murry, M. D. (2021). Xenophobia and racism: Immigrant youth experiences, stress, and resilience. In P. Tummala-Narra (Ed.), *Cultural, racial, and ethnic psychology. Trauma and racial minority immigrants: Turmoil, uncertainty, and resistance* (pp. 51–68). American Psychological Association. https://doi.org/10.1037/0000214-004

Masten, A. S. (2014). *Ordinary magic: Resilience in development*. Guilford Press.

Michael, T., Halligan, S. L., Clark, D. M., & Ehlers, A. (2007). Rumination in posttraumatic stress disorder. *Depression & Anxiety, 24*, 307–317. https://doi.org/10.1002/da.20228

Motti-Stefanidi, F., Berry, J., Chryssochoou, X., Sam, D. L., & Phinney, J. (2012). Positive immigrant youth adaptation in context: Developmental, acculturation, and social psychological perspectives. In A. S. Masten, K. Liebkind, & D. J. Hernández (Eds.), *Realizing the potential of immigrant youth* (pp. 117–158). Cambridge University Press. http://dx.doi.org/10.1017/CBO9781139094696.008

Perreira, K. M., & Ornelas, I. (2013). Painful passages: Traumatic experiences and post-traumatic stress among U.S. immigrant Latino adolescents and their primary caregivers. *International Migration Review, 47*(4), 976–1005. https://doi.org/10.1111/imre.12050

Pottie, K., Batista, R., Mayhew, M., Mota, L., & Grant, K. (2014). Improving delivery of primary care for vulnerable immigrants. *Canadian Family Physician, 60*(1), e32–e40. https://www.ncbi.nlm.nih.gov/pmc/articles/PMC3994840/

Shah, H., & Mishra, A. K. (2021). Trauma and children: Exploring posttraumatic growth among school children impacted by armed conflict in Kashmir. *American Journal of Orthopsychiatry, 91*, 132–148. https://doi-org.ezproxysuf.flo.org/10.1037/ort0000523

Silove, D., Austin, P., & Steel, Z. (2007). No refuge from terror: The impact of detention on the mental health of trauma-affected refugees seeking asylum in Australia. *Transcultural Psychiatry, 44*(3), 359–393. https://doi.org/10.1177/1363461507081637

Stockton, H., Hunt, N., & Stephen, J. (2011). Cognitive processing, rumination, and posttraumatic growth. *Journal of Traumatic Stress, 24*, 85–92. https://doi.org/10.1002/jts.20606

Suarez-Morales, L., & Lopez, B. (2009). The impact of acculturative stress and daily hassles on pre-adolescent psychological adjustment: Examining anxiety symptoms. *Journal of Primary Prevention, 30*(3–4), 335–349. https://doi.org/10.1007/s10935-009-0175-y

Suárez-Orozco, C. (2015). Family separations and reunifications. In C. Suárez-Orozco, M. M. Abo-Zena, & A. K. Marks: (Eds.), *Transitions: The development of children of immigrants* (pp. 32–46). Suárez-Orozco, Carola (Ed); Abo-Zena, Mona M. (Ed); Marks, Amy K. (Ed); Publisher: New York University Press; 2015, pp. 32–46.

Suarez-Orozco, C., Abo-Zena, M., & Marks, A. K. (2015). *Transitions: The development of immigrant children.* NYU Press.

Suárez-Orozco, C., Gaytán, F. X., Bang, H. J., Pakes, J., O'Connor, E., & Rhodes, J. (2010). Academic trajectories of newcomer immigrant youth. *Developmental Psychology, 46*, 602–618. http://dx.doi.org/10.1037/ a0018201

Suárez-Orozco, C., Motti-Stefanidi, F., Marks, A., & Katsiaficas, D. (2018). An integrative risk and resilience model for understanding the adaptation of immigrant-origin children and youth. *American Psychologist, 73*(6), 781–796. https://doi.org/10.1037/amp0000265

Szaflarski, M., & Bauldry, S. (2019). The effects of perceived discrimination on immigrant and refugee physical and mental health. *Advances in Medical Sociology, 19*, 173–204. https://doi.org/10.1108/S1057-629020190000019009

Taku, K., Kilmer, R. P., Cann, A., Tedeschi, R. G., & Calhoun, L. G. (2012). Exploring posttraumatic growth in Japanese youth. *Psychological Trauma: Theory, Research, Practice, and Policy, 4*, 411–419. https://doi-org.ezproxysuf.flo.org/10.1037/a0024363

Tedeschi, R. G., & Calhoun, L. G. (1996). The posttraumatic growth inventory: Measuring the positive legacy of trauma. *Journal of Traumatic Stress, 9*, 455–472. https://doi-org.ezproxysuf.flo.org/10.1002/jts.2490090305

Tedeschi, R. G., Park, C. L., & Calhoun, L. G. (1998). *Posttraumatic growth: Positive changes in the aftermath of a crisis.* Lawrence Erlbaum Associates Inc. Publishers.

Teodorescu, D.-S., Siqveland, J., Heir, T., Hauff, E., Wentzel-Larsen, T., & Lien, L. (2012). Posttraumatic growth, depressive symptoms, posttraumatic stress symptoms, post-migration stressors and quality of life in multi-traumatized psychiatric outpatients with a refugee background in Norway. *Health and Quality of Life Outcomes, 10*, 84–100.

Thibeault, M. A., Mendez, J. L., Nelson-Gray, R. O., & Stein, G. L. (2017). Impact of trauma exposure and acculturative stress on internalizing symptoms for recently arrived migrant-origin youth: Results from a community-based partnership. *Journal of Community Psychology, 45*(8), 984–998. https://doi.org/10.1002/jcop.21905

UNICEF. (2019, May 4). *Child migration - UNICEF data.* https://data.unicef.org/topic/child-migration-and-displacement/migration/

Yoshikawa, H. (2011). *Immigrants raising citizens: Undocumented parents and their children.* Russell Sage Foundation.

Zhang, L., Marks, A. K., Roberg, R., Murry, M., & Ramos, Z. (2020, May). *While COVID-19 does not discriminate, immigration status does determine families' and children's health and well-being.* Research to Policy Collaboration.

Zhou, M. (1997). Growing up American: The challenge confronting immigrant children and children of immigrants. *Annual Review of Sociology, 23*(1), 63–95. http://search.proquest.com.ezp-prod1.hul.harvard.edu/scholarly-journals/growing-up-american-challenge-confronting/docview/1750795348/se-2?accountid=11311

5

Resilience to Structural Violence

Learning From African Youth

LINDA THERON, SADIYYA HAFFEJEE, AND MICHAEL UNGAR ■

"As long as poverty, injustice and gross inequality exist in our world, none of us can truly rest" (Mandela, 2005). Mandela's words reflect a vision for a world without structural violence, that is, a world with equal life chances for all. His words echo the 1994 promise made to all South Africans on the eve of the country's first democracy. It was a promise of equality and freedom from poverty, discrimination, and injustice. For the majority of South Africans, this promise did not materialize. Instead, most South Africans—more particularly, South Africans of color—continue to be challenged by structural violence and its sequelae (i.e., death, illness, injury, stigmatization, and/or psychological trauma; Farmer, 2004). Despite the concerted efforts toward social transformation and alleviation of poverty (Leibbrandt et al., 2011), the "past legacy of race, class, gender and spatial inequality brought about by colonialism and imperialism persists" (Patel, 2011, p. 71). Notwithstanding the apparent intractability of structural violence in South Africa (Tshishonga, 2019), many South African youth aspire for futures unfettered by structural and historical chains (van Breda & Theron, 2018). In this chapter, we use a multisystemic social-ecological resilience framework (Ungar & Theron, 2019) to interrogate the factors and processes that support such resilience.

A social-ecological resilience framework emphasizes promotive and protective factors and processes (PPFPs) in the social and physical ecology when accounting for positive youth outcomes before, during, or after exposure to significant stress (Ungar, 2011). While promotive factors and processes are generally enabling, protective ones ameliorate the effects of higher risk exposure. The attention to social (e.g., relational) and ecological (e.g., environmental and structural) resources conveys that personal PPFPs do not account fully for youth resilience (Ungar & Theron, 2019). Instead, resilience is fueled by interactions between multiple systems, ranging from individual biological and psychological systems to relational, sociocultural, structural, and ecological ones (Masten & Motti-Stefanidi, 2020). In short, resilience is facilitated by multiple PPFPs at multiple systemic levels (Ungar & Theron, 2019). This understanding is particularly relevant in structurally violent contexts, such as South Africa, in that it encourages "new understandings of how people in the resource-constrained environment of South Africa work for their growth and development, and how social structures of inequality and opportunity can be mobilized to cultivate a society that cherishes social flourishing" (van Breda, 2018a, p. 13). Further, a socioecological perspective of resilience questions why youth are being tasked with transforming and/or resisting structural violence on their own; it redirects attention to structural intervention at multiple system levels and social justice agendas (Bottrell, 2013; Hart et al., 2016; Tol, 2020).

Accordingly, this chapter has four aims. First, it provides a brief explanation of structural violence and what is known about the resilience of South African youth who are exposed to structural violence. Second, it introduces the Resilient Youth in Stressed Environments (RYSE) study, with a focus on the structural violence that characterizes the South African RYSE site. Third, it draws on qualitative RYSE data to showcase three pathways of youth resilience to structural violence. Fourth, it problematizes these pathways and argues that resilience to structural violence requires social justice interventions that resource young people equitably.

STRUCTURAL VIOLENCE DEFINED

Structural violence is an indirect form of violence that is perpetrated against those whose social status is devalued (Farmer et al., 2006). It depends on economic, social, political, legal, and religious structures that manifest as social inequalities, oppression, and social injustices that deny equal life chances to all (Evans, 2016; Farmer, 2004; Farmer et al., 2006; Galtung, 1969). These structures are typically legitimized by individual and collective belief systems and ideologies (Galtung, 1969; Heinecken, 2020).

These problematic structures generate violence in that they prohibit people from realizing their full potential (Galtung & Höivik, 1971). In so doing, they cause injury that is corrosive, is often intergenerational, and undermines fundamental human rights (Farmer et al., 2006; Kabeer, 2010; Rohwerder, 2016; UN Department of Economic and Social Affairs [UNDESA], 2013). To be clearer, structural violence constricts individual agency (Farmer, 2004). While individuals and groups may resist structurally violent forces, the ability to affect comprehensive change is dependent on structural redress. Moreover, constricted personal agency can result in psychological oppression that is cyclical in nature (Gelkopf, 2018). For instance, there is an increased risk for trauma/psychological distress and recurring health, education, and employment difficulties in communities characterized by poorer education, exposure to family and communal violence, and heightened risk for sexual violence.

STRUCTURAL VIOLENCE IN SOUTH AFRICA AND ITS IMPACT ON YOUTH

In South Africa, structural violence is rooted in the country's complex, fractured, and traumatic social, political, and economic history (Patel, 2011) and the post-1994 democratic dispensation's failure to genuinely address the "ghosts of racism, discrimination and more importantly the socio-economic inequalities" (Tshishonga, 2019, p. 176). It manifests in pervasive poverty, food insecurity, malnutrition, uneven access to education and employment opportunities, inadequate social and health services, and high rates of interpersonal violence and crime (Fouché et al., 2019; Heinecken, 2020; Zizzamia et al., 2019).

South Africa's youth of color are disproportionately impacted by structural violence, predisposing them to poor quality of life (Mampane, 2014; Meinck et al., 2015). To illustrate: 59% of those younger than 18 (majority Black) live below the upper-bound poverty line; more than 35% are stunted; 30% have inadequate access to basic services and quality education; and 42% have been exposed to some form of abuse (Artz et al., 2016; Hall, 2019). Inadequate and unequal access to education results in poorer outcomes at school and reduced opportunities for employment (Van der Berg & Spaull, 2020). As it is, South Africa has among the highest youth unemployment rates in the world (Graham & Patel, 2020). Among youth, socioeconomic inequalities are associated with psychological distress and increased risk-taking (Small et al., 2019) and with limited relationship choices (Graham & Mphaphuli, 2018). The intersecting nature of structural inequalities also means that youth living in disadvantaged contexts are more likely to experience higher levels of crime and drug-related violence (Kabeer, 2010).

SOUTH AFRICAN YOUTH RESILIENCE TO STRUCTURAL VIOLENCE

A systematic review of studies documenting the resilience of South African children and youth (Van Breda & Theron, 2018) concluded that socioecological understandings of resilience hold true for South African youth in general. This is also true for youth challenged by structural violence. Their resilience, which is typically associated with engagement in education, disengagement from crime, and psychological well-being, is supported inter alia by personal PPFPs (e.g., agency, meaning making, problem-solving, self-esteem, hope, and mastery), relational PPFPs (e.g., immediate and extended family members, teachers, and religious figures), structural PPFPs (e.g., schools, churches, health/social services, and corporate entities), and cultural and religious PPFPs (Botha & van den Berg, 2016; Collishaw et al., 2016; Haffejee & Theron, 2019; Malindi & Machenjedze, 2012; Mampane, 2014; Mosavel et al., 2015; Van Breda, 2018b). While the full range of socioecological resources matter, neither structural PPFPs nor cultural/religious ones featured prominently in South African youth accounts of resilience (van

Breda & Theron, 2018). As in studies conducted in other contexts characterized by structural violence, including Palestine (Abualkibash & Lera, 2015), Afghanistan (Panter-Brick & Eggerman, 2012), Ghana (Wilson & Somhlaba, 2016), Kenya (King, 2020), and Cambodia (Wyatt & Nowlin, 2019), religious/spiritual beliefs were a source of hope for disadvantaged South African youth.

Relational PPFPs were most prominent in South African accounts of youth resilience (Van Breda & Theron, 2018). Family functioning and parental support are a particularly vital resource for youth (Zolkoski & Bullock, 2012). The extent to which these relationships are protective depends on the emotional stability and accessibility of adult caregivers (Soleimanpour et al., 2017). This may be compromised, for example, by poor mental health or parental absence as is often the case in disadvantaged South African communities where many parents live and work away from their families. In such cases, extended family (grandparents, siblings, aunts, and uncles) or relationships outside of the family are prominent (Dass-Brailsford, 2005; Theron & van Rensburg, 2020). However, the prominence of extended family and other relationships also fits with traditionally African, interdependent ways of being that encourage relatedness and generous support of all fellow human beings (Phasha, 2010). In Africa, this pattern of collective responsibility and sharing is often termed *ubuntu.*

Personal PPFPs were also prominently reported by South African youth (van Breda & Theron, 2018). In highlighting internal or personal pathways of resilience, Lewis (2018) references the Tibetan practice, grounded in Buddhist principles, of freeing oneself from the binds of negative emotion and focusing on inner stability and strength by cultivating compassion and an understanding that suffering is natural, expected, and experienced by others as well. Lewis (2018) adds that while this form of acceptance may appear paradoxical from a social justice perspective, it represents an internal choice and a freedom from fixation. This finding echoes many South African studies that speak to the ability to make meaning or reframe the experience of adversity (Van Breda & Theron, 2018), or as Van Breda (2020) said, acceptance of that which is beyond an individual's control. While this may not challenge or change structural factors, it does, however, enable coping and appears to be useful as a short-term resource (Lewis, 2018).

Very few South African studies have considered youth resilience over time (Van Breda & Theron, 2018). PPFPs that were consistent over time for youth exposed to chronic structural disadvantage included education and education-related future aspirations, faith-based support, and supportive peers (Theron & van Rensburg, 2018). In particular, education is viewed as a means to escape disadvantage and enable social and economic mobility (Maila & Ross, 2018; Mosavel et al., 2015; Walker & Mkwananzi, 2015). Although such hopes are not always realized, access to education—particularly quality education—is viewed as a hard-won right by those who were denied schooling in Apartheid times or subjected to inferior, racially segregated education. Education access in the post-1994 democratic South Africa signifies both transformation and hope for a better future. For many, education also offers access to structural resources; for example, schools may provide safety from familial and community violence, as well as access to food, electricity, water, and technology (Malindi & Machenjedze, 2012).

THE RYSE STUDY

RYSE is a multiyear study (2017–2021) investigating the resilience of Canadian and South African youth living in stressed environments (see Ungar et al., 2021; www.ryseproject.org). The study received ethical clearance from collaborating Canadian and South African institutions and all participants consented in writing. The data reported in this chapter are drawn from RYSE, South Africa. In particular, the reported data were generated by youth (aged 14 to 24) whose everyday environment was stressed by structural violence.

As reported previously (e.g., Theron & Ungar, 2019; Theron et al., 2020), the South African research site is in one of the country's poorer provinces. It comprises a town and adjacent township that were built to accommodate the employees of a large coal liquefaction plant. This chapter is concerned with the insights of the youth from the township. Historically, townships were the neighborhoods where South Africans of color were forced to live. Typically, they were spatially segregated communities (usually on the peripheries of towns or cities) with low-cost, cramped housing and poor infrastructure. Like many other townships in South Africa, the township in question is densely populated and characterized by structural violence (including extensive poverty and poor-quality schools). The township's proximity to the coal liquefaction plant and coal mines exposes residents to high levels of air and water pollution. Additionally, as in much of South Africa, the township in question has been characterized by recurring violent protests relating to residents' dissatisfaction with poor service delivery and local government corruption (Canham, 2018).

Following McCubbin and Moniz (2015), a community-based advisory panel (CAP) facilitated the recruitment of South African RYSE participants. The CAP invited voluntary participation from township youth aged 14 to 24 who were comfortable communicating in English and could contribute meaningful information about youth resilience. In total, 61 township-dwelling youth (average age, 18.5; majority male [57%]) participated in individual or group-facilitated qualitative work that explored what enables and constrains youth resilience. In order to understand what enables and constrains resilience, the RYSE team (including experienced researchers and postgraduate students) engaged these youth in interviews and/or arts-based activities (e.g., body-maps, De Jager et al., 2016; draw-write-and-talk activities, Mitchell et al., 2011). Various prompts/questions were used, including, for example, "What are the biggest challenges youth in your community face? What do the youth do to overcome these challenges? What/who makes it possible for young people to overcome these challenges?" These prompts/questions were grounded in a phenomenological approach that respected the youths' expert understanding of resilience in the face of structural violence (de Lange, 2008).

Participant responses were transcribed verbatim. In instances where participants used their mother tongue, research team members who were fluent in that mother tongue translated and the translations were independently checked for accuracy. Using the RYSE codebook (see Theron et al., 2020), the data were individually coded by the first author, various postgraduate students affiliated to RYSE, and an independent consultant. Consensus discussions were used to resolve isolated instances where coding was not unanimous. These coded data have been previously reported (e.g., Theron & Ungar, 2019; Theron et al., 2020). Nevertheless, these previous publications did not explicitly investigate youth resilience to structural violence.

Learning About Resilience to Structural Violence From RYSE Participants

Structural violence loomed large in how RYSE participants described their everyday lives and manifested as "dreams are limited." For the most part, resilience to a structurally violent everyday life, and its potential to limit young people's dreams for the future, entailed avoiding illegal or harmful behaviors (e.g., engaging in substance abuse). Instead, youth continued to hope for a meaningful future (e.g., a future characterized by financial independence, positive relationships, or a sense of fulfillment). Mostly, this was facilitated by a "warrior spirit," "something to keep busy," and a "not just for myself" orientation. Youth experiences of structural violence and related pathways of resilience are detailed next.

"Dreams Are Limited"

Experiences of structural violence related to poor-quality schooling, perennial resource constraints (including job scarcity), pollution-related health concerns, vulnerability to violent crime, and repeated experiences of exploitation were evident. Youth reported that these experiences were discouraging, particularly if they prompted beliefs that "dreams are limited" (Danny, 23-year-old). When dreams seemed limited, it was tempting to find illegal or harmful solutions to everyday hardship:

> Our mindset that we grew up with in the township . . . finishes us. The mentality is if you do not have money then you are not able to gel with other people, other people will never take you seriously. So, things such as those cause problems . . . and, if you don't know someone . . . you will not succeed here in [community]. You have to know someone . . . . The problem that we have is to find jobs through favours and things such as that . . . . In the suburbs, crime isn't an issue most of the time because most of the people in the suburbs are educated, they keep busy with other things . . . they have

something that keeps them busy . . . so they don't think of doing things that are out of hand. (Bongani, 23-year-old man)

The stress that you are educated and you still not getting a job, you are just sitting [at home] with your diploma or degree. . . . So, I feel like the youth in our area . . . majority of them are getting drunk, smoking [drugs], and all of those things. (Minkie, 19-year-old woman)

The lived experience of structural violence was often described as a form of entrapment, with little opportunity for an alternate existence. For example, Blessed, a young woman of 19, spoke of industry-related learnerships or bursaries that kept beneficiaries tied to the coal liquefaction industry and its limited opportunities for employment and upward trajectories:

They [coal liquefaction industry] are giving me the education just to come back and work for them and give them more money. . . . I am living, I am fed, but am I a dreamer? I'm not. Because, what I'm chasing is to get an education and come back and work here: become an artisan . . . get a car, get a family, my kids [will] live here, [I will] encourage them for the same things. No maths, no physics. Become an artisan. Go back again—it's a circle . . . there is nothing that we can do about it. It hurts—not being able to change your situation. . . . Because, you do not know where to start. Where do you start? Who do you talk to? The same person you're going to go to is the same person who is going to stab you in the back, because they want the same money. They want the same thing as the person who owns [coal liquefaction plant] is getting.

Tshepo, a young man (19 years old) who was employed at the local coal liquefaction plant, felt similarly stuck:

We have bad influences around this location, we have bad people, yeah. . . . I want to leave this place, but at the same time I have to work here, because on the other side [elsewhere] there are no jobs. People are struggling to find jobs. But when you are here, you can find a job. But, at the same time you get diseases—you benefit from working, but your health . . . you are dying . . . because of the pollution. When you breathe you don't know what you are breathing, because of [coal liquefaction plant]—that's why. Which means, I'm in the middle of nowhere. Where will I go? Will I stay, will I go? Yeah, that's how it is.

A "Warrior Spirit"

To manage the limitations of structural violence required "a warrior spirit and [will to] keep pushing forward" (Siya, 18-year-old man). This orientation directed participants' attention away from a limited present: "personally, I have a bigger dream" (Zenande, 17-year-old boy) and "get towards your goals and get exactly what you want, not being influenced by the community and environment you are living in" (Thokolo, 17-year-old boy). It facilitated pursuit of a vision that would support an improved future: "What gets me going through the day is just thinking about my goals, my possibilities, and what tomorrow might hold" (Thuso, 17-year-old boy) and "I think about what I want in the future. . . . That's what drives me every day" (Thandiwe, 21-year-old woman). It facilitated hope: "If you never surrender to life, you'll reach your success" (Siya, 18-year-old man). For the most part, a sense of personal agency was central to realizing this hope:

> I have this will to live. I want to live large. . . . What makes me to be strong is the faith that I have in myself, that I know that I am capable of being something, of making something out of myself . . . for me being strong means being able to stand up for yourself, even when the situation is working against you. (Blessed, 19-year-old woman)

> I believe that my future is in my hands and no one is coming to give it to me. . . . It's my responsibility to make my dreams a reality. (Simphiwe, 21-year-old man)

> I push myself to succeed . . . my vision gets me going. (Thoko, 17-year-old girl)

Immediate and extended family were instrumental in encouraging and/or sustaining participants' drive toward a better future, as were faith-based communities:

> I have the most supportive parents ever. . . . They're always there for me in everything and I think it's because they want the best for us. Maybe they've been through the worst and they don't want us ending up like them. So, they want the best. My father always says, "I want you in big places, I don't want you doing what we do. I want you to do better in everything." (Gugu, 17-year-old girl)

> My family makes my hope stronger because they always encourage me to look forward to my future and they always tell me that I have a bright future ahead of me. (Tshepo, 19-year-old man)

> My mother just tells me where she would like us to be. Basically, house-wise and car-wise, what she envisions for us. That's what kind of pushes me to go further, just knowing what her dreams are for us (Thuso, 17-year-old boy)

> My grandmother's always there for me. She's my pillar of strength. At school I was not that good a student, you know. I used to fail a lot. I reached a

point where I wanted to give up, but my grandmother told me to keep on. (Nhlanhla, 20-year-old man)

My brother told me that in life whatever you experience, you have to fight back. And, he also told me this environment that I'm living in, it's sort of full of obstacles. So, I must take [recognize] these disadvantages and the diseases that I have as obstacles that will stop me from pursuing my career [unless I fight back]. (Quphza, 17-year-old boy)

My church is more like a second home. I feel safe when I'm there and that's the only place I get guidance, except from my mom. We share so many ideas with my youth group and they help us to think positive about the future. (Minkie, 19-year-old woman)

There was occasional mention of friends being instrumental in a participant's warrior spirit, also indirectly via the example of their own warrior spirit. In this regard, Simphiwe (21-year-old man), related the following:

I am wearing a T-shirt of a production company that was opened by a very close friend of mine. We grew up together. . . . He pushed his dream to a point where he is now a celebrated, well-known guitarist and he plays for a few artists. He has been on TV quite a lot and now he is starting his own production company. So, I asked him what makes him strong and he said the situations where he failed in life and the passion and the love he had for his dream, and the drive he had for his dream and the courage to push for that dream.

Although most participants were ambivalent about the petrochemical industry's effects on their lives, there was some appreciation for its sponsorship of study opportunities. For instance: "Not everyone is fortunate enough for going to varsity, so a lot of us depend on bursaries from [petrochemical industry]" (Zenande, 17-year-old boy), and "There is opportunity, one of which is school . . . I am OK as a young person to be living in [community], because I get a lot of opportunities around [petrochemical industry]" (Happiness, 17-year-old girl).

"Something to Keep Busy"

Keeping busy was not easily achieved in the structurally disadvantaged context of the RYSE study, South Africa. Still, participants valued "something to keep busy" (Blessed, 19-year-old woman), partly because it took the focus off the negative and helped keep hopes up:

Books help me to relieve stress . . . they're something that keeps me busy . . . and, you know that you will not be busy only now, but it will pay off tomorrow as well. So ja [yes], that's what keeps me OK when life gets hard. (Lwande, 22-year-old woman)

I enjoy reading books; that's a good way to escape from reality. . . . I really enjoy music . . . it gets you out of your slump . . . you know, brings your mood up. (Thuso, 17-year-old boy)

Keeping busy also supported avoidance of peer pressure and related criminal or risky behaviors. In the words of Simphiwe (21-year-old man):

It [keeping busy] takes a lot of your time. . . . Time is the difference because another person is maybe going to smoke drugs or mug people . . . you're coming from training and you're tired. You want to just bath[e] and eat and sleep. So, it's less time for violence and drugs.

In this regard, access to structural resources (e.g., a local sports facility and community hall provided and maintained by the petrochemical industry) were key:

It's because of them [industry] that we have this [facility]. If it wasn't for them, there would be no [facility], no people gyming, there'd be no people singing because we wouldn't have the facilities similar to this. . . . These resources help the youth . . . keep them busy instead of doing negative things. (Danny, 23-year-old man)

Informal supports, such as family and prosocial peers, were helpful when institutional or state-sponsored resources, like sporting venues, were unavailable. They promoted keeping busy in other socially desirable ways and even joined in. For example, Minkie (19-year-old woman) said: "I run with my sister and with my friends and sometimes with my mom. . . . After I have taken a jog, I feel free. My mind opens up, it just becomes good."

"Not Just for Myself" Orientation

Participants' vision for a better future extended beyond themselves to their families and communities. They expressed a desire to compensate for the effects of structural violence by securing a future that would improve the fate of family and community. This desire fueled their warrior spirit:

When you look at our family backgrounds, they aren't all good. So, every day you have thoughts of my mother didn't study and my father didn't study, but then you have this desire to study so that you can change the situation at home. (Busi, 20-year-old woman)

I guess it's my siblings where I draw most of my strength, coz being the elder one, I just think to myself if I lose hope where do I put them? Coz for everything since Mom's not here they look up to me. So, I have to be strong. Not just for myself. I have to be positive for them as well. (Lwande, 22-year-old woman)

I see this problem [the resource-constrained community] as an opportunity to, you know, take it and make something better out if it. . . . We are lacking a lot of things, we don't have a lot of resources like . . . the only work . . . decent job you will find here is working at [coal liquefaction plant]. . . . I don't want to be famous, but I want to change this place. I want to change the mindset of the youth of this place. I want to build youth centers here in [community]. . . . I really want to help other people and give them hope. (Gugu, 17-year-old girl)

Employment has turned out to be very hard for someone who is from here . . . so it's something that's in my heart that if maybe not all of us can get a job in the petrochemical industry we can also create . . . I wanna create employment for other people, other than working there [coal liquefaction plant] because working there can also have an impact on your health. (Simphiwe, 21-year-old man)

In some instances, the inclination to make a positive difference to others was prompted by first-hand experience of successful local businesspeople caring too little for interdependent ways of being (e.g., "Everyone is thinking for themselves. Like people with business," Nomalanga, 22-year-old woman) and a desire to halt the negative trend. In other instances, the inclination was directly encouraged by immediate or extended family:

One thing my grandfather told me, "wake up every day and see that day as a new way to make your life better." That's why I keep going to school, learn whatever I have to learn to make my life better. . . . I'd just like to get a good job that satisfies—just like he said—take out my family from where they are right now, put them in a better place. (Siya, 18-year-old man)

Reflecting on the Learning From RYSE Participants: Prioritizing Facilitative (i.e., Enabling) Environments

Reflecting the findings from previous research (Evans, 2016; Farmer, 2004; Farmer et al., 2006; Galtung, 1969; Heinecken, 2020), the corrosive and cyclical impacts of structural violence were potent in the everyday lives of the township-dwelling RYSE participants. Young people were familiar with unemployment and hardship and their often-inevitable sequelae (e.g., despair, crime, substance abuse, corruption). To manage these, young people drew on three PPFPs: a "warrior spirit," "something to keep busy," and a "not just for myself" orientation. While the first (i.e., a "warrior spirit") suggested that resilience to structural violence required the capacity for counterviolence, resistance, or warlike ways, the third PPFP implied a generous interdependence that has long been associated with traditional African ways of being (Phasha, 2010) and with the resilience of South African youth of color (Van Breda & Theron, 2018). Taken together, the three PPFPs speak to resilience relying on interactions between multiple systems (Masten & Motti-Stefanidi, 2020; Ungar & Theron, 2019), including the psychological (e.g., hopeful meaning making), relational (e.g., family and peer encouragement), sociocultural (e.g., altruistic values), structural (e.g., supportive faith-based organizations), and ecological (e.g., outdoor spaces to jog). In short, resilience to structural violence may not be reduced to only a personal fight.

Even so, it would be easy to focus on the role of personal agency, part current and part aspirational, in how youth responded to the structural violence. Taking action, or being determined to do so, is salient in other South African youths' resilience (van Breda & Theron, 2018). While personal agency could be a default response in a context characterized by disabling structures (Theron et al., 2020), that would not make it any less problematic given the centrality of structural supports to realizing personal agency (Farmer, 2004). The feeble value of a completed education in a community/country characterized by exponential rates of youth unemployment (Graham & Patel, 2020)—as also reported by the RYSE participants—is a case in point.

In short, if resilience to structural violence requires some capacity for counterviolence or warlike ways, then these should be directed at disrupting continued valorizing of youth agency or any other personal resource, more particularly in the absence of structural transformation. Despite how youth accounts appeared to foreground personal agency, there were references to supports (mostly informal) that emboldened their agency. It is this facilitative environment—that is, one characterized by available, accessible, and meaningful social and ecological supports that facilitate resilience—that requires valorizing.

As in these pre-existing accounts of South African youth resilience, and as presaged by socioecological approaches to resilience (Masten, 2014; Ungar & Theron, 2019), youths' personal agency was buttressed by their families, peers, faith-based organizations, and, to some extent, the petrochemical industry (although its influence was somewhat mixed). These relational and institutional structures cofacilitated youth agency and so the resilience of these relational and structural systems is as important as that of youths themselves. Their facilitative value needs to be appreciated and sustained (e.g., via family or community support programs).

Further, institutional structures will likely be more facilitative of youth resilience if they are made aware of how their initiatives—including corporate social ones aimed at redressing structural violence—are perceived and taken up by youth. This directs researchers to purposefully disseminate research results to industry and corporations. Ideally, youth and researchers would partner in this dissemination. For instance, researchers and youth could coauthor and copresent a research report detailing the benefits of corporate social initiatives as experienced by youth living in close proximity to industry. Supporting youth to codisseminate the findings to industry (as is the case in the RYSE study) has the advantage of giving authoritative voice, so to speak, to those who are routinely silenced by structural violence.

Youth valued being gainfully occupied. Having something to do, be it education, employment, or recreation related, diminished attention to hardship and limited occasion to engage in crime or self-harming behaviors. While the value of keeping busy might seem obvious, the opportunities to do so are restricted in the face of structural violence. In this regard, the petrochemical industry's sponsorship of accessible recreational facilities must be acknowledged, and they should be encouraged to build on this in ways that will reduce discrepancies between the recreational opportunities in townships and more privileged communities. Further, they and other South African employers need to do more to create employment opportunities that will not only keep youth busy but also expedite social equality for youth whose past and present have been sabotaged by structural violence (Graham & Patel, 2020; Van der Berg & Spaull, 2020).

Youths' intention to uplift their families and communities suggests that resilience-enabling cultural values, such as African people's traditional commitment to generous and reciprocal interdependence (Phasha, 2010), have continued to thrive despite concerns that Western ways of being and/or widespread corruption are corroding such values (Ramphele, 2012). In other words, sociocultural values that encourage respect for humanity can contribute to environments that facilitate youth resilience. In the face of structural violence, such values must be resolutely protected and championed.

Finally, in countries such as South Africa where social violence is entrenched, an environment that is facilitative of youth resilience must necessarily be a socially just one. As with South African interim legislation that purposefully aimed to protect those most vulnerable to socioeconomic challenges during a national disaster (Fouché et al., 2020), economic, social, political, legal, and religious structures must be mobilized to redress social inequalities, oppression, and other social injustices (Evans, 2016; Farmer, 2004; Farmer et al., 2006). Doing so should result in a facilitative environment that will allow youth to believe that dreams are *un*limited, regardless of the dreamer's social status.

REFERENCES

Abualkibash, S. K. A., & Lera, M. J. (2015). Psychological resilience among Palestinian school students: An exploratory study in the West Bank. *International Humanities Studies*, 2(3), 1–20. https://idus.us.es/handle/11441/52704

Artz, L., Burton, P., Ward, C., Leoschut, L., Phyfer, J., Lloyd, S., & Le Mottee, C. (2016). *Sexual victimisation of children in South Africa. Final report of the Optimus Foundation study: South Africa.* http://www.ci.uct.ac.za/overview-violence/reports/sexual-victimisation-of-children-in-SA

Botha, A., & van den Berg, H. (2016). Trauma exposure and life satisfaction among at-risk black South African adolescents. *Journal of Psychology in Africa*, 26(6), 500–507. https://www.tandfonline.com/doi/full/10.1080/14330237.2016.1250422

Bottrell, D. (2013). Responsibilised resilience? Reworking neoliberal social policy texts. *M/C Journal, 16*(5). https://www.journal.media-culture.org.au/index.php/mcjour nal/article/view/708

Canham, H. (2018). Theorising community rage for decolonial action. *South African Journal of Psychology, 48*(3), 319–330. https://doi.org/10.1177/0081246318787682

Collishaw, S., Gardner, F., Lawrence Aber, J., & Cluver, L. (2016). Predictors of mental health resilience in children who have been parentally bereaved by AIDS in urban South Africa. *Journal of Abnormal Child Psychology, 44*(4), 719–730. https://link. springer.com/content/pdf/10.1007/s10802-015-0068-x.pdf

Dass-Brailsford, P. (2005). Exploring resiliency: Academic achievement among disad- vantaged black youth in South Africa. *South African Journal of Psychology, 35*, 574– 591. https://journals.sagepub.com/doi/pdf/10.1177/008124630503500311

De Jager, A., Tewson, A., Ludlow, B., & Boydell, K. (2016). Embodied ways of storying the self: A systematic review of body-mapping. *Forum Qualitative Sozialforschung/ Forum: Qualitative Social Research, 17*(2). https://www.qualitative-research.net/ index.php/fqs/article/view/2526/3986

de Lange, N. (2008). Visual participatory approaches to HIV and AIDS research as in- tervention in a rural community setting. *Journal of Psychology in Africa, 18*(1), 179– 185. https://www.tandfonline.com/doi/abs/10.1080/14330237.2008.10820184

Evans, M. (2016). Structural violence, socioeconomic rights, and transformative jus- tice. *Journal of Human Rights, 15*(1), 1–20. https://www.tandfonline.com/doi/pdf/ 10.1080/14754835.2015.1032223

Farmer, P. (2004). An anthropology of structural violence. *Current Anthropology, 45*(3), 305–326. https://www.journals.uchicago.edu/doi/pdfplus/10.1086/382250

Farmer, P. E., Nizeye, B., Stulac, S., & Keshavjee, S. (2006). Structural violence and clin- ical medicine. *PLoS Med, 3*(10), e449. https://journals.plos.org/plosmedicine/arti cle?id=10.1371/journal.pmed.0030449

Fouché, A., Fouché, F. D., & Theron, L. C. (2020). Child protection and resilience in the face of COVID-19 in South Africa: A rapid review of C-19 legislation. *Child Abuse & Neglect, 110*(2), 1–17. https://doi.org/10.1016/j.chiabu.2020.104710

Fouché, A., Truter, E., & Fouché, D. F. (2019). Safeguarding children in South African townships against child sexual abuse: The voices of our children. *Child Abuse Review, 28*(6), 455–472. https://onlinelibrary.wiley.com/doi/pdf/10.1002/car.2603

Galtung, J. (1969). Violence, peace and peace research. *Journal of Peace Research, 6*, 167– 191. https://www.jstor.org/stable/pdf/422690.pdf

Galtung, J., & Höivik, T. (1971). Structural and direct violence: A note on operationalization. *Journal of Peace Research, 8*(1), 73–76. https://doi.org/10.1177/ 002234337100800108

Gelkopf, M. (2018). Social injustice and the cycle of traumatic childhood experiences and multiple problems in adulthood. *JAMA Network Open, 1*(7), e184488. https:// jamanetwork.com/journals/jamanetworkopen/fullarticle/2713032

Graham, L., & Mphaphuli, M. (2018). "A guy 'does' and you don't, they do you in- stead": Young people's narratives of gender and sexuality in a low-income context of South Africa. *SAGE Open, 1*(11), 1–11. https://journals.sagepub.com/doi/pdf/ 10.1177/2158244018819041

Graham, L., & Patel, L. (2020, June 15). South Africa has taken steps to help young job- less people. Here's what's working. *The Conversation.* https://theconversation.com/

south-africa-has-taken-steps-to-help-young-jobless-people-heres-whats-working-140666

Haffejee, S., & Theron, L. (2019). "The power of me": The role of agency in the resilience process of adolescent African girls who have been sexually abused. *Journal of Adolescent Research, 34*(6), 683–712. https://doi.org/10.1177/0743558419833332.

Hall, K. (2019). Income poverty, unemployment and social grants. In M. Shung-King, L. Lake, D. Sanders, & M. Hendricks (Eds.), *South African child gauge 2019* (pp. 221–227). Children's Institute, University of Cape Town.

Hart, A., Gagnon, E., Eryigit-Madzwamuse, S., Cameron, J., Aranda, K., Rathbone, A., & Heaver, B. (2016). Uniting resilience research and practice with an inequalities approach. *SAGE Open, 6*(4), 1–13. https://journals.sagepub.com/doi/pdf/10.1177/2158244016682477

Heinecken, L. (2020, January 15). What's behind violence in South Africa: A sociologist's perspective. *The Conversation.* https://theconversation.com/whats-behind-viole nce-in-south-africa-a-sociologists-perspective-128130

Kabeer, N. (2010). *Can the MDGs provide a pathway to social justice? The challenge of intersecting inequalities.* Institute of Development Studies. https://www.ids.ac.uk/download.php?file=files/dmfile/MDGreportwebsiteu2WC.pdf

King, A. (2020). *Experiences of hope, resilience and spirituality in Kenyan children and adolescents* (Unpublished doctorate). George Fox University.

Leibbrandt, M., Wegner, E., & Finn, A. (2011). *The policies for reducing income inequality and poverty in South Africa.* A Southern Africa Labour and Development Research Unit Working Paper (Number 64). SALDR. http://137.158.104.7/bitstream/handle/11090/79/2011_64.pdf?sequence=1

Lewis, S. E. (2018). Resilience, agency, and everyday lojong in the Tibetan diaspora. *Contemporary Buddhism, 19*(2), 342–361. https://www.tandfonline.com/doi/pdf/10.1080/14639947.2018.1480153

Maila, P., & Ross, E. (2018). Perceptions of disadvantaged rural matriculants regarding factors facilitating and constraining their transition to tertiary education. *South African Journal of Education, 38*(1), 1–12. http://www.sajournalofeducation.co.za/index.php/saje/article/view/1360/748

Malindi, M. J., & Machenjedze, N. (2012). The role of school engagement in strengthening resilience among male street children. *South African Journal of Psychology, 42*(1), 71–81. https://journals.sagepub.com/doi/pdf/10.1177/008124631204200108

Mampane, M. R. (2014). Factors contributing to the resilience of middle-adolescents in a South African township: Insights from a resilience questionnaire. *South African Journal of Education, 34*(4), 1–11. http://www.sajournalofeducation.co.za/index.php/saje/issue/view/44

Mandela, N. (2005). Address by Nelson Mandela for the "Make Poverty History" campaign, London, UK. February 3, 2005. http://www.mandela.gov.za/mandela_speec hes/2005/050203_poverty.htm

Masten, A. S. (2014). *Ordinary magic: Resilience in development.* Guilford Publications.

Masten, A. S., & Motti-Stefanidi, F. (2020). Multisystem resilience for children and youth in disaster: Reflections in the context of COVID-19. *Adversity and Resilience Science, 1*(2), 95–106. https://link.springer.com/article/10.1007%2Fs42844-020-00010-w

McCubbin, L. D., & Moniz, J. (2015). Ethical principles in resilience research: Respect, relevance, reciprocity and responsibility. In L. C. Theron, L. Liebenberg, & M. Ungar

(Eds.), *Youth resilience and culture: Commonalities and complexities* (pp. 217–229). Springer.

Meinck, M., Cluver, L. D., & Boyes, M. E. (2015). Household illness, poverty and physical and emotional child abuse victimisation: Findings from South Africa's first prospective cohort study. *BMC Public Health, 15*(1), 1–13. https://link.springer.com/article/10.1186/s12889-015-1792-4

Mitchell, C., Theron, L. C., Stuart, J., Smith, A., & Campbell, Z. (2011). Drawings as a research method. In L. C. Theron, C. Mitchell, A. Smith, & J. Stuart (Eds.), *Picturing research: Drawings as visual methodology* (pp. 19–36). Sense.

Mosavel, M., Ahmed, R., Ports, K. A., & Simon, C. (2015). South African, urban youth narratives: Resilience within community. *International Journal of Adolescence and Youth, 20*(2), 245–255. https://www.tandfonline.com/doi/pdf/10.1080/02673843.2013.785439

Panter-Brick, C., & Eggerman, M. (2012). Understanding culture, resilience, and mental health: The production of hope. In M. Ungar (Ed.), *The social ecology of resilience: A handbook of theory and practice* (pp. 369–386). Springer.

Patel, L. (2011). Race, inequality and social welfare: South Africa's imperial legacy. In J. Midgley & D. Piachaud (Eds.), *Colonialism and welfare: Social policy and the British imperial legacy* (pp. 71–84). Edward Elgar Publishing.

Phasha, T. N. (2010). Educational resilience among African survivors of child sexual abuse in South Africa. *Journal of Black Studies, 40*(6), 1234–1253. https://journals.sagepub.com/doi/pdf/10.1177/0021934708327693

Ramphele, M. (2012). *Conversations with my sons and daughters*. Penguin Books.

Rohwerder, B. (2016). *Poverty and Inequality: Topic guide*. GSDRC, University of Birmingham.

Small, L. A., Parchment, T. M., Bahar, O. S., Osuji, H. L., Chomanczuk, A. H., & Bhana, A. (2019). South African adult caregivers as "protective shields": Serving as a buffer between stressful neighborhood conditions and youth risk behaviors. *Journal of Community Psychology, 47*(8), 1850–1864. https://onlinelibrary.wiley.com/doi/pdf/10.1002/jcop.22235

Soleimanpour, S., Geierstanger, S., & Brindis, C. D. (2017). Adverse childhood experiences and resilience: Addressing the unique needs of adolescents. *Academic Pediatrics, 17*(7), S108–S114. https://doi.org/10.1016/j.acap.2017.01.008

Theron, L. C., Levine, D., & Ungar, M. (2020). African emerging adult resilience: Insights from a sample of township youth. *Emerging Adulthood, 9*(4), 360–371. https://doi.org/10.1177/2167696820940077

Theron, L. C., & Ungar, M. (2019). Adolescent resilience in the face of relentless adversity: The role of strong, black women. In I. Eloff (Ed.), *Handbook of quality of life in African societies* (pp. 97–111). Springer.

Theron, L., & van Rensburg, A. (2018). Resilience over time: Learning from school-attending adolescents living in conditions of structural inequality. *Journal of Adolescence, 67*, 167–178. https://doi.org/10.1016/j.adolescence.2018.06.012

Theron, L. C., & van Rensburg, A. (2020). Parent-figures and adolescent resilience: An African perspective. *International Journal of School & Educational Psychology, 8*(2), 90–103. https://doi.org/10.1080/21683603.2019.1657994

Tol, W. A. (2020). Interpersonal violence and mental health: A social justice framework to advance research and practice. *Global Mental Health, 7*(e10), 1–8. https://doi.org/10.1017/gmh.2020.4

Tshishonga, N. (2019). The legacy of Apartheid on democracy and citizenship in post-Apartheid South Africa: An inclusionary and exclusionary binary? *AFFRIKA: Journal of Politics, Economics and Society, 9*(1), 167–191. https://www-proquest-com.uplib.idm.oclc.org/docview/2250960380?accountid=14717

UN Department of Economic and Social Affairs (UNDESA). (2013). *Inequality matters: Report of the world social situation 2013.* United Nations. https://www.un.org/esa/socdev/documents/reports/InequalityMatters.pd

Ungar, M. (2011). The social ecology of resilience: Addressing contextual and cultural ambiguity of a nascent construct. *American Journal of Orthopsychiatry, 81*(1), 1–17. https://doi.org/10.1111/j.1939-0025.2010.01067.x

Ungar, M., & Theron, L. (2019). Resilience and mental health: How multisystemic processes contribute to positive outcomes. *Lancet Psychiatry, 7*(5), 441–448. https://doi.org/10.1016/S2215-0366(19)30434-1

Ungar, M., Theron, L., Murphy, K., & Jefferies, P. (2021). Researching multisystemic resilience: A sample methodology. *Frontiers in Psychology, 11*, 3808. https://doi/10.3389/fpsyg.2020.607994

Van Breda, A. D. (2018a). A critical review of resilience theory and its relevance for social work. *Social Work/Maatskaplike Werk, 54*(1), 1–18. http://www.scielo.org.za/scielo.php?script=sci_arttext&pid=S0037-80542018000100002

Van Breda, A. D. (2018b). Resilience of vulnerable students transitioning into a South African university. *Higher Education, 75*(6), 1109–1124. https://link.springer.com/content/pdf/10.1007/s10734-017-0188-z.pdf

Van Breda, A. D. (2020). Resilience and culture in South Africa: The case of "acceptance." In U. Straub, G. Rott, & R. Lutz (Eds.), *Knowledge and social work: Social work of the South* (Vol. VIII, pp. 327–344). Paulo Freire Verlag.

Van Breda, A. D., & Theron, L. C. (2018). A critical review of South African child and youth resilience studies, 2009–2017. *Children and Youth Services Review, 91*, 237–247. https://doi.org/10.1016/j.childyouth.2018.06.022

Van der Berg, S., & Spaull, N. (2020). *Counting the cost: COVID-19 school closures in South Africa & its impacts on children.* Research on Socioeconomic Policy (RESEP), Stellenbosch University. http://resep.sun.ac.za/wp-content/uploads/2020/06/Van-der-Berg-Spaull-2020-Counting-the-Cost-COVID-19-Children-and-Schooling-15-June-2020-1.pdf

Walker, M., & Mkwananzi, F. (2015). Challenges in accessing higher education: A case study of marginalised young people in one South African informal settlement. *International Journal of Educational Development, 40*, 40–49. https://doi.org/10.1016/j.ijedudev.2014.11.010

Wilson, A., & Somhlaba, N. Z. (2016). Psychological well-being in a context of adversity: Ghanaian adolescents' experiences of hope and life satisfaction. *Africa Today, 63*(1), 85–103. https://doi.org/10.2979/africatoday.63.1.0085

Wyatt, Z., & Nowlin, M. (2019). Trauma, resilience and the power of human connection: Reflections from the field of Cambodia. *American Journal of Applied Psychology, 8*(2), 50–56. http://www.sciencepublishinggroup.com/j/ajap

Zizzamia, R., Schotte, S., & Leibbrandt, M. (2019). *Snakes and ladders and loaded dice: Poverty dynamics and inequality in South Africa between 2008–2017.* University of Cape Town. http://137.158.104.7/bitstream/handle/11090/950/2019_235_Saldr uwp.pdf?sequence=1

Zolkoski, S., & Bullock, L. (2012). Resilience in children and youth: A review. *Children and Youth Services Review, 34*(12), 2295–2303. https://doi.org/10.1016/j.childyo uth.2012.08.009

6

The Impact of Racism on Violence Exposure Among Black Children in the United States

DONTE L. BERNARD, HENRY A. WILLIS, AND
EFFUA E. SOSOO ■

The toxin of racism that runs through the veins of society has yet to find an antidote.

—HARRELL (2000, p. 1)

Globally, it is estimated that over 1 billion children between the ages of 2 and 17 are exposed to violence each year (Hillis et al., 2016). In North America alone, roughly 60% of youth have been found to report direct or vicarious experiences in their lifetime (Finkelhor et al., 2015; Hillis et al., 2016). The prevalence of child-hood violence exposure is alarming especially when considering the host of del-eterious physical and psychosocial consequences associated with these adverse experiences that can persist across the life course (Heinze et al., 2017; Mrug & Windle, 2010). Within the United States specifically, significant disparities exist with respect to the rates at which youth are exposed to violence, with Black[1] youth reporting exposure to violence at higher rates and with more severity relative to their White counterparts (Berg, 2014; Kilpatrick et al., 2003)—disparities that continue to be observed into adulthood (West, 2016).

---

1. The term *Black* is used throughout this chapter to broadly capture individuals across African diaspora who live within the United States.

According to the Centers for Disease Control and Prevention (CDC), the exposure to and perpetuation of violence does not exist in a vacuum, but rather is a product of interactions across social-ecological domains (CDC, n.d.; Dahlberg & Krug, 2006). To this end, recent work has demonstrated how socioecological approaches may be strengthened when factors such as race and racism are considered (Smith & Landor, 2018; West, 2016, 2019). Such literature underscores the work of N. Jones (2007), who asserts that it "is easier to talk about violence as an individual pathology than it is to think about violence as a product of systemic inequalities that act on and through individuals in ways we don't yet fully understand" (p. 128). Thus, literature would benefit from a more nuanced conceptualization of violence that anchors structural and systemic inequity as primary drivers.

To this end, research has highlighted that disparities in violence exposure are not coincidental, but rather stem from the historical and contemporary significance of racism that increases the likelihood that other forms of violence and adversity may occur (Bernardet al., 2021; Sanders-Phillips et al., 2009). Yet, the predominant focus of extant research seeking to expand conceptualizations of violence through a culturally informed lens have largely centered on the "downstream" effects of racism on mental health (e.g., psychological and physical health impact). Thus, akin to work by McCrea et al. (2019), the purpose of this chapter is to explicate the ways in which the potential "upstream" effects of racism (e.g., social position, income distribution) may place Black youth at greater risk for violence exposure and subsequent mental health concerns.

OPERATIONALIZING VIOLENCE

Violence can be broadly characterized as the establishment and use of power that is unjustly exerted against a person or group to cause psychological, emotional, or physical harm (Krug et al., 2002). The World Health Organization defines violence as the intentional use of physical force or power, threatened or actual, against oneself, another person, or a group or community that either results in or has a high likelihood of resulting in injury, death, psychological harm, maldevelopment, or deprivation (Krug et al., 2002). Emphasized within this definition is that violence is a multifaceted construct that can manifest as use of force *or* the threatened use of power. Therefore, violence captures not only occurrences of physical harm and maltreatment but also incidents of psychological injury that may result from acts of omission or neglect (Rutherford et al., 2007). Violence, then, can be self-directed, used toward an individual or specific group, or utilized to repress an entire racial and/or ethnic group (Rutherford et al., 2007).

Violence has been theorized to co-occur across societal domains, manifesting at the individual and structural level to negatively impact those exposed. For example, the use of physical or psychological violence is concurrently used to establish and maintain power through person-centered acts (e.g., interpersonal violence) and through more public or socially oriented means (e.g., political violence, war; Pine et al., 2005; Sanders-Phillips, 2009). In complement to research highlighting interpersonal and socially oriented forms of violence, research by Johan Galtung brings attention to structural and cultural forms of violence. According to Galtung, *structural violence* represents systemic processes in which political, economic, religious, cultural, or legal structures operate to harm or disadvantage individuals or groups (Galtung, 1969), whereas cultural violence represents the cultural-symbolic processes (i.e., religion, language, art, and empirical science) that are used to justify or legitimize structural forms of violence (Galtung, 1990). As a composite, this literature suggests that violence represents a multidimensional construct that may vary as a function of one's broader sociocultural and contextual environment (Hoffman et al., 2011).

Violence exposure among youth represents a salient risk factor for poor mental health outcomes including increases in anxiety, depression, and posttraumatic stress concerns (Evans et al., 2008; Polanin et al., 2021), in addition to other health risk behaviors such as antisocial behavior and suicide (Wilson et al., 2009; Zatti et al., 2017). Violence exposure early in development has also been demonstrated to alter social schemas relating to the normalcy and acceptability of violence when interacting with others (Su et al., 2010), increase perceptions of threat (Miller, 2015), detract from feelings of safety and security (Holden, 2003), and decrease perceptions of self-esteem and self-worth (Copeland et al., 2007). In light of this collective body of literature, the World Health Organization has positioned the perpetuation and exposure to violence among youth as a global health problem (World Health Organization, 2020).

SOCIOECOLOGICAL MODEL OF VIOLENCE

The literature is replete with theoretical frameworks that catalog the innumerable factors that undergird violence. One such framework that takes an etiological and preventative approach to conceptualizing violence is the social-ecological model (CDC, n.d.; Dahlberg & Krug, 2006). Informed by tenets of ecological theory (Bronfenbrenner, 1977), the social-ecological model suggests that violence results from a complex interaction between individual, relational, community, and societal level factors. At the *individual* level, the risk for a person to perpetrate or be victimized by violence is argued to be influenced by micro-level and personal history factors (e.g., age, education, income, substance use, or history of abuse). The *relational* level posits that an individual's closest familial and peer relationships influence their behavior and subsequently inform levels of risk for violence exposure. At the *community* level, characteristics associated with one's neighborhood, school, and workplace are noted to inform individual and relational processes and serve as important contextual determinants of violence. Finally, at the *societal* level, it is argued that broader macro-level factors such as educational and social policies, in addition to cultural norms, create a broader context that serves to encourage violence and maintain social inequity.

There are several benefits of conceptualizing violence from this social-ecological framework. First, such an approach moves beyond framing violence as a person-centered incident and instead as a product of the culmination of interacting factors across ecological domains. This important acknowledgment underscores research noting that violence can manifest in different ways to uniquely influence health (Finkelhor et al., 2007; Krug et al., 2002; Pine et al., 2005). Second, socioecological frameworks facilitate considerations of structural forms of violence (e.g., poverty) that may generate cascading effects that increase risk for future forms of violent victimization (Jonson-Reid, 1998). Third, a socioecological conceptualization of violence provides space to acknowledge that violence may be experienced differently based on a person's or group's sociodemographic profile, which resonates with the growing awareness that conceptualizations of violence need to be expanded to account for culturally relevant experiences (e.g., Daiute & Fine, 2003). Socioecological approaches have been utilized to catalog the relevance of racism across sociocultural domains to explain increased risk of violence exposure among Black adults in America (West, 2016, 2019) and can be extended to capture other culturally relevant drivers of social inequity across global contexts (Mahmudiono et al., 2019).

THE SIGNIFICANCE OF RACISM

As research begins to recognize the significance of racism within conceptualizations of violence, it is important to understand how racism is conventionally studied within psychological literature. Doing so will provide important context to highlight gaps and facilitate enhancements of extant socioecological models, further bolstering our understanding of violence exposure and consequent psychological experiences of Black youth. Racism represents a nearly ubiquitous experience among Black youth and has been defined in a number of ways to delineate its multifaceted nature. For example, Harrell (2000) operationalized racism as "a system of dominance, power, and privilege based on racial group designations; rooted in the historical oppression of a group defined or perceived by dominant-group members as inferior, deviant or undesirable" (p. 43). Similarly, Williams and Williams-Morris (2000) characterize racism as an "organized system that leads to the subjugation of some human population groups relative to others" (p. 244). Furthermore, Paradies (2006) defines racism as "a societal system in which actors are divided into 'races,' with power unevenly distributed (or produced) based on these racial classifications" (p. 145).

While the aforementioned definitions have unique variations, a shared area of emphasis among them all (in addition to several others) is that racism represents a *system* of oppression that excludes, isolates, and marginalizes nondominant groups through the differential access or disparate allocation of power and societal resources. That is, racism operates in distinct yet interrelated ways that can uniquely and collectively compromise health outcomes. In line with this notion, J. M. Jones's (1972) tripartite model of racism asserts that racism simultaneously occurs across person-mediated (individual), institutional, and cultural levels. Extending this work, Harrell (2000) suggests that these simultaneous occurrences of racism manifest across four contexts: *interpersonal* (i.e., direct and vicarious racial discrimination), *collective* (i.e., impacting the functioning of large groups as in disparities in health and treatment in the criminal legal system), *cultural-symbolic* (i.e., depictions of racism in art, entertainment, and science), and *sociopolitical* (i.e., political debate and public discourse about race and institutional policy, practices, and processes). It is important to acknowledge that racism is not a phenomenon that is unique to the United States. The systemic nature of racism can be observed across a variety of global contexts, serving to perpetuate and maintain health disparities through its impact on important health determinants including income, housing, education, and health care (Paradies, 2018).

Within the United States in particular, the impact of racism on the psychosocial functioning of Black youth is profound. For example, chronic person-centered experiences of racism (i.e., racial discrimination) have been shown to predict a range of internalizing (e.g., anxiety), externalizing (e.g., aggression), and traumatic stress symptoms, in addition to behavioral health concerns including substance use, risky behavior, and suicidality among Black youth (Benner et al., 2018; Bernard et al., 2022; Gibbons et al., 2007; Jernigan & Daniel, 2011; Priest et al., 2013). In addition, experiences of racial discrimination among Black youth have been found to increase the likelihood that relationships are perceived as hostile or threatening, the acceptability of defiant behaviors (e.g., physical assault), and the risk of engaging in violent crime such as assault with a weapon (Burt et al., 2012; Unnever et al., 2017).

LIMITATIONS IN THE STUDY OF RACISM WITHIN SOCIOECOLOGICAL FRAMEWORKS

Though the integration of racism within socioecological models may bolster our understanding of the complex set of factors contributing to experiences of violence, there are several limitations of the current state of the literature that are important to note. First, extant socioecological models of violence focus predominantly on the experiences of adults and thus overlook the developmental significance of violence and the conjoint effects of racism across important formative years. Second, despite research suggesting that racism co-occurs across different socioecological levels, research has seldom explicated how this co-occurrence may inform violence exposure and perpetuation. Third, manifestations of racism (i.e., racial discrimination) are conventionally discussed as culturally relevant psychosocial experiences that increase the risk for violence exposure. Yet, racism-related encounters also have the capacity to victimize individuals as a unique form of violence (Sanders-Phillips et al., 2009) and thus should be accounted for within the socioecological conceptualizations of violence, and not solely as a cultural "overlay" in which other experiences of violence are interpreted.

ENHANCING THE INTEGRATION OF RACISM WITHIN SOCIOECOLOGICAL MODELS

Given these limitations, the remainder of this chapter aims to demonstrate how considerations of racism within the socioecological model can enhance our understanding of violence exposure among Black youth within the United States. Consistent with the aforementioned conceptualization of violence, we will emphasize how anti-Black racism within the United States increases risk for psychological harm, maldevelopment, or injury among Black youth. Specifically, we draw upon theoretical frameworks that recognize the multilevel, potentially traumatic, and developmentally significant nature of racism within Black families (Bernard et al., 2021; Carter, 2007; García Coll et al., 1996; J. M. Jones, 1972) to delineate the violent nature of racism across individual (e.g., age, gender), relational (e.g., peer interactions, family systems), community (e.g., neighborhood disadvantage, school experiences), and societal (e.g., media, criminal legal system) levels. Though discussed separately, it is difficult to disentangle these socioecological domains as they inform and overlap with one another in significant ways. It is also important to acknowledge that the forthcoming discussion is by no means exhaustive, but rather serves to highlight salient examples of how racism may manifest across these socioecological levels to increase risk for violence exposure. Finally, it should be noted that this framework, while focused here on documenting harms to Black youth within the United States, is more broadly useful for interrogating how racism represents latent and manifested forms of violence and may therefore be applicable in other geographic and cultural contexts across the globe.

Individual-Level Risk Factors

Age. While racism-related experiences occur across the life course, the psychological impact of racism may be greatest among youth who may still be in the process of developing the sophisticated coping skills needed to adaptively navigate these adverse experiences (S. C. T. Jones et al., 2020). Notably, American children exhibit an awareness of racial stereotypes and anti-Black biases by age 6 (Baron & Banaji, 2006; McKown & Weinstein, 2003). As evidenced by the seminal Clark and Clark doll study (Clark & Clark, 1950), this awareness can have significant consequences as to how Black youth think about and value what it means to be Black in America, which can have lasting psychological consequences (Landor & McNeil Smith, 2019). One such consequence is the internalization of anti-Black rhetoric (i.e., internalized racism; T.-K. M. Bailey et al., 2011), which has been empirically linked to increases in aggressive behavior, more accepting attitudes toward gun violence, and an overall propensity for violence among Black youth (Bryant, 2011). Thus, in line with early developmental experiences of violence, racism-related encounters that occur early in development not only challenge feelings of safety and security (Saleem et al., 2019) but also increase the likelihood for other forms of violence to occur.

Gender. Several studies have denoted the importance of gender when under-standing the psychological effects of violence exposure (Hatch & Dohrenwend, 2007). Perhaps not surprisingly, the literature has also implicated gender as an important psychosocial factor with implications for how racism affects health (Chavous et al., 2008; Neblett et al., 2016). Across developmental markers, Black males report higher rates of discriminatory experiences relative to their female counterparts (Banks et al., 2006; Brownlow et al., 2019), which can be explained, in part, due to the gendered differences in racial stereotypes. As an example, the relevance of stereotypes characterizing Black males as dangerous or harmful (e.g., "super-predator"; Carter, 2007) may be directly related to the violent, and at times fatal, interactions with community members and law enforcement. A salient ex-ample of the deadly implications of these stereotypes among Black youth can be gleaned from the murder of Trayvon Martin, a Black 17-year-old who was followed at night and ultimately shot and killed by a neighborhood watchman for "looking suspicious." To be sure, Black women must also contend with these harmful stereotypes and experiences, in addition to stereotypes that position them as older and hypersexualized in nature (Epstein et al., 2017), which have been directly linked to increased encounters of interpersonal and sexual violence (Wun, 2018).

Relationship-Level Factors

Peer Relationships. As noted by Haynie and Payne (2006), "peer relations and friendship networks in adolescence may have important implications for un-derstanding how particular groups of individuals, such as racial and ethnic minorities, face higher or lower risks of violence" (p. 777). One particularly im-portant aspect of peer relationships that is important to consider for Black youth is peer victimization. Peer victimization is a prevalent and potentially violent ex-perience that affects youth across sociodemographic profiles. However, racial and ethnic minority youth may be victimized by peers with more frequency given their marginalized societal status in America (Felix & You, 2011; Scherr & Larson, 2010). Indeed, racial and ethnic peer victimization can co-occur with more generalized forms of peer victimization to increase risk for negative mental health concerns (Arens & Visser, 2020). As an example, work by Seaton et al. (2013) found that perceptions of racial discrimination among Black and Latino youth were associated with increases in being perceived by peers as victims of overt (e.g., being threatened or physically hurt) and relational (e.g., being excluded from an activity) peer victimization. Studies have also found that Black youth are more likely to be exposed to negative remarks related to their race or racist images on-line (Tynes et al., 2004), with potentially traumatic consequences (Tynes et al., 2019). In fact, higher levels of online forms of racial discrimination have also been linked to higher levels of hate crimes in U.S. cities, highlighting how cyber-racism can influence victimization offline (Relia et al., 2019). When these data are considered in tandem with evidence demonstrating that Black adolescents report five discriminatory experiences per day on average (English et al., 2020), it is evident that Black youth are particularly at risk of being subjected to peer victimization, which may come at a steep cost to their mental and physical wellness.

Family Systems. While there is significant heterogeneity in sociocultural experiences within the Black community, Black families are by and large burdened by institutionalized forms of oppression rooted within historical policies and practices that place them at greater risk to experience economic deprivation, be disproportionately embedded within impoverished neighborhoods, and be affected by mass incarceration—or the comparatively elevated rates by which Black individuals are imprisoned in America relative to White individuals (West, 2016). Such burdens can negatively affect the family system and subsequently increase risk for the violent victimization of Black youth. As an example, Black youth are 6 times more likely to have a parent incarcerated relative to their White peers (Sykes & Pettit, 2014), which can considerably reduce the economic resources of the family, in addition to disrupting positive parent-child relationships (Murray & Murray, 2010). A scarcity of financial resources can affect virtually every aspect of parenting, including the amount of time caregivers may have to appropriately monitor youth behaviors (Conger et al., 1992; Conger et al., 2010), due to the competing responsibilities that are necessary to provide basic resources. Moreover, low levels of parental monitoring can increase the likelihood that a child will associate with deviant peers and engage in violence themselves (Haggerty et al., 2013). Caregivers living in poverty are also at greater risk to utilize overly harsh forms of discipline (Neppl et al., 2016), which may partially explain why Black children are at higher likelihood to experience childhood maltreatment and child abuse—robust predictors of violent behavior (Topitzes et al., 2012)—relative to their Hispanic and White peers (U.S. Department of Health & Health Services, Administration for Children & Families, Administration on Children, Youth, & Families, Children's Bureau, 2019).

Community-Level Factors

Neighborhood Disadvantage. The unequal distribution of wealth between Black and White households has been argued to be among the most salient and far-reaching manifestations of racism within the United States (Thomas et al., 2020). Data from the Pew Research Center (2020) indicate that the median income generated by Black households represents only 61% of that of White households, even after accounting for explanatory factors such as home ownership and educational attainment (Darity et al., 2018). This income disparity has been implicated as a primary reason that Black families are overly concentrated within largely segregated, impoverished, and high-risk neighborhoods where violence is more likely to occur (Gaylord-Harden et al., 2015; Stockman et al., 2015; Williams, 2018; Williams & Collins, 2001). Racial disparities in policing (e.g., neighborhood surveillance, misconduct, and interpersonal treatment) further amplify the stress and risk for violence within disadvantaged neighborhoods (Lerman & Weaver, 2014; McLeod et al., 2020). As an example, residents within high-crime communities have been found to be perceived with greater suspicion by law enforcement and are also at greater risk to experience adverse interactions with police officers (Terrill & Reisig, 2003). Such issues are also relevant at early developmental stages, as Black youth have been found to characterize interactions with law enforcement as being violent, harassing, and disrespectful (Brunson & Miller, 2006). The implications of these adverse interactions are dire, with police being 6 times more likely to utilize lethal forms of intervention toward Black adolescents relative to White adolescents (Badolato et al., 2020).

Academic Environment. Prior research indicates "educational institutions are organized around and reflect the interests of dominant groups in the society; that the function of school is to reproduce the current inequities of our social, political, and economic system" (Ferguson, 2000, p. 50). Thus, it follows that within educational spaces, Black youth are at increased likelihood to experience chronic encounters of racial discrimination, negative stereotypes, and other negative race-centered interactions from peers and teachers that can detract from positive psychological adjustment outcomes (Rowley et al., 2010). The proliferation of racism-related experiences can give rise to increases in externalizing behaviors (e.g., fighting), school truancy, and other risky behaviors (e.g., substance use) that may place Black youth at greater risk for expulsion (Felice, 1981; Gibbons et al., 2007). This risk for school removal is further heightened by the inequitable school disciplinary practices (e.g., zero-tolerance policies) that characterize Black youth as more problematic and thus more likely than their White peers to be suspended or expelled for the same offense (Amemiya et al., 2020; Riddle & Sinclair, 2019; Welch & Payne, 2012). Racial disparities in how students are perceived and disciplined by teachers and administrators have been directly connected to the criminalization of Black youth within academic contexts (e.g., school arrests; Hirschfield, 2008), which increases early exposure to the criminal legal system, where experiences of violent victimization are more likely to occur.

Societal-Level Factors

Media. Previous research has highlighted how portrayals of Black Americans in the media can not only influence Black youth development but also shape both internalized racial attitudes and attitudes about Black Americans held by other racial and ethnic groups (Tynes & Ward, 2009; Williams & Mohammed, 2013). For example, negative portrayals of Black Americans via images and videos are related to priming of stereotypes among White individuals (e.g., Givens & Monahan, 2005). Similarly, negative portrayals of Black Americans in TV shows and local news reports have been linked to increased levels of racial prejudice and negative attitudes toward Black Americans (Gilliam & Iyengar, 2000; Mutz & Goldman, 2010). Additionally, scholars have found that exposure to Black rather than White suspects in the news led to increased support for punitive legislation for crime such as the death penalty and three-strikes legislation (Dixon, 2006; Gilliam & Iyengar, 2000). The implications of these primed stereotypes and negative attitudes are alarming and considerably increase risk for Black youth to experience or be exposed to violence. For instance, studies have found that newspaper articles are more likely to describe Black incarcerated persons as animalistic (i.e., "ape-like") and that these negative portrayals are linked to Black defendants being more likely to be executed relative to their White counterparts (Goff et al., 2008). These negative media portrayals have been associated with the dehumanization and criminalization of Black Americans (Smiley & Fakunle, 2016), which increases risk for Black youth to encounter instances of violence due to being perceived by law enforcement and other community members as deviant, violent, and threatening (Goff et al., 2014).

Criminal Legal System. Though designed for justice, the penal institutions that make up the criminal legal system within the United States (e.g., law enforcement, judicial system, sentencing board) disproportionally target and criminalize Black communities (Z. D. Bailey et al., 2017; Brewer & Heitzeg, 2008). In fact, Black individuals are at increased risk for arrest relative to their White counterparts; once arrested, they are also more likely to be convicted; and once convicted, they are more likely to experience longer and more severe sentences (Sentencing Project, 2018). Such discrepancies have been directly connected to biases held by law enforcement and judicial officials that associate Black individuals with criminality, dangerous behaviors, and presumptions of guilt (Eberhardt et al., 2004; Steffensmeier et al., 1998). While these disparities are alarming, they become even more concerning when considering that these disparities are detected relatively early in development. Specifically, research has found Black adolescents to be 5 times more likely to be incarcerated relative to their White counterparts (Sickmund et al., 2013). Thus, it is perhaps not surprising that Black youth have a higher rate of booked arrests (i.e., formally recorded arrests with subsequent fingerprinting) than White and Hispanic youth (Raphael & Rozo, 2019). Juvenile incarceration can have lasting impacts on youth that can indirectly and directly increase risk for violence exposure. In the context of direct effects, juvenile incarceration can increase exposure to antisocial peers, risk for serious mental health concerns, lower school completion rate, and future delinquent behavior (Aizer & Doyle, 2015; Gatti et al., 2009; Geerlings et al., 2020). Regarding indirect effects, juvenile incarceration has been linked to reductions in future employability and vocational earnings that can persist well into adulthood (Taylor, 2016), making Black youth disproportionately vulnerable to other forms of structural (i.e., poverty) and interpersonal forms of violence (e.g., gun violence) and future involvement with the criminal legal system (McCrea et al., 2019).

IMPLICATIONS AND CONCLUSION

The purpose of this chapter was to demonstrate how the omnipresent nature of racism permeates across individual, relational, community, and societal levels to position Black youth to be at an elevated risk for violence exposure and victimization relative to youth of other racial and ethnic groups, specifically in the United States. Although the predominant focus of this chapter centers on interrogating racism as a unique form of violence, this framework certainly has global relevance and can be used to challenge the deficit-based narratives that attribute violence disparities to person or group-centered characteristics (e.g., Lynam et al., 1993). To this end, it is important to reiterate that one's race or race and/or ethnicity does not in itself increase the likelihood that violence will occur; rather, violence is linked with the socioecological risk factors that disparately accumulate among particular racial and ethnic groups (Sampson et al., 2005; Sheats et al., 2018). Accordingly, while person-centered resilience approaches (e.g., psychotherapy) may be useful in promoting psychological resilience to violence exposure at a micro level, more systemic and policy-based approaches are needed to reduce the adverse societal conditions that undergird the etiology of violence among marginalized communities both domestically and globally. In line with this notion, Sheats et al. (2018) assert that to reduce violence exposure, "it is important for prevention efforts to consider societal conditions disproportionately experienced by Blacks, including concentrated poverty, residential segregation, and other forms of racism that limit opportunities to grow up in healthy, violence-free environments" (p. 466).

In conclusion, violence exposure represents a significant concern among Black youth that can have devastating physical and psychological consequences that can persist across the life course. As evidenced within the current chapter, violence exposure is the product of a complex set of socioecological factors that are considerably shaped by the pervasive effects of racism. As such, it is difficult to fully understand the factors that undergird violence exposure without consideration of the historical and contemporary significance of racism among Black families and other communities of color.

REFERENCES

Aizer, A., & Doyle, J. J., Jr. (2015). Juvenile incarceration, human capital, and future crime: Evidence from randomly assigned judges. *Quarterly Journal of Economics*, *130*(2), 759–803. https://doi.org/10.1093/qje/qjv003

Amemiya, J., Mortenson, E., & Wang, M.-T. (2020). Minor infractions are not minor: School infractions for minor misconduct may increase adolescents' defiant behavior and contribute to racial disparities in school discipline. *American Psychologist*, *75*(1), 23–36. https://doi.org/10.1037/amp0000475

Arens, A. K., & Visser, L. (2020). Personal peer victimization and ethnic peer victimization: Findings on their co-occurrence, predictors, and outcomes from a latent profile analysis. *Child Abuse & Neglect*, *99*, 104250. https://doi.org/10.1016/j.chiabu.2019.104250

Badolato, G. M., Boyle, M. D., McCarter, R., Zeoli, A. M., Terrill, W., & Goyal, M. K. (2020). Racial and ethnic disparities in firearm-related pediatric deaths related to legal intervention. *Pediatrics*, *146*(6), 1–3. https://doi.org/10.1542/peds.2020-015917

Bailey, T.-K. M., Chung, Y. B., Williams, W. S., Singh, A. A., & Terrell, H. K. (2011). Development and validation of the Internalized Racial Oppression Scale for Black individuals. *Journal of Counseling Psychology*, *58*(4), 481–493. https://doi.org/10.1037/a0023585

Bailey, Z. D., Krieger, N., Agénor, M., Graves, J., Linos, N., & Bassett, M. T. (2017). Structural racism and health inequities in the USA: Evidence and interventions. *The Láncet*, *389*(10077), 1453–1463. https://doi.org/10.1016/S0140-6736(17)30569-X

Banks, K. H., Kohn-Wood, L. P., & Spencer, M. (2006). An examination of the African American experience of everyday discrimination and symptoms of psychological distress. *Community Mental Health Journal*, *42*(6), 555–570. https://doi.org/10.1007/s10597-006-9052-9.

Baron, A. S., & Banaji, M. R. (2006). The development of implicit attitudes: Evidence of race evaluations from ages 6 and 10 and adulthood. *Psychological Science*, *17*(1), 53–58. https://doi.org/10.1111/j.1467-9280.2005.01664.x

Benner, A. D., Wang, Y., Shen, Y., Boyle, A. E., Polk, R., & Cheng, Y.-P. (2018). Racial/ethnic discrimination and well-being during adolescence: A meta-analytic review. *American Psychologist*, *73*(7), 855–883. https://doi.org/10.1037/amp0000204

Berg, M. T. (2014). Accounting for racial disparities in the nature of violent victimization. *Journal of Quantitative Criminology*, *30*(4), 629–650. https://doi.org/10.1007/s10940-014-9217-6

Bernard, D. L., Calhoun, C. D., Banks, D. E., Halliday, C. A., Hughes-Halbert, C., & Danielson, C. K. (2021). Making the "C-ACE" for a culturally-informed adverse childhood experiences framework to understand the pervasive mental health impact of racism on Black youth. *Journal of Child & Adolescent Trauma*, *14*(2), 233–247.

Bernard, D. L., Smith, Q., & Lanier, P. (2022). Racial discrimination and other adverse childhood experiences as risk factors for internalizing mental health concerns among Black youth. *Journal of Traumatic Stress*, *35*(2), 473–483.

Brewer, R. M., & Heitzeg, N. A. (2008). The racialization of crime and punishment: Criminal justice, color-blind racism, and the political economy of the prison industrial complex. *American Behavioral Scientist*, *51*(5), 625–644. https://doi.org/10.1177/0002764207307745

Bronfenbrenner, U. (1977). Toward an experimental ecology of human development. *American Psychologist*, *32*(7), 513–531. https://doi.org/10.1037/0003-066X.32.7.513

Brownlow, B. N., Sosoo, E. E., Long, R. N., Hoggard, L. S., Burford, T. I., & Hill, L. K. (2019). Sex differences in the impact of racial discrimination on mental health among Black Americans. *Current Psychiatry Reports*, *21*(11), 1–14. https://doi.org/10.1007/s11920-019-1098-9

Brunson, R. K., & Miller, J. (2006). Young Black men and urban policing in the United States. *British Journal of Criminology*, *46*(4), 613–640. https://doi.org/10.1093/bjc/azi093

Bryant, W. W. (2011). Internalized racism's association with African American male youth's propensity for violence. *Journal of Black Studies*, *42*(4), 690–707. https://doi.org/10.1177/0021934710393243

Burt, C. H., Simons, R. L., & Gibbons, F. X. (2012). Racial discrimination, ethnic-racial socialization, and crime: A micro-sociological model of risk and resilience.

American Sociological Review, 77(4), 648–677. https://doi.org/10.1177/000312241 2448648

Carter, R. T. (2007). Racism and psychological and emotional injury recognizing and assessing race-based traumatic stress. *Counseling Psychologist, 35*(1), 13–105. https://doi.org/10.1177/0011000006292033

Centers for Disease Control and Prevention (CDC). (n.d.). *The social-ecological model: A framework for violence prevention.* https://www.cdc.gov/violenceprevention/pdf/ sem_framewrk-a.pdf

Chavous, T. M., Rivas-Drake, D., Smalls, C., Griffin, T., & Cogburn, C. (2008). Gender matters, too: The influences of school racial discrimination and racial identity on academic engagement outcomes among African American adolescents. *Developmental Psychology, 44*(3), 637–654. https://doi.org/10.1037/0012-1649.44.3.637

Clark, K. B., & Clark, M. P. (1950). Emotional factors in racial identification and preference in Negro children. *Journal of Negro Education, 19*(3), 341–350. https://doi.org/ 10.2307/2966491

Conger, R. D., Conger, K. J., Elder, G. H., Lorenz, F. O., Simons, R. L., & Whitbeck, L. B. (1992). A family process model of economic hardship and adjustment of early adolescent boys. *Child Development, 63*(3), 526–541. https://doi.org/10.1111/j.1467-8624.1992.tb01644.x

Conger, R. D., Conger, K. J., & Martin, M. J. (2010). Socioeconomic status, family processes, and individual development. *Journal of Marriage and the Family, 72*(3), 685–704. https://doi.org/10.1111/j.1741-3737.2010.00725.x

Copeland, W. E., Keeler, G., Angold, A., & Costello, E. J. (2007). Traumatic events and posttraumatic stress in childhood. *Archives of General Psychiatry, 64*(5), 577–584. https://doi.org/10.1001/archpsyc.64.5.577

Dahlberg, L. L., & Krug, E. G. (2006). Violence: A global public health problem. *Ciência & Saúde Coletiva, 11,* 1163–1178. https://doi.org/10.1590/S1413-8123200600 0500007

Daiute, C., & Fine, M. (2003). Youth perspectives on violence and injustice. *Journal of Social Issues, 59*(1), 1–14. https://doi.org/10.1111/1540-4560.00001

Darity, W., Jr., Hamilton, D., Paul, M., Aja, A., Price, A., Moore, A., & Chiopris, C. (2018). *What we get wrong about closing the racial wealth gap* (pp. 1–67). Samuel DuBois Cook Center on Social Equity and Insight Center for Community Economic Development.

Dixon, T. L. (2006). Psychological reactions to crime news portrayals of Black criminals: Understanding the moderating roles of prior news viewing and stereotype endorsement. *Communication Monographs, 73*(2), 162–187. https://doi.org/ 10.1080/03637750600690643

Eberhardt, J. L., Goff, P. A., Purdie, V. J., & Davies, P. G. (2004). Seeing Black: Race, crime, and visual processing. *Journal of Personality and Social Psychology, 87*(6), 876–893. https://doi.org/10.1037/0022-3514.87.6.876

English, D., Lambert, S. F., Tynes, B. M., Bowleg, L., Zea, M. C., & Howard, L. C. (2020). Daily multidimensional racial discrimination among Black US American adolescents. *Journal of Applied Developmental Psychology, 66,* 1–12. https://doi.org/ 10.1016/j.appdev.2019.101068

Epstein, R., Blake, J., & González, T. (2017). *Girlhood interrupted: The erasure of Black girls' childhood.* Center on Poverty and Inequality. http://www.law.georgetown.edu/academics/centers-institutes/poverty-inequality/upload/girlhood-interrupted.pdf

Evans, S. E., Davies, C., & DiLillo, D. (2008). Exposure to domestic violence: A meta-analysis of child and adolescent outcomes. *Aggression and Violent Behavior, 13*(2), 131–140. https://doi.org/10.1016/j.avb.2008.02.005

Felice, L. G. (1981). Black student dropout behavior: Disengagement from school rejection and racial discrimination. *Journal of Negro Education, 50*(4), 415–424. https://doi.org/10.2307/2294802

Felix, E. D., & You, S. (2011). Peer victimization within the ethnic context of high school. *Journal of Community Psychology, 39*(7), 860–875. https://doi.org/10.1002/jcop.20465

Ferguson, A. A. (2000). *Bad boys: Public schools in the making of Black masculinity.* University of Michigan Press. http://ebookcentral.proquest.com/lib/musc/detail.action?docID=3414825

Finkelhor, D., Ormrod, R. K., & Turner, H. A. (2007). Polyvictimization and trauma in a national longitudinal cohort. *Development and Psychopathology, 19*(1), 149–166. https://doi.org/10.1017/S0954579407070083

Finkelhor, D., Turner, H., Shattuck, A., Hamby, S., & Kracke, K. (2015). *Children's exposure to violence, crime, and abuse: An update.* Office of Juvenile Justice and Delinquency Prevention. https://www.ojp.gov/pdffiles1/ojjdp/227744.pdf

Galtung, J. (1969). Violence, peace, and peace research. *Journal of Peace Research, 6*(3), 167–191. https://doi.org/10.1177/002234336900600301

Galtung, J. (1990). Cultural violence. *Journal of Peace Research, 27*(3), 291–305. https://doi.org/10.1177%2F0022343390027003005

García Coll, C., Lamberty, G., Jenkins, R., McAdoo, H. P., Crnic, K., Wasik, B. H., & Garcia, H. V. (1996). An integrative model for the study of developmental competencies in minority children. *Child Development, 67*(5), 1891. https://doi.org/10.2307/1131600

Gatti, U., Tremblay, R. E., & Vitaro, F. (2009). Iatrogenic effect of juvenile justice. *Journal of Child Psychology and Psychiatry, 50*(8), 991–998. https://doi.org/10.1111/j.1469-7610.2008.02057.x

Gaylord-Harden, N. K., Zakaryan, A., Bernard, D., & Pekoc, S. (2015). Community-level victimization and aggressive behavior in African American male adolescents: A profile analysis. *Journal of Community Psychology, 43*(4), 502–519. https://doi.org/10.1002/jcop.21699

Geerlings, Y., Asscher, J. J., Stams, G. J. J., & Assink, M. (2020). The association between psychopathy and delinquency in juveniles: A three-level meta-analysis. *Aggression and Violent Behavior, 50*, 101342. https://doi.org/10.1016/j.avb.2019.101342

Gibbons, F. X., Yeh, H.-C., Gerrard, M., Cleveland, M. J., Cutrona, C., Simons, R. L., & Brody, G. H. (2007). Early experience with racial discrimination and conduct disorder as predictors of subsequent drug use: A critical period hypothesis. *Drug and Alcohol Dependence, 88*(Suppl. 1), S27–S37. https://doi.org/10.1016/j.drugalcdep.2006.12.015

Gilliam, F. D., & Iyengar, S. (2000). Prime suspects: The influence of local television news on the viewing public. *American Journal of Political Science, 44*(3), 560–573. https://doi.org/10.2307/2669264

Givens, S. M. B., & Monahan, J. L. (2005). Priming mammies, jezebels, and other control-ling images: An examination of the influence of mediated stereotypes on perceptions of an African American woman. *Media Psychology*, *7*(1), 87–106. https://doi.org/10.1207/S1532785XMEP0701_5

Goff, P. A., Eberhardt, J. L., Williams, M. J., & Jackson, M. C. (2008). Not yet human: Implicit knowledge, historical dehumanization, and contemporary consequences. *Journal of Personality and Social Psychology*, *94*(2), 292–306. https://doi.org/10.1037/0022-3514.94.2.292

Goff, P. A., Jackson, M. C., Di Leone, B. A. L., Culotta, C. M., & DiTomasso, N. A. (2014). The essence of innocence: Consequences of dehumanizing Black children. *Journal of Personality and Social Psychology*, *106*(4), 526–545. https://doi.org/10.1037/a0035663

Haggerty, K. P., Skinner, M. L., McGlynn, A., Catalano, R. F., & Crutchfield, R. D. (2013). Parent and peer predictors of violent behavior of Black and White teens. *Violence and Victims*, *28*(1), 145–160. https://doi.org/10.1891/0886-6708.28.1.145

Harrell, S. P. (2000). A multidimensional conceptualization of racism-related stress: Implications for the well-being of people of color. *American Journal of Orthopsychiatry*, *70*(1), 42–57. https://doi.org/10.1037/h0087722

Hatch, S. L., & Dohrenwend, B. P. (2007). Distribution of traumatic and other stressful life events by race/ethnicity, gender, SES and age: A review of the research. *American Journal of Community Psychology*, *40*(3–4), 313–332. https://doi.org/ 10.1007/s10464-007-9134-z

Haynie, D. L., & Payne, D. C. (2006). Race, friendship networks, and violent delinquency. *Criminology*, *44*(4), 775–805. https://doi.org/10.1111/j.1745-9125.2006.00063.x

Heinze, J. E., Stoddard, S. A., Aiyer, S. M., Eisman, A. B., & Zimmerman, M. A. (2017). Exposure to violence during adolescence as a predictor of perceived stress trajectories in emerging adulthood. *Journal of Applied Developmental Psychology*, *49*, 31–38. https://doi.org/10.1016/j.appdev.2017.01.005

Hillis, S., Mercy, J., Amobi, A., & Kress, H. (2016). Global prevalence of past-year vi-olence against children: A systematic review and minimum estimates. *Pediatrics*, *137*(3), 1–13.

Hirschfield, P. J. (2008). Preparing for prison?: The criminalization of school discipline in the USA. *Theoretical Criminology*, *12*(1), 79–101. https://doi.org/10.1177/1362480607085795

Hoffman, J., Knox, L., & Cohen, R. (2011). Beyond suppression: Global perspectives on youth violence. In J. Hoffman, L. Knox, & R. Cohen (Eds.), *Global crime and justice series*. Praeger.

Holden, G. W. (2003). Children exposed to domestic violence and child abuse: Terminology and taxonomy. *Clinical Child and Family Psychology Review*, *6*(3), 151–160. https://doi.org/10.1023/a:1024906315255

Jernigan, M. M., & Daniel, J. H. (2011). Racial trauma in the lives of Black children and adolescents: Challenges and clinical implications. *Journal of Child & Adolescent Trauma*, *4*(2), 123–141. https://doi.org/10.1080/19361521.2011.574678

Jones, J. M. (1972). *Prejudice and racism*. Addison-Wesley.

Jones, N. (2007). A bad relationship: Violence in the lives of incarcerated Black women. In M. Marable, I. Steinberg, & K. Middlemass (Eds.), *Racializing justice*, *disenfranchising lives. The Critical Black Studies Series* (pp. 123–129). Palgrave Macmillan. https://doi.org/10.1057/9780230607347_11

Jones, S. C. T., Anderson, R. E., Gaskin-Wasson, A. L., Sawyer, B. A., Applewhite, K., & Metzger, I. W. (2020). From "crib to coffin": Navigating coping from racism-related stress throughout the lifespan of Black Americans. *American Journal of Orthopsychiatry, 90*(2), 267–282. https://doi.org/10.1037/ort0000430

Jonson-Reid, M. (1998). Youth violence and exposure to violence in childhood: An ecological review. *Aggression and Violent Behavior, 3*(2), 159–179. https://doi.org/10.1016/S1359-1789(97)00009-8

Kilpatrick, D. G., Saunders, B. E., & Smith, D. W. (2003). *Youth victimization: Prevalence and implications. Research in brief.* US Department of Justice, Office of Justice Programs.

Krug, E. G., Mercy, J. A., Dahlberg, L. L., & Zwi, A. B. (2002). The world report on violence and health. *The Lancet, 360*(9339), 1083–1088. https://doi.org/10.1016/S0140-6736(02)11133-0

Landor, A. M., & McNeil Smith, S. (2019). Skin-tone trauma: Historical and contemporary influences on the health and interpersonal outcomes of African Americans. *Perspectives on Psychological Science, 14*(5), 797–815. https://doi.org/10.1177/1745691619851781

Lerman, A. E., & Weaver, V. (2014). Staying out of sight? Concentrated policing and local political action. *Annals of the American Academy of Political and Social Science, 651*(1), 202–219. https://doi.org/10.1177/0002716213503085

Lynam, D., Moffitt, T., & Stouthamer-Loeber, M. (1993). Explaining the relation between IQ and delinquency: Class, race, test motivation, school failure, or self-control? *Journal of Abnormal Psychology, 102*(2), 187–196. https://doi.org/10.1037/0021-843X.102.2.187

Mahmudiono, T., Segalita, C., & Rosenkranz, R. R. (2019). Socio-ecological model of correlates of double burden of malnutrition in developing countries: A narrative review. *International Journal of Environmental Research and Public Health, 16*(19), 3730. https://doi.org/10.3390/ijerph16193730

McCrea, K. T., Richards, M., Quimby, D., Scott, D., Davis, L., Hart, S., Thomas, A., & Hopson, S. (2019). Understanding violence and developing resilience with African American youth in high-poverty, high-crime communities. *Children and Youth Services Review, 99*, 296–307. https://doi.org/10.1016/j.childyouth.2018.12.018

McKown, C., & Weinstein, R. S. (2003). The development and consequences of stereotype consciousness in middle childhood. *Child Development, 74*(2), 498–515. https://doi.org/10.1111/1467-8624.7402012

McLeod, M. N., Heller, D., Manze, M. G., & Echeverria, S. E. (2020). Police interactions and the mental health of Black Americans: A systematic review. *Journal of Racial and Ethnic Health Disparities, 7*(1), 10–27. https://doi.org/10.1007/s40615-019-00629-1

Miller, L. E. (2015). Perceived threat in childhood: A review of research and implications for children living in violent households. *Trauma, Violence, & Abuse, 16*(2), 153–168. https://doi.org/10.1177/1524838013517563

Mrug, S., & Windle, M. (2010). Prospective effects of violence exposure across multiple contexts on early adolescents' internalizing and externalizing problems. *Journal of Child Psychology and Psychiatry, 51*(8), 953–961. https://doi.org/10.1111/j.1469-7610.2010.02222.x

Murray, J., & Murray, L. (2010). Parental incarceration, attachment and child psycho-pathology. *Attachment & Human Development*, *12*(4), 289–309. https://doi.org/10.1080/14751790903416889

Mutz, D. C., & Goldman, S. K. (2010). Mass media. In J. F. Dovidio, M. Hewstone, P. Glick, & V. M. Esses (Eds.), *The Sage handbook of prejudice, stereotyping and discrim-ination* (pp. 241–257). Sage.

Neblett, E. W., Bernard, D. L., & Banks, K. H. (2016). The moderating roles of gender and socioeconomic status in the association between racial discrimination and psy-chological adjustment. *Cognitive and Behavioral Practice*, *23*(3), 385–397. https://doi.org/10.1016/j.cbpra.2016.05.002

Neppl, T. K., Senia, J. M., & Donnellan, M. B. (2016). Effects of economic hard-ship: Testing the family stress model over time. *Journal of Family Psychology*, *30*(1), 12–21. https://doi.org/10.1037/fam0000168

Paradies, Y. (2006). A systematic review of empirical research on self-reported racism and health. *International Journal of Epidemiology*, *35*(4), 888–901. https://doi.org/10.1093/ije/dyl056

Paradies, Y. (2018). "Racism and Indigenous Health." In Oxford Research Encyclopedia of Global Public Health. Oxford University Press. doi:10.1093/acrefore/9780190632366.013.86

Pew Research Center. (2020). *6 facts about economic inequality in the U.S.* https://www.pewresearch.org/fact-tank/2020/02/07/6-facts-about-economic-inequality-in-the-u-s/

Pine, D. S., Costello, J., & Masten, A. (2005). Trauma, proximity, and developmental psycho-pathology: The effects of war and terrorism on children. *Neuropsychopharmacology*, *30*(10), 1781–1792. https://doi.org/10.1038/sj.npp.1300814

Polanin, J. R., Espelage, D. L., Grotpeter, J. K., Spinney, E., Ingram, K. M., Valido, A., El Sheikh, A., Torgal, C., & Robinson, L. (2021). A meta-analysis of longitudinal partial correlations between school violence and mental health, school performance, and criminal or delinquent acts. *Psychological Bulletin*, *147*(2), 115–133. https://doi.org/10.1037/bul0000314

Priest, N., Paradies, Y., Trenerry, B., Truong, M., Karlsen, S., & Kelly, Y. (2013). A sys-tematic review of studies examining the relationship between reported racism and health and wellbeing for children and young people. *Social Science & Medicine*, *95*, 115–127. https://doi.org/10.1016/j.socscimed.2012.11.031

Raphael, S., & Rozo, S. V. (2019). Racial disparities in the acquisition of juvenile arrest records. *Journal of Labor Economics*, *37*(S1), S125–S159. https://doi.org/10.1086/701068

Relia, K., Li, Z., Cook, S. H., & Chunara, R. (2019). Race, ethnicity and national origin-based discrimination in social media and hate crimes across 100 U.S. cities. *Proceedings of the International AAAI Conference on Web and Social Media*, *13*, 417–427.

Riddle, T., & Sinclair, S. (2019). Racial disparities in school-based disciplinary actions are associated with county-level rates of racial bias. *Proceedings of the National Academy of Sciences*, *116*(17), 8255–8260. https://doi.org/10.1073/pnas.1808307116

Rowley, S. J., Kurtz-Costes, B., & Cooper, S. (2010). Schooling and the development of African American children. In J. Meece & J. Eccles (Eds.), *Handbook of research on schools, schooling, and human development* (pp. 275–292). Erlbaum

Rutherford, A., Zwi, A. B., Grove, N. J., & Butchart, A. (2007). Violence: A glossary. *Journal of Epidemiology & Community Health*, *61*(8), 676–680. https://doi.org/10.1136/jech.2005.043711

Saleem, F. T., Anderson, R. E., & Williams, M. (2019). Addressing the "myth" of racial trauma: Developmental and ecological considerations for youth of color. *Clinical Child and Family Psychology Review*, *23*, 1–14. https://doi.org/10.1007/s10 567-019-00304-1

Sampson, R. J., Morenoff, J. D., & Raudenbush, S. (2005). Social anatomy of racial and ethnic disparities in violence. *American Journal of Public Health*, *95*(2), 224–232. https://doi.org/10.2105/AJPH.2004.037705

Sanders-Phillips, K., Settles-Reaves, B., Walker, D., & Brownlow, J. (2009). Social inequality and racial discrimination: Risk factors for health disparities in children of color. *Pediatrics*, *124*(Suppl. 3), S176–S186.

Scherr, T. G., & Larson, J. (2010). Bullying dynamics associated with race, ethnicity, and immigration status. In S. R. Jimerson, S. M. Swearer, & D. L. Espelage (Eds.), *The international handbook of school bullying* (pp. 223–234). Routledge.

Seaton, E. K., Neblett, E. W., Cole, D. J., & Prinstein, M. J. (2013). Perceived discrimination and peer victimization among African American and Latino youth. *Journal of Youth and Adolescence*, *42*(3), 342–350. https://doi.org/10.1007/s10964-012-9848-6

Sentencing Project (US). (2018). *Report of the Sentencing Project to the United Nations Special Rapporteur on contemporary forms of racism, racial discrimination, xenophobia, and related intolerance: Regarding racial disparities in the United States criminal justice system.*

Sheats, K. J., Irving, S. M., Mercy, J. A., Simon, T. R., Crosby, A. E., Ford, D. C., Merrick, M. T., Annor, F. B., & Morgan, R. E. (2018). Violence-related disparities experienced by Black youth and young adults: Opportunities for prevention. *American Journal of Preventive Medicine*, *55*(4), 462–469. https://doi.org/10.1016/j.amepre.2018.05.017

Sickmund, M., Sladky, T. J., Kang, W., & Puzzanchera, C. (2013). *Easy access to the census of juveniles in residential placement.* http://www.ojjdp.gov/ojstatbb/ezacjrp/

Smiley, C., & Fakunle, D. (2016). From "brute" to "thug": The demonization and criminalization of unarmed Black male victims in America. *Journal of Human Behavior in the Social Environment*, *26*(3–4), 350–366. https://doi.org/10.1080/10911 359.2015.1129256

Smith, S. M., & Landor, A. M. (2018). Toward a better understanding of African American families: Development of the sociocultural family stress model. *Journal of Family Theory & Review*, *10*(2), 434–450. https://doi.org/10.1111/jftr.12260

Steffensmeier, D., Ulmer, J., & Kramer, J. (1998). The interaction of race, gender, and age in criminal sentencing: The punishment cost of being young, Black, and male. *Criminology*, *36*(4), 763–798. https://doi.org/10.1111/j.1745-9125.1998.tb01265.x

Stockman, J. K., Hayashi, H., & Campbell, J. C. (2015). Intimate partner violence and its health impact on disproportionately affected populations, including minorities and impoverished groups. *Journal of Women's Health*, *24*(1), 62–79. https://doi.org/10.1089/jwh.2014.4879

Su, W., Mrug, S., & Windle, M. (2010). Social cognitive and emotional mediators link violence exposure and parental nurturance to adolescent aggression. *Journal of Clinical Child and Adolescent Psychology*, *39*(6), 814–824. https://doi.org/10.1080/15374416.2010.517163

Sykes, B. L., & Pettit, B. (2014). Mass incarceration, family complexity, and the repro-
    duction of childhood disadvantage. *Annals of the American Academy of Political and
    Social Science, 654*(1), 127–149. https://doi.org/10.1177/0002716214526345

Taylor, M. (2016). Adult earnings of juvenile delinquents: The interaction of race/
    ethnicity, gender, and juvenile justice status on future earnings. *Justice Policy,
    13*(2), 1–24.

Terrill, W., & Reisig, M. D. (2003). Neighborhood context and police use of force. *Journal
    of Research in Crime and Delinquency, 40*(3), 291–321. https://doi.org/10.1177/
    0022427803253800

Thomas, M., Herring, C., Horton, H. D., Semyonov, M., Henderson, L., & Mason, P. L.
    (2020). Race and the accumulation of wealth: Racial differences in net worth over
    the life course, 1989–2009. *Social Problems, 67*(1), 20–39. https://doi.org/10.1093/
    socpro/spz002

Topitzes, J., Mersky, J. P., & Reynolds, A. J. (2012). From child maltreatment to violent
    offending: An examination of mixed-gender and gender-specific models. *Journal
    of Interpersonal Violence, 27*(12), 2322–2347. https://doi.org/10.1177/088626051
    1433510

Tynes, B., Reynolds, L., & Greenfield, P. M. (2004). Adolescence, race, and ethnicity
    on the Internet: A comparison of discourse in monitored vs. unmonitored chat
    rooms. *Journal of Applied Developmental Psychology, 25*(6), 667–684. https://doi.
    org/10.1016/j.appdev.2004.09.003

Tynes, B. M., & Ward, L. M. (2009). The role of media use and portrayals in African
    Americans' psychosocial development. In H. A. Neville, B. M. Tynes, & S. O. Utsey
    (Eds.), *Handbook of African American psychology* (pp. 143–158). Sage Publications.

Tynes, B. M., Willis, H. A., Stewart, A. M., & Hamilton, M. W. (2019). Race-related
    traumatic events online and mental health among adolescents of color. *Journal of
    Adolescent Health, 65*(3), 371–377. https://doi.org/10.1016/j.jadohealth.2019.03.006

Unnever, J. D., Cullen, F. T., & Barnes, J. C. (2017). Racial discrimination and pathways
    to delinquency: Testing a theory of African American offending. *Race and Justice,
    7*(4), 350–373. https://doi.org/10.1177/2153368716658768

U.S. Department of Health & Health Services, Administration for Children & Families,
    Administration on Children, Youth, & Families, Children's Bureau. (2019). *Child
    maltreatment, 2019.* https://acf.hhs.gov/cb/data-research/child-maltreatment

Welch, K., & Payne, A. A. (2012). Exclusionary school punishment: The effect of racial
    threat on expulsion and suspension. *Youth Violence and Juvenile Justice, 10*(2), 155–
    171. https://doi.org/10.1177/1541204011423766

West, C. (2016). Living in a web of trauma: An ecological examination of violence among
    African Americans. In C. Cuevas (Ed.), *The Wiley-Blackwell handbook on psychology
    and violence* (pp. 649–665). Wiley-Blackwell.

West, C. M. (2019). Toward an ecological model of violence among African Americans.
    In W. S. DeKeseredy, C. Rennison, & A. Sanchez (Eds.), *The Routledge international
    handbook of violence studies* (pp. 190–209). Routledge.

Williams, D. R. (2018). Stress and the mental health of populations of color: Advancing
    our understanding of race-related stressors. *Journal of Health and Social Behavior,
    59*(4), 466–485. https://doi.org/10.1177/0022146518814251

Williams, D. R., & Collins, C. (2001). Racial residential segregation: A fundamental cause of racial disparities in health. *Public Health Reports, 116*(5), 404–416. https://doi.org/10.1093/phr/116.5.404

Williams, D. R., & Mohammed, S. A. (2013). Racism and health I: Pathways and scientific evidence. *American Behavioral Scientist, 57*(8), 1152–1173. https://doi.org/10.1177/0002764213487340

Williams, D. R., & Williams-Morris, R. (2000). Racism and mental health: The African American experience. *Ethnicity & Health, 5*(3–4), 243–268. https://doi.org/10.1080/713667453

Wilson, H. W., Stover, C. S., & Berkowitz, S. J. (2009). Research review: The relationship between childhood violence exposure and juvenile antisocial behavior: A meta-analytic review. *Journal of Child Psychology and Psychiatry, 50*(7), 769–779. https://doi.org/10.1111/j.1469-7610.2008.01974.x

World Health Organization. (2020). *Youth violence.* Retrieved March 15, 2021, from https://www.who.int/news-room/fact-sheets/detail/youth-violence

Wun, C. (2018). Angered: Black and non-Black girls of color at the intersections of violence and school discipline in the United States. *Race Ethnicity and Education, 21*(4), 423–437. https://doi.org/10.1080/13613324.2016.1248829

Zatti, C., Rosa, V., Barros, A., Valdivia, L., Calegaro, V. C., Freitas, L. H., Ceresér, K. M. M., da Rocha, N. S., Bastos, A. G., & Schuch, F. B. (2017). Childhood trauma and suicide attempt: A meta-analysis of longitudinal studies from the last decade. *Psychiatry Research, 256*, 353–358. https://doi.org/10.1016/j.psychres.2017.06.082

Violence Against Children in Social Microsystems

7

Child Sex and Labor Trafficking

Psychological Perspectives on Risk Factors, Impacts, and Interventions

KELLY KINNISH, ELIZABETH W. PERRY, KATHERINE REUBEN, KATHRYN O'HARA, AND SHANNON SELF-BROWN ■

The trafficking of children[1] for sex and labor is a severe form of child maltreatment that causes immediate and long-term harm to victims and is a significant human rights concern (Curtis et al., 2008; Dank et al., 2015; Greenbaum, 2020; Institute of Medicine [IOM] and National Research Council [NRC], 2013; Murphy, 2017; United Nations Office on Drugs and Crime [UNODC], 2021). According to the United Nations *Global Report on Trafficking in Persons 2020*, 34% of all detected trafficking victims worldwide are children. Risk and vulnerability to being trafficked is multifaceted and intersects across individual, relational, and broader community and societal factors (Dalla et al., 2020; Hopper, 2017; IOM & NRC, 2013; Klatt et al., 2014; Laird et al., 2020; Stanford et al., 2021; Swaner et al., 2016). Trafficking experiences are highly heterogeneous (Greenbaum, 2020), although the trauma and adversity intrinsically embedded in trafficking feature especially prominently in understanding both the impacts of child trafficking and vulnerability to future trafficking (Cole et al., 2016; Hopper, 2017; Hossain et al., 2010; IOM and National Research Council, 2013; Self-Brown et al., 2021). Interventions that are responsive to the diverse experiences and needs of trafficked children and

---

1. The term *children* is used here to reflect inclusion of all minors (under the age of legal responsibility, in the United States under 18) and young people needing protection. Although it is recognized that this term often connotes younger children ("children and adolescents"), it is used here intentionally to shift historical perspective and counteract the alignment of adolescent victimization through child sex trafficking/commercial sexual exploitation of children with adult prostitution and the "adultification" especially of youth of color (Epstein et al., 2017). The term *youth* is also used.

directly address associated psychological harms are essential to recovery and well-being for these children.

DEFINING TRAFFICKING

The UNODC (2021) defines human trafficking as "the recruitment, transportation, transfer, harbouring or receipt of people through force, fraud or deception, with the aim of exploiting them for profit." The most common forms of trafficking are for sex and labor. The US Trafficking Victim Protection Act (TVPA) defines sex trafficking as "the recruitment, harboring, transportation, provision, obtaining, patronizing, or soliciting of a person for the purposes of a commercial sex act, in which the commercial sex act is induced by force, fraud, or coercion, or in which the person induced to perform such an act has not attained 18 years of age." In the United States, force, fraud, or coercion is not a required element of child sex trafficking (CST), nor is it a requirement that a third party benefit from or facilitate the exchange (although these elements are often present). Commercial sexual exploitation of children (CSEC) is a commonly used related (nonlegal) term that includes sex trafficking as well as other commercial sexual exploitation that may not meet the strict criteria of the TVPA (e.g., exchanges that may be sexual in nature but do not involve overt sex acts, such as dancing at strip clubs, and production of child sexual abuse materials).

Child labor trafficking (CLT) is defined by the TVPA as "the act of recruiting, harboring, transporting, providing, obtaining a child for labor or services, through the use of force, fraud, or coercion for the purposes of subjection to involuntary servitude, peonage, debt bondage, or slavery." *Labor exploitation* and *forced labor* are related terms that similarly capture the victimization of children through labor. The International Labour Organization (ILO, 2017) defines child labor as "work that deprives children of their childhood, potential and dignity, and that is harmful to physical and mental development." Common forms include domestic servitude, begging crews, and fishing, factory, and mining work. Particularly egregious forms of child labor include use of child soldiers in armed conflict (Machel, 2009; UNODC, 2021; Wessells, 2006). In comparison to CST and CSEC, the CLT scientific literature is less substantial, and thus, child labor trafficking is less well understood in terms of scope, pathways, impacts, and intervention. Because the literature is more robust regarding CST/CSEC in the United States and globally, it will be the primary focus of this chapter. Research specific to or inclusive of CLT will be included where possible.

PREVALENCE

Prevalence estimates of child trafficking are notoriously difficult to obtain due to its criminal and hidden nature, disparities in definitions, and methodological and other challenges (Finkelhor et al., 2017; IOM and National Research Council,

2013). The lack of clarity regarding the true scope of the problem is a key chal-lenge in effective trafficking response. Trafficking of children, however, does ap-pear to represent a significant subset of all human trafficking (34%, as noted). The percentage of detected child victims appears to have a strong relationship to pov-erty; high-income countries have a low percentage of detected child victimization (18% of all victimization) compared to low-income countries (50% of all victim-ization). Also, in low-income countries children are more often trafficked for forced labor (46%), whereas in high-income countries they are trafficked mainly for sexual exploitation, forced criminality, or begging (UNODC, 2021).

RISK FACTORS FOR CHILD TRAFFICKING

Research in both high-income countries and low- and middle-income countries (LMICs) has identified a complex array of factors that contribute to trafficking risk and vulnerability (e.g., Adjei & Saewyc, 2017; Choi, 2015; Dalla et al., 2020; Franchino-Olsen, 2021; Hossain et al., 2010; IOM and National Research Council, 2013; Klatt et al., 2014; Laird et al., 2020; Ranganathan et al., 2017; Reid & Piquero, 2014; Reid et al., 2017; Stanford et al., 2021; Swahn et al., 2016; Varma et al., 2015; Williams et al., 2012). Trauma and maltreatment (Stoltz et al., 2007), family-related vulnerabilities (including caregiver loss/separation and familial involve-ment in commercial sex; Fedina et al., 2019; Klatt et al., 2014; Reid et al., 2017; Self-Brown et al., 2018), poverty and economic factors (Dalla et al., 2020; Klatt et al., 2014; Swahn et al., 2016), and marginalization (Boswell et al., 2019; Dalla et al., 2020; UNODC, 2021) are especially common. It is important to note that the experience of being trafficked is often the endpoint of multiple, intersecting, and compounding vulnerabilities.

Caregiver Loss/Separation, Being Orphaned, Impaired Caregiving

Significant child trafficking risk is associated with caregiver loss, separation, and impairment (Reid, 2011; Self-Brown et al., 2021). Loss and separation may occur through many circumstances, including the death of a caregiver, caregiver incar-ceration, intensive medical treatment, migration separation, or removal from the family of origin by child welfare. In a mixed sample of sex- and labor-trafficked children from 21 countries who received mental health services in the United Kingdom, 38% had experienced the death of one or both parents. Death of a parent was reported by 38% of a sample of sex-trafficked girls and 48% of former child soldiers in the Democratic Republic of the Congo (DRC; McMullen et al., 2013; O'Callaghan et al., 2013). In a sample of 113 CST/CSEC youth in California, 55% experienced abandonment by parents (Basson et al., 2012). Not only are these losses/separations experienced as distressing (especially if traumatic, such as witnessed violent death), but also they often occur in the context of, or are precipitated by, other traumatic events, such as natural disasters, community violence, or armed conflict/civil unrest. Loss and separation from a caregiver sometimes result in a cascade of other negative effects that additionally contribute to CST/CSEC vulnerability, including unstable living circumstances and out-of-home placement (foster care); educational disruption; loss of peer relationships, community connection, and other social-emotional supports; and loss of financial security (IOM and National Research Council, 2013).

Children in LMICs may be especially vulnerable given high rates of orphanhood, resulting from numerous, intersecting contextual factors such as violence, armed conflict, extreme poverty, or infectious disease (HIV/AIDS). For instance, sub-Saharan Africa carries more than 70% of the global burden of HIV infection and the highest rates of extreme child poverty in the world, which can lead to high rates of trauma and adverse experiences, further contributing to trafficking risk (Kharsany & Karim, 2016). Swahn and colleagues (2016, 2017) reported high rates of orphaning (61% and 76%, respectively), and Self-Brown and colleagues (2018) reported high rates of CST/CSEC (39%) among youth living on the streets or in slums in Uganda. Cluver et al. (2011) found that AIDS orphanhood (i.e., loss of one or both parents to AIDS) and parent AIDS sickness predicted transactional sex among South African adolescents. In combination, the effects of AIDS, food insecurity, and exposure to abuse raised prevalence of transactional sex for girls from 1% to 57% (Cluver et al., 2011). Labor trafficking vulnerability is also a concern. In a study of orphaned and abandoned children ages 6 to 12 in five LMICs, 60.7% had engaged in work the past week and 10.5% had worked more than 28 hours (Whetten et al., 2011).

Impaired caregiving can also impact the ability to supervise and protect children from trafficking risk and vulnerability. Caregiver mental illness, substance use problems, cognitive or physical disability, and medical illness may compromise a caregiver's ability to meet a child's basic needs and provide emotional support, guidance, and monitoring and supervision (Basson et al., 2012; Moore et al., 2021; Reid, 2011; Reid & Piquero, 2014; Self-Brown et al., 2018). In a sample of predominantly male, juvenile justice-involved CST/CSEC youth, 37% reported maternal substance abuse and 44% reported caregiver arrest/incarceration (Chapple & Crawford, 2019). Hopper (2017) reported high rates of caregiver substance abuse or dependence (39%) and caregiver mental health impairment/trauma-related impacts (44%) among trafficked youth. Basson et al. (2012) found that poor supervision was a factor for 50% of CST/CSEC youth. Adolescents in sub-Saharan Africa with low levels of parental monitoring had a higher prevalence of CSEC compared with youth with higher levels of parental monitoring (Adjei & Saewyc, 2017). Lastly, Reid (2011) found that caregiver strain (substance abuse, mental illness, domestic violence) was associated with higher levels of child maltreatment, which led to running away, early alcohol or drug use, and sexual self-denigration (negative views and self-blame), all of which were associated with greater likelihood of sex trafficking in a sample of African American girls.

Familial involvement in commercial sex is also a significant risk factor for CST/CSEC (Fedina et al., 2019; Klatt et al., 2014; Reed et al., 2019). Sadly, some children are trafficked *by* caregivers or other family members (Finkelhor & Ormrod, 2004; Mitchell et al., 2013; Sprang & Cole, 2018; Reid et al., 2015). A caregiver may traffic youth directly through a family-controlled organized trafficking enterprise, sell a child to a trafficker, or traffic their child independently to meet an emergent financial need or obtain drugs in addiction (Sprang & Cole, 2018). Even if not trafficked directly by a caregiver, family involvement in the commercial sex industry may increase risk by normalizing or glorifying engagement in commercial sex (Fedina et al., 2019; Klatt et al., 2014).

Trauma, Child Maltreatment, and Violence Exposure

Rates of child trauma, maltreatment, and violence exposure are often very high in children who experience trafficking, including early experiences of sexual abuse, traumatic loss and separation, and exposure to violence in their homes and communities (physical abuse, intimate partner violence, community violence; Basson et al., 2012; Greenbaum et al., 2018; Hopper, 2017; Landers et al., 2017). O'Callaghan (2013) and McMullen et al. (2013) reported an average of 12 different trauma types in groups of sex-trafficked girls and former child soldiers in the DRC. In a U.S. sample, Self-Brown et al. (2021) reported an average of six different trauma types. The contribution of individual trauma and maltreatment types as well as cumulative impacts are described.

Sexual Abuse and Assault

Numerous studies have found that children with a history of sexual abuse or rape are at an increased risk of CST/CSEC (Adjei & Saewyc, 2017; Boyce et al., 2018; Fedina et al., 2019; Lalor & McElvaney, 2010; Reid et al., 2017; Stoltz et al., 2007; Svedin & Priebe, 2007; Swahn et al., 2016). In a sample of juvenile justice-involved youth, the odds of having been trafficked was 2.52 times greater for girls who had experienced sexual abuse and 8.21 times greater for boys who had experienced sexual abuse (Reid et al., 2017). A history of sexual molestation and rape were, likewise, each associated with increased odds of having transactional sex among girls aging out of the foster care system (Ahrens et al., 2012).

Child Maltreatment and Family/Interpersonal Violence

Physical abuse and exposure to violence also appear to contribute to trafficking risk (Green et al., 1999; Klatt et al., 2014). Numerous studies document high rates of violence victimization in trafficked children. For example, Varma and colleagues (2015) found that 44% of CSEC youth had a history of physical abuse. Hopper (2017) similarly reported that 78% of trafficked youth experienced physical violence and abuse. Emotional abuse by caregivers (e.g., belittling, intimidation, humiliation, and rejection) can profoundly impact children and increase trafficking victimization risk. Landers et al. (2017) reported that 54% of child welfare–involved trafficked youth had experienced repeated emotional abuse that spanned at least a year. Caregivers, as primary drivers of a child's low self-worth, negative cognitions, and unhealthy relationship norms, may specifically enhance child vulnerability to coercive control by potential exploiters (Roe-Sepowitz, 2012). Basson et al. (2012) reported that 53% of a sample of CST/CSEC youth had experienced emotional abuse and 56% experienced severe and repeated episodes of neglect.

Poverty and Economic Factors

Economic factors and poverty significantly impact trafficking vulnerability (Dalla et al., 2020; IOM and National Research Council, 2013; Klatt et al., 2014; Reid, 2012; Swaner et al., 2016; UNODC, 2021). Individuals with limited opportunities to meet basic needs and/or who have expectations to provide monetarily for others (children who are homeless, have impaired parents or siblings in need, have young children of their own) are especially at risk. Hopper (2017) reported that 72% of a sample of trafficked youth described financial stress or poverty in childhood, and 38% described some responsibility for financially contributing to the household as children. Lack of food or water was endorsed as a significant trauma by 83% of a sample of sex-trafficked girls and 86% of former child soldiers in the DRC (McMullen et al., 2013; O'Callahan et al., 2013). In a study of trafficked Bedia (Dalit) girls in India, participants were the sole or primary provider for their family (including food, clothing, medical, education, and wedding costs for siblings). Homeless and housing-insecure youth are also especially vulnerable. In the United States and globally, self-reported rates of CST/CSEC among homeless or "street" youth are very high (Curtis et al., 2008; Self-Brown et al., 2018). For example, among youth living in the slums of Kampala, Uganda, 39% endorsed engaging in transactional sex (Self-Brown et al., 2018). In a large sample ($n = 641$) of homeless youth in the United States and Canada, 30% reported having engaged in the sex trade and 8% experienced labor trafficking (Murphy, 2017).

Marginalized Individuals and Communities

Individuals who are members of marginalized classes or groups are at increased risk of trafficking due to a complex array of factors, including restricted access to economic and educational opportunities, discrimination and biases of formal systems including law enforcement, and negative perceptions and bullying that undermine self-worth (Butler, 2015; Chong, 2014; Dalla et al., 2020; Fedina et al., 2019; Reid, 2012, 2018; Reid & Piquero, 2014; UNODC, 2021). Indigenous populations are especially vulnerable in the United States and elsewhere (Pierce, 2012; Sethi, 2007; Stanford et al., 2021). In the United States, African American,

Latinx, and Native American youth are significantly overrepresented among trafficked youth (Rights4girls, n.d.). Immigrant and refugee children are also vulnerable to trafficking, especially those who are unaccompanied by a parent or guardian (Reid, 2012; UNODC, 2021). Trauma-related factors and other adversities prompting migration and/or that occur during or after migration may elevate the risk (violence, poverty, marginalization).

LGBTQ youth are also substantially overrepresented among CST/CSEC youth (Boswell et al., 2019; Murphy, 2017; Swaner et al., 2016). This is likely primarily due to family rejection (being "kicked out" or unwelcome in their homes) leading to homelessness, as LGBTQ youth are also overrepresented among homeless youth (Dank et al., 2015; Murphy, 2017; Ray, 2006). In a large sample of youth in the sex trade, 47% identified as something other than heterosexual (Swaner et al., 2016). Importantly, even among homeless youth, LGBTQ youth experience CST/CSEC at greater rates than their cisgender, heterosexual counterparts (Cochran et al., 2002; Murphy, 2017), which may be related to discrimination in services and employment (safe alternatives for meeting needs), especially for transgender youth (Dank et al., 2015).

Child Welfare and Foster Care

Research documents that approximately 50% to 90% of U.S. youth who experience CST/CSEC have histories of involvement with child welfare services (U.S. Department of Health and Human Services, Administration for Children, Youth and Families, 2013) and high rates of foster care placement (Dierkhising et al., 2018; Landers et al., 2017). Early placement in congregate care facilities and history of multiple placements appear to be significant risk factors for CST/CSEC (Dierkhising et al., 2021; Gibbs et al., 2018). In addition to experiences (child abuse, exposure to violence) resulting in foster care placement that are associated with CSE/CSEC risk, experiences *while in* care potentially exacerbate CST/CSEC risk. That is, foster care may erode a youth's sense of safety, security, connection, and self-worth and belief that others will care for them and keep them safe, at the same time that it also monetizes their care (Dierkhising et al., 2018; O'Neill, 2018; Walker, 2013). Aging out of foster care is a particular point of trafficking vulnerability for already very high-risk youth (Ahrens, 2012).

Leaving Home/Placement ("Running Away")

Youth who leave home or placement ("run away") are especially vulnerable to being trafficked (Bigelsen, 2013; Fedina et al., 2019; Gibbs et al., 2018; Greene et al., 1999; Murphy, 2017; Varma et al., 2015). Although leaving placement increases trafficking vulnerability for all youth, youth in foster care leave placement at greater rates, with risk increasing with number of placements (Courtney & Zinn, 2009; Kim et al., 2015; Lin, 2012). O'Brien et al. (2017) found that, among

youth with child welfare histories, youth who experienced CST/CSEC were significantly more likely than those without a CST/CSEC history to have run away
from a foster care placement. Landers et al. (2017) reported that 84% of child
welfare–involved CST/CSEC youth had left placement in the last month. Basson
et al. (2012) similarly found that 62% of a sample of CSEC girls left placement
multiple times per month. Of those with frequent episodes, 87% were running
to unsafe environments that could not meet their basic needs or where the likelihood of victimization was high.

Gender

Women and girls are overrepresented among all victims of human trafficking and
especially identified/detected CST/CSEC victims (UNODC, 2021; ILO, 2017).
Gender-based vulnerabilities are often rooted in societal and community norms and
values regarding the role of women, especially those that limit educational and economic opportunities for girls and women (Stanford et al., 2021; Williams et al., 2012).
Differences between girls and boys with regard to vulnerability factors have been
explored, such as greater likelihood of a third-party exploiter among girls, although
no consistent pattern of findings has emerged for major variables of interest (e.g.,
Ahrens et al., 2012; Cole, 2018; Reid, 2012; Reid et al., 2017).

Social Media

An increasingly important youth behavior that may serve as a risk factor for CST/
CSEC is engagement with social media as online platforms are increasingly being
used to recruit and market CSEC victims (Fredlund et al., 2013; UNODC, 2021;
Wells et al., 2012). One U.S. report found that 80% of CST/CSEC investigations included technology (Mitchell & Boyd, 2014). Similar rates have been documented in
LMICs as well, with the UNODC estimating that 76% of transactions were initiated
on the internet.

Posttraumatic Stress Disorder and Complex Trauma

As described previously, exposure to multiple, chronic, and complex trauma[2] is
common among trafficked children (Basson et al., 2012; Hopper, 2017; Landers
et al., 2017). These experiences can negatively impact emotional regulation,

---

2. The National Child Traumatic Stress Network defines complex trauma as "children's exposure
to multiple traumatic events—often of an invasive, interpersonal nature—and the wide-ranging,
long-term effects of this exposure." In the *International Classification of Diseases*, 11th edition
(ICD -11), complex posttraumatic stress disorder (PTSD) diagnostic criteria are comprised
of the three core PTSD features of re-experiencing, avoidance and persistent perceptions of

relationships, and self-concept in ways that appear to contribute to trafficking vulnerability. Hopper (2017) reported that in a sample of trafficked girls, 94% described emotional neglect and attachment disturbance and 81% reported emotional dysregulation prior to trafficking. Youth may engage in behaviors that elevate vulnerability in an effort to cope with dysregulation. Substance use, which is a significant risk factor for trafficking (Cook et al., 2018; Klatt et al., 2014; Moore et al., 2021), is an especially salient example. More broadly, in Hopper (2017), emotional needs such as a desire for affection, love, or support were a vulnerability factor in 59% of the cases reviewed. Exploitation of disrupted attachment and relational impairments is considered a hallmark of trafficker grooming and control tactics (Reid, 2016; Smith et al., 2009).

CHILD TRAFFICKING EXPERIENCES

Violence and Abuse

Children trafficked for sex and labor experience a range of traumatic and harmful experiences while being trafficked (Curtis et al., 2008; Hopper, 2017; Kiss et al., 2015; Nodzenski et al., 2020; O'Callaghan et al., 2013; Ottisova et al., 2018; Sprang & Cole, 2018; Swaner et al., 2016; Twis et al., 2020). Specifically, sex-trafficked children often report experiences of coerced, forced, and multiple sex acts including violent sexual assault, with sexual violence lasting from a few days to years (Curtis et al., 2008; Hopper, 2017). They may also experience physical assault by traffickers who maintain control through the use of direct violence, threats, and the witnessing of and forced participation in violence toward others (Curtis et al., 2008; Moore et al., 2021; Reid, 2016). Emotional abuse by traffickers may include verbal aggression and threats, belittling, and humiliation, often purposely employed to maintain dependence and control (Casassa et al., 2021; Hopper, 2017). In Hopper (2017), nearly all youth (97%) described some means by which they were monitored and controlled by their trafficker. Specifically, 91% described social isolation; 78% reported resource deprivation; 84% described psychological coercion in the form of threats, verbal abuse, and the instillation of fear; and 47% described being hit, pushed, slapped, or beaten as a means of control. In a sample of 387 children ages 10 to 17 who experienced sex and labor trafficking (52% forced sex; 5% child bride; 29% labor, e.g., begging, factory, fishing, entertainment, domestic) in Southeast Asia (Kiss et al., 2015), 41% of boys and 19% of girls reported physical violence, 23% of girls and 1% of boys reported sexual violence, and 30% experienced threats of harm to themselves or someone they cared about while being trafficked. Among those reporting physical or sexual violence, 23% sustained a serious injury. In the same study, most children worked 7 days per

current threat, as well prominent symptoms of affective dysregulation, negative self-concept, and interpersonal disturbance.

week (53% of girls, 73% of boys), an average of 10.3 hours per day for boys and 7.2 hours for girls (likely an underestimate, as 33% of girls stated they did not have fixed hours). Further, serious occupational injuries were sustained by 21% of boys and 7% of girls.

Harm to Others

As previously stated, trafficking victims sometimes are forced to witness or inflict harm against others (Hopper, 2017; Kiss et al., 2015; McMullen et al., 2013; Reid, 2016). Kiss et al. (2015) reported that 17% of a sample of sex- and labor-trafficked children in Southeast Asia witnessed the trafficker beat or intentionally hurt someone else. Among a group of former child soldiers, personally killing or torturing other people was identified as the worst thing that had happened during the war by 32% of boys (McMullen et al., 2013).

Neglect

Trafficking harm is notable not only for what children experience but also for of what they are deprived. While being trafficked, youth may experience neglect by traffickers in a quasi-caregiving role, including poor nutrition, sleep hygiene, and medical neglect (Greenbaum, 2020; UNODC, 2021). Trafficked youth who are homeless or missing from care (who "run away") similarly often experience neglect in the form of unmet basic needs, chronic food insecurity, lack of housing, poor medical care, and neglect of chronic medical conditions and may not be attending school, engaging in prosocial activities with peers, or having other interactions and doing other activities that contribute to healthy development (Bigelsen, 2013; Dank et al., 2015; Murphy, 2017).

TRAFFICKING IMPACTS

Child trafficking experiences can lead to severe physical, psychological, social, educational, legal, and economic impacts (Greenbaum, 2020; IOM and National Research Council, 2013; UNODC, 2021). This includes significant traumatic stress symptoms, as well as depression, anxiety, substance abuse, unplanned or forced pregnancy, sexually transmitted infections, malnutrition, suicide and self-harm, incarceration, social isolation, educational disruption, and revictimization (Cole et al., 2016; Greenbaum et al., 2018; Hossain et al., 2010; IOM and National Research Council, 2013; Lederer & Wetzel, 2014; Ray, 2006). Mental health impacts are especially severe and often additionally interfere with obtaining the services and supports needed to achieve full physical and psychological recovery (Reid, 2010).

Mental Health Impacts

Trafficked children often have complex mental health needs. Numerous studies document very high rates of psychiatric diagnoses, especially PTSD, depression, and anxiety as well as conduct disorder, attention-deficit hyperactivity disorder (ADHD), and bipolar disorder (Basson et al., 2012; Cole et al., 2016; Hossain et al., 2010; IOM and National Research Council, 2013; Lederer & Wetzel, 2014; Ottisova et al., 2018; Palines et al., 2020). It is emphasized that mental health concerns often precede trafficking experiences and may be an important contributor to vulnerability; however, trafficking experiences appear to substantially contribute to the breadth and severity of mental health concerns over and above prior trauma and victimization experiences. For example, when compared to other youth with significant history of trauma without a history of trafficking, trafficked youth have a greater severity of symptoms and comorbid mental health diagnoses (Chapple & Crawford, 2019; Cole et al., 2016; Cook et al., 2018; Lanctôt et al., 2020).

Posttraumatic Stress Symptoms, PTSD, and Complex PTSD

Unsurprisingly, given the history of trauma prior to and while being trafficked, trauma impacts are especially prominent in the mental health presentation of trafficked children. Numerous studies document very high rates of posttraumatic stress (PTS) symptoms and PTSD diagnosis. PTS symptoms are significantly higher among youth who have experienced CST/CSEC compared to other vulnerable youth (Lanctôt et al., 2020) and specifically youth who have experienced other forms of child sexual abuse but not CST/CSEC (Cole et al., 2016; Landers et al., 2017). Cole et al. (2016) compared service-seeking youth who had experienced sexual abuse and CSEC with a matched sample of youth who experienced sexual abuse but not CSEC. The CSEC group endorsed significantly greater overall PTSD symptoms as well as avoidance and hyperarousal subdomain symptoms. Dissociative responses have also been found for as many as 81% of trafficked youth. In Kenny et al. (2019), 20% of child trafficking victims met criteria for PTSD dissociative subtype, while only 7.7% of at-risk youth did.

Research also demonstrates the compounded impacts of multiple traumas among trafficked children. Self-Brown et al. (2021) found that CST/CSEC youth who reported a history of multiple traumas were significantly more likely to meet PTSD criteria and endorse higher rates of emotional distress than youth who had not experienced multiple types of victimization. Violence exposure in multiple categories of violence was a better predictor of mental health symptoms than individual categories of victimization, consistent with polyvictimization research with other child populations (Finkelhor et al., 2007; Holt et al., 2007; Turner et al., 2010; Vranceanu et al., 2007). Among trafficked children in Southeast Asia (Kiss et al., 2015), PTSD was associated with having experienced violence premigration/ pretrafficking and extremely excessive work hours, poor living conditions, and having been threatened while being trafficked. Hossain et al. (2010) similarly found that injuries and sexual violence during trafficking were associated with higher levels of PTSD (as well as depression and anxiety). Regarding complex PTSD (C-PTSD), trafficked children had greater rates of C-PTSD than matched nontrafficked controls in a mixed sample of boys and girls trafficked for sex and labor in the United Kingdom (Ottisova et al., 2018). Consistent with the documented effects of complex trauma/C-PTSD, Hopper (2017), reported high rates of impairments in emotion dysregulation and impulse control (88%), attention (59%), dissociation/consciousness (81%), interpersonal relationships (91%), and self-perception and attributions (91%) in a sample of sex-trafficked youth, with fully 56% having symptoms in all categories.

Depression, Anxiety, Suicidal Ideation, and Self-Harm

Although elevated rates of PTSD and C-PTSD are a common focus in the literature, depression and anxiety are also frequently experienced by CST/CSEC youth. In Basson et al. (2012), 75% of CST/CSEC youth experienced depression and 55% experienced anxiety. Kiss et al. (2015) reported that 56% of a sample of trafficked youth in Southeast Asia met criteria for probable depression and 33% for anxiety. Trafficking experiences associated with depression and anxiety were severe physical violence, sexual violence, restricted freedom, adverse living conditions, and having been threatened.

Relatedly, rates of suicidal ideation and suicide attempts are also very high among trafficked children (Basson et al., 2012; Ottisova et al., 2018; Sprang & Cole, 2018). In Hopper (2017), 59% of the youth endorsed experiencing suicidal ideation, and 38% acknowledged a history of suicide attempts. Half of a sample of familial sex-trafficked children reported having attempted suicide (Sprang & Cole, 2018). Of 51 trafficked children from 21 countries receiving services in the United Kingdom, 27% reported having attempted suicide (Ottisova et al., 2018). Experiences while being trafficked, including severe physical violence, sexual violence, extremely excessive work hours, restricted freedom, and threats by trafficker, increased the likelihood of suicidal ideation in a mixed sample of sex- and labor-trafficked children in Southeast Asia (Kiss et al., 2015). Underscoring the contributions of early trauma experiences, children reporting pretrafficking physical or sexual violence were at increased risk for self-harm.

Negative Cognitive Appraisals

Alterations of views of the self, the world, and the future, especially poor self-concept, stigma, and shame, are significant to the experience of being trafficked (Nodzenski et al., 2020). Clinically significant posttraumatic cognitions, as measured by the Child Post-Traumatic Cognitions Inventory (CPTCI), were reported by 52% of a sample of service-seeking CST/CSEC youth, with higher CPTCI scores associated with polyvictimization and greater PTS symptoms (Perry et al., 2022). In Hopper (2017), 91% of youth described trafficking impacts on their sense of self. Specifically, the youth described being blamed for early sexual abuse and being labeled "promiscuous," "bad," and "damaged." In Kiss et al. (2015), 54% of trafficked youth worried about how they would be treated upon their return home, 56% reported feelings of guilt or shame, 34% were still afraid of the trafficker or his or her associates, and 5% said they had no hopes for the future. Children's concerns about social ostracization and maltreatment by others in their community of origin were associated with greater negative mental health outcomes (e.g., PTSD, depression, anxiety). Self-harm, specifically, was significantly associated with feelings of guilt or shame. Poor self-concept/ low self-worth is recognized as both a risk factor and impact of trafficking (Reid, 2011).

Substance Use and Substance Use Disorder

CST/CSEC youth also have very high rates of substance use problems (Basson et al., 2012; Cole et al., 2016; Cook et al., 2018; Hopper, 2017; Landers et al., 2017; Moore et al., 2021; Varma et al., 2015). Cole et al. (2016) found significantly greater substance abuse among service-seeking CSEC youth compared to sexually abused non-CSEC youth (68% vs. 26%). Cook et al. (2018) similarly found high rates of substance use (88%) among youth involved in a juvenile justice CSEC specialty court program, with greater substance use problems associated with a history of child abuse and co-occurring mental health problems. For some youth, substance use preceded trafficking and may have been a means of coping, albeit a maladaptive one, with prior trauma and adversity. Substance use is also a tool of recruitment and grooming as well as a method for coping with trafficking experiences, sometimes supplied by traffickers to maintain control and dependence. Hopper (2017) reported that 47% of survivors in the study described the use of alcohol or drugs during their trafficking initiation process. Posttrafficking, substance use may (continue to) be a strategy for coping with trafficking experiences specifically and trauma and dysregulation more broadly.

Labor Trafficking Impacts

Little is known about the specific impacts of child labor trafficking, although it is generally understood that dangerous, physically harmful work tasks and excessive work hours have physical, psychological, social/relational, and educational harms (Ibrahim et al., 2019; Whetten et al., 2011). In a systematic review of studies of CLT impact in LMICs, Ibrahim et al. (2019) found that child labor was associated with a number of adverse health outcomes, including behavioral and emotional disorders, decreased coping efficacy, poor growth, malnutrition, and higher incidence of infectious and system-specific diseases.

Notably, few studies have explored the mental health impacts of CLT, and fewer still have compared mental health outcomes of youth who have experienced CLT to those who have experienced CST/CSEC. In one of the few such studies conducted with adults (Hopper & Gonzales, 2018), sex trafficking survivors reported more severe posttrauma reactions than labor trafficking survivors, including more PTSD and C-PTSD symptoms. Sex trafficking survivors also had higher prevalence rates of pretrafficking child abuse and a higher incidence of physical and sexual violence during trafficking than those who had experienced labor trafficking. It is unknown if these findings would hold true for children as well. Kiss et al. (2015) found that working extremely excessive hours (>10 hours/day), experienced by 14.5% of the sample, was a risk factor for PTSD, depression, and suicidal ideation among trafficked children in Southeast Asia. However, the authors did not compare the two groups on mental health outcomes.

INTERVENTION WITH TRAFFICKED CHILDREN

The psychological impacts of child trafficking are typically severe and complex, as described; therefore, mental health treatment is a significant and prioritized need for survivors. Although there are effective interventions that target the primary mental health impacts of trafficking (e.g., PTSD, depression, anxiety, substance use problems, suicidal ideation, and self-harm), treatment research specifically with child trafficking survivors is sparse.

Trauma-Focused Treatment

Trauma-focused treatments are especially important given the prevalence of trauma experiences and high rates of PTS symptoms, PTSD, and other trauma-related difficulties. Trauma impacts, especially difficulties with emotional and behavioral regulation, attachment and relationships, attention and consciousness, and self-concept, also often negatively affect engagement in and completion of other services (e.g., housing/placement, education, occupational services) that support recovery and reduce revictimization risk.

Trauma-focused cognitive behavioral therapy (TF-CBT; Cohen, Mannarino, & Deblinger, 2017) is one treatment that has been utilized with trafficked children in an array of settings globally. This has included LMICs (Cambodia, the DRC) as well as high-income countries (United States). In a randomized controlled trial (RCT) (O'Callaghan et al., 2013), 52 girls recovered from a brothel in the DRC were assigned to TF-CBT or a waitlist control group. The TF-CBT treatment was delivered in a 15-session culturally modified group format by nonclinical lay facilitators. There was a significant reduction in PTS symptom scores for youth in TF-CBT treatment compared to the waitlist control group, with reductions sustained at 3-month follow-up. There were also significant improvements in symptoms of depression, anxiety, conduct problems, and prosocial behavior in the TF-CBT group, which were maintained at follow-up. In a contemporaneous study with former child soldiers in the DRC (McMullen et al., 2013), boys in the TF-CBT treatment group similarly reported significant reductions in PTS symptoms compared to the waitlist control group, as well as improvements in depression, anxiety, conduct problems, psychosocial distress, and prosocial behavior. These effects were also sustained at 3-month follow-up. TF-CBT has also been successfully implemented with trafficked girls in Cambodia (Bass et al., 2011) as well as in the United States (Kinnish et al., 2020). Narrative exposure therapy (NET) was also found to be effective in reducing trauma symptoms in child soldiers in Uganda randomly assigned to NET, an academic catch-up program, or waitlist control (Ertl et al., 2011). TF-CBT and other trauma-focused evidence-based treatments (EBTs) typically have multiple elements that contribute to improvements and are often shared to some degree across treatments (e.g., psychoeducation about trauma, coping and relaxation skills building, gradual/prolonged exposure).

The aforementioned studies support the value of cognitive processing and narrative elements in treatment. In fact, trafficking's greatest impact may be in the way victims' views of themselves, the world, and the future are profoundly altered by their trafficking experiences. These alterations may directly contribute to revictimization risk (e.g., youth thinking they are "ruined" or "only good for sex"; Countryman-Rosewurm & DiLollo, 2017; Salami et al., 2018). Countryman-Rosewurm and DiLollo assert, "Sex trafficked women and girls may be 'rescued' from the streets (i.e., provided shelter, a vehicle, educational and career development opportunities, and an alternative form of income) but, if some form of cognitive restructuring does not occur, then it is likely that they will continue to be drawn into the life that validates who they believe they have always been and always will be. . . . [I]t is the cognitive story—formed as a result of early childhood risk factors—that is often the biggest risk of sex trafficking" (p. 59).

Other trauma-focused EBTs for children and adolescents that may be helpful with trafficked youth include eye movement desensitization and reprocessing (EMDR) (Rodenberg et al., 2009; Shapiro, 2018), prolonged exposure therapy for adolescents (PE-A) (Foa et al., 2013), and Risk Reduction through Family Therapy (RRFT; Danielson et al., 2010, 2020). These therapies all include enhancement of coping and regulatory capacities and exposure elements. RRFT is a model of particular relevance, in that it addresses both trauma and substance use and includes components to address family communication, risky sexual behaviors, cognitive coping, and trauma-specific cognitive processing, all of which are prioritized needs of trafficked youth. Treatments targeting complex trauma (e.g., Attachment Regulation and Competency, Blaustein & Kinniburgh, 2018; Integrative Treatment of Complex Trauma for Adolescents, Briere & Lanktree, 2013) are also of significant potential benefit. Systematic efforts to tailor these models and evaluate their effectiveness with trafficked children are a clear priority.

Group Interventions. At least in part because of the shame, stigma, and isolation of trafficking victims, group treatments may be especially beneficial

(McMullen et al., 2013; O'Callaghan et al., 2013; Usacheva et al., 2021). Ending the Game is a group intervention that targets shame, isolation, regulation of emotion and behavior, maladaptive cognitions, identity disturbance, and dissociation and has demonstrated positive trends in improving regulation, relational capacity, sense of self, and future orientation (Usacheva et al., 2021). It is noted that the TF-CBT treatment in the previously described RCTs was delivered in a group setting. Group treatments may also address resource challenges in LMICs and other low-resource settings.

There are additional well-supported models and strategies of potentially high value with trafficked children. Dialectical Behavioral Therapy (DBT) is effective at reducing suicidal ideation and self-harm, specifically, and building coping and regulation more generally (Linehan, 1993; McCauley et al., 2018). Motivational interviewing (Miller & Rollnick, 2013) may be useful in enhancing treatment engagement and trafficking/exploitation desistence, especially when utilized in concert with the Stages of Change model adapted for CSEC (Girls Educational and Mentoring Services, 2011; Prochaska & DiClemente, 1983). Harm reduction approaches are also potentially beneficial in reducing the harms of ongoing commercial sex and other risky behaviors (e.g., substance use, self-injury; Hickle & Hallett, 2016; Pierce, 2012).

Reintegration

It is especially important for overall recovery that response incorporates opportunities to establish or re-establish healthy supportive relationships and connection with family and community, if and when it is safe to do so. A child's specific needs for reintegration with a family of origin, a new caregiving relationship, and/or mentoring are quite individualized and dependent on both their pretrafficking circumstances and relationships that contributed to trafficking vulnerability and their specific trafficking experiences. In particular, caregiver perspectives that may contribute to shame and stigma are especially important considerations for this population (Cohen, Mannarino, & Kinnish, 2017; Kiss et al., 2015). Mentoring, especially connection to survivor mentors, can be especially beneficial in building safe, supportive relationships and reducing shame and stigma (e.g., My Life My Choice Survivor Mentoring Program; Rothman et al., 2019).

Especially promising are comprehensive service models that establish levels of care based on individualized needs and incorporate significant case management and survivor mentoring/coaching. For example, the CHANCE program in Florida (Landers et al., 2017) provides individual and group therapy for trafficked youth and their caregivers to reduce shame and isolation and teach practical skills, individual TF-CBT treatment to address trauma impacts, specialized placement, life coaches with lived experiences of commercial sexual exploitation, intensive case management, and 24/7 youth and caregiver support access.

Although treatment outcome research specifically with trafficked children is quite limited, there are many treatment models and intervention strategies that are effective in addressing the needs of trafficked children. There are also increasing efforts to develop comprehensive service approaches that integrate effective mental health treatment into a broad array of services and supports. It is essential that the knowledge base regarding the trafficking of children is expanded, specifically addressing the intersection of risk factors and trafficking experiences on psychological functioning to inform treatment development, including rigorous mental health treatment outcome research to guide the field.

IMPLICATIONS FOR PUBLIC POLICY AND FUTURE RESEARCH

In this chapter we broadly summarized the data on factors that increase risk for child trafficking, the experiences of youth during trafficking victimization, the common mental health outcomes of trafficked youth, and what we currently understand to be the best practices for intervention approaches. Clearly, there is mounting research to help us in understanding child trafficking risk, experiences, and impact, but it is important to consider how to translate the existing knowledge into a call to action for the next decade of work to critically inform this field.

First is a call for prevention. Many identified trafficking vulnerabilities (e.g., poverty, child trauma and maltreatment) are risk factors for a multitude of interrelated health outcomes. Research is needed to identify whether there are unique risk pathways that are more likely to result in youth trafficking victimization. In particular, high-quality prospective studies of vulnerable youth are needed. Enhanced research is also needed to identify protective factors and strategies for effectively bolstering these factors among high-risk youth and reduce trafficking victimization. Screening that then identifies youth at high risk but not (yet) trafficked and funnels youth to interventions addressing identified vulnerability factors is key. The proliferation of trauma and adverse childhood experiences (ACEs) screening may serve as a foundation, augmented by items and measures that more accurately pinpoint trafficking risk. Finally, the ubiquitousness of technology/social media in everyday life and its use in recruitment and facilitation of trafficking of young people warrant attention in both research and policy initiatives. Greater understanding of how youth social media behavior affects trafficking risk is important to explore, while also recognizing its benefits for marginalized youth (e.g., socially and geographically isolated youth, LGBTQ youth).

Second is a call for a better understanding of the unique intervention needs of trafficked youth and effective strategies to meet those needs. Although there are many evidence-based interventions that address the identified mental health needs of trafficked children, application with trafficked children and rigorous research to determine the efficacy and effectiveness of these interventions with this population are quite limited. Integrated trauma and substance abuse treatments are also a clear priority. Further, implementation science research is needed to identify trafficking-specific tailoring strategies that may crosscut EBTs and improve the dissemination and implementation of these interventions in the field so that all identified youth have access. Development and funding of comprehensive service models that recognize and address the multidimensional needs of trafficked youth should also be prioritized. In the context of these models, the specific mental health interventions utilized are more focused and tailored to the needs of trafficked youth, and resources are in place to address trafficking-specific barriers to treatment. The importance of relational supports in these models is also strongly underscored.

Lastly, a more granular approach to understanding the unique and comparable experiences of trafficking in LMICs versus high-income countries, as well as domestic versus transnational trafficking of children, is needed. Little is known about and few services are specific to labor trafficking of children. Thus, research and policy initiatives that focus on the risk, experiences, outcomes, and interventions for children who have experienced labor trafficking are warranted. In conclusion, the trafficking of children for sex and labor is a significant and complex global public health concern. Multiple and intersecting individual, relational, and contextual factors often contribute to trafficking vulnerability and compound the physical and psychological harm to children of being trafficked. Early trauma and adversity are particularly underscored, with mental health interventions to address the impacts of trauma prior to and while being trafficked especially important to recovery. Targeted research is needed to better understand intersecting risk factors and pathways of vulnerability and trafficking impacts, guide necessarily complex prevention and intervention efforts, and drive continued enhancement of overall response to this important global issue.

REFERENCES

Adjei, J. K., & Saewyc, E. M. (2017). Boys are not exempt: Sexual exploitation of adolescents in sub-Saharan Africa. *Child Abuse & Neglect, 65,* 14–23. https://doi.org/10.1016/j.chiabu.2017.01.001

Ahrens, K. R., Katon, W., McCarty, C., Richardson, L. P., & Courtney, M. E. (2012). Association between childhood sexual abuse and transactional sex in youth aging out of foster care. *Child Abuse & Neglect, 36*(1), 75–80. https://doi.org/10.1016/j.chiabu.2011.07.009

Bass, J., Bearup, L., Bolton, P., Murray, L., & Skavenski, S. (2011). *Implementing trauma focused cognitive behavioral therapy (TF-CBT) among formerly trafficked-sexually exploited and sexually abused girls in Cambodia: A feasibility study.* World Vision.

Basson, D., Rosenblatt, E., & Haley, H. (2012). *Research to action: Sexually exploited minors needs and strengths.* West Coast Children's Clinic.

Bigelsen, J. (2013). *Homelessness, survival sex and human trafficking: As experienced by the youth of Covenant House New York.* Covenant House New York. https://humantraffickinghotline.org/sites/default/files/Homelessness%2C%20Survival%20Sex%2C%20and%20Human%20Trafficking%20-%20Covenant%20House%20NY.pdf

Blaustein, M., & Kinniburgh, K. (2018). *Treating traumatic stress in children and adolescents: How to foster resilience through attachment, self-regulation, and competency* (2nd ed.). Guilford Press.

Boswell, K., Temples, H. S., & Wright, M. E. (2019). LGBT youth, sex trafficking, and the nurse practitioner's role. *Journal of Pediatric Health Care, 33*(5), 555–560. https://doi.org/10.1016/j.pedhc.2019.02.005

Boyce, S. C., Brouwer, K. C., Triplett, D., Servin, A. E., Magis-Rodriguez, C., & Silverman, J. G. (2018). Childhood experiences of sexual violence, pregnancy, and marriage associated with child sex trafficking among female sex workers in two US–Mexico border cities. *American Journal of Public Health, 108*(8), 1049–1054. https://doi.org/10.2105/AJPH.2018.304455

Briere, J., & Lanktree, C. B. (2013). *Integrative Treatment of Complex Trauma for Adolescents (ITCT-A): A guide for the treatment of multiply-traumatized youth* (2nd ed.). University of Southern California-Adolescent Trauma Training Center, National Child Traumatic Stress Network, U.S. Department of Substance Abuse and Mental Health Services Administration.

Butler, C. N. (2015). The racial roots of human trafficking. *UCLA Law Review, 62,* 1464–1514.

Casassa, K., Knight, L., & Mengo, C. (2021). Trauma bonding perspectives from service providers and survivors of sex trafficking: A scoping review. *Trauma, Violence, & Abuse, 23*(3), 969–984. https://doi.org/10.1177/1524838020985542

Chapple, C., & Crawford, B. (2019). Mental health diagnoses of youth commercial sex exploitation victims: An analysis within an adjudicated delinquent sample. *Journal of Family Violence, 34,* 723–732. https://doi.org/10.1007/s10896-019-00065-z

Choi, K. R. (2015). Risk factors for domestic minor sex trafficking in the United States: A literature review. *Journal of Forensic Nursing, 11*(2), 66–76. https://doi.org/10.1097/JFN.0000000000000072

Chong, N. (2014). Human trafficking and sex industry: Does ethnicity and race matter? *Journal of Intercultural Studies, 35,* 196–213. https://doi.org/10.1080/07256868.2014.885413

Cluver, L., Orkin, M., Boyes, M., Gardner, F., & Meinck, F. (2011). Transactional sex amongst AIDS-orphaned and AIDS-affected adolescents predicted by abuse and extreme poverty. *JAIDS Journal of Acquired Immune Deficiency Syndromes, 58*(3), 336–343. https://doi.org/10.1097/QAI.0b013e31822f0d82

Cochran, B. N., Stewart, A. J., Ginzler, J. A., & Cauce, A. M. (2002). Challenges faced by homeless sexual minorities: Comparison of gay, lesbian, bisexual, and transgender homeless adolescents with their heterosexual counterparts. *American Journal of Public Health, 92*(5), 773–777. https://doi.org/10.2105/AJPH.92.5.773

Cohen, J. A., Mannarino, A. P., & Deblinger, E. (2017). *Treating trauma and traumatic grief* (2nd ed.). Guilford Press.

Cohen, J. A., Mannarino, A. P., & Kinnish, K. (2017). Trauma-focused cognitive behavioral therapy for commercially sexually exploited youth. *Journal of Child and Adolescent Trauma, 10*(2), 175–185. https://doi.org/10.1007/s40653-015-0073-9

Cole, J. (2018). Service providers' perspectives on sex trafficking of male minors: Comparing background and trafficking situations of male and female victims. *Child and Adolescent Social Work Journal, 35*(4), 423–433. https://doi.org/10.1007/s10560-018-0530-z

Cole, J., Sprang, G., Lee, R., & Cohen, J. (2016). The trauma of commercial sexual exploitation of youth: A comparison of CSE victims to sexual abuse victims in a clinical sample. *Journal of Interpersonal Violence, 31*, 122–146. https://doi.org/10.1177/0886260514555133

Cook, M. C., Barnert, E., Ijadi-Maghsoodi, R., Ports, K., & Bath, E. (2018). Exploring mental health and substance use treatment needs of commercially sexually exploited youth participating in a specialty juvenile court. *Behavioral Medicine, 44*(3), 242–249. https://doi.org/10.1080/08964289.2018.1432552

Countryman-Roswurm, K., & DiLollo, A. (2017) Survivor: A narrative therapy approach for use with sex trafficked women and girls. *Women & Therapy, 40*, 55–72. https://doi.org/10.1080/02703149.2016.1206782

Courtney, M. E., & Zinn, A. (2009). Predictors of running away from out-of-home care. *Children and Youth Services Review, 31*(12), 1298–1306. https://doi.org/10.1016/j.childyouth.2009.06.003

Curtis, R., Terry, K., Dank, M., Dombrowski, K., & Khan, B. (2008). *The commercial sexual exploitation of children in New York City, Volume 1: The CSEC population in New York City: Size, characteristics, and needs.* NCJ Publication No. 225083. Bureau of Justice Statistics. https://www.ncjrs.gov/pdffiles1/nij/grants/225083.pdf

Dalla, R. L., Panchal, T. J., Erwin, S., Peter, J., Roselius, K., Ranjan, R., Mischra, M. & Sahu, S. (2020). Structural vulnerabilities, personal agency, and caste: An exploration of child sex trafficking in rural India. *Violence and Victims, 35*(3), 307–330.

Danielson, C. K., Adams, Z., McCart, M. R., Chapman, J. E., Sheidow, A. J., Walker, J., Smalling, A., & de Arellano, M. A. (2020). Safety and efficacy of exposure-based risk reduction through family therapy for co-occurring substance use problems and posttraumatic stress disorder symptoms among adolescents: A randomized clinical trial. *JAMA Psychiatry, 77*(6), 574–586. https://doi.org/10.1001/jamapsychiatry.2019.4803

Danielson, C. K., McCart, M., de Arellano, M. A., Macdonald, A., Silcott, L., & Resnick, H. (2010). Risk reduction for substance use and trauma-related psychopathology in adolescent sexual assault victims: Findings from an open trial. *Child Maltreatment, 15*(3), 261–268. https://doi.org/10.1177/1077559510367939

Dank, M., Yahner, J., Madden, K., Banuelos, I., Yu, L., Ritchie, A., Mora, M., & Conner, B. (2015). *Surviving the streets of New York: Experiences of LGBTQ youth, YMSM, YWSW engaged in survival sex.* Urban Institute.

Dierkhising, C. B., Walker Brown, K., Ackerman-Brimberg, M., & Newcombe, A. (2018). *Commercially sexually exploited girls and young women involved in child welfare and juvenile justice in Los Angeles County: An exploration and evaluation of placement experiences and services received.* National Center for Youth Law, California State University, Los Angeles. https://youthlaw.org/publication/csec_la_childwelfare_juvenilejustice/

Dierkhising, C. B., Eastman, A. L., & Walker Brown, K. (2022). Examining housing instability among females who are system-involved: comparing females with and without histories of commercial sexual exploitation. *Child Maltreatment*, http://doi.org/10.1177/10775595211039463

Epstein, R., Blake, J., & González, T. (2017). *Girlhood interrupted: The erasure of Black girls' childhood.* Georgetown Law, Center on Poverty and Inequality. http://dx.doi.org/10.2139/ssrn.3000695

Ertl, V., Pfeiffer, A., Schauer, E., Elbert, T., & Neuner, F. (2011). Community-implemented trauma therapy for former child soldiers in Northern Uganda: A randomized controlled trial. *JAMA, 306*(5), 503–512. https://doi.org/10.1001/jama.2011.1060

Fedina, L., Williamson, C., & Perdue, T. (2019). Risk factors for domestic child sex trafficking in the United States. *Journal of Interpersonal Violence, 34*(13), 2653–2673. https://doi.org/10.1177/0886260516662306

Finkelhor, D., & Ormrod, R. K. (2004). *Prostitution of juveniles: Patterns from NIBRS.* Juvenile Justice Bulletin – NCJ203946 (pp. 1–12). US Government Printing Office. (CV67)

Finkelhor, D., Ormrod, R. K., & Turner, H. A. (2007). Poly-victimization: A neglected component in child victimization trauma. *Child Abuse & Neglect, 31*, 7–26. https://doi.org/10.1016/j.chiabu.2006.06.008

Finkelhor, D., Vaquerano, J., & Stranski, M. (2008, revised 2017). *Sex trafficking of minors: How many juveniles are being prostituted in the US?* Crimes Against Children Research Center.

Foa, E. B., McLean, C. M., Capaldi, S., & Rosenfield, D. (2013). Prolonged exposure vs supportive counseling for sexual abuse–related PTSD in adolescent girls: A randomized clinical trial. *JAMA, 310*(24), 2650–2657. https://doi.org10.1001/jama.2013.282829

Franchino-Olsen, H. (2021). Vulnerabilities relevant for commercial sexual exploitation of children/domestic minor sex trafficking: A systematic review of risk factors. *Trauma, Violence & Abuse, 22*(1), 99–111. https://doi.org/10.1177/1524838018821956

Fredlund, C., Svensson, F., Svedin, C. G., Priebe, G., & Wadsby, M. (2013). Adolescents' lifetime experience of selling sex: Development over five years. *Journal of Child Sexual Abuse, 22*(3), 312–325. https://doi.org/10.1080/10538712.2013.743950

Gibbs, D. A., Feinberg, R. K., Dolan, M., Latzman, N. E., Misra, S., & Domanico, R. (2018). *Report to Congress: The child welfare system response to sex trafficking of children.* U.S. Department of Health and Human Services, Administration for Children and Families.

Girls Educational and Mentoring Services. (2011). Stages of change in CSEC counseling. *Connections, 13*, 7–10.

Greenbaum, V. J. (2020). A public health approach to global child sex trafficking. *Annual Review of Public Health, 41*, 481–497.

Greenbaum, V. J., Dodd, M., & McCracken, C. (2018). A short screening tool to identify victims of child sex trafficking in the health care setting. *Pediatric Emergency Care, 34*(1), 33–37. https://doi.org/10.1097/PEC.0000000000000602

Greene, J. M., Ennett, S. T., & Ringwalt, C. L. (1999). Prevalence and correlates of survival sex among runaways and homeless youth. *American Journal of Public Health, 89*, 1406–1409.

Hickle, K., & Hallett, S. (2016). Mitigating harm: Considering harm reduction principles in work with sexually exploited young people. *Child & Society, 30*, 302–313. https://doi.org/10.1111/chso.12145

Holt, M. K., Finkelhor, D., & Kantor, G. K. (2007). Multiple victimization experiences of urban elementary school students: Associations with psychosocial functioning and academic performance. *Child Abuse & Neglect, 31*(5), 503–515. https://doi.org/10.1016/j.chiabu.2006.12.006

Hopper, E. (2017). Polyvictimization and developmental trauma adaptations in sex trafficked youth. *Journal of Child and Adolescent Trauma, 10*, 161–173. https://doi.org/10.1007/s40653-016-0114-z

Hopper, E. K., & Gonzalez, L. D. (2018). A comparison of psychological symptoms in survivors of sex and labor trafficking. *Behavioral Medicine, 44*(3), 177–188. https://doi.org/10.1080/08964289.2018.1432551

Hossain, M., Zimmerman, C., Abas, M., Light, M., & Watts, C. (2010). The relationship of trauma to mental disorders among trafficked and sexually exploited girls and women. *American Journal of Public Health, 100*(12), 2442–2449.

Ibrahim, A., Abdalla, S. M., Jafer, M., Abdelgadir, J., & de Vries, N. (2019). Child labor and health: A systematic literature review of the impacts of child labor on child's health in low- and middle-income countries. *Journal of Public Health, 41*(1), 18–26. https://doi.org/10.1093/pubmed/fdy018

Institute of Medicine and National Research Council. (2013). *Confronting commercial sexual exploitation and sex trafficking of minors in the United States.* National Academies Press.

International Labour Organization (ILO). (2017). *Global estimates of modern slavery: Forced labour and forced marriage.* http://www.ilo.org/global/topics/forced-labour/statistics/lang--en/index.htm

Kenny, M. C., Helpingstine, C. E., & Weber, M. (2019). Treatment of a commercially sexually abused girl using trauma-focused cognitive behavioral therapy and legal interventions. *Clinical Case Studies, 18*(1), 18–35. https://doi.org/10.1177/1534650118800809

Kharsany, A. B., & Karim, Q. A. (2016). HIV infection and AIDS in sub-Saharan Africa: Current status, challenges and opportunities. *Open AIDS Journal, 10*, 34–48. https://doi.org/10.2174/1874613601610010034

Kim, H., Chenot, D., & Lee, S. (2015). Running away from out-of-home care: A multi-level analysis. *Children & Society, 29*, 109–121. https://doi.org/10.1111/chso.12019.

Kinnish, K., McCarty, C., Tiwari, A., Osborne, M., Glasheen, T., Franchot, K. K., Kramer, C., & Self-Brown, S. (2020). Featured counter-trafficking program: Project intersect. *Child Abuse & Neglect, 100*, 104132. https://doi.org/10.1016/j.chiabu.2019.104132

Kiss, L., Yun, K., Pocock, N., & Zimmerman, C. (2015). Exploitation, violence, and suicide risk among child and adolescent survivors of human trafficking in the Greater Mekong subregion. *JAMA Pediatrics, 169*(9), e152278. https://doi.org/10.1001/jamapediatrics.2015.2278

Klatt, T., Cavner, D., & Egan, V. (2014). Rationalising predictors of child sexual exploitation and sex-trading. *Child Abuse & Neglect, 38*(2), 252–260. https://doi.org/10.1016/j.chiabu.2013.08.019

Laird, J. J., Klettke, B., Hall, K., Clancy, E., & Hallford, D. (2020). Demographic and psychosocial factors associated with child sexual exploitation: A systematic review and meta-analysis. *JAMA Network Open, 3*(9), e2017682. https://doi.org/10.1001/jamanetworkopen.2020.17682

Lalor, K., & McElvaney, R. (2010). Child sexual abuse, links to later sexual exploitation/high- risk sexual behavior, and prevention/treatment programs. *Trauma, Violence, & Abuse, 11*(4), 159–177. https://doi.org/10.1177/1524838010378299

Lanctôt, N., Reid, J. A., & Laurier, C. (2020). Nightmares and flashbacks: The impact of commercial sexual exploitation of children among female adolescents placed in residential care. *Child Abuse & Neglect, 100,* 104195. https://doi.org/10.1016/j.chi abu.2019.104195

Landers, M., McGrath, K., Johnson, M. H., Armstrong, M. I., & Dollard, N. (2017). Baseline characteristics of dependent youth who have been commercially sexually exploited: Findings from a specialized treatment program. *Journal of Child Sexual Abuse, 26*(6), 692–709. https://doi.org/10.1080/10538712.2017.1323814

Lederer, L., & Wetzel, C. (2014). The health consequences of sex trafficking and their implications for identifying victims in healthcare facilities. *Annals of Health Law, 23,* 61–91.

Lin, C.-H. (2012). Children who run away from foster care: Who are the children and what are the risk factors? *Children and Youth Services Review, 34,* 807–813. https://doi.org10.1016/j.childyouth.2012.01.009

Linehan, M. M. (1993). *Cognitive-behavioral treatment of borderline personality disorder.* Guilford Press.

Machel, G. (2009). *Machel study 10-year strategic review: Children and conflict in a changing world.* Office of the Special Representative of the Secretary-General for Children and Armed Conflict in collaboration with UNICEF UN Children's Fund.

McCauley, E., Berk, M. S., Asarnow, J. R., Adrian, M., Cohen, J., Korslund, K., Avina, C., Hughes, J., Harned, M., Gallop, R., & Linehan, M. M. (2018). Efficacy of dialectical behavior therapy for adolescents at high risk for suicide: A randomized clinical trial. *JAMA Psychiatry, 75*(8), 777–785. https://doi.org/10.1001/jamapsychia try.2018.1109

McMullen, J., O'Callaghan, P., Shannon, C., Black, A., & Eakin, J. (2013). Group trauma-focused cognitive-behavioural therapy with former child soldiers and other war-affected boys in the DR Congo: A randomised controlled trial. *Journal of Child Psychology and Psychiatry, and Allied Disciplines, 54*(11), 1231–1241. https://doi.org/10.1111/jcpp.12094

Miller, W. R., & Rollnick, S. (2013). *Motivational interviewing: Helping people change.* Guilford Press.

Mitchell, K. J., & Boyd, D. (2014). *Understanding the role of technology in the commercial sexual exploitation of children: The perspective of law enforcement.* Crimes Against Children Research Center, University of New Hampshire.

Mitchell, K. J., Finkelhor, D., & Wolak, J. (2013). *Sex trafficking cases involving minors.* Crimes Against Children Research Center, University of New Hampshire. (CV 313). http://www.unh.edu/ccrc/pdf/CV313_Final_Sex_Trafficking_Minors_Nov_2 013_rev.pdf

Moore, J. L., Goldberg, A. P., & Barron, C. (2021). Substance use in a domestic minor sex trafficking patient population. *Pediatric Emergency Care, 37*(4), e159–e162. https://doi.org/ 10.1097/PEC.0000000000001749

Murphy, L. (2017). *Labor and sex trafficking among homeless youth—A ten-city study: Full report.* Modern Slavery Research Project, Loyola University New Orleans.

Nodzenski, M., Kiss, L., Pocock, N., Stöckl, H., Zimmerman, C., & Buller, A. M. (2020). Post- trafficking stressors: The influence of hopes, fears and expectations on the mental health of young trafficking survivors in the Greater Mekong sub-region. *Child Abuse & Neglect, 100,* 104067. https://doi.org/10.1016/j.chiabu.2019.104067.

O'Brien, J., White, K., & Rizo, C. (2017). Domestic minor sex trafficking among child welfare– involved youth: An exploratory study of correlates. *Child Maltreatment, 22,* 107755951770999. https://doi.org/10.1177/1077559517709995

O'Callaghan, P., McMullen, J., Shannon, C., Rafferty, H., & Black, A. (2013). A randomized controlled trial of trauma-focused cognitive behavioral therapy for sexually exploited, war-affected Congolese girls. *Journal of the American Academy of Child & Adolescent Psychiatry, 52*(4), 359–369. https://doi.org/10.1016/j.jaac.2013.01.013

O'Neill, C. (2018). *From foster care to trafficking: An analysis of contributory factors.* EPCAT-USA. https://www.ecpatusa.org/from-foster-care-to-trafficking

Ottisova, L., Smith, P., & Oram, S. (2018). Psychological consequences of human trafficking: Complex posttraumatic stress disorder in trafficked children. *Behavioral Medicine, 44*(3), 234–241. https://doi.org/10.1080/08964289.2018.1432555

Palines, P. A., Rabbitt, A. L., Pan, A. Y., Nugent, M. L., & Ehrman, W. G. (2020). Comparing mental health disorders among sex trafficked children and three groups of youth at high-risk for trafficking: A dual retrospective cohort and scoping review. *Child Abuse & Neglect, 100,* 104196. https://doi.org/10.1016/j.chiabu.2019.104196

Perry, E. W., Osborne, M. C., Lee, N., Kinnish, K., & Self-Brown, S. (2022). Posttraumatic cognitions and posttraumatic stress symptoms among young people who have ex-perienced commercial sexual exploitation and trafficking. *Public Health Report, 137*(Supplement 1), 91S–101S. https://doi.org/10.1177/00333549211041552

Pierce, A. S. (2012). American Indian adolescent girls: Vulnerability to sex trafficking, intervention strategies. *American Indian and Alaska Native Mental Health Research, 19*(1), 37–56. https://doi.org/10.5820/aian.1901.2012.37

Prochaska, J. O., & DiClemente, C. C. (1983). Stages and processes of self-change of smoking: Toward an integrative model of change. *Journal of Consulting and Clinical Psychology, 51*(3), 390–395. https://doi.org/10.1037/0022-006X.51.3.390

Ranganathan, M., MacPhail, C., Pettifor, A., Kahn, K., Khoza, N., Twine, R., . . . Heise, L. (2017). Young women's perceptions of transactional sex and sexual agency: A quali-tative study in the context of rural South Africa. *BMC Public Health, 17,* 666. https://doi.org/10.1186/s12889-017-4636-6

Ray, N. (2006). *Lesbian, gay, bisexual and transgender youth: An epidemic of homelessness.* National Gay and Lesbian Task Force Policy Institute and the National Coalition for the Homeless.

Reed, S. M., Kennedy, M. A., Decker, M. R., & Cimino, A. N. (2019). Friends, family, and boyfriends: An analysis of relationship pathways into commercial sexual exploita-tion. *Child Abuse & Neglect, 90,* 1–12. https://doi.org/10.1016/j.chiabu.2019.01.016

Reid, J. A. (2010). Doors wide shut: Barriers to the successful delivery of victim services for domestically trafficked minors in a southern U.S. metropolitan area. *Women & Criminal Justice, 20*(1–2), 147–166. https://doi.org/10.1080/08974451003641206

Reid, J. A. (2011). An exploratory model of girl's vulnerability to commercial sexual exploitation in prostitution. *Child Maltreatment, 16*(2), 146–157. https://doi.org/10.1177/1077559511404700

Reid, J. A. (2012). Exploratory review of route-specific, gendered, and age-graded dy-namics of exploitation: Applying life course theory to victimization in sex trafficking in North America. *Aggression and Violent Behavior, 7,* 42–57. https://doi.org/10.1016/j.avb.2012.02.005.

Reid, J. A. (2016). Entrapment and enmeshment schemes used by sex traffickers. *Sex Abuse, 28*(6), 491–511. https://doi.org/10.1177/1079063214544334

Reid, J. A. (2018). Sex trafficking of girls with intellectual disabilities: An exploratory mixed methods study. *Sexual Abuse, 30*(2), 107–131. https://doi.org/10.1177/10790 63216630981

Reid, J. A., Baglivio, M. T., Piquero, A. R., Greenwald, M. A., & Epps, N. (2017). Human trafficking of minors and childhood adversity in Florida. *American Journal of Public Health, 107*(2), 306–311. https://doi.org/10.2105/AJPH.2016.303564

Reid, J. A., Huard, J., & Haskell, R. A. (2015). Family-facilitated juvenile sex trafficking. *Journal of Crime and Justice, 38,* 361–376. https://doi.org/10.1080/07356 48X.2014.967965

Reid, J. A., & Piquero, A. R. (2014). Age-graded risks for commercial sexual exploitation of male and female youth. *Journal of Interpersonal Violence, 29*(9), 1747–1777. https://doi.org/10.1177/0886260513511535

Rights4girls. (n.d.). *Racial and gender disparities in the sex trade.* https://rights4girls.org/ wp-content/uploads/2019/05/Racial-Disparties-FactSheet-_Jan-2021.pdf

Rodenburg, R., Benjamin, A., de Roos, C., Meijer, A. M., & Stams, G. J. (2009). Efficacy of EMDR in children: A meta-analysis. *Clinical Psychology Review, 29,* 599–606.

Roe-Sepowitz, D. E. (2012). Juvenile entry into prostitution: The role of emotional abuse. *Violence Against Women, 18*(5), 562–579. https://doi.org/10.1177/107780121 2453140

Rothman, E. F., Preis, S. R., Bright, K. T., Paruk, J., Bair-Merritt, M., & Farrell, A. (2019). A longitudinal evaluation of a survivor-mentor program for child survivors of sex trafficking in the United States. *Child Abuse & Neglect, 100,* 104083. https://doi.org/ 10.1016/j.chiabu.2019.104083

Salami, T., Gordon, M., Coverdale, J., & Nguyen, P. T. (2018). What therapies are favored in the treatment of the psychological sequelae of trauma in human trafficking victims? *Journal of Psychiatric Practice, 24*(2), 87–96. https://doi.org/10.1097/ PRA.0000000000000288

Self-Brown, S., Culbreth, R., Wilson, R., Armistead, L., Kasirye, R., & Swahn, M. H. (2018). Individual and parental risk factors for sexual exploitation among high-risk youth in Uganda. *Journal of Interpersonal Violence, 36*(5–6), NP3263–NP3284. https://doi.org/10.1177/0886260518771685

Self-Brown, S. R., Osborne, M. C., Lee, N., Perry, E. W., & Kinnish, K. (2021). Exploring the impact of trauma history on the mental health presentations of youth who have experienced commercial sexual exploitation and trafficking. *Behavioral Medicine,* 1–19. https://doi.org/10.1080/08964289.2020.1865255

Sethi, A. (2007). Domestic sex trafficking of Aboriginal girls in Canada: Issues and implications. *First Peoples Child & Family Review, 3*(3), 57–71. https://fpcfr.com/ index.php/FPCFR/article/view/50

Shapiro, F. (2018). *Eye movement desensitization and reprocessing (EMDR) therapy: Basic principles, protocols, and procedures* (3rd ed.). Guilford Press.

Smith, L. A., Vardman, S. H., & Snow, M. A. (2009). *The national report on domestic minor trafficking: America's prostituted children.* Shared Hope International. https:// sharedhope.org/wp-content/uploads/2012/09/SHI_National_Report_on_DMST_2 009.pdf

Sprang, G., & Cole, J. (2018). Familial sex trafficking of minors: Trafficking conditions, clinical presentation, and system involvement. *Journal of Family Violence, 33*(3), 185–195. https://doi.org/10.1007/s10896-018-9950-y

Stanford, K., Cappetta, A., Ahn, R., & Macias-Konstantopoulos, W. (2021). Sex and labor trafficking in Paraguay: Risk factors, needs assessment, and the role of the health care system. *Journal of Interpersonal Violence, 36*, 4806–4831. https://doi.org/10.1177/0886260518788364

Stoltz, J. A., Shannon, K., Kerr, T., Zhang, R., Montaner, J. S., & Wood, E. (2007). Associations between childhood maltreatment and sex work in a cohort of drug-using youth. *Social Science & Medicine, 65*(6), 1214–1221. https://doi.org/10.1016/j.socscimed.2007.05.005

Svedin, C. G., & Priebe, G. (2007). Selling sex in a population-based study of high school seniors in Sweden: Demographic and psychosocial correlates. *Archives of Sexual Behavior, 36*, 21–32. https://doi.org/10.1007/s10508-006-9083-x

Swahn, M. H., Culbreth, R., Salazar, L. F., Kasirye, R., & Seeley, J. (2016). Prevalence of HIV and associated risks of sex workers among youth in the slums of Kampala. *AIDS Research and Treatment, 2016*, 5360180. https://doi.org/10.1155/2016/5360180

Swahn, M. H., Culbreth, R., Staton, C., & Kasirye, R. (2017). Psychosocial health concerns among service-seeking orphans in the slums of Kampala. *Vulnerable Children and Youth Studies, 12*(3), 258–263. https://doi.org/10.1080/17450128.2017.1290306

Swaner, R., Labriola, M., Rempel, M., Walker, A., & Spadafore, J. (2016). *Youth involvement in the sex trade: A national study*. Center for Court Innovation.

Trafficking Victims Protection Act of 2000, 22 U.S.C. §7102 (9)(a)(4)(10) (2017).

Turner, H. A., Finkelhor, D., & Ormrod, R. (2010). Poly-victimization in a national sample of children and youth. *American Journal of Preventive Medicine, 38*(3), 323–330. https://doi.org/10.1016/j.amepre.2009.11.012

Twis, M. K., Gillespie, L., & Greenwood, D. (2020). An analysis of romantic partnership dynamics in domestic minor sex trafficking case files. *Journal of Interpersonal Violence, 37*(7-8), NP5394–NP5418. https://doi.org/10.1177/0886260520960302

United Nations Office on Drugs and Crime (UNODC). (2021). *Global report on trafficking in persons 2020* (Sales No. E.20.IV.3). United Nations.

U.S. Department of Health and Human Services, Administration for Children, Youth and Families. (2013). *Guidance to states and services on addressing human trafficking of children and youth in the United States*.

Usacheva, M., Smalley, C., Hafer, N., & Brooks, S. (2021) Ending the Game: A new psychoeducational curriculum for victims of commercial sexual exploitation. *Women & Criminal Justice, 32*(3), 257–276. https://doi.org/10.1080/08974454.2021.1885568

Varma, S., Gillespie, S., McCracken, C., & Greenbaum, V. J. (2015). Characteristics of child commercial sexual exploitation and sex trafficking victims presenting for medical care in the United States. *Child Abuse & Neglect, 44*, 98–105. https://doi.org/10.1016/j. chiabu.2015.04.004

Vranceanu, A. M., Hobfoll, S. E., & Johnson, R. J. (2007). Child multi-type maltreatment and associated depression and PTSD symptoms: The role of social support and stress. *Child Abuse & Neglect, 31*(1), 71–84. https://doi.org/10. 1016/j.chiabu.2006.04.010

Walker, K. (2013). *California Child Welfare Council, ending the commercial sexual exploitation of children: A call for multi-system collaboration in California*. http://www.chhs.

ca.gov/Child%20Welfare/Ending%20CCSEC%20-%20A%20Call%20for%20Multi-System%20Collaboration%20in%20CA%20-%20February%202013.pdf

Wells, M., Mitchell, K. J., & Ji, K. (2012). Exploring the role of the Internet in juvenile prostitution cases coming to the attention of law enforcement. *Journal of Child Sexual Abuse, 21*, 327–342. https://doi.org/10.1080/10538712.2012.669823

Wessells, M. (2006). Child soldiering: Entry, reintegration, and breaking cycles of violence. In M. Fitzduff & C. Stout (Eds.), *The psychology of resolving global conflicts: From war to peace* (pp. 243–266). Praeger Security International.

Whetten, R., Messer, L., Ostermann, J., Whetten, K., Pence, B., Buckner, M., . . . Positive Outcomes for Orphans (POFO) Research Team. (2011). Child work and labour among orphaned and abandoned children in five low and middle income countries. *BMC International Health and Human Rights, 11*, 1. https://doi.org/10.1186/1472-698X-11-1

Williams, T. P., Binagwaho, A., & Betancourt, T. S. (2012). Transactional sex as a form of child sexual exploitation and abuse in Rwanda: Implications for child security and protection. *Child Abuse & Neglect, 36*(4), 354–361. https://doi.org/10.1016/j.chiabu.2011.11.006

8

Global Perspectives on Family Violence

Prevalence and Effects on Children across Cultural Contexts

KATHRYN H. HOWELL, TAYLOR R. NAPIER,
KARI N. THOMSEN, CECILIA MARTINEZ-TORTEYA, AND
ÅSA KÄLLSTRÖM ■

Family violence is a broadly defined construct that includes any act or threat of physical, sexual, or psychological violence perpetrated against one individual by another who is connected through marriage or family relation. Such violence represents attempts to control or harm a family member or intimate partner and typically includes intimate partner violence (IPV), child abuse and neglect (CAN), sibling abuse, parent/in-law abuse, and elder abuse. This chapter first reviews the global rates and prevalence of family violence, including diverse conceptualizations of family violence across countries. Next, the concept of polyvictimization is introduced to capture the intersection of different types of family violence. This is followed by a review of the short- and long-term consequences of family violence on children from a global perspective. The unique cultural contexts of two countries, Mexico and Sweden, are explored in depth to assess how qualities and consequences of family violence impact children and families. The chapter concludes with reflections and future directions to address family violence on the world stage.

GLOBAL ESTIMATES OF FAMILY VIOLENCE

Global conceptualizations of family violence identify different forms of violence under the family violence "umbrella," which has resulted in significant variability in the legal and clinical definitions of this construct (see Cutland, 2012 for review), as well as difficulties ascertaining international prevalence rates. Although contextual factors, such as cultural practices and traditions, societal beliefs about gender norms, and resource access, contribute to diverse definitions, research on family violence has consistently focused on IPV and CAN.

DEFINITIONS OF FAMILY VIOLENCE

Intimate Partner Violence

IPV is a pervasive societal problem that occurs in nearly all countries. IPV includes any form of psychological (e.g., intimidation, threats, humiliation), physical (e.g., slapping, hitting, kicking), or sexual (e.g., forced sexual acts) abuse, as well as controlling behaviors (e.g., social isolation, restricting access to finances, monitoring movement), by a current or past romantic partner. Per World Health Organization (WHO) data from 2018, rates of IPV range from 16% to 23% in Europe to 35% in Southeast Asia, with nearly 30% of ever-partnered women experiencing physical or sexual violence in their lifetime. While 10% of men also report lifetime exposure to IPV (Smith et al., 2018), women experience IPV at disproportionate rates. Indeed, research across global contexts suggests that occurrences of IPV are maintained by patriarchal beliefs that uphold men as the ultimate authority over their family, providing them with the power to discipline their wives (WHO, 2006; Medina Nuñez & Medina Villegas, 2019). For example, in Mexico, violence against women is maintained by strong beliefs in gender roles and machismo that limit women's power and autonomy within the relationship (Medina Nuñez & Medina Villegas, 2019). Though IPV in Sweden is typically viewed as an uncommon experience, some research has identified a Nordic paradox that highlights the high levels of both gender equality and IPV in this region (Wemrell et al., 2021). Thus, despite changing gender norms, IPV remains an acceptable practice in many countries.

Rates of IPV are difficult to ascertain because incidents differ substantially even between regions in a single country (e.g., urban vs. rural locations; Guruge et al., 2010). Further, the prevalence of IPV may be impacted by contextual resources, as research suggests that IPV estimates center around 23% in higher income areas (e.g., North America, Europe, Japan) compared to 37% in lower income regions (e.g., parts of Africa, Eastern Mediterranean, Southeast Asia regions; WHO, 2013). Moreover, recent calls to action emphasize that economic abuse, or financial entrapment through the restriction of economic resources, should also be included in definitions of IPV (Postmus et al., 2020), as it has been documented as a habitual element of violent relationships worldwide (Gibbs et al., 2018). The undermining of women's economic independence facilitates family violence as a lack of financial resources, which may contribute to a longer relationship duration (Antai et al., 2014), thus increasing the likelihood of children being exposed to IPV. Indeed, IPV has rippling effects across the family system, with an estimated

25% of children under the age of 5 exposed to IPV that occurs in the home (UNICEF, 2017).

Child Abuse and Neglect

Researchers estimate that nearly 1 billion children are exposed to at least one form of CAN annually (Hillis et al., 2016). Traditionally, CAN refers to physical abuse, sexual abuse, emotional abuse, and neglect (i.e., failure of a caregiver to provide for a child's physical or emotional needs); however, cultural norms and expectations contribute to widely varying definitions in different countries. Childhood sexual violence has received the most widespread global attention, with substantially higher prevalence rates for females (18%) than males (7.6%; Stoltenborgh et al., 2011). Meta-analyses found higher childhood sexual abuse prevalence rates in Africa and Australia, whereas the lowest rates were reported in Europe and Asia (Stoltenborgh et al., 2011). Further, global prevalence rates show that 23% of children experience physical abuse, though these rates vary widely due to societal beliefs about corporal punishment and parental authority (Straus, 2010). Only 59 out of 199 countries have banned corporal punishment practices (Waterston & Janson, 2020), with 83% of children in Africa reporting severe physical punishment at home (Gershoff, 2017). Importantly, many families across cultures wish to keep discipline practices private to preserve their family reputation, which likely contributes to suppressed estimates of CAN (Chan, 2011; Guruge et al., 2010).

The prevalence of neglect is high across the globe, but the highest rates of neglect occur in countries with the most limited resource access, which may prohibit families from meeting their children's basic needs (Kobulsky et al., 2020). In higher income countries, estimates of physical and emotional neglect are 16% and 18%, respectively (Stoltenborgh et al., 2013), yet children in East Asia report rates between 23% and 44% compared to 89% to 94% in Burundi, which was the country with the highest prevalence of neglect (Charak et al., 2017).

Elder Abuse, Sibling Abuse, In-Law Abuse

In addition to IPV and CAN, some researchers have extended their definition of family violence to include aggression toward other family members (Chan et al., 2021; Raj et al., 2006). Elder abuse is the type most consistently included in definitions of family violence, with international estimates ranging from 2% to 36% (Pillemer et al., 2016). Despite evidence that sibling abuse is the most widespread form of family violence, research on this topic is scarce and primarily concentrated in higher income countries (e.g., United States, Australia, Portugal). Available prevalence rates suggest that 83% of youth report minor acts of sibling victimization, whereas 56% report physical injury because of sibling abuse (Mackey et al., 2010). Even fewer countries have included in-law or parent abuse in conventional definitions of family violence, and global estimates of its occurrence are not available. However, women from multiple countries report high levels of in-law and parent conflict (Raj et al., 2006; Chan et al., 2009), highlighting the need for further research.

FAMILY POLYVICTIMIZATION FRAMEWORK

Family violence experiences typically co-occur and intersect with other forms of adversity (e.g., peer victimization, community violence). Polyvictimization is defined as exposure to two or more types of adversity (Bidarra et al., 2016), which contributes to a higher stress burden for individuals. Research on family violence has been relatively slow to adopt a polyvictimization framework, instead largely focusing on single types of violence (Bidarra et al., 2016). Due to different conceptualizations of what constitutes polyvictimization, reported rates vary substantially across the globe, ranging from 4% in Malaysia to 38% in Kenya and Tanzania (Le et al., 2018). IPV and CAN are two types of family violence that often co-occur. In the United States and Great Britain, upwards of 40% of children who are exposed to IPV also experience physical abuse (Appel & Holden, 1998), while 31% of those exposed to IPV also experience sexual abuse (Bidarra et al., 2016). In the only known study that included CAN, IPV, elder abuse, and in-law abuse in the definition of polyvictimization, reported co-occurrence was 10% of adults in community samples and 36% in clinical populations in China (Chan et al., 2021). Such research underscores that a polyvictimization approach to conceptualizing family violence as both chronic and cumulative may best capture the unique, detrimental impact of family violence on individual functioning.

SHORT-TERM EFFECTS OF FAMILY VIOLENCE

Short-term effects of family violence represent negative impacts on children from birth through age 18. Chronic exposure to family violence can challenge a child's physiological response systems (Glaser & Kiecolt-Glaser, 2005) and negatively impact psychosocial development and health, even during infancy (Koen et al., 2014). A robust international literature has demonstrated a significant association between CAN and child psychopathology, including internalizing and externalizing difficulties and challenges with socialization (English et al., 2005; Huguenel et al., 2021). CAN also contributes to posttraumatic stress disorder (PTSD) and risk for substance abuse among youth (Spinazzola et al., 2014). Researchers have begun to parse apart how aspects of the abuse may relate to youth functioning, with studies demonstrating that type, severity, and age of CAN exposure (English et al., 2005) uniquely affect child outcomes.

International research has also explored the consequences of IPV exposure on children. For example, Dutch children who witnessed IPV reported more frequent health complaints, including more regulatory and pain problems, as well as higher rates of self-harm compared to children not exposed to IPV (Lamers-Winkelman et al., 2012). In a longitudinal study in Brazil, young children who were exposed to IPV had higher risk of behavioral difficulties; moreover, age of first exposure and type of IPV placed children at risk of developing behavior problems (Silva et al., 2019). Further, research has shown that exposure to family violence is associated with poorer receptive vocabulary (i.e., the collection of words that is understood by an individual), general language abilities, and pragmatic language skills (i.e., the social language skills that are used in daily interactions with others) in an Australian sample of school-aged children (Conway et al., 2021). Similar challenges are also seen in math and reading performance among youth experiencing family violence (Kiesel et al., 2016).

LONG-TERM EFFECTS OF FAMILY VIOLENCE

The detrimental impact of family violence on child functioning can persist into adulthood. Research shows significant associations between CAN and depression, anxiety, substance dependence, somatic symptoms, body dysmorphic concerns, and trauma exposure into adulthood (Fitzgerald & Gallus, 2020; Krakau et al., 2021; Min et al., 2013). In a German sample, as the number of childhood maltreatment experiences increased, the likelihood of health risks also increased, including obesity, diabetes, cancer, and hypertension (Clemens et al., 2018). In a Swiss sample, individuals identified as high risk who experienced significantly more CAN than individuals in a comparison group reported higher rates of mental health difficulties, including anxiety, phobias, PTSD, and somatic symptoms (Thoma et al., 2021).

The impact of family violence is not contained within the individual, as there are effects across generations. For example, a history of family violence exposure during childhood increases the risk of perpetrating IPV or CAN or of being a victim of IPV as an adult (Assink et al., 2018). The long-term effects of family violence on adult psychological functioning may help explain the intergenerational nature of family violence. McFarlane and colleagues (2014) explored the relation between maternal and child psychopathology among mothers who experienced IPV; they found that the mother's mental health (i.e., PTSD, depression, anxiety) was directly associated with her children's mental health difficulties. Others have suggested parenting practices (i.e., responsiveness, emotional availability; Greene et al., 2018) or parental health problems (Fredland et al., 2015) may be mechanisms of risk transmission. The magnitude of negative effects linked to family violence has made it a worldwide public health concern.

RESILIENCE FOLLOWING FAMILY VIOLENCE

Despite substantial evidence of the maladaptive effects of family violence, many individuals demonstrate resilience in the midst of this adversity. Current conceptualizations of resilience use a multisystemic and resource-driven definition that accounts for the role of relational and contextual factors (Ungar, 2021). Although research on multisystemic resilience following family violence is limited, some studies have explored factors related to positive adaptation. Kassis and colleagues (2013) found that optimism, self-acceptance, and help-seeking promoted resilience, as did limiting risk factors, such as alcohol misuse, inconsistent parenting, and beliefs that support aggression. Resilience in children exposed to family violence has often been associated with positive maternal parenting practices (e.g., Graham-Bermann et al., 2009).

The definitions, rates, and consequences of family violence are vast, with evidence of substantial variability within and across countries. Examining the unique experiences of family violence in specific countries allows for an in-depth exploration of how historical and cultural factors contribute to the conceptualization and expression of family violence and its effects on children. Mexico and Sweden are two countries that showcase how family violence is uniquely defined and how its impact on the family system is charted from two different perspectives.

FAMILY VIOLENCE IN MEXICO

Definitions of Family Violence in Mexico

Historically, family violence research in Mexico focused on the physical and sexual abuse of children as well as violence from male to female romantic partners, highlighting severe abuse that results in injury or death (Medina et al., 1994). Contemporary conceptualizations incorporate physical, sexual, psychological, and economic abuse, coercive control, and neglect as types of family violence, including violence between romantic partners (IPV) and from parents to children (CAN), as well as violence that involves other household members (e.g., siblings, grandparents). Both direct victimization (i.e., being abused or neglected) and indirect victimization (i.e., witnessing violence) are included in current views of family violence in Mexico (Secretaria de Salud, 2015).

Prevalence Rates of Family Violence in Mexico

Studies of family violence in Mexico have reported a wide range of prevalence estimates, likely due to differences in study methodology and sample characteristics. For IPV victimization, a national survey showed that 44% of women reported lifetime IPV, with the most common type being psychological (40%), followed by economic (21%), physical (18%) and sexual (7%) (INEGI, 2017). Although maltreatment is the leading cause of death and injury for children in Mexico, it is difficult to determine its prevalence, as official records vastly underestimate the scope of the problem (Villatoro et al., 2006). Women's retrospective reports of CAN indicate that 10% experienced sexual abuse in childhood, 35% experienced physical or emotional abuse, and 34% witnessed physical or emotional abuse in their family (INEGI, 2017). Youth self–reports suggest higher rates of physical (16% to 55%) and psychological (48 to 64%) abuse (Caballero et al., 2010; Villatoro et al., 2006). Self-reports of child abuse perpetration vary widely based on sample characteristics and the study's definition of abuse, with 36% of women in a large national study and 70% of women in a sample seeking healthcare reporting they hit their children (INEGI, 2017; Gaxiola Romero & Frías Armenta, 2005).

Family Violence in the Mexican Context

Associations between family violence and psychosocial risk in Mexican samples mirror the findings of research in other contexts, which indicate that family violence often occurs in the context of multiple adversities, including lacking financial resources to fulfill basic needs, caring for a child with a disability, parental substance use, and community violence (Erolin et al., 2014; Tovar Domínguez et al., 2016; Rey et al., 2021). In addition, contemporary definitions underscore that violence against women is a reflection of the historical power imbalance between men and women in Mexican society (Medina Nuñez & Medina Villegas, 2019), which is maintained by traditional gender roles and machismo. Interviews with IPV survivors suggest violence is frequently explained by external factors (e.g., family of origin discord, economic pressures, alcohol use), or as a way of punishing women for not adhering to a submissive role (e.g., domestic activities vs. employment; Doubova et al., 2007). Further, large gender disparities exist in employment, but counterintuitively, women who work are more likely to have experienced IPV during the past year, especially in rural areas of Mexico where female employment is still rare (17% employed vs. 41% in urban areas; INEGI, 2017; Canedo & Morse, 2021). In addition, close family ties may present opportunities for abuse, with aunts and uncles being the most frequently reported perpetrators of child sexual abuse (Castro, 2019). Other context-specific issues that contribute to enduring problems include the higher prevalence of CAN in urban (versus rural) regions, children staying home alone or being supervised by siblings, and child marriage (Castro, 2019; Valdez-Santiago et al., 2020).

Polyvictimization and Intergenerational Violence in Mexico

Research in Mexico documents that victims of family violence often experience multiple types of abuse, such that child exposure to family violence increases risk for adult IPV victimization and child abuse perpetration (Castro, 2019; Orozco-Vargas et al., 2021). One national study found that women who experienced physical or sexual child abuse were three times more likely to experience IPV during the last 12 months (Rivera-Rivera et al., 2006). Similarly, Orozco-Vargas and colleagues (2021) reported that witnessing IPV in the family of origin increased risk for IPV victimization in adulthood. Experiences of violence in the family of origin, and polyvictimization specifically, increase risk for perpetrating child abuse. Castro and Frias (2019) found that 61% of women who experienced family violence in childhood and also experienced IPV as adults reported hitting their children, as compared to 20% of the women not exposed to violence, with each type of experienced violence increasing risk for child abuse. Notably, the ubiquitous nature of family violence can lead to the normalization of abuse. One qualitative study with twenty-six school-aged children found they frequently experienced emotional abuse and witnessed IPV, but they did not conceptualize their experiences as maltreatment (Tovar Domínguez et al., 2016).

Short- and Long-term Effects of Family Violence in Mexico

Research on the effects of family violence in Mexico is sparse and limited by methodological challenges (e.g., cross-sectional designs, self-report measures). Available studies document mental health impacts during childhood and adolescence, including PTSD, conduct problems, depression, and anxiety (Frías Armenta & Gaxiola Romero, 2008; Erolin et al., 2014). For example, Rizo Martinez and colleagues (2018) reported very high rates of PTSD, depression, and anxiety (50% to 92%) among female adolescents who experienced any type of child abuse. Scolesce and colleagues (2020) also found increased risk for alcohol and substance use, poor functioning, and lower school attendance among youth exposed to family violence. The lasting impact of direct and indirect family violence exposure into adulthood has also been documented, including the use of maladaptive emotion regulation strategies, depression, anxiety, suicide risk, physical health problems, and alcohol use (Orozco-Vargas et al., 2021; Ortiz-Guzmán et al., 2018), as well as work disruptions (Gupta et al., 2018), lower economic earnings (Knaul & Ramirez, 2003), and more arrests (Rey et al., 2007).

Resilience in Mexican Families Exposed to Family Violence

A small but emerging literature characterizes resilience among individuals exposed to family violence. In one of the only studies to explore multisystemic resilience, Gaxiola Romero and Frías Armenta (2012) evaluated protective factors among a sample of high-risk women, including social supports, neighborhood cohesion, quality of romantic relationships, self-esteem, and quality of life. They found that protective factors at the individual, relational, and community levels reduced risk for perpetration of child abuse, even in the midst of IPV and other family-based adversity. Recent qualitative data also highlights individual and environmental resilience among women exposed to IPV, including parenting strengths (e.g., protecting children from IPV, motivation to leave a violent relationship for their children), religion, family support, and positive experiences with helping systems (Carney et al., accept pending minor revision). Additional research is needed in this area, particularly as it relates to the experiences of youth.

Clinical and Policy Implications in the Mexican Context

Despite significant efforts to document the urgency of addressing family violence, more multi-method longitudinal research is needed to explore its long-term effects and the mechanisms (e.g., physiological, regulatory) of risk transmission. Studies that utilize a broader definition of family violence (e.g., between siblings, perpetrated by other family members) and explore the experiences of men and LGBTQ individuals are also essential. In addition, studies that address family violence intervention effectiveness in the Mexican context are scarce. One large randomized controlled trial (RCT) of a nurse-delivered brief intervention for women exposed to IPV found no significant differences between the intervention and control groups at follow-up, but decreases in IPV and increases in safety planning and quality of life were found for both the intervention and control groups (Gupta et al., 2017). These findings, along with the very low rates of formal help-seeking among family violence victims (Ambriz-Mora et al., 2014), suggest the need for evaluating holistic approaches to intervention that involve training primary care staff, police officers, and other first responders. This work should be paired with continued efforts to modify community norms about the acceptability of family violence and practical policies to address the health, economic, housing, and work problems that often accompany family violence exposure.

FAMILY VIOLENCE IN SWEDEN

Definitions of Family Violence in Sweden

The term "family violence" (*familjevåld, våld i familjen*) is not commonly used in Sweden; instead, this form of violence is refered to as "violence in close relationships" (*våld i nära relationer*) and typically includes IPV, and sometimes child abuse. Child abuse is defined as an adult exposing a child to physical or psychological violence, sexual abuse, harm or neglecting to meet a child's basic needs. This definition does not distinguish between intentional and unintentional, nor active and passive, acts (SOU, 2001). It is officially recognized that violence in close relationships includes a range of anything from subtle actions to severe crimes and can include experiences of being ridiculed or threatened to being raped or severely abused (Socialstyrelsen, 2021). Elder abuse and sibling abuse are sometimes included in these definitions, but have received very minimal attention in research and practice, whereas violence in relationships with in-laws has not been assessed.

Research and public debate has led to several legal statutes that have had a significant impact on how family violence is defined in Sweden. In 1998, Sweden enacted legislation explicitly aimed at combating men's repeated criminal acts of violence against women (Gross Violation of a Woman's Integrity Law, 1998). This legislation is applied when a woman's self-confidence is severely damaged by her current or former partner's repeated abuse (Strand et al., 2021). All forms of child corporal punishment were prohibited in Sweden in 1979 and the UN convention of the rights of the child was ratified in 1990 and became Swedish law in 2020. In 2021, it became a criminal offence to allow a child to witness crimes in a close relationship (LViolation of a Child's Integrity Law, 2021), enabling children to be a plaintiff, have a plaintiff's counsel, and receive criminal damage compensation if they are exposed to IPV. These laws reflect how family violence is conceptualized and tracked in Sweden.

Prevalence Rates of Family Violence in Sweden

In Nordic countries, including Denmark, Finland, and Sweden, rates of IPV are as high as 32% (Gracia et al., 2020). One study that specifically assessed Sweden found that 14% of women and 5% of men have experienced physical violence or threat of violence in an ongoing or previous intimate relationship. Further, 20% of women (8% of men) have experienced repeated or systematic violence (NCK, 2014). A nationally representative survey found that sexual violence was the most common form of violence against women (Ahnlund et al., 2017). Of children in Sweden, approximately 10% have witnessed physical IPV between their parents and 28% have been exposed to some form of physical and/or verbal conflict between their parents (Cater et al., 2015).

Regarding CAN, 10-22% of children have been physically victimized by a parent (Annerbäck et al., 2010; Glatz et al., 2019) and 6% by a sibling (Glatz et al., 2019). In a population-based sample of Swedish adolescents including 4,339 youth, 65% of females and 23% of males reported having experienced child sexual abuse, which in this study included pawing or indecent touching, as well as non-contact abuse; participants seldom reported that the offender was a family member (Priebe & Svedin, 2009). Notably, relatively few children experience neglect, possibly related to Sweden's generous social insurance system, free parent education programs, and child health services (Cater et al., 2014). One nationally representative, retrospective study found that 5% of male and 10% of female Swedish young adults reported emotional neglect as children, which was described as having no one who could help them, protect them, comfort them, or take their concerns seriously (Cater et al., 2014). Thus, family violence is experienced in myriad ways among individuals in Sweden.

Family Violence in the Swedish Context

A number of factors related to the Swedish context impact how family violence is conceptualized. A relatively large proportion of Swedes live in rural areas, where the severity of IPV is higher and more chronic than in urban areas (Strand & Storey, 2019). Thus, the geographic region in which violence transpires is an important consideration. Another unique facet of family violence in Sweden relates to the experiences of indigenous people, specifically the Sami. Burman (2017) argues that men's violence against Sami women is a blindspot in Sweden and knowledge about Sami women's experiences of all forms of violence, including IPV, is lacking. An additional contextual consideration is the experience of foreign-born parents and their children. Jernbro and Janson (2017) note that children born outside the Nordic countries may experience greater financial hardship and more challenging social conditions, which may contribute to more frequent reports of family violence. Annerbäck and colleagues (2010) found that this explanation for the higher rates of family violence among foreign-born families was relevant, but not sufficient. They proposed that differences in child rearing views may contribute to violence being more generally accepted in non-Nordic households.

Polyvictimization and Intergenerational Violence in Sweden

Polyvictimization has received some empirical attention in Sweden; this research consistently finds overlap in experiences of children witnessing IPV and experiencing CAN (Annerbäck et al., 2010; Broberg et al., 2011; Glatz et al., 2019). Gender differences are also evident, with females reporting greater polyvictimization by their parents (14% of females compared to 5% of males). Cater et al. (2014) found that 29% of young adults reported lifetime exposure to at least three forms of victimization within and outside the family. Additional polyvictimization research is needed that is specifically focused on family violence, as most of the available polyvictimization literature examines exposure to any type of adversity. A small body of research has explored intergenerational facets of family violence in Sweden. One study found that childhood beliefs regarding violence were associated with future aggressive behavior, with individuals who believed that IPV was due to the use of alcohol or drugs showing greater aggression in romantic relationships in adulthood (Graham-Bermann et al., 2017). Intergenerational family violence research is an area in need of deeper exploration in Sweden.

Short- and Long-term Effects of Family Violence in Sweden

Experiencing physical abuse or witnessing parental IPV during childhood has been associated with a variety of indicators of poor health and low well-being during childhood and adolescence, including high emotional reactivity, emotional dysregulation, and risk-taking behaviors such as smoking, using alcohol or drugs, shoplifting, and earlier age of sexual debut (Annerbäck et al., 2012; Broberg et al., 2011). These associations grow stronger when children are exposed to chronic abuse, as evidenced by one study of 7,262 adolescents age 15-17 that showed a strong relationship between chronic and cumulative violence and negative health outcomes (Annerbäck et al., 2012).

Regarding long-term effects, exposure to parental IPV in Sweden has been associated with higher symptoms of anxiety, depression, posttraumic stress, and self-harm behaviors (Cater et al., 2015). Miller-Graff and colleagues (2016) also found it to be positively associated with adult psychopathology symptoms and negatively associated with life satisfaction in adulthood. Generally, the more types of victimization a child is subjected to, the higher the prevalence of many types of adult mental health and behavioral problems, illustrating the deleterious consequences of polyvictimization (Cater et al., 2014). One study highlighted the importance of the perpetrator's relationship to the child, with violence perpetrated specifically by fathers being related to adult-reported anxiety and PTSD symptoms (Miller et al., 2014). Another study underscored the role of how violence is interpreted; the belief during childhood that the perpetrator used violence in a cruel or sadistic manner, or to punish the child, was linked with more mental health problems during adulthood (Graham-Bermann et al., 2017). Although the research on long-term effects of family violence in Sweden is sparse, the available studies shed light on key factors that may be impactful over time.

Resilience in Swedish Families Exposed to Family Violence

Research conducted in Sweden on resilience following family violence is limited. One study showed the important role of parental warmth in mediating the association between childhood IPV exposure and positive outcomes in adulthood (Miller et al., 2016). A second study examined the role of reporting and found that young Swedish adults who retrospectively reported confiding in someone about the interparental violence they witnessed during childhood described this experience to be cathartic and helpful (Howell et al., 2015). Finally, a qualitative study of adult women who perceived themselves to be functioning well despite experiencing childhood maltreatment described the process of resilience as an ongoing endeavor to thrive rather than just survive. These women highlighted the importance of external processes connected to social relations and environmental conditions that promoted resilience. Themes of resilience were captured by four domains: establishing and maintaining command of life, employing personal resources, surrounding oneself with valuable people, and reaching acceptance (Gunnarsdottir et al., 2021). This mix of quantitative and qualitative research provides valuable information on how resilience is conceptualized in Sweden.

Clinical and Policy Implications in the Swedish Context

A number of clinical and policy implications emerge from the work on family violence in Sweden. Interventions for children exposed to family violence need to be developed and rigorously evaluated. One national evaluation of methods for helping children exposed to IPV showed that the available interventions had only moderate positive effects on children's health and well-being (Broberg et al., 2011). In particular, addressing children's anger was challenging for practitioners and available treatment modalities showed modest benefits (Broberg et al., 2015). Additionally, the sparse population of Sweden limits intervention development and evaluation. Indeed, Sweden has only 10 million inhabitants and few researchers who study family violence, which makes large-scale intervention evaluations of culturally-informed programs difficult to conduct. Adapting evidence-based interventions from other cultural contexts is also challenging and requires significant modifications to be fully accepted and relevant to Swedish families (Källström & Grip, 2019).

Another implication relates to the Swedish laws that have been enacted regarding family violence. Laws in Sweden prioritize ongoing contact between the child and the non-resident parent, so most children continue to have contact with both caregivers after parental separation (Forssell & Cater, 2015). There is a firmly held belief in children's rights to be protected from violence and abuse; however, beliefs in gender equality and children's rights to have continued contact with both parents are also strong, so sometimes there is conflict between ensuring children spend time with both parents and shielding them from potential abuse or violence. Finding ways to fulfill the goals of Sweden's ambitious legislation related to family violence remains an ongoing pursuit.

REFLECTIONS AND FUTURE DIRECTIONS

This global exploration of family violence provides novel information on the variations in definition, prevalence, and effects across cultural contexts. An in-depth assessment of how family violence is conceptualized in Mexico and Sweden, including polyvictimization, resilience, short- and long-term consequences, and policy and clinical implications offer evidence for commonalities and points of divergence across countries. Although family violence is an expansive term, most research and clinical work has focused on child abuse, neglect, and IPV. Minimal global work has examined sibling abuse, parent/in-law abuse, or elder abuse, as many countries do not consider these as types of family violence. More research is also needed on co-occurring family violence. A focus on polyvictimization would allow researchers and clinicians to develop a more complete understanding of how forms of family violence interact and affect children's functioning. Further, resilience has received much less empirical attention than the problematic short- and long-term effects of family violence. Identifying what individual, relational, community, and cultural factors promote multisystemic resilience on a global scale is a necessary direction for intervention science.

CONCLUSION

Family violence is a worldwide public health concern. Despite significant variations across countries in definition and prevalence, there is universal agreement
that children who experience family violence are profoundly affected in the short-
and long-term. Culturally-informed interventions that consider both resilience
and problematic functioning are critical to address the consequences of family
violence and place youth on a pathway towards well-being. This chapter compares
data from a country in Latin America to a country in Northern Europe. Although
in future research it could be helpful to consider experiences of family violence
from other regions across the globe, examining these two countries provides a valuable perspective on the occurrence of violence in unique geographic locations, as
well as recommendations for further research on resilience and effective methods
of intervention and violence-reduction.

REFERENCES

Ahnlund, P., Andersson, T., Snellman, F., Sundström, M., Heimer, G. (2017). Prevalence
and correlates of sexual, physical, and psychological violence against women and
men of 60 to 74 years in Sweden. *Journal of Interpersonal Violence* 35(5–6), 1539–
1561. https://doi.org/10.1177/0886260517696874

Ambriz-Mora, M. I., Zonana-Nacach, A., & Anzaldo-Campos, M. C. (2014). Intimate
partner violence and family dysfunction among Mexican women seen a primary
care unit. *Semergen*, 41(5), 241–246. https://doi.org/10.1016/j.semerg.2014.07.004

Annerbäck, E. M., Sahlqvist, L., Svedin, C. G., Wingren, G., & Gustafsson, P. A. (2012).
Child physical abuse and concurrence of other types of child abuse in Sweden—
Associations with health and risk behaviors. *Child Abuse & Neglect*, 36(7-8), 585–
595. https://doi.org/10.1016/j.chiabu.2012.05.006

Annerbäck, E. M., Wingren, G., Svedin, C. G., & Gustafsson, P. A. (2010). Prevalence
and characteristics of child physical abuse in Sweden—Findings from a population-
based youth survey. *Acta Paediatrica*, 99, 1229–1236. https://doi.org/10.1111/
j.1651-2227.2010.01792.x

Antai, D., Antai, J., & Anthony, D. S. (2014). The relationship between socio-economic
inequalities, intimate partner violence and economic abuse: A national study of
women in the Philippines. Global public health, 9(7), 808–826. http://dx.doi.org/
10.1080/17441692.2014.917195

Appel, A. E., & Holden, G. W. (1998). The co-occurrence of spouse and physical child
abuse: a review and appraisal. *Journal of Family Psychology*, *12*(4), 578.

Assink, M., Spruit, A., Schuts, M., Lindauer, R., van der Put, C. E., & Stams, G.
J. J. (2018). The intergenerational transmission of child maltreatment: A three-level
meta-analysis. *Child Abuse & Neglect*, *84*, 131–145. https://doi.org/10.1016/j.chi
abu.2018.07.037

Bidarra, Z. S., Lessard, G., & Dumont, A. (2016). Co-occurrence of intimate partner violence and child sexual abuse: Prevalence, risk factors and related issues. *Child Abuse
& Neglect*, *55*, 10–21. https://doi.org/10.1016/j.chiabu.2016.03.007

Broberg, A., Almqvist, L., Axberg, U., Grip, K., Almqvist, K., Sharifi, U., Cater, A. K., Forssell, A., Eriksson, M., & Iversen, C. (2011). *Stöd till barn som upplevt våld mot mamma: Resultat från en nationellutvärdering.* Göteborg: Göteborg University.

Broberg, A., Almqvist, K., Appell, P., Axberg, U., Cater, Å. K., Draxler, H., Eriksson, M., Grip, K., Hjärthag, F., Ole Hultmann, Iversen, C., & Röbäck de Souza, K. (2015). *Utveckling av bedömningsinstrument och stödinsatser för våldsutsatta barn.* Göteborg: Göteborg University.

Burman, M. (2017). Men's intimate partner violence against Sami women: A Swedish blind spot. *Nordic Journal on Law and Society*, 1(01-02), 194–215. https://doi.org/10.36368/njolas.v1i01-02.18

Caballero, M. Á., Ramos, L., González, C., & Saltijeral, M. T. (2010). Family violence and risk of substance use among Mexican adolescents. *Child Abuse & Neglect, 34*(8), 576–584. https://doi.org/10.1016/j.chiabu.2010.02.001

Canedo, A. P., & Morse, S. M. (2021). An estimation of the effect of women's employment on the prevalence of intimate partner violence in Mexico. *Journal of Interpersonal Violence*, 36(19-20), NP10594–NP10618. https://doi.org/10.1177/0886260519876016

Carney, J.R., Martinez-Torteya, C., Miller-Graff, L.E., Gilliam, H., Howell, K.H. (accept with minor revisions). A Thematic Analysis of Barriers to and Facilitators of Wellbeing and Resource Access for IPV-Exposed, Pregnant Women in Mexico. *Journal of Family Violence.*

Castro, R. (2019). Hacia una revisión de la Endireh y sus resultados. In R. Castro (Ed.) De parejas, hogares, instituciones y espacios comunitarios: Violencias contra las mujeres en México (Endireh 2016) (pp. 385–411). Centro Regional de Investigaciones Multidisciplinarias-Universidad Nacional Autónoma de México & Inmujeres.

Castro, R. & Frias, S. (2019). Obstetric Violence in Mexico: Results From a 2016 National Household Survey. *Violence Against Women, 26*, 555–572. https://doi.org/10.1177/1077801219836732

Cater, Å. K., Andershed, A-K., & Andershed, H. (2014). Youth Victimization in Sweden: Prevalence, Characteristics and Relation to Mental Health and Behavioral Problems in Young Adulthood, *Child Abuse & Neglect, 38*(8), 1290–1302. https://doi.org/10.1016/j.chiabu.2014.03.002

Cater, Å. K., Miller, L. E., Howell, K. H., & Graham-Bermann, S. A. (2015). Childhood exposure to intimate partner violence and adult mental health problems: Relationships with gender and age of exposure. *Journal of Family Violence, 30*(7), 875–886.

Chan, K. L. (2011). Children exposed to child maltreatment and intimate partner violence: A study of co-occurrence among Hong Kong Chinese families. *Child Abuse & Neglect, 35*(7), 532–542. https://doi.org/10.1016/j.chiabu.2011.03.008

Chan, K. L., Tiwari, A., Fong, D. Y., Leung, W. C., Brownridge, D. A., & Ho, P. C. (2009). Correlates of in-law conflict and intimate partner violence against Chinese pregnant women in Hong Kong. *Journal of Interpersonal Violence*, 24(1), 97–110. https://doi.org/10.1177/0886260508315780

Chan, K. L., Chen, Q., & Chen, M. (2021). Prevalence and correlates of the co-occurrence of family violence: A meta-analysis on family polyvictimization. *Trauma, Violence, & Abuse*, 22(2), 289–305. https://doi.org/10.1177/1524838019841601

Charak, R., de Jong, J. T. V. M., Berckmoes, L. H., Ndayisaba, H., & Reis, R. (2017). Assessing the factor structure of the childhood trauma questionnaire, and cumulative effect of abuse and neglect on mental health among adolescents in conflict-affected Burundi. *Child Abuse & Neglect*, 72, 383–392. https://doi.org/10.1016/j.chiabu.2017.09.009

Clemens, V., Huber-Lang, M., Plener, P. L., Brähler, E., Brown, R. C., & Fegert, J. M. (2018). Association of child maltreatment subtypes and long-term physical health in a German representative sample. *European Journal of Psychotraumatology*, 9(1), 1510278. https://doi.org/10.1080/20008198.2018.1510278

Conway, L. J., Cook, F., Cahir, P., Brown, S., Reilly, S., Gartland, D., Mensah, F., & Giallo, R. (2021). Children's language abilities at age 10 and exposure to intimate partner violence in early childhood: Results of an Australian prospective pregnancy cohort study. *Child Abuse & Neglect*, 111, 104794. https://doi.org/10.1016/j.chiabu.2020.104794

Cutland, M. (2012). Child abuse and its legislation: the global picture. *Archives of Disease in Childhood*, 97(8), 679–684. http://dx.doi.org/10.1136/archdischild-2012-301648

Doubova, S. V., Pámanes-González, V., Billings, D. L., & del Pilar Torres-Arreola, L. (2007). Partner violence against pregnant women in Mexico City. *Revista de Saude Publica*, 41(4), 582–590. https://doi.org/10.1590/S0034-89102007000400012

English, D. J., Upadhyaya, M. P., Litrownik, A. J., Marshall, J. M., Runyan, D. K., Graham, J. C., & Dubowitz, H. (2005). Maltreatment's wake: The relationship of maltreatment dimensions to child outcomes. *Child Abuse & Neglect*, 29(5), 597–619. https://doi.org/10.1016/j.chiabu.2004.12.008

Erolin, K. S., Wieling, E., & Parra, R. E. A. (2014). Family violence exposure and associated risk factors for child PTSD in a Mexican sample. *Child Abuse & Neglect*, 38(6), 1011–1022. https://doi.org/10.1016/j.chiabu.2014.04.011

Fitzgerald, M., & Gallus, K. (2020). Emotional support as a mechanism linking childhood maltreatment and adult's depressive and social anxiety symptoms. *Child Abuse & Neglect*, 108, 104645. https://doi.org/10.1016/j.chiabu.2020.104645

Forssell, A. M., & Cater, Å. (2015). Patterns in child–father contact after parental separation in a sample of child witnesses to intimate partner violence. *Journal of Family Violence*, 30(3), 339–349. https://doi.org/10.1007/s10896-015-9673-2

Fredland, N., Symes, L., Gilroy, H., Paulson, R., Nava, A., McFarlane, J., & Pennings, J. (2015). Connecting partner violence to poor functioning for mothers and children: Modeling intergenerational outcomes. *Journal of Family Violence*, 30(5), 555–566. https://doi.org/10.1007/s10896-015-9702-1

Frías Armenta, M., & Gaxiola Romero, J. C. (2008). Consecuencias de la violencia familiar experimentada directa e indirectamente en niños: depresión, ansiedad, conducta antisocial y ejecución académica. Revista Mexicana de Psicología, 25(2), 237–248. http://www.redalyc.org/articulo.oa?id=243016308004

Gracia, E., Lila, M., & Santirso, F. A. (2020). Attitudes toward intimate partner violence against women in the European Union: A systematic review. *European Psychologist*, 25(2), 104–121. https://doi.org/10.1027/1016-9040/a000392

Gaxiola Romero, J. C., & Frías Armenta, M. (2005). Las consecuencias del maltrato infantil: un estudio con madres mexicanas. Revista Mexicana de Psicología, 22(2), 363–374. http://www.redalyc.org/articulo.oa?id=243020634001

Gaxiola Romero, J. C., & Frías Armenta, M. (2012). Factores protectores, estilos de crianza y maltrato infantil: un modelo ecológico. *Psyecology*, *3*(3), 259–270. https://doi.org/10.1174/217119712802845769

Gershoff, E. T. (2017). School corporal punishment in global perspective: prevalence, outcomes, and efforts at intervention. *Psychology, Health & Medicine*, 22(sup1), 224–239. https://doi.org/10.1174/217119712802845769

Gibbs, A., Dunkle, K., & Jewkes, R. (2018). Emotional and economic intimate partner violence as key drivers of depression and suicidal ideation: A cross-sectional study among young women in informal settlements in South Africa. *PloS one*, *13*(4), e0194885. https://doi.org/10.1371/journal.pone.0194885

Glaser, R., & Kiecolt-Glaser, J. K. (2005). Stress-induced immune dysfunction: implications for health. *Nature Reviews Immunology*, *5*(3), 243–251.

Glatz, T., Källström, Å., Hellfeldt, K., & Thunberg, S. (2019) Physical violence in family sub-systems: Links to peer victimization and long-term emotional and behavioral problems. *Journal of Family Violence*, *34*(5), 423–433.

Graham-Bermann, S. A., Cater, Å. K., Miller-Graff, L., & Howell, K. (2017) Adults' Explanations for Intimate Partner Violence (IPV) During Childhood and Associated Effects. *Journal of Clinical Psychology 73*(6), 652–668. https://doi.org/10.1002/jclp.22345

Graham-Bermann, S. A., Gruber, G., Howell, K. H., & Girz, L. (2009). Factors discriminating among profiles of resilience and psychopathology in children exposed to intimate partner violence (IPV). *Child Abuse & Neglect*, *33*(9), 648–660. https://doi.org/10.1016/j.chiabu.2009.01.002

Greene, C. A., Chan, G., McCarthy, K. J., Wakschlag, L. S., & Briggs-Gowan, M. J. (2018). Psychological and physical intimate partner violence and young children's mental health: The role of maternal posttraumatic stress symptoms and parenting behaviors. *Child Abuse & Neglect*, *77*, 168–179. https://doi.org/10.1016/j.chiabu.2018.01.012

Gross Violation of a Woman's Integrity Law, 367 S.C.C § 1998. https://evaw-global-database.unwomen.org/fr/countries/europe/sweden/1998/act-on-violence-against-women--government-bill-1997-98-55

Gunnarsdottir, H., Löve, J., Hensing, G., & Källström, Å. (2021) To live and not only survive—an ongoing endeavor. Resilience experiences among adult women abused as children, *Frontiers in Public Health*, *9*, 599921. https://doi.org/10.3389/fpubh.2021.599921

Gupta, J., Falb, K. L., Ponta, O., Xuan, Z., Campos, P. A., Gomez, A. A., Valades, J., Cariño, G. & Olavarrieta, C. D. (2017). A nurse-delivered, clinic-based intervention to address intimate partner violence among low-income women in Mexico City: findings from a cluster randomized controlled trial. *BMC Medicine*, *15*(1), 1–12. https://doi.org/10.1186/s12916-017-0880-y

Gupta, J., Willie, T. C., Harris, C., Campos, P. A., Falb, K. L., Moreno, C. G., Olavarrieta, C. D., & Okechukwu, C. A. (2018). Intimate partner violence against low-income women in Mexico City and associations with work-related disruptions: A latent class analysis using crosssectional data. *Journal of Epidemiology and Community Health*, *72*(7), 605–610. http://dx.doi.org/10.1136/jech-2017-209681

Guruge S., Tiwari A., Lucea, M., International Perspectives on Family Violence. (Pgs. 411–446) Humphreys, J., & Campbell, J. C. (Eds.). (2010). *Family Violence and Nursing Practice*. Springer Publishing Company.

Hillis, S., Mercy, J., Amobi, A., & Kress, H. (2016). Global prevalence of past-year violence against children: A systematic review and minimum estimates. *Pediatrics*, *137*(3), 1–13. https://doi.org/10.1542/peds.2015-4079

Howell, K. H., Cater, Å. K., Miller-Graff, L. E., & Graham-Bermann, S. A. (2015). The process of reporting and receiving support following exposure to intimate partner violence during childhood. *Journal of Interpersonal Violence*, 30(16), 2886–2907. https://doi.org/10.1177/0886260514554289

Huguenel, B. M., Leon, S. C., Hindt, L. A., Lutz, N., & Osborne, J. (2021). Profiles of maltreatment in the child welfare system: predicting mental health outcomes and examining age as a moderator. *Journal of Traumatic Stress*, *3*(4), 721–732. https://doi.org/10.1002/jts.22685

Instituto Nacional de Estadistica y Geografia (INEGI) (2017). Encuesta Nacional sobre la Dinamica de las Relaciones Familiares—Prinicipales Resulados. Retrieved from https://www.inegi.org.mx/contenidos/programas/endireh/2016/doc/endireh2016_presentacion_ejecutiva.pdf

Jernbro, C. & Janson, S. (2017) *Violence against children in Sweden 2016 - A national survey*, The Children's Welfare Foundation, Sweden.

Källström, A., & Grip, K. (2019). Thinking critically about cross-cultural implementation— Swedish social workers' experiences of testing the Kids' Club method for helping child and mother victims of intimate partner violence. *European Journal of Social Work*, *22*(4), 587–598. https://doi.org/10.1080/13691457.2018.1441130

Kassis, W., Artz, S., & Moldenhauer, S. (2013). Laying down the family burden: A cross-cultural analysis of resilience in the midst of family violence. *Child & Youth Services*, *34*(1), 37–63. https://doi.org/10.1080/0145935X.2013.766067

Kiesel, L. R., Piescher, K. N., & Edleson, J. L. (2016). The relationship between child maltreatment, intimate partner violence exposure, and academic performance. *Journal of Public Child Welfare*, *10*(4), 434–456. https://doi.org/10.1080/15548 732.2016.1209150

Knaul, F., & Ramirez, M. (2003). El Impacto De La Violencia Intrafamiliar En La Probabilidad De Violencia Intergeneracional, La Progresión Escolar Y El Mercadfo Laboral En México. En F. M. Knaul & G. Nigenda (Eds.), *Caleidoscopio de la Salud. De la Investigación a las Políticas y de las Políticas a la Accion*, (pp. 69–88). Mexico, Fundacion Mexicana para la Salud.

Kobulsky, J. M., Dubowitz, H., & Xu, Y. (2020). The global challenge of the neglect of children. *Child Abuse & Neglect*, 110, 104296. https://doi.org/10.1016/j.chiabu.2019.104296

Koen, N., Wyatt, G. E., Williams, J. K., Zhang, M., Myer, L., Zar, H. J., & Stein, D. J. (2014). Intimate partner violence: associations with low infant birthweight in a South African birth cohort. *Metabolic Brain Disease*, *29*(2), 281–299.

Krakau, L., Tibubos, A. N., Beutel, M. E., Ehrenthal, J. C., Gieler, U., & Brähler, E. (2021). Personality functioning as a mediator of adult mental health following child maltreatment. *Journal of Affective Disorders*, *291*, 126–134. https://doi.org/10.1016/j.jad.2021.05.006

Lamers-Winkelman, F., Schipper, J. C. D., & Oosterman, M. (2012). Children's physical health complaints after exposure to intimate partner violence. *British Journal of Health Psychology*, *17*(4), 771–784. https://doi.org/10.1111/j.2044-8287.2012.02072.x

Le, M. T., Holton, S., Romero, L., & Fisher, J. (2018). Polyvictimization among children and adolescents in low-and lower-middle-income countries: A systematic review and meta-analysis. *Trauma, Violence, & Abuse, 19*(3), 323–342. https://doi.org/ 10.1177/1524838016659489

Mackey, A. L., Fromuth, M. E., & Kelly, D. B. (2010). The association of sibling relationship and abuse with later psychological adjustment. *Journal of Interpersonal Violence*, 25(6), 955–968. https://doi.org/10.1177/0886260509340545

McFarlane, J., Symes, L., Binder, B. K., Maddoux, J., & Paulson, R. (2014). Maternal-child dyads of functioning: the intergenerational impact of violence against women on children. *Maternal and Child Health Journal, 18*(9), 2236–2243. https://doi.org/ 10.1007/s10995-014-1473-4

Medina, M. H., Yañez, J. R. T., & Pacheco, R. A. R. (1994). Mortalidad por homicidio en niños. México, 1979-1990. Salud Pública de México, 36(5), 529–537.

Medina Núñez, I., & Medina Villegas, A. (2019). Violencias contra las mujeres en las relaciones de pareja en México. *Intersticios sociales, 18*, 269–302.

Miller, L.E., Cater, A.K., Howell, K.H., & Graham-Bermann, S.A. (2014). Perpetration patterns and environmental contexts of IPV in Sweden: Relationships with adult mental health. *Child Abuse & Neglect, 38*(1), 147–158.

Miller-Graff, L. E., Cater, Å. K., Howell, K. H., & Graham-Bermann, S. A. (2016). Parent–child warmth as a potential mediator of childhood exposure to intimate partner violence and positive adulthood functioning. *Anxiety, Stress, & Coping, 29*(3), 259–273. https://doi.org/10.1080/10615806.2015.1028030

Min, M. O., Minnes, S., Kim, H., & Singer, L. T. (2013). Pathways linking childhood maltreatment and adult physical health. *Child Abuse & Neglect, 37*(6), 361–373. https:// doi.org/10.1016/j.chiabu.2012.09.008

NCK (2014). *Våld och hälsa—En befolkningsundersökning om kvinnors och mäns våldsutsatthet samt kopplingen till hälsa*, Nationellt Centrum för Kvinnofrid.

Ortiz-Guzmán, J. A., Ibarra-Alcantar, M. C., Alvarado-Cruz, F. J., Graciano-Morales, H., & Jiménez-Genchi, A. (2018). Características clínicas de mujeres con depresión mayor que sufrieron abuso sexual en la infancia. Gaceta Medica Mexico, 154(3), 295–301. https://dx.doi.org/10.24875/GMM.18003221

Orozco-Vargas, A. E., Venebra-Muñoz, A., Aguilera-Reyes, U., & García-López, G. I. (2021). The mediating role of emotion regulation strategies in the relationship between family of origin violence and intimate partner violence. Psicologia: Reflexão e Crítica, *34*(23), 1–15. https://doi.org/10.1186/s41155-021-00187-8

Pillemer, K., Burnes, D., Riffin, C., & Lachs, M. S. (2016). Elder abuse: global situation, risk factors, and prevention strategies. *The Gerontologist, 56*(Suppl_2), 194–S205. https://doi.org/10.1093/geront/gnw004

Priebe, G. & Svedin, C.G. (2009). Prevalence, characteristics, and associations of sexual abuse with sociodemographics and consensual sex in a population-based sample of Swedish adolescents. *Journal of Child Sexual Abuse*, 18:1, 19–39. Doi: 10.1080/ 10538710802584635

Postmus, J. L., Hoge, G. L., Breckenridge, J., Sharp-Jeffs, N., & Chung, D. (2020). Economic abuse as an invisible form of domestic violence: A multicountry review. *Trauma, Violence, & Abuse*, 21(2), 261–283. https://doi.org/10.1177/152483801 8764160

Raj, A., Livramento, K. N., Santana, M. C., Gupta, J., & Silverman, J. G. (2006). Victims of intimate partner violence more likely to report abuse from in-laws. *Violence against women*, 12(10), 936–949. https://doi.org/10.1177/1077801206292935

Rey, G. N., Garcia, F. J., Medina-Mora Icaza, M. E., & Sainz, M. T. (2007). Alcohol and drug consumption, depressive features, and family violence as associated with complaints to the Prosecutor's Office in Central Mexico. *Substance Use & Misuse*, 42(10), 1485–1504. https://doi.org/10.1080/10826080701202817

Rey, G. N., López, M. M., Toledano-Toledano, F., García, F. J., & Velázquez, J. V. (2021). Intimate-partner violence and its relationship with substance consumption by Mexican men and women: National Survey on Addictions. *Salud Mental*, 44(3), 135–143. https://doi.org/10.1080/10826080701202817

Rivera-Rivera L, Allen B, Chávez-Ayala R, Avila-Burgos L. (2006). Abuso físico y sexual durante la niñez y revictimización de las mujeres mexicanas durante la edad adulta. *Salud Publica de Mexico*, 48(2), 268–278. http://www.redalyc.org/articulo.oa?id=10604807

Rizo Martínez, L. E., Guevara Pérez, M. A., Hernández González, M., Sánchez Sosa, J. J. (2018). A preliminary study of the prevalence of post-traumatic stress disorder, depression and anxiety symptoms in female adolescents maltreatment victims in Mexico. *Salud Mental*, 41(3), 139–144. https://doi.org/10.17711/SM.0185-3325.2018.018

Secretaria de Salud (2015). Programa de Acción Específico: Prevención y Atención a la Violencia Familiar y de Género 2013—2018. Retrieved from https://www.gob.mx/salud/acciones-y-programas/programa-de-accion-especifico-prevencion-y-atencion-de-la-violencia-familiar-y-de-genero-2013-2018-9279

Scolesce, A., Willie, T. C., Falb, K. L., Sipsma, H., Campos, P. A., Olavarrieta, C. D., & Gupta, J. (2020). Intimate partner violence against low-income women in Mexico City and associations with child school attendance: A latent class analysis using cross-sectional data. *Maternal and Child Health Journal*, 24(3), 360–368. http://dx.doi.org/10.1136/jech-2017-209681

Silva, E. P., Ludermir, A. B., de Carvalho Lima, M., Eickmann, S. H., & Emond, A. (2019). Mental health of children exposed to intimate partner violence against their mother: a longitudinal study from Brazil. *Child Abuse & Neglect*, 92, 1–11. https://doi.org/10.1016/j.chiabu.2019.03.002

Smith, S. G., Zhang, X., Basile, K.C., Merrick, M.T., Wang, J., Kresnow, M., Chen, J. (2018). The National Intimate Partner and Sexual Violence Survey (NISVS): 2015 Data Brief—Updated Release. Atlanta, GA: National Center for Injury Prevention and Control, Centers for Disease Control and Prevention.

SOU (2001). *Barnmisshandel: Att förebygga och åtgärda*, Slutbetänkande av Kommittén mot barnmisshandel, 72, Stockholm: Fritzes.

Socialstyrelsen (2021). *Våld i nära relationer*. Retrieved from www.socialstyrelsen.se/stod_i_arbetet/vald_och_brott/vald_i_nara_relationer

Spinazzola, J., Hodgdon, H., Liang, L.-J., Ford, J. D., Layne, C. M., Pynoos, R., Briggs, E. C., Stolbach, B., & Kisiel, C. (2014). Unseen wounds: The contribution of psychological maltreatment to child and adolescent mental health and risk outcomes. *Psychological Trauma: Theory, Research, Practice, and Policy*, 6(Suppl 1), S18–S28. https://doi.org/10.1037/a0037766

Strand, S.J.M., Selenius, H., Petersson, J. & Storey, J.E. (2021). Repeated and Systematic Intimate Partner Violence in Rural Areas in Sweden. International Criminology, 1, 220–233. https://doi.org/10.1007/s43576-021-00026-x

Strand, S.J.M., & Storey, J. E. (2019). Intimate partner violence in urban, rural, and remote areas: An investigation of offense severity and risk factors. *Violence against Women*, 25(2), 188–207. https://doi.org/10.1177/1077801218766611

Stoltenborgh, M., Bakermans-Kranenburg, M. J., & Van Ijzendoorn, M. H. (2013). The neglect of child neglect: A meta-analytic review of the prevalence of neglect. *Social Psychiatry and Psychiatric Epidemiology*, 48(3), 345–355. https://doi.org/10.1007/s00127-012-0549-y

Stoltenborgh, M., Van Ijzendoorn, M. H., Euser, E. M., & Bakermans-Kranenburg, M. J. (2011). A global perspective on child sexual abuse: Meta-analysis of prevalence around the world. *Child Maltreatment*, 16(2), 79–101. https://doi.org/10.1177/1077559511403920

Straus, M. A. (2010). Prevalence, societal causes, and trends in corporal punishment by parents in world perspective. *Law and Contemporary Problems*, 73(2), 1–30.

Thoma, M. V., Bernays, F., Eising, C. M., Maercker, A., & Rohner, S. L. (2021). Child maltreatment, lifetime trauma, and mental health in Swiss older survivors of enforced child welfare practices: Investigating the mediating role of self-esteem and self-compassion. *Child Abuse & Neglect*, 113, 104925. https://doi.org/10.1016/j.chiabu.2020.104925

Tovar Domínguez, A. G., Almeraya Quintero, S. X., Guajardo Hernández, L. G., & Borja Bravo, M. (2016). El maltrato infantil desde la voz de la niñez. *Revista Mexicana de Ciencias Agrícolas*, 7(1), 195–207. doi: https://doi.org/10.29312/remexca.v7i1.383

Ungar, M. (2021). Modeling multisystemic resilience: Connecting Biological, Psychological, Social, and Ecological Adaptation in Contexts of Adversity. In M. Ungar (Ed.), *Multisystemic Resilience, Adaption and Transformation in Contexts of Change* (pp. 6–34). Oxford University Press. htpps://doi.org/10.1093/oso/9780190095888.001.0001

UNICEF Humanitarian Action for Children. (2017). Overview. https://www.unicef.org/publications/files/HAC_2017_Overview_ENG.pdf.

Valdez-Santiago, R., Villalobos, A., Arenas-Monreal, L., Flores-Celis, K., & Ramos-Lira, L. (2020). Abuso sexual infantil en México: conductas de riesgo e indicadores de salud mental en adolescentes. *Salud Pública de México, 62*(6), 661–671. https://doi.org/10.21149/11924

Villatoro, J. A. V., del Valle, N. Q., López, M. D. L. G., Santos, M. D., Buenabad, N. G. A., Oteo, A. E., . . . Salazar, I. C. C. (2006)¿ Cómo educamos a nuestros/as hijos/as? Encuesta de Maltrato Infantil y Factores Asociados. Instituto Nacional de las Mujeres (INMUJERES). Instituto Nacional de Psiquiatría Ramón de la Fuente Muñiz (INPRFM), 1, 15–165.

Violation of a Child's Integrity Law, 397 S.C.C § Chapter 4, Section 3 (2021). https://www.government.se/492a92/contentassets/7a2dcae0787e465e9a2431554b5eab03/the-swedish-criminal-code.pdf

Waterston, T., & Janson, S. (2020). Hitting children is wrong. *BMJ Paediatrics Open*, 4(1), 1–3. https://doi.org/10.1136/bmjpo-2020-000675

Wemrell, M., Stjernlöf, S., Lila, M., Gracia, E., & Ivert, A. K. (2021). The Nordic paradox. professionals' discussions about gender equality and intimate partner violence against women in Sweden. *Women & Criminal Justice*, 1–23. https://doi.org/10.1111/soc4.12699

World Health Organization (WHO) (2006). Multi-country study on women's health and domestic violence against women: Summary report. Initial results on prevalence, health outcomes and women's responses. Geneva, Switzerland: WHO.

World Health Organization (WHO) (2013). *Global and Regional Estimates of Violence Against Women: Prevalence and Health Effects of Intimate Partner Violence and Non-partner Sexual Violence* (Illustrated ed.). Geneva, Switzerland: WHO.

. World Health Organization (WHO) (2021). Violence against women prevalence estimates, 2018: global, regional and national prevalence estimates for intimate partner violence against women and global and regional prevalence estimates for non-partner sexual violence against women. Geneva, Switzerland: WHO.

9

Navigating Violent Spaces

Violence Against Children in Alternative Care

SCOTT L. MOESCHBERGER AND BREEANNA WHITE ■

Globally, rates of violence against children persist at alarming levels, with almost 1 billion children experiencing some form of violence (Hillis et al., 2016). There has been significant attention in recent years on caring for the rights of children (United Nations, 2019), alongside the recognition that they are often among the most vulnerable members of society. Although all children are vulnerable, orphans face particular risks. There are an estimated 145 million orphans around the globe, 15 million of which are double orphans (UNICEF, 2015). This latter term is used to describe a child who has lost both parents, while children who lose one parent are considered "single orphans." Of children who are orphaned, much consensus has emerged related to the risk of violence faced by children in institutional care (Sherr et al., 2017). Broad coalitions of academics, caregivers, advocates, and nongovernmental organizations (NGOs) have collected data and disseminated recommendations to move toward family-based care whenever possible (Goldman et al., 2020).

While children are at risk for a variety of different types of violence (Hillis et al., 2016), the breakdown of protective family structures represents a key vulnerability factor. This can lead to transition to alternative care placements such as family-based care environments (i.e., foster care) or larger institutionalized settings such as orphanages and group homes (Faith to Action Initiative, 2015). The aftermath of the dissolution of or disruption to children's families of origin is complex: Children face increased risks of violence as they enter alternative care and move through a system, eventually reaching the point where they "age out" whether or not they have been given a chance to develop skills and relationships that will support them in their young adult life. Most of these children are considered orphans, a population that bears an increased level of vulnerability. It is challenging to accurately account for the number of children currently living in institutional care, but estimates range from 3 to 9 million children who live in institutional care worldwide (Desmond et al., 2020). Institutional care is a broad term used to describe orphanages, group homes, and any facility that houses more than 10 children outside of what would be considered a family environment (Browne, 2009). These facilities can be government funded or run by private organizations. Of the children in institutional care, an estimated four out of five are single orphans (Pinheiro, 2006). In some cases, this is because parents have placed the child in care due to financial pressures, because the child has special needs, or because they feel unable to care for the child for some reason. In some of the worst cases it has become common for recruiters to take children from their families and display them as orphans to gain a profit (van Doore, 2016).

As public and professional attention on orphans has increased, there has also been an increased understanding of the severe limitations of once-traditional, institutional forms of care (Goldman et al., 2020), particularly those that are underresourced (Carr et al., 2020a). The negative impact of institutional care has been well documented over recent years and includes disrupted attachment, developmental delays, and peer and caregiver violence (Carr et al., 2020b; Goldman et al., 2020; Sherr et al., 2017). This chapter will consider the trajectory of children who become "orphaned" and move into alternate and institutional care— including circumstances that precipitate the need for care, the rates and context of violence experienced while in care, and the risks when transitioning out of care. It will also review trends in institutional and family care as well as implications for policy.

WHY CHILDREN ENTER CARE

Across the globe, the reasons children become institutionalized are complex and highly contextual. There are, however, some common risk factors that precipitate children ending up in institutional care. These include factors such as poverty and HIV/AIDS (Williamson & Greenberg, 2010), COVID-19 (Hillis, 2021), neglect and substance abuse (Lipari & VanHorn, 2017), and other cultural and political dynamics such as conflict, disasters, and migration (Sherr et al., 2017). Although outside the scope of this chapter, it is important to acknowledge that significant numbers of children also navigate life without any adult care, due to circumstances including families separated by war and displacement, fleeing violence in the home or community, separation during attempts to immigrate, or trafficking (UNICEF, 2017). These children may survive on the streets or in gangs and other informal affiliative groups.

For those who end up in institutional or other alternative forms of care, myriad circumstances may precipitate that event. They may be removed from an abusive or neglectful home, or they may be orphaned by the loss of parents due to sickness or a sudden accident. In places such as the United States, substance abuse–related neglect is a primary reason for children being removed from the home (National

Center on Substance Abuse and Child Welfare [NCSACW], 2019). These numbers continue to rise, showing an increase in the prevalence of parental alcohol or drug abuse as a condition for removal from the home, which has grown by over 20% from 18.5% in 2000 to 30.9% in 2019. These rates highlight the devastating impact of the U.S. opioid crisis on the lives of children. More than 8.7 million children in the United States are believed to live in households with parents who are substance users (Lipari & VanHorn, 2017). One of every 13 children living with a substance-abusing parent experiences severe maltreatment each year (Smith et al., 2007). This can begin a toxic, intergenerational spiral as research indicates that children who experience violence are at greater risk of abusing substances themselves (World Health Organization, 2016). Although there is not space to consider every circumstance, these broad categories will provide the backdrop for why children enter care outside their family of origin.

TYPES OF CARE: CONTINUUM OF FAMILY TO INSTITUTIONAL CARE

The types of care can be considered on a continuum, ranging from family care, which involves direct placement of the child with a host family, to institutional care. Institutional care provides for the physical needs of a child but may be lacking in emotional warmth, caring attention from adults, and other nurture typically provided in the family context (Faith to Action, 2015). In the middle of the continuum are forms of institutional care that are intended to imitate aspects of family life such as smaller group homes and orphanages structured on a smaller scale.

Throughout history, societies have used this range of methods to care for children who become orphaned, and at one time orphanages seemed to offer the most feasible and economical solution for children who were not adopted into a family (McKenzie, 1999). While certainly a more humane option than living alone in the streets (Ayaya et al., 2021), the detriments of the institutionalized approach have become increasingly clear to the psychological community and all those concerned with the welfare of children (van IJzendoorn et al., 2020). Caregivers and staff, who may feel ill-equipped or stretched thin, are often focused on maintaining routines and conformity, rather than on creating an environment where individual children have the opportunity to flourish (Groark et al., 2011). In some cases, staff are ill-equipped, lacking the training to understand and adequately care for children who have experienced trauma and abuse. Their level of exhaustion frequently results in lack of patience and viewing the children as "objects" (Salomão et al., 2014). Other risk factors for poor quality of care include low staff/child ratios, limited staff autonomy, lack of specialized training, and minimal experience. Studies also reveal developmental issues for children who are separated from their families at a young age and then institutionalized (van IJzendoorn et al., 2020). In general, the risk of harm to children in institutional care, particularly those under the age of 5, is well documented (Browne, 2009; Goldman et al., 2020).

Cumulatively, these risk factors amount to what van IJzendoorn et al. (2011) termed "structural neglect," referencing the toll of an environment deficient in stable caring parent figures. For example, due to strict routines, institutions may be lacking in opportunities for free play or for intellectual stimulation through books, equipment, and outdoor play, and the child may not be able to experience celebrations, wider social interaction, and everyday experiences outside the institution (Browne, 2009). Children raised in institutions consistently perform more poorly in cognitive functioning than their peers, exhibiting cognitive delays as well as impaired social functioning (Sherr et al., 2017; Zimmerman, 2005). In summary, children in institutions are delayed in most aspects of cognitive and socioemotional development when compared to their noninstitutionalized peers (McCall & Groark, 2015). Any amount of orphanage experience is harmful, with the greatest damage experienced during the critical first years of life and increasing with the length of stay in an institution (van IJzendoorn et al., 2020). This provides a foundation for the trend away from more institutionalized forms of care, buoyed by the growing body of evidence on family-based care as providing the best outcomes for children on a number of measures. The global community of scholars, faith leaders, and others who care for the vulnerable has recognized the detriments of institutional care and has therefore shifted attention and recommendations away from institutions toward family-based models of care (Goldman et al., 2020).

NAVIGATING VIOLENCE SPACES: EXPOSURE TO VIOLENCE AND NEGLECT PRIOR TO CARE

Children in care are more vulnerable to various types of violence, including physical and sexual abuse, and their developmental trajectory is encumbered by additional layers of challenge. There are risks of violence in all types of alternative care (Sherr et al., 2017), but this risk is particularly high in institutional settings that are underresourced (Carr et al., 2020a). Sadly, children and adolescents must navigate abuse and neglect prior to care, within care, as they transition in and out of care, and with peers in care. This all occurs within systems and structures that may look for ways to profit from their care through some type of trafficking. In this regard, conceptualizing these children as polyvictims (Finkelhor et al., 2007) widens the scope of policies and interventions aimed at addressing violence at every step of their harrowing journey.

While a significant number of children experience violence after entering care, there is also evidence that many children have experienced violence prior to their transition into alternative care, either at the community or interpersonal level. Although children across the world enter care for a variety of reasons, none of them are positive—all of the circumstances that precipitate care are inherently traumatic. In the United States and United Kingdom, the majority of children and young people now enter care as a result of neglect (Font & Maguire-Jack, 2021; Rahilly & Hendry, 2014). However, there seems to be comparable rates of physical maltreatment prior to entering care (Katz et al., 2017). In a systemic review of 21 primary studies representing eight countries, Carr et al. (2020b) found that an average of 38% of children experienced some unspecified type of maltreatment prior to entering long-term care. In the United States, the majority of children in institutional care arrive with a history of traumatic experiences, including witnessing violence, physical abuse, sexual abuse, and neglect, often arriving with a previous diagnosis related to trauma (S. M. Brown et al., 2012).

Across the globe, many children in care come from families with a lower socioeconomic status, where parents feel under stress due to financial pressures and a lack of resources for child care and necessities such as shelter, food, and clothing (Browne, 2009). They also may lack access to clean water and basic health care (McGuinness & Schneider, 2007; Salomão et al., 2014). Parents under these kinds of stress with minimal resources are less able to effectively care for their children (McLoyd, 2021). In addition to potential violence within the home, many children are exposed to violence in their community prior to entering care. Some communities have seen an increase in orphans due to war and displacement (Ahmad et al., 2005; Sherr et al., 2017). Despite the case against institutions, it must be acknowledged that in some locations there are few alternatives, particularly those suffering under the impact of war, famine, and natural disasters, and orphanages may serve a critical role in survival for orphaned children (Margoob et al., 2006).

NAVIGATING VIOLENT SPACES: VIOLENCE WITHIN ALTERNATIVE CARE

Violence in Foster Care

It is clear that many children who enter institutional care have had past experiences of violence, whether that directly precipitated their shift to the institution or whether it was part of the landscape of their previous environment (Katz et al., 2017; Rahilly & Hendry, 2014). Tragically, many children then face ongoing violence in their new home or caregiving institution (Salomão et al., 2014). Occurrences of physical abuse have been widely documented in recent decades and are considered endemic in settings of institutional care (Carr et al., 2020b). In an examination of foster youth in the Midwest of the United States, for example, 30% of youth reported neglect by a foster caregiver and almost 25% reported physical abuse by a foster caregiver (Katz et al., 2017). Some populations are at higher risk for abuse, including females (Katz et al., 2017), those who are Black or American Indian/Alaskan Native (Yi et al., 2020), and LGBTQ youth of color (Robinson, 2018). Experiences of violence can lead into a vicious cycle of mistreatment and multiple placements for higher risk youth. Those who act out are more likely to be treated harshly and also to be moved to a different placement; multiple placements then lead to more negative outcomes for the child, such as mental health issues and poor physical health (Katz et al., 2017; Smith et al., 2007;

Yi et al., 2020). To best care for children, foster parents need to be supported and resourced in order to interrupt negative cycles of mistreatment in response to challenging behaviors.

Violence in Institutional Care

For children who have experienced some form of neglect and violence, entering care is an important protective factor, but one that does not remove vulnerability to ongoing abuse. Institutions such as orphanages also hold increased risks for children to suffer additional recurring violence (Salomão et al., 2014). For the approximately 8 million children residing in orphanages or residential care facilities globally (Pinheiro, 2006), there is increasing evidence that they will experience higher rates of violence than those in the general population (Sherr et al., 2017). In Southeast Asia, residential care and institutions serve as the third most common site of child sexual abuse, outranked only by the streets and commercial establishments such as brothels and clubs (Groark et al., 2011). In a recent systematic review of child abuse in long-term settings, Carr et al. (2020b) reviewed 21 primary studies that examined child abuse experiences across Canada, Ireland, the United States, Australia, the Netherlands, Germany, Austria, and Switzerland. In this analysis, reports of child abuse in long-term care showed significant ranges between samples, but overall an average of 88% experiencing unspecified child abuse, 67% experiencing sexual abuse, and 63% experiencing physical abuse. Several country-specific studies provide a snapshot of the experiences of children in care. In Vietnam, Pham et al. (2021) found the prevalence of both neglect and abuse to be significantly higher in institutionalized adolescents compared to their noninstitutionalized counterparts; however, these findings could reflect experiences prior to entering care. Similarly, in Tanzania, Hermenau et al. (2015) found that children raised in orphanages reported more types of neglect than the nonorphan matched sample. However, no differences between the types of abuse were reported between the two matched samples, indicated by high rates of child abuse for both orphaned and nonorphaned children (Hermenau et al., 2015). In another Tanzanian study, Hermenau et al. (2014) compared adverse experiences and age of entry into orphanages (birth to 4 years) compared with children who entered the orphanage as an older child (5 to 14 years). The findings indicated that early-institutionalized children reported more types of adverse experiences than later-entry children, with 89% of both samples experiencing or witnessing at least one type of abuse while in care (Hermenau et al., 2014).

While the high rates of abuse and neglect in care are troublingly high, there are mixed findings in comparing institutional care versus other forms of alternative care. Euser et al. (2014) utilized random sampling methods to examine physical abuse in adolescents across multiple forms of alternative care in the Netherlands. Overall, their data indicated a threefold increase in the risk for physical abuse for out-of-home care and the general population. In comparing types of out-of-home care (or "alternative care" by this chapter's definition), Euser et al. (2014) found that adolescents in residential care ($N = 161$) have an increased risk for physical abuse compared to adolescents in foster care ($N = 141$). Several other multicountry studies indicate more mixed evidence when comparing types of care. In a robust five-country study of over 1,000 children living in institutional care, Gray et al. (2015) found that 50.3% of the children had experienced physical or sexual abuse by the age of 13. The same study also considered over 1,000 children in family-based care. By comparison, the number was slightly higher (54.0%) for children living in family-based alternative care. This study also found that the annual incidence of physical or sexual abuse was actually significantly higher in family-based care (19%) than institutional care (13%). Similar findings in another large-scale study conducted in Western Kenya (Ayaya et al., 2021) provide comparisons between children living in institutional facilities ($N = 782$), family-based care ($N = 1,056$), and street-connected living ($N = 72$). Overall, 47% of the participants reported some type of abuse in the baseline assessment and 54% reported experiences of abuse "recently" while in their living environment. Comparing prevalence of abuse between institutional care and family-based care did not show statistically significant differences, but reported rates of physical abuse were still higher in family-based care, at 39% in institutional care versus 46% in family-based care, and sexual abuse of 14% in institutional care versus 23% in family-based care. Overall, when examining both Gray et al. (2015) and Ayaya et al. (2021), there is some evidence that family-based care does not offer sufficient protection against violence in the form of physical, sexual, or emotional abuse. Undoubtedly, there needs to be more precise research in comparing types of care, country/context variables, levels of resourcing, and caregiver qualities. As the case to deinstitutionalize care and move to more family-based care continues to grow (van IJzendoorn et al., 2020), further study is needed to monitor both the prevalence and types of violence occurring in care. While research has helped build a case against institutionalization, it is essential to collaborate across sectors to continue to refine the understanding of the elements that contribute to the best environment for children to flourish. Sweeping generalizations may have limited applicability to specific contextual settings.

NAVIGATING VIOLENCE SPACES: MULTIPLE TRANSITIONS IN AND OUT OF CARE

In addition to experiences of violence, orphaned children also experience significant disruption in key attachment relationships, with frequent transitions in caregivers (Zimmerman, 2005). When a child experiences the disruption of being uprooted from one family or setting and moving to another, they have to relearn routines, expectations, discipline styles, and perhaps most importantly whom to trust and how to attach to a caring adult (Quiroga & Hamilton-Giachritsis, 2016).

In the United States, there is concern about youth in foster care who transition through multiple home placements and mental health issues related to trauma (Engler et al., 2020). However, the challenges of multiple placements can be found in many countries. For example, a study in Malawi found that about a third of the children in care transitioned to new caretakers one to five times for a wide variety of reasons including financial circumstances, health, schooling, etc. (Zimmerman, 2005). Transitions may be due to a change in circumstances but can also be due to violence or neglect in foster homes. Youth who experience greater transition in combination with childhood violence exposure (CVE) face increased psychosocial problems (Garrido et al., 2011). While navigating one change to a new family could indicate an improved circumstance for the child in some cases, multiple transitions will more typically be associated with a negative cycle of frustration or withdrawal on the part of the child, which in turn is likely to elicit negative reactions from the caretakers, leading to additional changes in placement (Unrau et al., 2008).

After navigating years of foster care or institutional care, children often find themselves at the threshold of adulthood being "released" from formalized care, but without the skills and family support that are needed to successfully transition to adult life. This phenomenon of "aging out" is the most acute for those who have not experienced a stable family environment. Without attention to this vulnerability, this population is at high risk for trafficking or turning to illegal or maladaptive modes of survival (Zimmerman, 2005).

NAVIGATING VIOLENCE SPACES: RISK OF VIOLENCE FROM PEERS

Many children and adolescents in care experience additional abuse and bullying at the hands of peers, with rates ranging from 50% to 75% depending on the study (Mazzone et al., 2018). Children in care often witness the physical abuse of others in an institutional setting, which then in turn emboldens peer abuse and maltreatment. This is a particular risk for younger children, who are easily bullied by older youth (Khoury-Kassabri & Attar-Schwartz, 2014). A study of children's homes in England found that over half of the youth (53.5%) had experienced physical violence and 43.9% had been bullied (Gibbs & Sinclair, 2000). A study of Jewish and Arab youth in residential care found similar levels of bullying (56%). Peer-to-peer violence seems to be influenced by both individual traits and the context and culture of many institutions. In their study, Khoury-Kassabri and Attar-Schwartz (2014) found that youth self-efficacy can be a protective factor in these environments.

NAVIGATING VIOLENCE SPACES: PROFITING THROUGH TRAFFICKING

In the last decade, there is a growing amount of evidence that connects orphanages and trafficking (Brubacher et al., 2021). This was most notable in 2018 when the

Australian government recognized orphanage trafficking as a form of modern-day slavery (van Doore & Nhep, 2019). Lyneham and Facchini (2019) note that orphanages can serve as a destination for children to be further exploited or as a transit hub to route children through to other destinations. Children exploited in these schemes are often used to increase profit by increasing donations from donors, illicit adoptions, or sexual exploitations (Lyneham & Facchini, 2019). In many ways, orphanage trafficking mirrors the violence of other types of trafficking, including removal from the home under deception at an age they can recall the events, common threats of violence, and abusive forms of manipulation to keep them in care (Brubacher et al., 2021).

The connection between tourism and orphan trafficking has received increased attention in the literature (van Doore, 2016). The practice of including short term visits to orphanages during travel has been dubbed "voluntourism," a trend that has led to the unintended consequence of corrupt practices aimed at increasing the number of children in orphanages hosting tourists. Those who traffic children into orphanages manipulate the misplacedd compassion of visitors into a moneymaking scheme (Lyneham & Facchini, 2019). A danger in these settings has been the unfettered access that is often granted to visitors, without adequate protections in place to ensure the safety of the children. In some cases, adults may be permitted to take children off-site, which creates additional risks for this vulnerable population (van Doore, 2016).

CONCLUSIONS AND IMPLICATIONS

For children who end up in institutional settings through removal from the home, fleeing, or abandonment, the threat of violence exists along every step of the journey from entering into a system to aging out when they are considered an adult. While the evidence to rethink orphanages and other forms of institutional care is clearly warranted, this shift does not necessarily remove the potential for violence and harm during the child's journey through alternative care. Given the complex and polyvictimized nature of the violence in these settings, there is an urgent need for psychologists to join faith leaders, policymakers, and NGO leaders in creating a culture of peace. While family-based care is preferred, it is imperative to provide training and resources for caregivers in all settings and to develop protective measures against peer violence, trafficking, and abuse. It is also essential to continue to build our understanding of the types of violence faced by children who move through alternative care, to minimize unnecessary transitions, to build resilience, and to address socioecological factors that contribute to structural violence. In all of these areas, it is key to collaborate across sectors to work toward a world where all children have the opportunity to grow, learn, and flourish. In conclusion, a few broad recommendations for policy, research, and practice include the following:

Policy Implications

1. **It is essential to continue multisector efforts to deinstitutionalize care, ensuring movement toward quality, peaceful family-based care.** While the majority of evidence on institutional care is focused on cognitive and developmental delays (Sherr et al., 2017), there is increasing evidence that children in institutional facilities experience multiple forms of violence across multiple contexts. However, one important caveat to this recommendation is that the transition away from institutional care must be strategic in ensuring that the "replacement" care is peaceful and high-quality care. With some evidence that children experience violence across all types of alternative care (Ayaya et al., 2021; Gray et al., 2015), there should be a focus on increasing collaboration across care sectors (NGOs, faith-based groups, academic institutions, foundations, etc.), with significant attention given to the experience of children in these systems. ReThink Orphanages (www.rethinkorphanages.org) is a prime example of this type of cross-sectoral work to deinstitutionalize care; however, a more substantial focus on the impact of violence against children across all types of care would be a helpful complement to these ongoing conversations.

2. **Create a culture of child protection in orphanages and other forms of alternative care.** Where orphanages and institutional care are the norm, implement child protection policies before allowing access to foreign visitors, and limit visitors to those who meet stringent requirements such as providing meaningful training or enrichment experiences for staff and children. During the global movement to transition to family-based care, continued focus on policies and procedures to protect children will be even more important. While some countries will move proactively away from institutional care based on recommendations in the field, others will be much slower to pivot from existing models of care. In both cases, but particularly where institutional care persists in significant numbers, it will be helpful to have worldwide recommendations and ethical standards that prioritize the safety and care of children.

Research Implications

1. **Develop a more precise understanding and tracking of violence across care contexts.** The majority of evidence regarding children in alternative care is based on assessing cognitive, emotional, and developmental outcomes. Increased monitoring and research on the prevalence and impact of violence against children before, during, and after care will provide a more robust understanding of the various formats

and contexts in which children are experiencing violence. With the movement away from institutional care toward family-based care/foster care, it is essential to identify and document trends in occurrences and types of violence. For instance, does a shift in care context shift the types and intensity of violence that a child experiences?

Practice Implications

1. **Increase the focus on supporting caregivers working in underresourced care settings.** Those who care for vulnerable children in orphanages and group homes often experience stress due to the intensity of providing care for traumatized children, pressures to maintain schedules and structure, and long hours. Caregivers may lack training in child development, behavioral management techniques, and other strategies for feeling successful in working with children who may present challenging behaviors (Salomão et al., 2014). For those who provide care in these settings, communities should invest in training and professional development that allow staff to feel an increased sense of agency and self-efficacy in caring for a vulnerable population. Increasing the focus on staff development can support the goal of fostering a therapeutic milieu for children, where they receive support, care, and individual attention, rather than a functional approach that focuses on minimal standards of meeting basic needs. This training should not have a critical approach but instead focus on building capacity in staff through education and developing empathy. Violence from caregivers is more likely when there is frustration in managing children's behavior, and so developing empathy and a broader skill set in positive responses can provide alternatives to reactionary and sometimes violent responses.

2. **Continue enhancement of trauma-informed care training.** Much has been learned in recent years about the multifaceted impacts of trauma on the brain, the body, and human functioning. This knowledge needs to be carried over into professional development in caregiving settings. Caregivers who understand the dynamics of trauma in children will be better equipped to create an environment where children have the potential to follow a healthy developmental trajectory and even to flourish (Lotty et al., 2020). Knowledge about the impact of trauma and understanding characteristic ways that children may express negative experiences from the past will lead to greater empathy and support from caregivers (Purvis et al., 2007). Instead of labeling a child as "difficult" based on "bad behavior," caregiving training in understanding the effects of trauma can foster an environment where behavior is understood in the context of regulation of emotional states and lead to improved outcomes for the child (A. D. Brown et al., 2013).

3. **Educate peers in institutional facilities in nonviolent conflict resolution.** As discussed, children in care experience higher levels of peer-to-peer violence. It is important to find ways to mitigate against bullying and similar types of violence. This may include focusing on developing resilience and self-efficacy in the child, which serve as protective factors. It is also valuable to consider their socioecological context beyond their place of residence. Schools can be a location of additional violence, such as when bullying or peer violence occurs, but they can also provide a place of support, such as when a child has positive relationships with teachers. Khoury-Kassabri and Attar-Schwartz (2014) found that the child who has positive relationships with school staff experiences decreased levels of violence from peers. They recommend a consideration of ecological factors in designing policies and practices that reduce violence for this vulnerable population. Providing specific training in institutional settings in conflict-solving skills, anger management, and positive communication can contribute to efforts to minimize bullying and peer violence (Mazzone et al., 2018).

REFERENCES

Ahmad, A., Qahar, J., Siddiq, A., Majeed, A., Rasheed, J., Jabar, F., & Von Knorring, A. L. (2005). A 2-year follow-up of orphans' competence, socioemotional problems and post-traumatic stress symptoms in traditional foster care and orphanages in Iraqi Kurdistan. *Child: Care, Health and Development, 31*(2), 203–215. https://doi.org/10.1111/j.1365-2214.2004.00477.x

Ayaya, S., DeLong, A., Embleton, L., Ayuku, D., Sang, E., Hogan, J., Kamanda, A., Atwoli, L., Makori, D., Ott, M.A., Ombok, C., & Braitstein, P. (2021). Prevalence, incidence and chronicity of child abuse among orphaned, separated, and street-connected children and adolescents in western Kenya: What is the impact of care environment? *Child Abuse & Neglect, 10*, 4920. https://doi.org/10.1016/j.chiabu.2020.104920

Brown, A. D., McCauley, K., Navalta, C. P., & Saxe, G. N. (2013). Trauma systems therapy in residential settings: Improving emotion regulation and the social environment of traumatized children and youth in congregate care. *Journal of Family Violence, 28*(7), 693–703. doi:10.1007/s10896-013-9542-9

Brown, S. M., Baker, C. N., & Wilcox, P. (2012). Risking connection trauma training: A pathway toward trauma-informed care in child congregate care settings. *Psychological Trauma: Theory, Research, Practice, and Policy, 4*(5), 507–515. https://doi.org/10.1037/a0025269

Browne, K. (2009). *The risk of harm to young children in institutional care.* Save the Children Resource Center. https://resourcecentre.savethechildren.net/node/1474/pdf/1474.pdf

Brubacher, S. P., van Doore, K. E., & Powell, M. (2021). Responding to orphanage trafficking from an information gathering perspective. *Child Abuse & Neglect, 120*, 105222. https://doi.org/10.1016/j.chiabu.2021.105222

Carr, A., Duff, H., & Craddock, F. (2020a). A systematic review of reviews of the outcome of severe neglect in underresourced childcare institutions. *Trauma, Violence,
& Abuse, 21*(3), 484–497. https://doi.org/10.1177/1524838018777788

Carr, A., Duff, H., & Craddock, F. (2020b). A systematic review of the outcome of child
abuse in long-term care. *Trauma, Violence, & Abuse, 21*(4), 660–677. https://doi.
org/10.1177/1524838018789154

Desmond, C., Watt, K., Saha, A., Huang, J., & Lu, C. (2020). Prevalence and number
of children living in institutional care: Global, regional, and country estimates.
Lancet Child & Adolescent Health, 4(5), 370–377. https://doi.org/10.1016/
s2352-4642(20)30022-5

Engler, A. D., Sarpong, K. O., Van Horne, B. S., Greeley, C. S., & Keefe, R. J. (2020).
A systematic review of mental health disorders of children in foster care. *Trauma,
Violence, & Abuse, 23*(1), 255–264. https://doi.org/10.1177/1524838020941197

Euser, S., Alink, L. R., Tharner, A., van IJzendoorn, M. H., & Bakermans-Kranenburg,
M. J. (2014). Out of home placement to promote safety? The prevalence of physical
abuse in residential and foster care. *Children and Youth Services Review, 37*, 64–70.
https://doi.org/10.1016/j.childyouth.2013.12.002

Faith to Action Initiative. (2015). *A continuum of care for orphans and vulnerable
children.* https://www.faithtoaction.org/wpcontent/uploads/2015/08/Faith2Act
ion_ContinuumOfCare.pdf

Finkelhor, D., Ormrod, R. K., & Turner, H. A. (2007). Poly-victimization: A neglected
component in child victimization. *Child Abuse & Neglect, 31*(1), 7–26. https://doi.
org/10.1016/j.chiabu.2006.06.008

Font, S., & Maguire-Jack, K. (2021). The organizational context of substantiation in child
protective services cases. *Journal of Interpersonal Violence, 36*(15–16), 7414–7435.
https://doi.org/10.1177/0886260519834996

Garrido, E. F., Culhane, S. E., Petrenko, C. L. M., & Taussig, H. N. (2011). Psychosocial
consequences of caregiver transitions for maltreated youth entering foster
care: The moderating impact of community violence exposure. *American Journal of
Orthopsychiatry, 81*(3), 382–389. https://doi.org/10.1111/j.1939-0025.2011.01106.x

Gibbs, I., & Sinclair, I. (2000). Bullying, sexual harassment and happiness in residential
children's homes. *Child Abuse Review, 9*(4), 247–256. https://doi.org/10.1002/1099-
0852(200007/08)9:4<247::AID-CAR619>3.0.CO;2-Q

Goldman, P. S., Bakermans-Kranenburg, M. J., Bradford, B., Christopoulos, A., Ken,
P. L. A., Cuthbert, C., . . . Sonuga-Barke, E. J. (2020). Institutionalisation and
deinstitutionalisation of children 2: Policy and practice recommendations for
global, national, and local actors. *Lancet Child & Adolescent Health, 4*(8), 606–633.
https://doi.org/10.1016/S2352-4642(20)30060-2

Gray, C. L., Pence, B. W., Ostermann, J., Whetten, R. A., O'Donnell, K., Thielman, N. M.,
& Whetten, K. (2015). Prevalence and incidence of traumatic experiences among
orphans in institutional and family-based settings in 5 low-and middle-income
countries: A longitudinal study. *Global Health: Science and Practice, 3*(3), 395–404.
https://doi.org/10.9745/GHSP-D-15-00093

Groark, C. J., McCall, R. B., Fish, L., & Whole Child International Evaluation Team.
(2011). Characteristics of environments, caregivers, and children in three Central
American orphanages. *Infant Mental Health Journal, 32*(2), 232–250. https://doi.
org/10.1002/imhj.20292

Hermenau, K., Eggert, I., Landolt, M. A., & Hecker, T. (2015). Neglect and perceived stigmatization impact psychological distress of orphans in Tanzania. *European Journal of Psychotraumatology, 6*(1), 28617. https://doi.org/10.3402/ejpt.v6.28617

Hermenau, K., Hecker, T., Elbert, T., & Ruf-Leuschner, M. (2014). Maltreatment and mental health in institutional care—Comparing early and late institutionalized children in Tanzania. *Infant Mental Health Journal, 35*(2), 102–110. https://doi.org/10.1002/imhj.21440

Hillis, S., Mercy, J., Amobi, A., & Kress, H. (2016). Global prevalence of past-year violence against children: A systematic review and minimum estimates. *Pediatrics, 137*(3), 1–13. https://doi.org/10.1542/peds.2015-4079

Hillis, S. D., Unwin, H. J. T., Chen, Y., Cluver, L., Sherr, L., Goldman, P. S., . . . Flaxman, S. (2021). Global minimum estimates of children affected by COVID-19-associated orphanhood and deaths of caregivers: A modelling study. *The Lancet, 398*(10298), 391–402. https://doi.org/10.1016/S0140-6736(21)01253-8

Katz, C., Courtney, M., & Novotny, E. (2017). Pre-foster care maltreatment class as a predictor of maltreatment in foster care. *Child & Adolescent Social Work Journal, 34*(1), 35–49. https://doi.org/10.1007/s10560-016-0476-y

Khoury-Kassabri, M., & Attar-Schwartz, S. (2014). Adolescents' reports of physical violence by peers in residential care settings: An ecological examination. *Journal of Interpersonal Violence, 29*(4), 659–682. https://doi.org/10.1177/0886260513505208

Lipari, R. N., & Van Horn, S. L. (2017). Children living with parents who have a substance use disorder. *CBHSQ report.* https://www.samhsa.gov/data/sites/default/files/report_3223/ShortReport-3223.html

Lotty, M., Dunn-Galvin, A., & Bantry-White, E. (2020). Effectiveness of a trauma-informed care psychoeducational program for foster carers—Evaluation of the Fostering Connections Program. *Child Abuse & Neglect, 102,* 104390. https://doi.org/10.1016/j.chiabu.2020.104390

Lyneham, S., & Facchini, L. (2019). Benevolent harm: Orphanages, voluntourism and child sexual exploitation in South-East Asia. *Trends and Issues in Crime and Criminal Justice, 574,* 1–16.

Margoob, M. A., Rather, Y. H., Khan, A. Y., Singh, G. P., Malik, Y. A., Firdosi, M. M., & Ahmad, S. A. (2006). Psychiatric disorders among children living in orphanages—Experience from Kashmir. *JK-Practitioner, 13*(11), S53–S55.

Mazzone, A., Nocentini, A., & Menesini, E. (2018). Bullying and peer violence among children and adolescents in residential care settings: A review of the literature. *Aggression and Violent Behavior, 38,* 101–112. https://doi.org/10.1016/j.avb.2017.12.004

McCall, R. B., & Groark, C. J. (2015). Research on institutionalized children: Implications for international child welfare practitioners and policymakers. *International Perspectives in Psychology, 4*(2), 142–159. http://dx.doi.org/10.1037/ipp0000033

McGuinness, T. M., & Schneider, K. (2007). Poverty, child maltreatment, and foster care. *Journal of the American Psychiatric Nurses Association, 13*(5), 296–303. doi:10.1177/1078390307308421

McKenzie, R. B. (1999). *Rethinking orphanages for the 21st century.* Sage Publications. https://doi.org/10.4135/9781452232904.n1

McLoyd, V. C. (2021). Poverty, parenting, and policy: Meeting the support needs of poor parents. In H. E. Fitzgerald & B. M. Lester (Eds.), *Children of poverty* (pp. 269–303). Routledge.

National Center on Substance Abuse and Child Welfare (NCSACW). (2019). *Child welfare and alcohol and drug use statistics*. https://ncsacw.samhsa.gov/research/child-welfare-and-treatment-statistics.aspx

Pham, T. S., Qi, H., Chen, D., Chen, H., & Fan, F. (2021). Prevalences of and correlations between childhood trauma and depressive symptoms, anxiety symptoms, and suicidal behavior among institutionalized adolescents in Vietnam. *Child Abuse & Neglect, 115*, 105022. 10.1016/j.chiabu.2021.105022

Pinheiro, P. S. (2006). *World report on violence against children*. United Nations Secretary-General's Study on Violence Against Children. https://www.unicef.org/violencestudy/reports.html

Purvis, K. B., Cross, D. R., & Sunshine, W. L. (2007). *The connected child: Bring hope and healing to your adoptive family*. McGraw-Hill.

Quiroga, M. G., & Hamilton-Giachritsis, C. (2016). Attachment styles in children living in alternative care: A systematic review of the literature. *Child & Youth Care Forum, 45*(4), 625–653. https://doi.org/10.1007/s10566-015-9342-x

Rahilly, T., & Hendry, E. (2014). *Promoting the wellbeing of children in care messages from research*. National Society for the Prevention of Cruelty to Children. http://clok.uclan.ac.uk/14634/1/promoting-wellbeing-children-in-care-messages-from-research.pdf

Robinson, B. A. (2018). Child welfare systems and LGBTQ youth homelessness: Gender segregation, instability, and intersectionality. *Child Welfare, 96*(2), 29–45.

Salomão, P. R., Wegner, W., & Canabarro, S. T. (2014). Children and teenagers living in orphanages victims of violence: Dilemmas and nursing perspectives. *Northeast Network Nursing Journal, 15*(3), 391–401 10.15253/2175-6783.2014000300003

Sherr, L., Roberts, K. J., & Gandhi, N. (2017). Child violence experiences in institutionalised/orphanage care. *Psychology, Health & Medicine, 22*(Suppl. 1), 31–57. https://doi.org/10.1080/13548506.2016.1271951

Smith, D. K., Johnson, A. B., Pears, K. C., Fisher, P. A., & DeGarmo, D. S. (2007). Child maltreatment and foster care: Unpacking the effects of prenatal and postnatal parental substance use. *Child Maltreatment, 12*(2), 150–160. https://doi.org/10.1177/1077559507300129

UNICEF. (2017, September). *Harrowing journeys*. https://data.unicef.org/resources/harrowing-journeys/

UNICEF. (2015). *Orphans*. https://www.unicef.org/media/orphans

United Nations. (2019). *Promotion and protection of the rights of children*. https://undocs.org/A/74/395

Unrau, Y. A., Seita, J. R., & Putney, K. S. (2008). Former foster youth remember multiple placement moves: A journey of loss and hope. *Children and Youth Services Review, 30*(11), 1256–1266. https://doi.org/10.1016/j.childyouth.2008.03.010

van Doore, K. E. (2016). Paper orphans: Exploring child trafficking for the purpose of orphanages. *International Journal of Children's Rights, 24*(2), 378–407. https://doi.org/10.1163/15718182-02402006

van Doore, K., & Nhep, R. (2019). Orphanage trafficking, modern slavery and the Australian response. *Griffith Journal of Law & Human Dignity, 7*(2), 114–138.

van IJzendoorn, M. H., Bakermans-Kranenburg, M. J., Duschinsky, R., Fox, N. A., Goldman, P. S., Gunnar, M. R., . . . Sonuga-Barke, E. J. (2020). Institutionalisation and deinstitutionalisation of children 1: A systematic and integrative review of evidence regarding effects on development. *Lancet Psychiatry, 7*(8), 703–720. https://doi.org/10.1016/S2215-0366(19)30399-2

van IJzendoorn, M. H., Palacios, J., Sonuga-Barke, E. J., Gunnar, M. R., Vorria, P., McCall, R. B., . . . Juffer, F. (2011). I. Children in institutional care: Delayed development and resilience. *Monographs of the Society for Research in Child Development, 76*(4), 8–30. https://doi.org/10.1111/j.1540-5834.2011.00626.x

Williamson, J., & Greenberg, A. (2010). *Families, not orphanages.* Better Care Network.

World Health Organization. (2016). *INSPIRE: Seven strategies for ending violence against children.*

Yi, Y., Edwards, F. R., & Wildeman, C. (2020). Cumulative prevalence of confirmed maltreatment and foster care placement for US children by race/ethnicity, 2011–2016. *American Journal of Public Health, 110*(5), 704–709. https://doi.org/10.2105/AJPH.2019.305554

Zimmerman, B. (2005). Orphan living situations in Malawi: A comparison of orphanages and foster homes. *Review of Policy Research, 22,* 881–917. https://doi.org/10.1111/j.1541-1338.2005.00180.x

10

A Holistic Approach to Understanding the Sexual Exploitation and Abuse of Girls

Direct and Structural Violence in Two Urban Slums in Mombasa, Kenya

MICHAEL G. WESSELLS, KATHLEEN KOSTELNY, AND KEN ONDORO ■

A major impediment to cultures of peace is pervasive violence against children (VAC), defined under international law as people under 18 years of age. The fact that nearly half of children worldwide experience violence in a particular year (Hillis et al., 2016) should evoke strong global concern and corrective action. Of particular concern is the sexual exploitation and abuse against children, which is defined as any actual or attempted abuse of a position of vulnerability, differential power, or trust, for sexual purposes, including, but not limited to, threatening or profiting monetarily, socially or politically from the sexual exploitation of another, while sexual abuse is defined as the actual or threatened physical intrusion of a sexual nature, whether by force or under unequal or coercive conditions (World Health Organization [WHO], 2017 b, p. 4). For expository purposes, we will use the term *sexual violence against children* to refer to all forms of sexual exploitation as well as the sexual abuse of children.

Though sexual violence against children is widespread globally, it is underreported for many reasons, including fear, shame, and stigma (Murray et al., 2014; UNICEF, 2014). In most societies, girls rather than boys are the main victims, although in many conflict settings, sexual violence against boys and men may also be widespread (Human Rights Watch, 2020). UNICEF (2020) estimates that worldwide, approximately 1 in 10 females under the age of 20 have been sexually abused, with the first perpetrator of sexual abuse usually being someone they know, such as a peer, school staff, relative, family acquaintance, or community member. Although this chapter focuses on girls, it is not meant to diminish the importance of sexual violence against boys or children with gender nonconforming identities.

To address sexual violence against girls, it is essential to develop an adequate understanding of the causes of sexual violence, with attention to diverse cultures and contexts. Since adult analyses of causes may not accurately reflect the understandings of children, it is of critical importance to focus on the lived experience of girls in a particular context. Thus, this chapter focuses on the contexts and causes of sexual violence against girls in urban slums in Mombasa, Kenya. Sexual violence against girls in slums is of interest because globally, people live increasingly in crowded, urban environments. The extreme poverty, deprivation, and weakening of social controls that are visible in many slums may combine to increase risk for sexual violence against girls (Ernst et al., 2013).

This chapter will briefly review the nature and impact of sexual violence against girls using a social-ecological theory (Bronfenbrenner, 1979) that emphasizes the importance of sexual violence at different levels (e.g., family, peers, community, and societal levels) and the interactions across levels (Sabri et al., 2013). The brief literature review will attend to both global literature and studies from sub-Saharan Africa. Next, it presents the situation of girls in two urban slums in the Mombasa, Kenya, area from the perspective of girls and young women (13 to 25 years of age). Using a systems approach that interweaves the insights of peace psychology and feminist theory, the chapter then analyzes sexual violence against girls in terms of the dynamic interaction between structural violence and direct violence. It concludes with a reflection on the need to expand current efforts to end violence against children by addressing further the interactions between structural and direct violence.

THE SOCIAL ECOLOGIES AND IMPACT OF SEXUAL VIOLENCE AGAINST GIRLS

An example of the nature, varieties, and pervasiveness of sexual violence against girls can be illustrated by considering how sexual violence occurs across children's different social environments in sub-Saharan African countries. At the household level, girls may be subjected to inappropriate touching, display, fondling, forced sexual acts, or rape (Lalor, 2004). Sexual violence may be committed against girls by family members, such as a father who sexually abuses his daughter. The COVID-19 pandemic, which necessitated long periods of lockdown and isolation at home, is believed to have enabled an increase in sexual violence against girls inside their own homes (Mlambo-Ngcuka, 2020). To meet basic needs, girls may also be exploited by having to trade sex for money or other items with someone in their household (Leach et al., 2003).

At school, girls may be abused by peers, teachers, and school staff through inappropriate touching, display, or fondling, or by forced sexual acts, including rape (International Women's Human Rights Clinic, 2018). At the community level, girls may be subjected to rape by intimate partners or strangers, sexual abuse by older men and community authority figures, practices such as forced early marriage, sexual exploitation via transactional sex, and exposure to violent pornography, among others (Wessells et al., 2014).

At the societal level, girls may be affected by social norms of female genital mutilation/cutting (FGM/C) (Mpinga et al., 2016) or pervasive problems of sexual trafficking (Deshpande et al., 2013), sexual abuse of girls inside armed forces or groups (Wessells, 2006), sexual abuse of girls living in institutions or juvenile detention (Pinheiro, 2006), online sexual abuse and exploitation (Ligiero et al., 2019), and rape of girls as an act of war (Card, 1996), among others (Pinheiro, 2006). Globally, an estimated 35% of girls and women experience physical or sexual violence in their lifetimes (WHO, 2017a).

Importantly, these forms of violence frequently do not occur in isolation but in a context in which other types of physical and psychological violence co-occur (Finkelhor et al., 2007). The interactions between different kinds of violence may significantly worsen girls' health, including their mental health and psychosocial well-being. Worldwide, girls frequently witness physical and sexual violence in their homes as part of intimate partner violence (Mootz et al., 2019; Tenkorang & Owusu, 2018). As a result, sexual violence may become normalized in girls' childhood experience.

Experiencing sexual violence can have a powerful, lifelong impact on girls (Finkelhor, 1979; Trickett et al., 2011). The mental health impact may include disorders such as posttraumatic stress disorder, continuous stress disorder, depression, and anxiety disorders (Murray et al., 2014). Survivors may develop HIV or other sexually transmitted infections, unwanted pregnancy, or reproductive health problems such as pain, damage, or dysfunction (Grose et al., 2021). These disorders create an enormous burden of distress, which may be amplified by the stigma, discrimination, and social isolation that usually accompany them (Murray et al., 2014). Evidence also indicates that early exposure to violence, including sexual violence, can impair subsequent cognitive development (Jouriles et al., 2008) and reduce success in education (Schnurr & Lohman, 2013). Child survivors of violence, including sexual violence, can sustain damaged health and well-being lifelong (Choi et al., 2019; Felitti et al., 1998).

No less profound are the psychosocial effects of sexual violence. Girl survivors of sexual violence are frequently stigmatized and socially isolated, and they may be blamed for what had happened to them. As a means of coping with their situation, girl survivors may engage in risky behavior such as substance abuse (WHO, 2020). Seen in some Muslim societies as having dishonored their families, girl survivors may be shamed and blamed, and even subjected to honor killings (Dayan, 2021).

The strong, diverse, multilevel effects of sexual violence on girls underscore the need for systemic approaches, and particularly for steps to prevent sexual violence from occurring. With this in mind, we present a brief case study that highlights issues of sexual violence against girls in two urban slums in Mombasa.

SEXUAL VIOLENCE AGAINST GIRLS IN TWO URBAN SLUMS IN MOMBASA

This case study is derived from a larger, rapid ethnographic study that was conducted in two slum areas (designated as informal settlements by the Kenyan government) in the Mombasa district (now designated as a county) in 2012 as a foundation for subsequent action research. The larger study's aim was to learn about local views of childhood, harms to children as identified by different subgroups (women, men, young women, young men, teenage girls, teenage boys, and young girls and young boys), pathways of response to those harms, and sources of prevention for children (Kostelny et al., 2013). This brief case study focuses specifically on the context and practices surrounding sexual violence as perceived and experienced by teenage girls and young women. It should be noted that the focus group and in-depth interviews were used to learn about harms to children in the community in general, and they did not include specific questions about sexual abuse. Furthermore, questions were asked about children in the community in general, and not about personal experiences, in order to avoid opening wounds from their previous experiences.

In the county of Mombasa, two of the largest slums are Bangladesh (with eight distinct subareas) and Tudor Moroto (with three distinct subareas), with a population of approximately 20,000 and 15,000 people, respectively. These slums were viewed by local stakeholders as typical of urban slums in the area. Residents live in overcrowded conditions and lack basic services such as running water, electricity, paved roads, and government health services. One subarea from each of the two areas was selected, partly on the basis of security, as the study population after consultation with local stakeholders about the characteristics of the subareas. The two subareas, which had a population of approximately 8,000, were judged to be comparable in size, mode of living, socioeconomic status, ethnicity, issues of children's vulnerability, access to resources such as hospitals and schools, and external child protection supports such as nongovernmental organizations and government child protection services.

The research team included both national and international researchers. The national team consisted of five Kenyan researchers who were divided into two teams, each of which worked in one of the slums and was guided by an experienced ethnographer who served as team leader. Two international researchers oversaw the data collection, had responsibility for the technical aspects of the research, and were responsible for data analysis.

A total of eight focus group discussions (FGD) with 78 teenage girls (aged 13 to 17) and young women (aged 18 to 25) were conducted. Two Kenyan researchers (one interviewer and one notetaker) facilitated each focus group discussion, which included 8 to 12 participants and lasted approximately 90 to 120 minutes.

The discussions focused on identifying what participants saw as the most serious harms to children other than poverty and health problems and then identifying and ranking the three most serious harms.

Additionally, 19 in-depth interviews, approximately 60 minutes in duration, were conducted individually with teenage girls and young women. The interviews also aimed to identify the most serious harms to girls and boys yet were conducted in a contextual, flexible manner that took into account the participants' gender, situation and social position, and interests and willingness to discuss particular topics. The interviews were open-ended in that they were not strictly scripted, and probing questions were used to follow the interests of the participants. The interviews and focus group discussions were conducted in Kiswahili, or for youth, Sheng (a combination of Kiswahili, English, and other languages).

Two international researchers analyzed the data using a grounded methodology (Charmaz, 2004). Before, during, and after the analysis, they consulted with the team leaders to check the appropriateness of particular categorizations, obtain additional information, and explore the interactions among and causes of particular issues. The triangulation of data was a key part of this search for consistent categories and patterns.

In group discussions and in-depth individual interviews, teenage girls and young women in both of the areas overwhelmingly identified various forms of sexual exploitation and abuse as the most serious harms to girls in their communities. In these discussions, girls and young women consistently raised and explored themes related to unequal power relations, rape, family members as perpetrators, transactional sex, prostitution, the sale of alcohol as a contributing factor, and hotspots for sexual violence. Although these are discussed separately, strong connections existed between them, as discussed later in the chapter.

Power Relations

Men in positions of authority such as teachers, community police, and village elders reportedly used their power to sexually exploit girls. In schools, teachers sexually abused girls during tutoring sessions and demanded sex in exchange for promoting girls to the next grade.

> Respondent 1: *That's why we don't want tuition* [after-school tutoring] *because teachers tell us to stay in school up to eight o'clock in the night, and then they come at that time and start touching you on the thighs.*
>
> Respondent 2: *And some do bad things to girls at that time.* (Teenage girls, group discussion, Bangladesh)

Men's position of power and their willingness to abuse that power figured prominently in regard to each of the problems discussed next.

Family Members as Perpetrators

Girls also identified family members—especially uncles, fathers, and stepfathers—as sexually abusing and exploiting girls. In addition to using terms such as *rape*, girls also spoke of "a father making his daughter a wife" when the mother was away from home and of having to sleep with fathers, stepfathers, or uncles in exchange for school fees or supplies.

> *When your mother has gone for a journey and you are left with your sisters and brothers, the father will come and force you to sleep with him. It is normally the stepfather, or even the father.* (Teenage girl, group discussion, Tudor Moroto)

> *When your mother dies and then you are taken to stay with your uncle, the uncle will now be the person who buys you everything, including clothes and uniforms for going to school. Then after some time, the uncle comes to you and tells you that you have to sleep with him for him to buy you a pen, and if you don't, he tells you that he won't buy you a pen. So he keeps on sleeping with you until you get pregnant.* (Teenage girl, group discussion, Tudor Moroto)

Rape

Rape occurred in both areas by nonrelatives as well as by family members. Nonrelatives included strangers but also members of the community, including single mothers' boyfriends, community police, and village elders. Young children were reported to be easily "cheated" (lured) by men in the area who offered them food and then afterward were taken into the men's homes and raped. Girls who worked as domestic help were raped by the men they worked for.

> *Aaaah! As early as 6 years the child has already slept with men. It is not all, but sometimes a child may be raped. They are many* [cases of rape]. *They happen.* (Teenage girl, group discussion, Tudor Moroto)

Transactional Sex

Transactional sex has been defined as extramarital, noncommercial sexual relationships involving the exchange of sex for material support or other benefits (Wamoyi et al., 2019). Transactional sex was widespread due to high levels of deprivation and inability to meet basic needs such as food. Teenage girls and young women reported that girls had sex with men in order to obtain school supplies and sanitary pads.

When the girl gets her period the first time and your mother cannot buy for her
the pad, she goes and has sex with someone so that she can get money to buy the
"Always" pads. (Teenage girl, group discussion, Tudor Moroto)

Prostitution

Girls also engaged in prostitution, which was reportedly widespread. Prostitution was closely
tied to transactional sex as most girls engaged in prostitution to get money for basic needs.

Prostitution is very common here in Bangladesh and is a very big harm to chil-
dren and also is a cause to other harms to children. Prostitution here does not
choose age. Be it 10 years or whichever age, prostitution is widespread. (Young
woman, group discussion, Bangladesh)

We do it [prostitution] to get money. We don't have money. It's the only part-
time job and it is a lot (of work) with small tokens. But when you get someone
who is willing, you go to do it for a short time and make money. So when they
come, to hell, you sleep with him. We do this to help our parents, siblings, and
also our children. (Teenage girl, group discussion, Tudor Moroto)

Teenage girls and young women also reported that some parents were complicit
in the girls' prostitution. Such parents not only failed to provide essential items for
their daughters but also told the girls to go out and earn money, with awareness
that prostitution was the girls' only means of earning money. Typically, when the
girls brought money back home, the parents would not ask how they got it.

Sale of Alcohol

In both areas, the main source of income for many women who were heads
of household was selling locally brewed alcohol such as palm wine from their
homes. Sexual abuse occurred frequently in the context of selling alcohol. Some
mothers used their daughters to attract customers by having them stand in front
of the home. Later men would become drunk and fondle the girls, and even rape
them. Mothers did little to stop the abuse out of fear of losing their customers and
livelihood. As one head teacher reported:

There are some girls here who tell us things like "my mother was selling chang'aa
[local brew] and then a drunk man came and took me behind there and put his
thing inside" so when I hear that I get sad. Many children are sexually abused.
(In-depth interview, teacher, Tudor Moroto)

In some cases, parents were clearly exploitative, and even looked for men for their
daughters to have sex with.

Other mothers force their children to sleep with a man so they look for you a man. It is those mothers who are selling alcohol so the men come to the house and takes you then pays the mother. Another man comes sleeps with you then gives your mother some money. (Teenage girl, group discussion, Tudor Moroto)

Hotspots Where Sexual Violence Occurs

Participants identified particular contexts such as disco clubs as places where sexual violence against girls was especially widespread. In Tudor Moroto, teenage girls and young women went to disco clubs and engaged in prostitution or consensual sex with men, which often led to early pregnancy and dropping out of school.

There are girls who go to the disco at night and they meet men there, have sex with them, and then they get pregnant and drop out of school. (Teenage girl, group discussion, Tudor Moroto)

Especially dangerous hotspots were *disco matangas*—fundraisers that help the family of the deceased raise money to cover the burial costs and that feature music, dancing, and the sale of alcohol. People saw *disco matanga* as a site at which rape and also consensual sex occurred frequently, contributing to HIV/AIDS, early pregnancy, and children being out of school.

Disco matanga is another issue. When someone dies here in Bangladesh, instead of people mourning, people are so excited they are going to attend the disco thing. This is where most children are exposed to various harm like raping, pregnancy, alcohol and so on. (Young woman, group discussion, Bangladesh)

Collectively, these findings indicate that sexual violence against girls in the two slums was widespread, variegated, and damaging to the girls' well-being and warrants concerted action, particularly around prevention. Still, it would be a mistake to conclude that the girls were severely traumatized and unable to cope with and navigate a very challenging environment. As observed in subsequent action research, the girls and their communities exhibited remarkable agency and resilience as they collectively organized themselves and worked to reduce early sex (Kostelny et al., 2020).

THE INTERPLAY OF STRUCTURAL AND DIRECT VIOLENCE

To build cultures of peace, it is essential to end sexual violence against children. Since effective prevention of sexual violence requires an understanding of the causes, it is vital to develop a holistic analysis of the causes of sexual violence against girls. Following important lines of work in peace psychology, feminist psychology, and gender-based violence, this section calls for attention to the importance of structural determinants of sexual violence and their systemic interaction with direct forms of sexual violence.

Structural Violence, Cultural Violence, and Patriarchy

Galtung (1969), the peace researcher who coined the term *structural violence*, defined it as harm caused by unequal social arrangements and institutions, noting that there may not be any person who directly harms another person in the structure. Galtung and many other peace psychologists (e.g., Christie et al., 2008; Mazurana & McKay, 2001; Pilisuk, 2001; Pilisuk & Rountree, 2015; Winter & Layton, 2001) agree that structural violence reflects conditions of social injustice and inequalities that are embedded in social, economic, political, religious, and cultural institutions. Because structural violence can seem to be "normal" and exists on a mass scale, it can be challenging to change. Although this section focuses on patriarchy, it is important to note that patriarchy interacts with diverse forms of structural violence (Hunnicutt, 2009) such as poverty, racism, and discrimination against people who have nondominant sexual orientations.

Also relevant is cultural violence, which may be thought of as cultural narratives that support or justify violence (Christie & Wessells, 2008). According to Galtung (1990), culture violence refers to "those aspects of culture, the symbolic sphere of our existence—exemplified by religion and ideology, language and art . . . that can be used to justify or legitimate direct or structural violence" (p. 291). With respect to ecological perspectives on sexual violence against girls, cultural violence may also be thought of as gendered, symbolic representations at different ecological levels (e.g., individual, family, peers, community, and societal) that privilege men over women and that may give men a sense of sexual entitlement and also rationalizations of violence in forms such as "she really wanted it."

Globally, patriarchy is one of the most widespread and entrenched forms of structural violence, one that causes extensive harm to girls and women. Patriarchy is a social system of male domination that subjugates women in social, political, economic, religious, and cultural institutions, norms, values, and practices (Brownmiller, 1975; Reardon, 1985). Patriarchy is theorized not as a homogeneous construct but as a driver of ongoing gender disparities that are manifest at different levels; are shaped by historic, sociopolitical, and cultural factors; and contribute to inequities in the power and status of men and women (see Hunnicutt, 2009). Worldwide, women constitute 39% of the workforce but receive an hourly pay 12% less than men. Further, women hold only 27% of managerial positions (United Nations, 2019). Although women are half the global population, they comprise only 24.3% of the members of national parliaments, and female heads of state remain rare (World Economic Forum, 2018). Similar patterns are visible in Kenya (Maseno & Kilonzo, 2011), which has never had a female president.

Patriarchy is also a key enabler of sexual violence and other violence against women (Brownmiller, 1975; Dworkin, 1976; Hunnicutt, 2009; Jones, 2000) in that norms and ideologies of patriarchy afford men a sense of power and entitlement over women, including in sexual interaction. Men may feel that it is their entitlement or right to rape or otherwise impose themselves sexually on women (Jewkes et al., 2011). They may also feel that forced sex is acceptable in particular circumstances such as being married. Similarly, men may feel entitled to control women's sexuality and bodies through practices such as FGM/C (Monagan, 2010). This is not to imply that all men in patriarchal societies are rapists or proponents of FGM/C but to indicate that there are institutionalized, structural forces that influence men in this direction. That they influence women's decisions too is seen in the fact that in some sub-Saharan African societies, women have become the keepers and key enablers of practices such as FGM/C. Girls' and women's learning and internalization of subjugated, sexually instrumentalized roles is a core element of patriarchal systems.

The influence of patriarchy, which is one among multiple causes of sexual violence globally, is visible in numerous respects in the sexual violence against children in Kenya. The widespread rape of girls, whether at the hands of teachers or by men at *disco matangas*, is undergirded by norms and ideologies of male power over women. These norms and ideologies assume (incorrectly) that men are entitled to dominate and take women as they please. In the purchase of alcohol from women's homes in the slums too, men felt entitled to sexually abuse girls in the women's households. Also, structural violence in the form of abject poverty likely contributed to the women's decisions to allow such abuse in their homes. As these examples illustrate, ideologies of male power and entitlement can hide the horror of rape and sexual abuse, normalize it, and even make it seem natural and legitimate.

The ideology of male supremacy and power helps to create an environment ripe for the sexual exploitation of girls through transactional sex (Williams et al., 2012). Locally, men and girls may adhere to a norm of reciprocity wherein a man gives a girl something (food, transportation, money for sanitary pads, etc.) and the girl is expected to give something in return (Wamoyi et al., 2019). This perceived norm of reciprocity, however, is only the proximal source of the social exchange. Undergirding the reciprocity are the ideologies and norms that afford men power over women and girls—sexually and physically as well as psychologically—and that make it seem legitimate to require sex as payment.

Patriarchy frequently exerts powerful influence in the family, where men are seen as the heads of the household, whereas women are infantilized and subjugated into secondary, support roles (Namy et al., 2017). With men seen as "kings" of their households, it can seem natural for men to demand sex from their wives even when the wives do not want it. It can also seem natural for fathers, stepfathers, or uncles to "take" sex from girls in the household, as was evident in this case study. Seen through the lens of extreme patriarchal beliefs, such sexual abuse of girls is an extension of men's dominance over women and an assertion of the primacy of men's needs.

As this analysis implies, violence against children is closely interconnected with violence against women (Carlson et al., 2020; Namy et al., 2017; Rubenstein et al.,

2020). Carlson et al. (2020) estimate that violence against children and intimate partner violence overlap by as much as one-third in many settings. In addition, both forms of violence have similar, overlapping risk factors such as everyday stress levels, alcohol and drug use, economic factors, and weakened social support systems (Bermudez et al., 2019; Rubenstein et al., 2020). In both, patriarchal norms exert a strong but often hidden influence.

Although this discussion has emphasized how structural violence influences direct violence such as sexual violence against children, it is essential to recognize that the causal pathway is not linear but circular. Circular causation is probably most visible in regard to intimate partner violence, which typically involves violence by a man toward a woman or girl with whom he has a relationship. Because patriarchy confers on men a sense of total power over women, a man who has traditional beliefs about masculinity may feel challenged, or even undermined and humiliated, by real or perceived disobedience by his female partner (Hunnicutt, 2009). The disobedience is seen as a transgression that is answerable by violence, which may be an expression of anger and frustration but is also instrumental in "keeping the woman in line." When men use violence against women or girls in this manner, it serves to restore what men regard as the natural balance of power, thereby strengthening the structural violence. In this web of circular causation, the structural violence and the direct violence against women and girls are mutually reinforcing. This dynamic likely makes it harder to disrupt and even end cycles of violence against women and girls.

Implications for Action

A key implication of this analysis is that efforts to reduce or end sexual violence against children in such forms as rape, partner abuse, or transactional sex require a systemic, long-term approach. For example, legal punishments against perpetrators who rape girls at *disco matangas* are necessary and highly important. Yet they will likely not be sufficient to achieve the longer term reduction of rape against girls that is needed. After all, if patriarchal beliefs about men's power over women and entitlement to sex remain strong, it is likely that rising generations of boys will be socialized in a manner that puts them at risk of becoming perpetrators. Similarly, if men having sex with girl prostitutes is seen as normal and as men's entitlement, the practice of prostitution with girls will likely continue.

What is needed, then, is a holistic approach to reducing or ending sexual violence against girls that systematically addresses both structural and direct forms of violence and their interaction. Thus far, this kind of holistic approach is quite rare. In fact, the main initiative, notably the global Partnership to End Violence Against Children, focuses overwhelmingly on direct violence (Wessells & Kostelny, 2021). This is likely due in part to the significant increase in the complexity of addressing violence against children through changing structural violence (Christie, in press; Dawes, in press). Structural violence such as patriarchy is very challenging to change because it is deeply entrenched in most societies, and men in power have the will, influence, and resources to resist change. Also, if it is challenging to change individual attitudes, beliefs, and behavior, it is far more challenging to transform ideologies that affect masses of people, are interwoven with masculine identity, and create the veneer of normalcy. Deep social change in power relations is likely measured in decades, whereas efforts to address a particular form of abuse such as sexual harassment could have more immediate effects.

These complexities, however, are no excuse for inaction. As shown by the global MeToo movement, it is possible to create deep change on a mass level and to challenge systems of entrenched male power. Further, there are a variety of programs and initiatives in different countries—including Kenya—that enjoy some success in helping to relax the grip of male dominance and reduce sexual violence against girls (e.g., Abramsky et al., 2014; Baiocchi et al., 2017; Ellsberg et al., 2015). Our challenge now is to build on these foundations, helping to establish gender equity and respect for all people that are core parts of a culture of peace.

REFERENCES

Abramsky, T., Devries, K., Kiss, L., Nakuti, J., Kyegombe, N., Starmann, E., Cundill, B., Francisco, L., Kaye, D., Musuya, T., Michau, L., & Watts, C. (2014). Findings from the SASA! Study: A cluster randomized controlled trial to assess the impact of a community mobilization intervention to prevent violence against women and reduce HIV risk in Kampala, Uganda. *BMC Medicine, 12*(1), 122. https://doi.org/10.1186/s12916-014-0122-5

Baiocchi, M., Omondi, B., Langat, N., Boothroyd, D. B., Sinclair, J., Pavia, L., Mulinge, M., Githua, O., Golden, N. H., & Sarnquist, C. (2017). A behavior-based intervention that prevents sexual assault: The results of a matched-pairs, cluster-randomized study in Nairobi, Kenya. *Prevention Science, 18*(7), 818–827. https://doi.org/10.1007/s11121-016-0701-0

Bermudez, L. G., Stark, L., Bennouna, C., Jensen, C., Potts, A., Kaloga, I. F., Tilus, R., Buteau, J. E., Marsh, M., Hoover, A., & Williams, M. L. (2019). Converging drivers of interpersonal violence: Findings from a qualitative study in post-hurricane Haiti. *Child Abuse & Neglect, 89*, 178–191. https://doi.org/10.1016/j.chiabu.2019.01.003

Bronfenbrenner, U. (1979). *The ecology of human development: Experiments by nature and design.* Harvard University Press. https://doi.org/10.1126/science.207.4431.634

Brownmiller, S. (1975). *Against our will: Men, women, and rape.* Simon & Schuster. https://doi.org/10.1177/001112877702300415

Card, C. (1996). Rape as a weapon of war. *Hypatia, 11*(4), 5–18. https://doi.org/10.1111/j.1527-2001.1996.tb01031.x

Carlson, C., Namy, S., Norcini Pala, A., Wainberg, M. L., Michau, L., Nakuti, J., Knight, L., Allen, E., Ikenberg, C., Naker, D., & Devries, K. (2020). Violence against children and intimate partner violence against women: Overlap and common contributing factors among caregiver-adolescent dyads. *BMC Public Health, 20*(1), 124. https://doi.org/10.1186/s12889-019-8115-0

Charmaz, K. (2004). Grounded theory. In S. Nagy Hesse-Biber & P. Leavy (Eds.), *Approaches to qualitative research* (pp. 496–521). Oxford University Press.

Choi, J.-K., Wang, D., & Jackson, A. P. (2019). Adverse experiences in early childhood and their longitudinal impact on later behavioral problems of children living in poverty. *Child Abuse & Neglect, 98*, 104181. https://doi.org/10.1016/j.chiabu.2019.104181

Christie, D. (2021). The moonshot and ending violence against children. *Peace & Conflict: Journal of Peace Psychology, 27*(1), 39–41. https://doi.org/10.1037/pac0000514

Christie, D., Tint, B., Wagner, R., & Winter, D. (2008). Peace psychology for a peaceful world. *American Psychologist, 63*(6), 540–552. https://doi.org/10.1037/0003-066X.63.6.540

Christie, D. J., & Wessells, M. (2008). Social psychology of violence. In L. Kurtz (Ed.), *Encyclopedia of violence, peace, and conflict* (2nd ed., pp. 1955–1963). Elsevier.

Dawes, A. (2021). Commentary on Wessells and Kostelny: Understanding and ending violence against children: A holistic approach. *Peace & Conflict: Journal of Peace Psychology, 27*(1), 28–32. https://doi.org/10.1037/pac0000511

Dayan H. (2021). Female Honor Killing: The Role of Low Socio-Economic Status and Rapid Modernization. *Journal of Interpersonal Violence, 36*(19-20), NP10393–NP10410. doi:10.1177/0886260519872984. Epub 2019 Sep 15. PMID: 31524058.

Deshpande, N. A., & Nour, N. M. (2013). Sex trafficking of women and girls. *Reviews in Obstetrics and Gynecology, 6*(1), 22–27.

Dworkin, A. (1976). *Our blood: Prophecies and discourses on sexual politics*. Perigee Books. https://doi.org/10.12681/grsr.470

Ellsberg, M., Arango, D. J., Morton, M., Gennari, F., Kiplesund, S., Contreras, M., & Watts, C. (2015). Prevention of violence against women and girls: What does the evidence say? *The Lancet, 385*(9977), 1555–1566. https://doi.org/10.1016/S0140-6736(14)61703-7

Ernst, K. C., Phillips, B. S., & Duncan, B. D. (2013). Slums are not places for children to live. *Advances in Pediatrics, 60*, 53–87. https://doi.org/10.1016/j.yapd.2013.04.005

Felitti, V., Anda, R., Nordenberg, D., Williamson, D. F., Spitz, A. M., Edwards, V., Koss, M. P., & Marks, J. S. (1998). Relationship of childhood abuse and household dysfunction to many of the leading causes of death in adults. The Adverse Childhood Experiences (ACE) Study. *American Journal of Preventive Medicine, 14*(4), 245–258. https://doi.org/10.1016/S0749-3797(98)00017-8

Finkelhor, D. (1979). *Sexually victimized children*. Free Press. https://doi.org/10.1093/sw/25.6.504-a

Finkelhor, D., Ormrod, R. K., & Turner, H. A. (2007). Poly-victimization: A neglected component in child victimization. *Child Abuse & Neglect, 31*, 7–26. https://doi.org/10.1016/j.chiabu.2006.06.008

Galtung, J. (1969). Violence, peace and peace research. *Journal of Peace Research, 6*(3), 167–191. https://doi.org/10.1177/002234336900600301

Galtung, J. (1990). Cultural violence. *Journal of Peace Research, 27*(3), 291–305. https://doi.org/10.1177/0022343390027003005

Grose, G., Chen, J. S., Roof, K. A., Rachel, S., & Yount, K. M. (2021). Sexual and reproductive health outcomes of violence against women and girls in lower-income countries: Review of reviews. *Journal of Sex Research, 58*(1), 1–20. https://doi.org/10.1080/00224499.2019.1707466

Hillis, S., Mercy, J., Amobi, A., & Kress, H. (2016). Global prevalence of past-year vi-
    olence against children: A systematic review and minimum estimates. *Pediatrics,*
    137(3), e20154079. https://doi.org/10.1542/peds.2015-4079

Human Rights Watch. (2020). *"They treated us in monstrous ways": Sexual violence*
    against men, boys, and transgender women in the Syrian conflict. https://www.hrw.
    org/report/2020/07/29/they-treated-us-monstrous-ways/sexual-violence-against-
    men-boys-and-transgender

Hunnicutt, G. (2009). Varieties of patriarchy and violence against women: Resurrecting
    "patriarchy" as a theoretical tool. *Violence Against Women, 15,* 553–573. https://doi.
    org/10.1177/1077801208331246

International Women's Human Rights Clinic. (2018). Girls' education under attack: The
    detrimental impact of sexual abuse by teachers on school girls' human rights in
    Kenya. *Georgetown Journal of International Law, 49,* 241–416.

Jewkes, R., Sikweyiya, Y., Morrell, R., & Dunkle, K. (2011). Gender inequitable mas-
    culinity and sexual entitlement in rape perpetration South Africa: Findings of a
    cross-sectional study. *PLoS One, 6*(12), e29590. https://doi.org/10.1371/journal.
    pone.0029590

Jones, S. (2000). *Feminist theory and Christian theology: Cartographies of grace.*
    Fortress Press.

Jouriles, E. N., Brown, A. S., McDonald, R., Rosenfield, D., Leahy, M. M., & Silver, C. (2008).
    Intimate partner violence and preschoolers' explicit memory functioning. *Journal of*
    Family Psychology, 22, 420–428. https://doi.org/10.1037/0893-3200.22.3.420

Kostelny, K., Ondoro, K., & Wessells, M. (2020). *Community action to end "early sex"*
    in Kenya: Endline report on community-led child protection. Report for the Oak
    Foundation. Child Resilience Alliance. https://gdc.unicef.org/resource/community-
    action-end-early-sex-kenya-endline-report-community-led-child-protection

Kostelny, K., Wessells, M., Chabeda-Barthe, J., & Ondoro, K. (2013). *Learning about chil-*
    dren in urban slums: A rapid ethnographic study in two urban slums in Mombasa of
    community-based child protection mechanisms and their linkage with the Kenyan na-
    tional child protection system. Interagency Learning Initiative on Community-Based
    Child Protection Mechanisms and Child Protection Systems. https://resourcecen
    tre.savethechildren.net/document/learning-about-children-urban-slums-rapid-
    ethnographic-study-two-urban-slums-mombasa/

Lalor, K. (2004). Child sexual abuse in sub-Saharan Africa: A literature review. *Child*
    Abuse & Neglect, 28(4), 439–460. https://doi.org/10.1016/j.chiabu.2003.07.005

Leach, F., Fiscian, V., Kadzamira, E., Lemani, E., & Machakanja, P. (2003). *An investi-*
    gative study of the abuse of girls in African schools. Department for International
    Development.   https://www.researchgate.net/publication/23508573_An_
    Investigative_Study_of_the_Abuse_of_Girls_in_African_Schools

Ligiero, D., Hart, C., Fulu, E., Thomas, A., & Radford, L. (2019). *What works to prevent*
    sexual violence against children: Evidence review. Together for Girls. https://www.
    togetherforgirls.org/svsolutions/

Maseno, L., & Kilonzo, S. M. (2011). Engendering development: Demystifying patri-
    archy and its effects on women in rural Kenya. *International Journal of Sociology and*
    Anthropology, 3(2), 45–55. http://www.academicjournals.org/ijsa

Mazurana, D., & McKay, S. (2001). Women, girls, and structural violence: A global analysis. In D. Christie, R. V. Wagner, & D. A. Winter (Eds.), *Peace, conflict, and violence: Peace psychology for the 21st century* (pp. 130–138). Prentice-Hall.

Mlambo-Ngcuka, P. (2020). *Violence against women and girls: The shadow pandemic.* UN Women. https://www.unwomen.org/en/news/stories/2020/4/statement-ed-phumzile-violence-against-women-during-pandemic

Monagan, S. L. (2010). Patriarchy: Perpetuating the practice of female genital mutilation. *Journal of Alternative Perspectives in the Social Sciences, 2*(1), 160–181. https://www.researchgate.net/publication/44199729_Patriarchy_Perpetuating_the_Practice_of_Female_Genital_Mutilation

Mootz, J. J., Stark, L., Meyer, E., Asgar, K., Roa, A. H., & Potts, A. (2019). Examining intersections between violence against women and violence against children: Perspectives of adolescents and adults in displaced Colombian communities. *Conflict and Health, 13,* 25. https://doi.org/10.1186/s13031-019-0200-6

Mpinga, E. K., Macias, A., Hasselgard-Rowe, J., Kandala, N., Felicien, T. K., Verloo, H., Bukonda, N. K. Z., & Chstonay, P. (2016). Female genital mutilation: A systematic review of research on its economic and social impacts across four decades. *Global Health Action, 9:1,* https://doi.org/10.3402/gha.v9.31489

Murray, L. K., Nguyen, A., & Cohen, J. A. (2014). Child sexual abuse. *Child and Adolescent Psychiatric Clinics of North America, 23*(2), 321–337. https://doi.org/10.1016/j.chc.2014.01.003

Namy, S., Carlson, C., O'Hara, K., Nakuti, J., Bukuluki, P., Lwanyaaga, J., Namakula, S., Nanyunja, B., Wainberg, M. L., Naker, D., & Michau, L. (2017). Towards a feminist understanding of intersecting violence against women and children in the family. *Social Science & Medicine, 184,* 40–48. https://doi.org/10.1016/j.socscimed.2017.04.042

Pilisuk, M. (2001). Globalism and structural violence. In D. Christie, R. V. Wagner, & D. A. Winter (Eds.), *Peace, conflict, and violence: Peace psychology for the 21st century* (pp. 149–157). Prentice-Hall.

Pilisuk, M., & Rountree, J. A. (2015). *The hidden structure of violence: Who benefits from global violence and war.* New York Press.

Pinheiro, P. S. (2006). *World report on violence against children.* United Nations. https://violenceagainstchildren.un.org/content/un-study-violence-against-children

Reardon, B. A. (1985). *Sexism and the war system.* Teachers College Press.

Rubenstein, B., Lu, L. Z. N., MacFarlane, M., & Stark, L. (2020). Predictors of interpersonal violence in the household in humanitarian settings: A systematic review. *Trauma, Violence, & Abuse, 21*(1), 31–44. https://doi.org/10.1177/1524838017738724

Sabri, B., Hong, J. S., Campbell, J. C., & Cho, H. (2013). Understanding children and adolescents' victimizations at multiple levels: An ecological review of the literature. *Journal of Social Service Research, 39*(3), 322–334. https://doi.org/10.1080/01488376.2013.769835

Schnurr, M. P., & Lohman, B. J. (2013). Longitudinal impact of toddlers' exposure to domestic violence. *Journal of Aggression Maltreatment and Trauma, 22,* 1015–1031. https://doi.org/10.1080/10926771.2013.834019

Tenkorang, E. Y., & Owusu, A. Y. (2018). A life course understanding of domestic and intimate partner violence in Ghana. *Child Abuse & Neglect, 79*, 384–394. https://doi.org/10.1016/j.chiabu.2018.02.027

Trickett, P. K., Noll, J. G., & Putnam, F. W. (2011). The impact of sexual abuse on female development: Lessons from a multigenerational, longitudinal research study. *Developmental Psychopathology, 23*(2), 453–476. https://doi.org/10.1017/S0954579411000174

UN Women. (2021). *Facts and figures: Ending violence against women.* https://www.unwomen.org/en/what-we-do/ending-violence-against-women/facts-and-figures

UNICEF. (2014). *Hidden in plain sight: A statistical analysis of violence against children.* https://www.unicef.org/documents/hidden-plain-sight-statistical-analysis-violence-against-children

UNICEF. (2020). *Sexual violence against children.* https://www.unicef.org/protection/sexual-violence-against-children#:~text=Sexual violence results in severe, social isolation and psychological trauma

United Nations. (2019). *The sustainable development goals report 2019.* https://unstats.un.org/sdgs/report/2019/

Wamoyi, J., Heise, L., Meiksin, R., Kyegombe, N., Nyato, D., & Buller, A. M. (2019). Is transactional sex exploitative? A social norms perspective, with implications for interventions with adolescent girls and young women in Tanzania. *PLoS One, 14*(4), e0214366. https://doi.org/10.1371/journal.pone.0214366

Wessells, M. G. (2006). *Child soldiers: From violence to protection.* Harvard University Press.

Wessells, M. G., & Kostelny, K. (2021). Understanding and ending violence against children: A holistic approach. *Peace & Conflict: Journal of Peace Psychology, 27*(1), 3–23. https://doi.org/10.1037/pac0000475

Wessells, M., Kostelny, K., & Ondoro, K. (2014). *A grounded view of community-based child protection mechanisms and their linkage with the wider child protection system in three urban and rural areas of Kenya: Summary and integrated analysis.* Save the Children. https://resourcecentre.savethechildren.net/document/grounded-view-community-based-child-protection-mechanisms-and-their-linkages-wider-child/

Williams, T. P., Binagwaho, A., & Betancourt, T. S. (2012). Transactional sex as a form of child sexual exploitation and abuse in Rwanda: Implications for child security and protection. *Child Abuse & Neglect, 36*(4), 354–361. https://doi.org/10.1016/j.chiabu.2011.11.006

Winter, D. D., & Layton, D. C. (2001). Structural violence: Introduction. In D. Christie, R. V. Wagner, & D. A. Winter (Eds.), *Peace, conflict, and violence: Peace psychology for the 21st century* (pp. 99–101). Prentice-Hall.

World Economic Forum. (2018). *The global gender gap report 2018.* https://www.weforum.org/reports/the-global-gender-gap-report-2018

World Health Organization (WHO). (2017a). *Violence against women.* https://www.who.int/en/news-room/fact-sheets/detail/violence-against-women

World Health Organization (WHO). (2017b). *WHO sexual exploitation and abuse prevention and response.* https://www.who.int/publications/m/item/who-sexual-exploitation-and-abuse-prevention-and-response

World Health Organization (WHO). (2020). *Violence against children.* htpps://www.who.int/news-room/fact-sheets/detail/violence-against-children

Practice and Policy to Redress Violence Against Children

11

Teacher Violence

*A Global Perspective on Prevalence, Contributing
Factors, Consequences, and Prevention*

TOBIAS HECKER, FAUSTINE BWIRE MASATH,
JOSEPH SSENYONGA, MABULA NKUBA, AND
KATHARIN HERMENAU ■

The ratification of the United Nations' Convention on the Rights of the Child and the adoption of the Sustainable Development Goals document the international community's efforts to protect all children from any form of violence in their environment. Children and adolescents spend much of their time at school in an environment that should be safe, where they are supposed to be protected against violence, nurtured, mentored, and educated. However, in many countries, schools are still places where children experience and/or witness violence. Teachers' use of violence against students at school is highly prevalent and a global concern that persists to date (Gershoff, 2017; Pinheiro, 2006). Teacher violence is defined as physical or emotional violence that is intended to cause physical or emotional pain to the students (Gershoff, 2017). These violent disciplinary measures may include beatings with the use of hands or objects (such as a cane or stick); shaking, pinching, or kicking students; forcing them to adopt painful bodily postures for a long time; and threats, name-calling, labeling, and public humiliation (Gershoff, 2017; Ssenyonga et al., 2019; Straus, 2010). Overall, the magnitude of violence against children is much better known for physical violence; however, for emotional violence the prevalence remains largely unknown (Scharpf, Kızıltepe, Kirika, & Hecker, 2022).

When using violence, teachers are typically motivated by the desire to assert their authority, instill respect and obedience, deter future misbehavior, and ensure that children meet their expectations (Antonowicz, 2010; Feinstein & Mwahombela, 2010; Naker, 2005). Consequently, the anticipated outcomes, including behavioral control and the belief that utilization of violence is time efficient, is effective, and leads to immediate compliance (Dubanoski et al., 1983; Mweru, 2010; Naong, 2007), maintain the use of violence (Heekes et al., 2020; Merrill et al., 2017). Violent disciplinary approaches are particularly prevalent in societies where violence is a widely accepted part of child upbringing (Gershoff, 2017).

GLOBAL PREVALENCE OF TEACHER VIOLENCE

Gershoff (2017) used data from 63 countries (including 29 countries that legally prohibit school corporal punishment) from Africa, the Americas and the Caribbean, Asia and the Pacific, Europe, and the Middle East to estimate the global prevalence of school corporal punishment. Prevalence rates were over 90% in 9 countries and between 70% and 80% in 11 countries, with higher prevalence in low- and middle-income countries. Likewise, data from a systematic review (Heekes et al., 2020) indicated that the prevalence of school violence varied across the regions. Children in Africa and Central America reported the highest lifetime prevalence of school violence (greater than 70%). More than 60% of the students experienced violence at school in the Eastern Mediterranean and Southeast Asia in the past year (Heekes et al., 2020).

Countries in Africa account for 39% of all countries that lawfully allow physical punishment in the educational context. Not surprisingly, they have a particularly high prevalence of school violence. For instance, over 70% of the students experienced school violence in their lifetime, and around 40% experienced school violence in the past week (Gershoff, 2017; Heekes et al., 2020). The consensus between studies based on both teachers' and schoolchildren's reports is that violence is very common in educational settings. For instance, 96% of pupils in Tanzanian primary schools were subjected to a minimum of one act of violence by teachers in the past month (Hecker et al., 2021). Also, 96% of teachers reported having used violence against pupils in the last month (Masath et al., 2021). Likewise, between 60% and 69% of pupils experienced hits with a hand or stick, and over 75% of the pupils witnessed teachers beating other pupils with a hand or stick for various reasons including poor academic performance and perceived misbehavior. Additionally, pupils also experienced emotional violence including insults (54%) and threats of being beaten (46%). Moreover, over 80% of secondary school students experienced violence, while more than 75% of the teachers admitted to having used violence against students at the secondary school level (Feinstein & Mwahombela, 2010; Hecker et al., 2018; Stein et al., 2019; Yaghambe & Tshabangu, 2013). Notably, prevalence rates were also high in countries where physical violence in schools is unlawful, suggesting that a legal ban may be a necessary but not sufficient condition for ending the use of violence against students. For example, 13% to 97% of students experienced violence by teachers in schools in countries with legislation in place that prohibits school corporal punishment (Gershoff, 2017; Heekes et al., 2020). In Uganda, over 90% of primary school pupils experienced physical violence by teachers in their lifetime, and about 52% in the past week.

The situation is similar in other African countries. For instance, student reports from South Africa found that 60% of teachers used violence at secondary schools (Ncontsa & Shumba, 2013). About 80% of children in primary school aged 8 to 17 years from Ghana, Kenya, and Mozambique experienced school violence in the past year (Parkes & Heslop, 2011). Moreover, in the previous week in Ethiopian primary schools, 12% of pupils aged 8 and 38% of pupils aged 15 years experienced violence, and 49% aged 8 and 76% aged 15 years witnessed teachers using violence to discipline schoolmates (Ogando Portela & Pells, 2015). Furthermore, pupils experienced physical violence (74% to 87%) and emotional violence (15% to 26%) in Nigerian schools (Smiley et al., 2021).

FACTORS CONTRIBUTING TO TEACHER VIOLENCE

In this chapter, we review the most important factors that have been identified as potential drivers of violent disciplining of children by teachers. About 732 million school-going children aged 6 to 7 years reside in countries where they are not legally protected from experiencing violence in the educational setting (Global Initiative to End All Corporal Punishment of Children, 2021; UNICEF, 2017, 2018). This is reflected in some countries' legal frameworks, in which the law permits the use of violent discipline in all settings. For instance, in Tanzania, despite the restrictions provided by the Law of the Child Act (United Republic of Tanzania, 2009) protecting children from all forms of violence and maltreatment, the Corporal Punishment Guideline (United Republic of Tanzania, 2002) and the Education Act of 1978 still permit the use of violence in schools.

The role of societal norms, attitudes, and beliefs regarding the use of violent discipline is also reported in research and seems to play a significant role. Among the common societal norms associated with the use of violence against children is that violent discipline teaches respect and compliance (Naker, 2005) and has positive effects on students' academic performance (Feinstein & Mwahombela, 2010; Semali & Vumilia, 2016; Tafa, 2002). With positive attitudes approving the application of violence for these ends, the use of violent discipline increases (Hecker et al., 2018). The use of violent discipline can also stem from religious beliefs (Ellison & Bradshaw, 2009). Parents as well as teachers may believe that religious verses or commands, such as the Bible or the Koran, promote violent discipline. Together, personal beliefs and positive attitudes toward the use of violent discipline may be further intensified by a lack of knowledge of nonviolent discipline strategies (Hecker et al., 2018) and the negligence of the negative consequences associated with it (Naker & Sekitoleko, 2009).

In societies in which children grow up witnessing and experiencing violence at home and school, social acceptance of violence against children is higher and the use of violence against children is more likely. This is supported by the cycle-of-violence hypothesis stating that exposure to (physical) violence in childhood increases the likelihood to be (physically) violent in adulthood (Widom, 1989). For instance, childhood maltreatment and intimate partner violence were shown to predict aggressive parenting behavior in Uganda (Saile et al., 2014). Parents with experiences of corporal punishment in their own childhood were at higher risk to use violence against their children (Ellonen et al., 2017). Similarly, for teachers in the United States, the use of violent discipline was high for those with past experiences of aversive disciplinary strategies (S. W. Lee & Weis, 1992). This is similar to findings in Tanzania and Uganda in which teachers' own experiences of violence were significantly associated with their use of violence against their students (Devries et al., 2014; Masath et al., 2021).

In addition, stress affects an individual's use of violent behavior. Teaching is considered one of the most stressful professions (Kyriacou, 2001), and the working conditions at schools are linked to teachers' use of violence. This association is particularly relevant in low- and middle-income countries where working conditions are characterized by extremely large classes, few teaching resources, and long working hours for low payment (Hecker et al., 2018). In such circumstances, teachers who report higher perceived stress levels resort more often to violent classroom management strategies than opting for nonviolent strategies that seem dysfunctional, time-consuming, and hard to implement to them (Hecker et al., 2018). In other studies, higher levels of stress were found to increase the potential for aggression (Knezevic et al., 2011). Unsurprisingly, teachers working under more demanding conditions were more likely to respond to students' misbehavior with violent punishment (Mweru, 2010).

Similarly, stress is influenced by different sociodemographic characteristics. For instance, the family economic conditions and income highly predict psychological aggression, physical aggression, and neglect (S. J. Lee et al., 2009). Similarly, lower socioeconomic status and high demands intensify teachers' stress, which in turn influences their use of violent discipline (Hecker et al., 2018; Nkuba, Hermenau, & Hecker, 2018). Furthermore, multiple studies indicated that teaching experience (Louw et al., 2011), educational background (Luk et al., 2010), weekly working hours (Otero-López et al., 2008), and class size (Bümen, 2010) significantly correlated with stress, which in turn increased the level of violence against students (Butchart et al., 2006; Hecker et al., 2018). In addition, the association between teachers' stress and their violent disciplining was influenced by their attitudes toward violent discipline (Ssenyonga et al., 2019).

CONSEQUENCES OF TEACHER VIOLENCE

The common consequences of teacher violence range from injury to mental health problems to reduced psychosocial and academic functioning (Gershoff, 2017). Global studies indicate that the outcomes for children have been far more negative than teachers or parents believe; teachers and parents often report positive outcomes like immediate compliance (Gershoff, 2017; Global Initiative to End All Corporal Punishment of Children, 2019). However, available global research findings point to negative consequences of teacher violence (Gershoff, 2017; Kiziltepe et al., 2020; Nkuba, Hermenau, Goessmann, & Hecker, 2018a; Portela &

Pells, 2015). For example, Gershoff et al. (2015) insist that teacher violence is not only ineffective in reducing students' misbehavior but also puts children at risk for physical injury as well as negative unintended consequences such as increased behavioral problems.

Several studies show that pupils experience a range of physical injuries associated with teacher violence, including muscle damage, cuts, and broken bones (e.g., Block, 2013). Even several cases of students' deaths due to teacher violence have been reported in Malaysia, South Africa, Nigeria, India, Sri Lanka, and the Philippines (Chianu, 2000; Covell & Becker, 2011; Morrow & Singh, 2014). However, in most cases the results of teacher violence are psychological and interpersonal, including feelings of humiliation among pupils when punished in front of the class (Feinstein & Mwahombela, 2010). Teachers' use of violence is associated with children's embarrassment and feelings of revenge (Donald & Clacherty, 2005). Teacher violence negatively affects the quality of the student-teacher relationship (Gershoff, 2017; Mulvaney & Mebert, 2007). As a result, teacher violence has also been associated with higher rates of school dropout, leading to a great economic loss to societies in which teacher violence is highly prevalent (Pereznieto et al., 2010).

Furthermore, schoolchildren who have experienced violence by their teachers or other caregivers are at a higher risk of developing a range of psychopathology, including posttraumatic stress disorder, internalizing problems (such as anxiety and depression), and externalizing problems (which include aggression and conduct problems; De Bellis et al., 2013; Hecker et al., 2016; Lansford et al., 2014; Palosaari et al., 2013). For example, exposure to teacher violence was linked to mental health problems, rule breaking, and delinquent behavior (Kabiru et al., 2010, 2014; Kiziltepe et al., 2020; Nkuba et al., 2019; Nkuba, Hermenau, Goessmann, & Hecker, 2018a). School corporal punishment by teachers was also highly associated with depression, greater hostility, and pessimism in schoolchildren (Csorba et al., 2001; Naz et al., 2011). In Tanzania, teacher violence has also been associated with a range of antisocial behaviors and externalizing problems such as theft, truancy, cigarette consumption, aggression, fighting, and alcohol and drug use (Yaghambe & Tshabangu, 2013).

Likewise, exposure to teacher violence has been associated with lower levels of academic achievement that may persist into adulthood (Boden et al., 2007; Mills et al., 2019), impairing the socioeconomic well-being and livelihoods of individuals, families, communities, and societies (Currie & Widom, 2010). Low socioeconomic status and poverty, in turn, increase the risk of child maltreatment both in families and in schools (van IJzendoorn et al., 2020), implying a vicious cycle. A study by Baker-Henningham et al. (2009) in Jamaica reported that pupils who were exposed to different forms of violence scored lower grades in mathematics and language skills. Moreover, a study from Nigeria indicates that children who attended schools where teachers used violent disciplinary methods in managing misbehaviors had a lower receptive vocabulary, inferior executive functioning, and less intrinsic motivation than children who attended schools where teachers did not use violence (Talwar et al., 2011). A study by UNICEF

(Portela & Pells, 2015) in Ethiopia, India, Peru, and Vietnam reported that the use of violent discipline by teachers at school predicted learning difficulties and dislike of school among children.

Despite these findings, most studies used correlational designs that do not allow any conclusions to be drawn about causality. Furthermore, children usually experience violence in different settings (e.g., at home and at school). Only a few studies considered the experience of violence in other settings, which, however, can also influence the possible outcome parameters. Nevertheless, as already stated in the United Nations' Convention on the Rights of the Child, violence against children in schools is a violation of children's rights, and the positive effects of violence that reportedly teachers expect could not even be shown in correlative studies. This alone suggests that nonviolent methods may be more useful and, more importantly, less likely to cause harm.

PREVENTION OF TEACHER VIOLENCE

The high prevalence of violence by teachers, the social acceptance of it, and the negative consequences of violence observed across various cultural settings, communities, and societies call for joint global and national efforts targeting multiple levels, including legislative reforms prohibiting and sanctioning the use of violence at schools, public education and awareness programs about the negative consequences of violence, the strengthening of structures for reporting the use of violence at schools, and the provision of alternative nonviolent discipline methods to educators. Global and continental initiatives such as goal 16.2 of the United Nations' Sustainable Development Goals 2030 and the African Charter on the Rights and Welfare of the Child may pave the way for legal and political changes. However, the stably high prevalence of teacher violence, especially in countries with legal regulations, clearly shows that neither legal restrictions nor awareness campaigns are sufficient to substantially reduce teacher violence. Interventions for teachers in schools are needed that both challenge social norms and teach practical nonviolent methods.

More and more countries are working to change these practices and to follow guidelines that emphasize the need to promote children's rights. Difficult working conditions, group pressure, and a lack of alternative strategies may lead to the common use of physical and emotional violence. Besides the negative consequences for the healthy development and the school performance of children, many teachers report that they feel stressed by using physical and/or emotional violence, that it does not solve problems in the long term, and that the relationship with students suffers due to its use. However, they lack alternative strategies and feel overwhelmed with how to start a change (Kaltenbach et al., 2018; Nkuba, Hermenau, Goessmann, & Hecker, 2018b). School-based interventions provide a possible promising solution to reduce teacher violence. Yet very few school--based interventions that aim to prevent violence by teachers have been rigorously evaluated. This underlines the need to develop, implement, and test intervention approaches that aim to reduce violent disciplining and provide teachers with nonviolent and effective action alternatives.

One such example is the Good Schools Toolkit, a complex behavioral intervention designed by the Ugandan not-for-profit organization Raising Voices. The intervention content is based on behavioral change techniques that have been shown to be effective in a variety of fields. Drawing on the transtheoretical model (Prochaska & Velicer, 1997), the toolkit uses a six-step process to engage teachers, students, administration, and parents to reflect on how they can promote quality of education in their school. The intervention support materials consist of booklets, posters, and facilitation guides for 60 different activities (e.g., setting school-wide goals, developing action plans with specific dates for deliverables, encouraging empathy by facilitating reflection on experiences of violence, providing new knowledge on alternative nonviolent discipline, and providing opportunities to practice new behavioral skills). These activities are related to creating a better learning environment, respecting each other, understanding power relationships, using nonviolent discipline, and improving teaching techniques (Devries et al., 2013). Schools are encouraged to self-monitor their progress according to their action plans. Reinforcement of new information and ideas, feedback on progress, and modeling of new techniques and behaviors is provided by visits from the Raising Voices team, and within the school by "protagonists" to their peers as they gain new knowledge and skills. Children participate actively and form committees and groups related to different activities. Schools reward successful achievement of their goals and action plan deliverables by creating celebrations. Social support for behavioral change is also created because the intervention engages multiple groups within a school (teachers, administration, students, and parents) to change ideas and attitudes. The Good Schools Toolkit has been evaluated in a cluster-randomized controlled trial (CRCT) at primary school level in one district in Uganda. Results showed a reduction in violence experienced by pupils in the past week (Devries et al., 2015).

Another example intervention is the Irie Classroom Toolbox, a universal, early childhood, violence prevention teacher training program designed for use in low- and middle-income countries that aims to reduce violence against children by teachers and prevent the early development of antisocial behavior in children aged 3 to 8 years. The toolbox also aims to improve the quality of the classroom environment and to promote child mental health, self-regulation, and prosocial skills. It consists of four modules: (a) creating an emotionally supportive classroom environment, (b) preventing and managing child behavior problems, (c) teaching social and emotional skills, and (d) individual and class-wide behavior planning. Intervention materials for teachers include (a) a tools book that provides simple guidelines on how to use each strategy and the underpinning rationale; (b) an activity book of songs, games, activities, lesson plans, and behavior planning forms; (c) three sets of picture cards to help teachers teach classroom rules, friendship skills, and understanding emotions; and (d) a problem-solving stories book consisting of 14 pictorial stories depicting common classroom problems that children encounter in school and strategies that children can use to overcome them (e.g., how to work together as a team and how to share class-room materials). The Irie Classroom Toolbox has been evaluated in CRCTs at pre- and primary school level in Jamaica. Results showed fewer counts of violence against children by teachers in the intervention schools compared with control schools at postintervention and 1-year follow-up (Baker-Henningham et al., 2019, 2021).

INTERACTION COMPETENCIES WITH CHILDREN—FOR TEACHERS (ICC-T)

Interventions targeting teacher violence at school should primarily work with teachers as the ones who use violence, focusing on both changing teachers' attitudes toward violence and providing them with alternative nonviolent discipline strategies. In addition, interventions should be applicable to a wide target group of teachers and students (i.e., different educational stages). Furthermore, interventions need to be brief, require relatively few resources, and emphasize transfer of intervention content to teachers' daily work to support dissemination in low-income settings (Scharpf et al., 2021). The intervention Interaction Competencies with Children—for Teachers (ICC-T) meets all these criteria (Kaltenbach et al., 2018; Nkuba, Hermenau, Goessmann, & Hecker, 2018b). Based on attachment, behavioral, and social learning theories, ICC-T aims to reduce the use of physical and emotional violence by teachers against students and to improve teacher-student interactions by enabling teachers to learn and practice essential interaction competencies with children. ICC-T is particularly suitable in societies in which violence by teachers is socially accepted and offers a basic introduction to essential interaction competencies in working with children. This introduction focuses mainly on nonviolent interaction strategies and encouraging warm, sensitive, and reliable teacher-child relationships. ICC-T was developed to prevent physical and emotional violence and to improve the teacher-student relationship. The key principles that guide the implementation of ICC-T are a participatory approach, an atmosphere of trust, confidentiality, and a practical orientation. The ICC-T intervention components include sessions on (a) teacher-student interaction, (b) maltreatment prevention, (c) effective discipline strategies, (d) identifying and supporting burdened students, and (e) using ICC-T components in everyday school life. The ICC-T training workshop occurs over 5½ half days.

ICC-T is designed to address the extent to which teachers lack alternative strategies and feel overwhelmed about how to start a change. ICC-T can help to fill this gap with knowledge, food for thought, reflections, exchange with colleagues, alternative interaction strategies, and practices that are based on teachers' experiences in everyday life. ICC-T aims to motivate attitudinal change, equip participants with knowledge and competencies, and give time and space to practice the skills being taught.

Structure and Application of ICC-T

With the help of a manual and some preparation, suitable professionals (e.g., teachers, psychologists) can train teachers successfully in ICC-T. A careful preparation phase is necessary to be able to answer possible questions from participants and to guide discussions on controversial topics. It is helpful if the facilitators are familiar with the everyday work-life of teachers. Five core components form the content of the ICC-T training (more information is provided in Table 11.1):

1. *Teacher-student interaction*: These sessions aim to foster empathy and understanding of the students' behavior, to raise awareness of the responsibility of teachers as a role model, to create a good learning atmosphere, and to improve teacher-student interactions. *(three sessions)*

2. *Violence prevention*: This component focuses on raising awareness of the negative consequences of corporal and emotional punishment for children's well-being. Participants reflect on their own experiences of corporal and emotional punishment as a child and their use of harsh punishment as a teacher, with intention to connect their own experiences and feelings to their current behavior and its consequences. *(five sessions)*

3. *Non-violent strategies*: This component introduces different behavior modification strategies to provide teachers with additional tools when maintaining and reinforcing good behavior and ways to effectively change or improve misbehavior. The aim is to reduce the use of emotional and physical violence by learning nonviolent alternatives' and reducing feelings of helplessness that teachers may sometimes experience. These sessions also provide participants with opportunities to practice these skills. *(eight sessions)*

4. *Supporting burdened students*: Sessions on identifying and supporting students facing a variety of challenging circumstances aim to raise awareness for common emotional and behavioral problems that may occur due to the stress related to navigating difficult life challenges. Guidance is also provided in effectively identifying and supporting such students within the school setting. *(two sessions)*

5. *Implementation*: It is one thing to know something, and another thing altogether to put it into practice! These sessions focus on ways the ICC-T components can be used in everyday school life. Daily use of the ICC-T skills is essential for the sustainability and effectiveness of the ICC-T approach. In addition, support strategies to improve the working atmosphere for teachers are discussed, including collegial supervision and collaboration with school counselors and parents. *(two sessions)*

In the 5½ days of the ICC-T training workshop, each full day has four sessions. There are breaks scheduled between sessions, which give time for participants to

Table 11.1. OVERVIEW OF INTERACTION COMPETENCIES WITH CHILDREN—TEACHER
VERSION (ICC-T)

Component	Content[a]
Teacher-student interaction	• Communication skills • Instructions and expectations • Teachers as role models and implications • Structure, rituals, and rules in the classroom
Maltreatment prevention	• Discussion of common discipline strategies in the relevant country • Consequences of emotional and physical violence • Self-reflection about participants' own experiences of corporal and emotional punishment as a child • Self-reflection about participants' own experiences when using corporal and emotional punishment • Debunking myths about the effectiveness of corporal punishment • Practicing alternative strategies to use instead of corporal or emotional punishment (connected with the *effective discipline strategies* component)
Effective discipline strategies	• Introduction of nonviolent strategies to maintain good behavior (e.g., reinforcement systems, contracts, etc.) • Introduction of strategies to change misbehavior (e.g., time-out, privilege removal, etc.) • Practicing the introduced strategies in role plays
Identifying and supporting burdened students	• Externalizing problems: aggressive and oppositional behavior • Internalizing problems: depression and social withdrawal • Discussion about specific cases • Elaboration of strategies to support burdened children
Implementation	• Putting the new knowledge into action in everyday school life • Collaborating with other teachers and school counselors • Organizing a peer consulting system

[a] The components include presentations by the trainers, discussions (in the full group and in small groups), record of the results, role plays, and repetitions. This table is an adapted version of the table in Kaltenbach et al. (2018).

refresh. Games and songs are used to engage the group in the morning and after the lunch break. These games and songs are also opportunities to practice possible activities that can be used with children and in the classroom. The training workshop starts with a welcome session, which includes an introduction and a pre-evaluation. The workshop ends with a session on evaluation and a time for participants to process and reflect on what they have learned throughout the training. The evaluation is recommended to monitor the uptake and feasibility of the training. Participants also receive the ICC-T certificate of participation for their work during the training.

Different methods are used to make the workshop practical and foster the active involvement of the participants, including theoretical inputs, discussions, small group works, self-reflection, and practice in role plays. In many sessions different methods are combined. For example, a session may start with a short theoretical didactic, which is then followed by small group work. The results of the small group work may then be discussed by the full group.

Feasibility and Effectiveness of ICC-T

Research demonstrating the feasibility and effectiveness of the ICC-T approach is underway, with several studies completed, additional work underway, and several studies planned in the future. In this section, we will summarize the findings to date and provide an overview of current studies as well as an outlook on planned studies.

Prior to any large-scale trials, the team first tested the feasibility of ICC-T in a pilot study. This study was conducted in one selected primary school in Tanzania (Kaltenbach et al., 2018). Participating teachers were highly motivated to be involved in the intervention and reported a high level of satisfaction with ICC-T as well as good integration of ICC-T content into their daily work. Expanding the evaluation, researchers next tested both the feasibility and the effectiveness of ICC-T using a CRCT in secondary schools in Tanzania (Nkuba, Hermenau, Goessmann, & Hecker, 2018b). The CRCT showed similar findings as the initial pilot study regarding the feasibility of ICC-T and provided initial evidence of the program's effectiveness. Teachers who participated in ICC-T intervention showed less positive attitudes toward the use of violent discipline compared to teachers from control schools. Furthermore, the use of violent discipline by teachers (self-reported and reported by students) was reduced in the intervention schools compared to the control schools (Nkuba, Hermenau, Goessmann, & Hecker, 2018b). The authors have conducted a similar CRCT in secondary schools in Uganda (Ssenyonga et al., 2022). Researchers found similar results as in Tanzania, demonstrating the feasibility of the intervention in Ugandan schools. Also, the data regarding effectiveness replicated the findings in Tanzania (Nkuba, Hermenau, Goessmann, & Hecker, 2018b). The same applies to a CRCT recently conducted in primary schools in Tanzania (Masath et al., 2020). In summary, ICC-T has shown convincing effects on both attitude and behavior change in several controlled studies. However, the studies to date have been limited to East Africa. Moreover, the longer term effects are still insufficiently studied. Therefore, ICC-T is currently implemented in several countries beyond East Africa, such as Ghana and Haiti, and larger multisite CRCTs test the effectiveness and the sustainability of effects (Scharpf et al., 2021). Further studies are being conducted and planned in the coming years that may demonstrate the feasibility and effectiveness of ICC-T in different cultural and societal contexts (Lopez Garcia et al., 2022).

SUMMARY AND OUTLOOK

The chapter shows that teacher violence is still highly prevalent around the world. Both the legal framework and the social acceptance of violence as a disciplinary method contribute to this. In addition, stressful working conditions and perceived stress also play a role. Violence against children, whether at school or at home, is associated with a whole range of negative consequences. Nevertheless, the findings on factors that contribute to violence against children as well as its consequences are mainly based on cross-sectional studies, which only allow conclusions about correlations. The few longitudinal studies are also of little help here. Experimental studies are needed to investigate causal mechanisms. Experimental field studies would be ideal for this because they reflect the reality of children's lives and therefore have high ecological validity (Toth & Cicchetti, 2013). However, the use of randomized controlled trials (RCT) in the study of violence against children is problematic, primarily due to ethical considerations (Gershoff et al., 2018; Hoeffler, 2017). However, RCTs implementing violence-reducing interventions offer an alternative as they allow for manipulation at the level of violence between the intervention and control group. Intervention studies are thus helpful not only because they test interventions that protect children from teacher violence but also because they help to better understand causal mechanisms in terms of contributing factors and consequences.

The high prevalence, social acceptance, and negative consequences of teacher violence call for global efforts to tackle this issue. Global and continental initiatives such as the United Nations' Sustainable Development Goals 2030 and the African Charter on the Rights and Welfare of the Child may pave the way for legal and political changes. In addition, interventions for teachers in schools are needed that both challenge social norms and teach practical, nonviolent methods. However, the field dedicated to preventing teacher violence is very small and is still in the early stages of research efforts. Early results are promising, but further evidence of effectiveness in other cultural contexts, stability of effects, and scaling-up is still pending. These steps are on the agenda for the coming years.

REFERENCES

Antonowicz, L. (2010). *Too often in silence: A report on school-based violence in West and Central Africa*. UNICEF, Plan West Africa, Save the Children Sweden West Africa and ActionAid. https://www.unicef.org/wcaro/documents_publications_4271.html

Baker-Henningham, H., Bowers, M., Francis, T., Vera-Hernández, M., & Walker, S. P. (2021). The Irie Classroom Toolbox, a universal violence-prevention teacher-training programme, in Jamaican preschools: A single-blind, cluster-randomised controlled trial. *Lancet Global Health*, *9*(4), e456–e468. https://doi.org/10.1016/S2214-109X(21)00002-4

Baker-Henningham, H., Meeks-Gardner, J., Chang, S., & Walker, S. (2009). Experiences of violence and deficits in academic achievement among urban primary school children in Jamaica. *Child Abuse and Neglect*, *33*(5), 296–306. https://doi.org/10.1016/j.chiabu.2008.05.011

Baker-Henningham, H., Scott, Y., Bowers, M., & Francis, T. (2019). Evaluation of a violence-prevention programme with Jamaican primary school teachers: A cluster randomised trial. *International Journal of Environmental Research and Public Health*, *16*(15), 1–197. https://doi.org/10.3390/ijerph16152797

Block, N. A. (2013). *Breaking the paddle: Ending school corporal punishment*. Center for Effective Discipline.

Boden, J. M., Horwood, L. J., & Fergusson, D. M. (2007). Exposure to childhood sexual and physical abuse and subsequent educational achievement outcomes. *Child Abuse and Neglect*, *31*(10), 1101–1114. https://doi.org/10.1016/j.chiabu.2007.03.022

Bümen, N. T. (2010). The relationship between demographics, self efficacy, and burnout among teachers. *Eurasian Journal of Educational Research*, *10*(40), 1–14. http://www.ejer.com.tr/index.php?git=archives&categori=87

Butchart, A., Harvey, A. P., Mian, M., & Fürniss, T. (2006). *Preventing child maltreatment: A guide to taking action and generating evidence*. World Health Organization & International Society for Prevention of Child Abuse and Neglect. https://doi.org/10.1192/bjp.170.3.205

Chianu, E. (2000). Two deaths, one blind eye, one imprisonment: Child abuse in the guise of corporal punishment in Nigerian schools. *Child Abuse & Neglect*, *24*(7), 1005–1009. https://doi.org/10.1016/S0145-2134(00)00154-X

Covell, K., & Becker, J. (2011). *Five years on: A global update on violence against children, report for Against, the NGO Advisory Council for Follow-Up to the UN Secretary-General's Study on Violence Against Children*. NGO Advisory Council for Follow-up to the UN Study on Violence Against Children. https://www.crin.org/en/docs/Five_Years_On.pdf

Csorba, J., Rózsa, S., Vetro, A., Gadoros, J., Makra, J., Somogyi, E., Kaczvinszky, E., & Kapornay, K. (2001). Family- and school-related stresses in depressed Hungarian children. *European Psychiatry*, *16*(1), 8–26. https://doi.org/10.1016/S0924-9338(00)00531-9

Currie, J., & Widom, C. S. (2010). Long-term consequences of child abuse and neglect on adult economic well-being. *Child Maltreatment*, *15*(2), 111–120. https://doi.org/10.1177/1077559509355316

De Bellis, M. D., Woolley, D. P., & Hooper, S. R. (2013). Neuropsychological findings in pediatric maltreatment: Relationship of PTSD, dissociative symptoms, and abuse/neglect indices to neurocognitive outcomes. *Child Maltreatment*, *18*(3), 171–183. https://doi.org/10.1177/1077559513497420

Devries, K. M., Allen, E., Child, J. C., Walakira, E., Parkes, J., Elbourne, D., Watts, C., & Naker, D. (2013). The Good Schools Toolkit to prevent violence against children in Ugandan primary schools: Study protocol for a cluster randomised controlled trial. *Trials*, *14*, 232. https://doi.org/ 10.1186/1745-6215-14-232

Devries, K., Child, J. C., Allen, E., Walakira, E., Parkes, J., & Naker, D. (2014). School violence, mental health, and educational performance in Uganda. *Pediatrics*, *133*(1), e129–e137. https://doi.org/10.1542/peds.2013-2007

Devries, K., Knight, L., Child, J. C., Mirembe, A., Nakuti, J., Jones, R., Sturgess, J., Allen, E., Kyegombe, N., Parkes, J., Walakira, E., Elbourne, D., Watts, C., & Naker, D. (2015). The Good School Toolkit for reducing physical violence from school staff to primary school students: A cluster-randomised controlled trial in Uganda. *Lancet Global Health*, *3*(7), e378–e386. https://doi.org/10.1016/S2214-109X(15)00060-1

Donald, D., & Clacherty, G. (2005). Developmental vulnerabilities and strengths of children living in child-headed households: A comparison with children in adult-headed households in equivalent impoverished communities. *African Journal of AIDS Research*, *4*(1), 21–28. https://doi.org/10.2989/16085900509490338

Dubanoski, R. A., Inaba, M., & Gerkewicz, K. (1983). Corporal punishment in schools: Myths, problems and alternatives. *Child Abuse & Neglect*, *7*, 271–278.

Ellison, C. G., & Bradshaw, M. (2009). Religious beliefs, sociopolitical ideology, and attitudes toward corporal punishment. *Journal of Family Issues*, *30*(3), 320–340. https://doi.org/10.1177/0192513X08326331.

Ellonen, N., Peltonen, K., Pösö, T., & Janson, S. (2017). A multifaceted risk analysis of fathers' self-reported physical violence toward their children. *Aggressive Behavior*, *43*(4), 317–328. https://doi.org/10.1002/ab.21691

Feinstein, S., & Mwahombela, L. (2010). Corporal punishment in Tanzania's schools. *International Review of Education*, *56*(4), 399–410. https://doi.org/10.1007/s11159-010-9169-5

Gershoff, E. T. (2017). School corporal punishment in global perspective: Prevalence, outcomes, and efforts at intervention. *Psychology, Health & Medicine*, *22*(1), 224–239. https://doi.org/10.1080/13548506.2016.1271955

Gershoff, E. T., Purtell, K. M., & Holas, I. (2015). Corporal punishment in U.S. public schools: Legal precedents, current practices, and future policy. In B. H. Fiese (Ed.), *Springer briefs in psychology series: Advances in child and family policy and practice* (pp. 1–109). Springer International Publishing. https://doi.org/10.1007/978-3-319-14818-2

Gershoff, E. T., Sattler, K. M. P., & Ansari, A. (2018). Strengthening causal estimates for links between spanking and children's externalizing behavior problems. *Psychological Science*, *29*(1), 110–120. https://doi.org/10.1177/0956797617729816

Global Initiative to End All Corporal Punishment of Children. (2019). *Global progress towards prohibiting all corporal punishment*. http://endcorporalpunishment.org/wp-content/uploads/legality-tables/Global-progress-table-commitment.pdf

Global Initiative to End All Corporal Punishment of Children. (2021, April). *Prohibiting all corporal punishment of children: Laying the foundations for non-violent childhoods together to #ENDviolence*.

Hecker, T., Dumke, L., Neuner, F., & Masath, F. B. (2021). Mental health problems moderate the association between teacher violence and children's social status in East Africa: A multi-informant study combining self- and peer-reports. *Development and Psychopathology*, 1–10. https://doi.org/10.1017/S095457942000228X

Hecker, T., Goessmann, K., Nkuba, M., & Hermenau, K. (2018). Teachers' stress intensifies violent disciplining in Tanzanian secondary schools. *Child Abuse & Neglect*, *76*, 173–183. https://doi.org/10.1016/j.chiabu.2017.10.019

Hecker, T., Hermenau, K., Salmen, C., Teicher, M., & Elbert, T. (2016). Harsh discipline relates to internalizing problems and cognitive functioning: Findings from a cross-sectional study with school children in Tanzania. *BMC Psychiatry, 16*, 118. https://doi.org/10.1186/s12888-016-0828-3

Heekes, S. L., Kruger, C. B., Lester, S. N., & Ward, C. L. (2022). A systematic review of corporal punishment in schools: Global prevalence and correlates. *Trauma, Violence, and Abuse, 23*(1), 52–72. https://doi.org/10.1177/1524838020925787

Hoeffler, A. (2017). Violence against children: A critical issue for development. *European Journal of Development Research, 29*(5), 945–963. https://doi.org/10.1057/s41287-017-0107-2

Kabiru, C. W., Beguy, D., Crichton, J., & Ezeh, A. C. (2010). Self-reported drunkenness among adolescents in four sub-Saharan African countries: Associations with adverse childhood experiences. *Child and Adolescent Psychiatry and Mental Health, 4*, 17. https://doi.org/10.1186/1753-2000-4-17

Kabiru, C. W., Elung'ata, P., Mojola, S. A., & Beguy, D. (2014). Adverse life events and delinquent behavior among Kenyan adolescents: A cross-sectional study on the protective role of parental monitoring, religiosity, and self-esteem. *Child and Adolescent Psychiatry and Mental Health, 8*, 24. http://www.capmh.com/content/8/1/24

Kaltenbach, E., Hermenau, K., Nkuba, M., Goessmann, K., & Hecker, T. (2018). Improving interaction competencies with children—A pilot feasibility study to reduce school corporal punishment. *Journal of Aggression, Maltreatment and Trauma, 27*(1), 35–53. https://doi.org/10.1080/10926771.2017.1357060

Kiziltepe, R., Irmak, T. Y., Eslek, D., & Hecker, T. (2020). Prevalence of violence by teachers and its association to students' emotional and behavioral problems and school performance: Findings from secondary school students and teachers in Turkey. *Child Abuse & Neglect, 107*, 104559. https://doi.org/10.1016/j.chiabu.2020.104559

Knezevic, B., Milosevic, M., Golubic, R., Belosevic, L., Russo, A., & Mustajbegovic, J. (2011). Work-related stress and work ability among Croatian university hospital midwives. *Midwifery, 27*(2), 146–153. https://doi.org/10.1016/j.midw.2009.04.002

Kyriacou, C. (2001). Teacher stress: Directions for future. *Educational Review, 53*(1), 27–35. https://doi.org/10.1080/0013191012003362

Lansford, J. E., Sharma, C., Malone, P. S., Woodlief, D., Dodge, K. A., Oburu, P., Pastorelli, C., Skinner, A. T., Sorbring, E., Tapanya, S., Tirado, L. M. U., Zelli, A., Al-Hassan, S. M., Alampay, L. P., Bacchini, D., Bombi, A. S., Bornstein, M. H., Chang, L., Deater-Deckard, K., & Di Giunta, L. (2014). Corporal punishment, maternal warmth, and child adjustment: A longitudinal study in eight countries. *Journal of Clinical Child and Adolescent Psychology, 43*(4), 670–685. https://doi.org/10.1080/15374416.2014.893518

Lee, S. J., Bellamy, J. L., & Guterman, N. B. (2009). Fathers, physical child abuse, and neglect: Advancing the knowledge base. *Child Maltreatment, 14*(3), 227–231. https://doi.org/10.1177/1077559509339388

Lee, S. W., & Weis, G. (1992). *Origins of teachers ' selection of aversive interventions.* Paper presented at the annual meeting of the National Association of School Psychologists, Nashville, TN.

López García, A. I., Scharpf, F., Hoeffler, A., & Hecker, T. (2021). Preventing violence by teachers in primary schools: Study protocol for a cluster randomized controlled trial in Haiti. *Frontiers in Public Health, 9,* 797267. https://doi.org/10.3389/fpubh.2021.797267

Louw, D., George, E., & Esterhuyse, K. (2011). Burnout amongst urban secondary school teachers in Namibia. *SA Journal of Industrial Psychology, 37*(1), 1–7. https://doi.org/10.4102/sajip.v37i1.1008

Luk, A. L., Chan, B. P. S., Cheong, S. W., & Ko., S. K. K. (2010). An exploration of the burnout situation on teachers in two schools in Macau. *Social Indicators Research, 95*(3), 489–502. https://doi.org/10.1007/s11205-009-9533-7

Masath, F. B., Hermenau, K., Nkuba, M., & Hecker, T. (2020). Reducing violent discipline by teachers using Interaction Competencies with Children for Teachers (ICC-T): Study protocol for a matched cluster randomized controlled trial in Tanzanian public primary schools. *Trials, 21,* 4. https://doi.org/10.1186/s13063-019-3828-z

Masath, F. B., Hinze, L., Nkuba, M., & Hecker, T. (2021). Factors contributing to violent discipline in the classroom: Findings from a representative sample of primary school teachers in Tanzania. *Journal of Interpersonal Violence.* Advance online publication. https://doi.org/10.1177/08862605211015219

Merrill, K. G., Knight, L., Glynn, J. R., Allen, E., Naker, D., & Devries, K. (2017). School staff perpetration of physical violence against students in Uganda: A multilevel analysis of risk factors. *BMJ Open, 7,* e015567. https://doi.org/10.1136/bmjopen-2016-015567

Mills, R., Kisely, S., Alati, R., Strathearn, L., & Najman, J. M. (2019). Cognitive and educational outcomes of maltreated and non-maltreated youth: A birth cohort study. *Australian and New Zealand Journal of Psychiatry, 53*(3), 248–255. https://doi.org/10.1177/0004867418768432

Morrow, V., & Singh, R. (2014). *Corporal punishment in schools in Andhra Pradesh, India: Children's and parents' views.* Young Lives.

Mulvaney, M. K., & Mebert, C. J. (2007). Parental corporal punishment predicts behavior problems in early childhood. *Journal of Family Psychology, 21,* 389–397. https://doi.org/10.1037/0893-3200.21.3.389

Mweru, M. (2010). Why are Kenyan teachers still using corporal punishment eight years after a ban on corporal punishment? *Child Abuse Review, 19*(4), 248–258. https://doi.org/10.1002/car.1121

Naker, D. (2005). *Violence against children: The voices of Ugandan children and adults.* Raising Voices and Save the Children in Uganda.

Naker, D., & Sekitoleko, D. (2009). *Positive discipline: Creating a good school without corporal punishment.* Raising Voices.

Naong, M. (2007). The impact of the abolition of corporal punishment on teacher morale: 1994–2004. *South African Journal of Education, 27*(2), 283–300.

Naz, A., Khan, W., Daraz, U., Hussain, M., & Khan, Q. (2011). The impacts of corporal punishment on students' academic performance/career and personality development up-to secondary level education in Khyber Pakhtunkhwa Pakistan. *International Journal of Business and Social Science, 2*(12), 130–140.

Ncontsa, V. N., & Shumba, A. (2013). The nature, causes and effects of school violence in South African high schools. *South African Journal of Education, 33*(3), Article 671.

Nkuba, M., Hermenau, K., Goessmann, K., & Hecker, T. (2018a). Mental health problems and their association to violence and maltreatment in a nationally representative sample of Tanzanian secondary school students. *Social Psychiatry & Psychiatric Epidemiology*, *53*(7), 699–707. https://doi.org/10.1007/s00127-018-1511-4

Nkuba, M., Hermenau, K., Goessmann, K., & Hecker, T. (2018b). Reducing violence by teachers using the preventive intervention Interaction Competencies with Children for Teachers (ICC-T): A cluster randomized controlled trial at secondary schools in Tanzania. *PLoS One*, *13*(8), e0201362. https://doi.org/https://doi.org/10.1371/jour nal.pone.0201362

Nkuba, M., Hermenau, K., & Hecker, T. (2018). Violence and maltreatment in Tanzanian families—Findings from a nationally representative sample of secondary school students and their parents. *Child Abuse & Neglect*, *77*, 110–120. https://doi.org/ 10.1016/j.chiabu.2018.01.002

Nkuba, M., Hermenau, K., & Hecker, T. (2019). The association of maltreatment and socially deviant behavior––Findings from a national study with adolescent students and their parents. *Mental Health and Prevention*, *13*, 159–168. https://doi.org/ 10.1016/j.mhp.2019.01.003

Ogando Portela, M. J., & Pells, K. (2015, November). *Corporal punishment in schools: Longitudinal evidence from Ethiopia, India, Peru and Viet Nam, Innocenti Discussion Paper 2015-02.* UNICEF Office of Research.

Otero-López, J. M., Mariño, M. J. S., & Bolaño, C. C. (2008). An integrating approach to the study of burnout in University Professors. *Psicothema*, *20*(4), 766–772.

Palosaari, E., Punamäki, R. L., Qouta, S., & Diab, M. (2013). Intergenerational effects of war trauma among Palestinian families mediated via psychological maltreatment. *Child Abuse and Neglect*, *37*(11), 955–968. https://doi.org/10.1016/j.chi abu.2013.04.006

Parkes, J., & Heslop, J. (2011). *Stop violence against girls in school: A cross-country analysis of baseline research from Ghana, Kenya and Mozambique.* https://actionaid.org/ sites/default/files/svags-_a_cross_country_analysis_of_baseline_research_from_ ghana_kenya_and_mozambique.pdf

Pereznieto, P., Harper, C., Clench, B., & Coarasa, J. (2010). *The economic impact of school violence: A report for Plan International.* Plan International & Overseas Development Institute.

Pinheiro, P. S. (2006). *World report on violence against children. United Nations Secretary-General's study on violence against children.* United Nations: Secretary-General's Study on Violence against Children.

Portela, M. J. O., & Pells, K. (2015). *Corporal punishment in schools: Longitudinal evidence from Ethiopia, India, Peru and Viet Nam.* UNICEF Office of Research.

Prochaska, J. O., & Velicer, W. F. (1997). The transtheoretical model of health behavior change. *American Journal of Health Promotion*, *12*(1), 38–48.

Saile, R., Ertl, V., Neuner, F., & Catani, C. (2014). Does war contribute to family violence against children? Findings from a two-generational multi-informant study in Northern Uganda. *Child Abuse and Neglect*, *38*(1), 135–146. https://doi.org/ 10.1016/j.chiabu.2013.10.007

Scharpf, F., Kızıltepe, R., Kirika, A., & Hecker, T. (2022). A systematic review of the prevalence and correlates of emotional violence by teachers. *Trauma, Violence, & Abuse. Advance Online Publication.* doi:10.1177/15248380221102559

Scharpf, F., Kirika, A., Masath, F. B., Mkinga, G., Ssenyonga, J., Nyarko-Tetteh, E., Nkuba, M., Karikari, A. K., & Hecker, T. (2021). Reducing physical and emotional violence by teachers using the intervention Interaction Competencies with Children for Teachers (ICC-T): Study protocol of a multi-country cluster randomized controlled trial in Ghana, Tanzania, and Uganda. *BMC Public Health, 21*, 1930. https://doi.org/10.1186/s12889-021-11950-y

Semali, L. M., & Vumilia, P. L. (2016). Challenges facing teachers' attempts to enhance learners' discipline in Tanzania's secondary schools. *World Journal of Education, 6*(1), 50–67. https://doi.org/10.5430/wje.v6n1p50

Smiley, A., Moussa, W., Ndamobissi, R., & Menkiti, A. (2021). The negative impact of violence on children's education and well-being: Evidence from Northern Nigeria. *International Journal of Educational Development, 81*, 102327. https://doi.org/10.1016/j.ijedudev.2020.102327

Ssenyonga, J., Hermenau, K., Mattonet, K., Nkuba, M., & Hecker, T. (2022). Reducing teachers' use of violence toward students: A cluster-randomized controlled trial in secondary schools in Southwestern Uganda. *Children and Youth Services Review, 138*, 106521. https://doi.org/10.1016/j.childyouth.2022.106521

Ssenyonga, J., Hermenau, K., Nkuba, M., & Hecker, T. (2019). Stress and positive attitudes towards violent discipline are associated with school violence by Ugandan teachers. *Child Abuse & Neglect, 93*, 15–26. https://doi.org/10.1016/j.chiabu.2019.04.012

Stein, M., Steenkamp, D., & Tangi, F. (2019). Relations of corporal punishment to academic results and achievements in secondary schools in Tanzania. *International Journal of Education and Research, 7*(8), 85–104. https://www.ijern.com/journal/2019/August-2019/08.pdf

Straus, M. A. (2010). Prevalence, societal causes, and trends in corporal punishment by parents in world perspective. *Law and Contemporary Problems, 31*, 1–30. http://scholarship.law.duke.edu/lcp/vol73/iss2/2

Tafa, E. M. (2002). Corporal punishment: The brutal face of Botswana's authoritarian schools. *Educational Review, 54*(1), 17–26. https://doi.org/10.1080/00131910120110848

Talwar, V., Carlson, S. M., & Lee, K. (2011). Effects of a punitive environment on children's executive functioning: A natural experiment. *Social Development, 20*(4), 805–824. https://doi.org/10.1111/j.1467-9507.2011.00617.x

Toth, S. L., & Cicchetti, D. (2013). A developmental psychopathology perspective on child maltreatment. *Child Maltreatment, 18*(3), 135–139. https://doi.org/10.1177/1077559513500380

UNICEF. (2017, November). *A familiar face: Violence in the lives of children and adolescents.* https://doi.org/10.1111/j.1365-2044.1982.tb01804.x

UNICEF. (2018). *An everyday lesson: ENDviolence in schools.* https://www.unicef.org/eap/media/2081/file/violence.pdf

United Republic of Tanzania. (2002). *The Government of Tanzania School Corporal Punishment Administration Guideline, Article 24 of the year 2002.*

United Republic of Tanzania. (2009). *The Law of the Child Act.* http://mcdgc.go.tz/data/Law_of_the_Child_Act_2009.pdf

van IJzendoorn, M. H., Bakermans-Kranenburg, M. J., Coughlan, B., & Reijman, S. (2020). Annual research review: Umbrella synthesis of meta-analyses on child maltreatment antecedents and interventions: Differential susceptibility perspective on risk and resilience. *Journal of Child Psychology and Psychiatry, 61*(3), 272–290. https://doi.org/10.1111/jcpp.13147

Widom, C. S. (1989). The cycle of violence. *Science, 244*(4901), 160–166. https://doi.org/
    10.1126/science.2704995

Yaghambe, R. S., & Tshabangu, I. (2013). Disciplinary networks in secondary
    schools: Policy dimensions and children's rights in Tanzania. *Journal of Studies in
    Education, 3*(4), 42–56. https://doi.org/10.5296/jse.v3i4.4167

12

Education in Crisis

Exploring the Effectiveness of Accelerated Education Programs in the Democratic Republic of the Congo and Tanzania[1]

NEIL BOOTHBY, ABIGAIL L. MILLS, YGAL SHARON, AND
SHUKRANI SALVATORY ■

Globally, the negative impact of armed conflict on children and their education is well recognized (Akresh & de Walque, 2011; Alderman et al., 2006; Chamarbagwala & Moran 2010; Shemyakina, 2011). Children affected by armed conflict face significant challenges, such as exposure to violence, loss of family members, changes in family roles, recruitment by armed groups, food insecurity, disease, and injury (Alexander et al., 2010). These challenges are frequently compounded by disruptions to education, with children often falling months or years behind in their school curriculum due to conflict (UNICEF, 2016). Moreover, when students drop out of school, they are at a heightened risk of never returning, leading to limited agency and skills needed to participate in civil society and community in the future. Humanitarian work in contexts of armed conflict such as these is essential and aligns well with the United Nations' 17 Sustainable Development Goals designed to achieve a better future for all.

Furthermore, research indicates that even minor disruptions to education can lead to significant impacts on future development and human capital (Justin et al., 2013). Currently, humanitarian crises such as war, natural disasters, and other phenomena disrupt access to, as well as quality of, education for 75 million children and young people on a yearly basis (Nicolai et al., 2016; United Nations Office for the Coordination of Humanitarian Affairs, 2019). When children experience disruptions to their education, the lack of learning and skill development puts

1. The research was part of the Building Resilience in Crisis Through Education—BRICE—project supported by the European Commission (DG-DEVCO) and the European Union.

youth at risk of future unemployment, low wages, stigmatization, and other social and economic disadvantages (IASC Reference Group, 2010). Research suggests that "the consequences of distressing events, such as lack of access to education, may have a more damaging and lasting impact on a child's well-being and development than the events themselves" (Alexander et al., 2010, p. 13). Historically, evidence also suggests that gaps in education lead to higher dropout rates. For example, after the Ebola crisis in Sierra Leone, girls were 16% less likely to be in school (Rogers et al., 2020), and after the 2008 global financial crisis, rural Ethiopia experienced an increase in school dropout probability for students ages 15 and older by nearly 8%. The effects reached 13% of girls (Rogers et al., 2020).

One way to ensure that conflict-affected youth receive the education they need is through accelerated education programs (AEPs). AEPs provide access to a flexible, age-appropriate curriculum on an accelerated time frame. These programs are specifically designed for out-of-school, overage children and youth who have not received any formal education or who experienced an interruption in education due to conflict and displacement. Globally, AEPs are employed with increasing frequency to address the overwhelming numbers of out-of-school children and youth. However, while there is widespread agreement on the need for such programming among agencies and governments, there is insufficient validated documentation to guide their design, implementation, and improvement (Baxter et al., 2016). In practice, AEPs take different forms in each context of implementation. Moreover, there is little documentation on the impact of such programming, including how they contribute to learning achievement and how successful they are at facilitating pathways between accelerated programming and formal and nonformal education. A 2016 literature review on the definition and impact of AEPs conducted by the U.S. Agency for International Development (USAID) indicates that AEPs, in general, may outperform formal or government schools; however, more robust research is needed as the comparison between AEP and formal schooling metrics is not always equivalent (Baxter et al., 2016).

THE PRESENT STUDY

Recognizing these gaps in evidence and the realities of armed conflict on student learning and well-being, in 2017, the Interagency Network for Emergency Education (INEE) established a Working Group on Accelerated Education (AEWG) to guide AEP research and learning. The AEP Learning Agenda that evolved through consultative processes consists of a set of research questions in priority development areas that the AEWG would like to pursue, leveraging academic research, program evaluations, and multimethod tests—the assumptions and principles that have been developed to guide AEPs (AEWG, 2017).

Recognizing that children develop within dynamic and interacting social-ecological contexts including family, school, and communities as the most proximate (Bronfenbrenner, 1977, 1979), the study frames its analysis within an ecological perspective. The ecological systems theory (Bronfenbrenner,

1992) posits that development is nested within multiple systems (or contexts), and these systems are all contributing to one's specific pathway of development. Bronfenbrenner (1979, 1986) identified four major systems within which the individual is influenced: (a) the microsystem, (b) the mesosystem, (c) the exosystem, (d) the macrosystem, and (e) the chronosystem. The present study considers individual student learners and their affiliations to people, schools, and wider communities (micro- and mesosystems). It employs a multilevel, mixed-methods model to examine how risk and protective factors in schools, homes, peer groups, and neighborhoods interact to affect student learners' behavior, academic performance, and educational outcomes while also exploring how national and cross-border dynamics influence student learner outcomes in these two distinct contexts (macrosystems).

In consultation with the INEE, a prospective, mixed-methods cohort study was designed to address two evidence gaps: (a) *How successful are AEPs in integrating student learners into formal education or vocational education?* and (b) *To what extent are AEPs successful in reaching and supporting marginalized student learners?* Answers to these questions could provide the emergency education sector with a better understanding of the extent to which AEPs can foster resilience in conflict-affected and displaced children at scale and what additional supports are required to serve war-affected and out-of-school children and youth.

METHOD

Participants

At the initiation of project implementation, it was expected that 6,300 learners (50% girls) would be enrolled in the programs (3,600 in the Democratic Republic of the Congo [DRC] and 2,700 in Tanzania). These learners were out-of-school children and youth aged 10 to 17 years who were unable to enroll in formal school due to being too old for primary school enrollment, having never attended school, or having missed significant schooling. A sample size of roughly 420 learners from each context (828 total) was selected. In the DRC, the sample included 421 students (233 girls and 188 boys), all of whose education had been disrupted by conflict and/or displacement in their home country. The sample from Tanzania included 418 students (197 girls and 221 boys), all of whom are refugees from Burundi.

Student learners participating in the DRC AEP live in a context that has been plagued by internal conflict since 1960 when the DRC won its independence from Belgium. Political instability, exacerbated by 20 years of tumultuous presidential elections, has only led to further internal instability, often at the hands of armed rebel groups. Today, armed conflict frequently forces civilians to relocate from their homes and even major cities lack the political stability to ensure the safety of their citizens. The AEP studied in this chapter is located in a rural, agrarian section of the DRC, plagued by gangs and high crime rates.

The context in Tanzania is similarly troubling. Hundreds of thousands of people fled Burundi for neighboring countries following the controversial 2015 presidential election, which incited violence and protests (International Federation of Human Rights, 2016). Nearly half of those who escaped, approximately 150,000 people, were in Tanzania, where they continue to suffer human rights violations, including arbitrary arrests and enforced disappearance carried out by Tanzania police and intelligence services in cooperation with Burundian counterparts (United Nations, 2021). In addition to living in fear, the capacity to provide Burundian refugee students with "catch-up" education programs is adversely affected by the Tanzania government's "austerity" measures aimed at forcing refugees to return to their homeland, including reduction of teacher salaries.

Procedures

Data collection occurred across three phases. Phase 1 of data collection took place between June and August of 2018 and focused on children and youth who had registered for AEPs to ensure that the baseline was established before learners received the intervention and that research activities would not compete with program rollout. The initial phase of research sought to provide a baseline to better understand the experiences of learners enrolled in the international nongovernmental organization's (INGO's) AEPs, including elements such as social continuity, economic realities, previous access to education, and experiences that may have influenced psychosocial well-being, such as exposure to violence.

Phase 2 of the study—April to August of 2019—focused on collecting a second round of data through follow-up interviews with the original 841 learners as well as in-depth interviews with a select group of high- and low-achieving learners. In order to create the sample for the interviews, the study team in each country analyzed the test scores of each cohort of students that completed the International Social Emotional Learning Assessment (ISELA) interview (described in "Measures") in 2018 and sorted them from highest to lowest scores, dividing the scores into quartiles. The study team then drew a randomized sample of 80 students, 40 from the top 25th percentile (denoted as high performers) and 40 from the bottom 25th percentile (denoted as low performers), to be interviewed. In addition, Phase 2 included data collection on student academic performance and teacher performance, as well as matriculation, dropout, and transition rates. Phase 2 activities, however, were compromised by several interactive factors: logistics, higher than anticipated attrition from baseline (36%), and delays in implementing formative academic measures and teacher observations. These challenges impacted the quality of data collected and limited the research team's ability to examine academic performance as originally planned; therefore, the research team also engaged a second cohort of learners to better assess their academic progress.

Finally, during Phase 3 of the study—October 2019 to December 2020—Annual Status of Education Report (ASER) and Child and Youth Resilience

Measure (CYRM) assessments were administered to student learners from both cohorts who continued in the AEPs or transitioned to formal schools. Cohort 2 included 633 learners (408 in the DRC and 225 in Tanzania). In the DRC, of the total 408 student learners assessed, 204 (50%) were female, and 204 (50%) were male. Of the 255 student learners assessed in Tanzania, 169 (66%) were female, and 86 (34%) were male. In total, an additional 189 individual interviews were conducted with learners and their parents from Cohort 1, based on four learner outcomes: (a) those who stayed in AEPs, (b) those who transitioned to formal school, (c) those who dropped out of AEPs, and (d) those who dropped out of formal school. Recorded interviews were transcribed word for word and translated from native languages to English.

A total of 120 learner interviews (40 in the DRC and 80 in Tanzania) were conducted and 67 with parents (40 in the DRC, 27 in Tanzania) focused on understanding what factors influenced why learners stayed in or dropped out of the AEP or formal school. An additional 52 interviews were conducted with teachers (33 in the DRC and 19 in Tanzania) to understand their training, experience in the classroom, and perception of why learners stay in school or drop out. In both country contexts, interviews were conducted with trained research teams in native languages (French, Swahili, and Kinyarwanda in the DRC and Kirundi in Tanzania). Interviews were recorded and then subsequently translated and transcribed. Data analysis was guided by the qualitative principles of thematic analysis and the constant comparative method (Kolb, 2012), in which interviews are coded inductively and themes are compared in a spreadsheet. A comprehensive codebook was developed, and interviews were coded in Dedoose.

Measures

A package of tools, each described next, was employed at different points in time throughout the study to address the key research questions and create a holistic understanding of learners. See Table 12.1 for a summative visual depicting the data collection timeline and indicators collected at each time point.

Demographic Profiles

The social-ecological component of the International Social and Emotional Learning Assessment (ISELA) was contextualized through a cognitive interview process and used to establish a demographic profile of student learners at baseline, including previous education experiences, conflict-related events, current living situations, household economic status, and social relationships of the students. Demographic information was collected in Phase 1.

Table 12.1. SUMMARY OF DATA COLLECTION PHASES AND INDICATORS COLLECTED
AT EACH TIME POINT

Phase 1	Phase 2	Phase 3
Enrollment	**Performance**	**Transition**
June–August 2018	April–August 2019	October 2019–December 2020
Enrollment	**Performance**	**Dropping out & formal school**
Demographics (ISELA)	Academics (grades)	Dropped out of AEP
Social & emotional learning (ISELA)	Social & emotional learning (ISELA)	Enrolled in formal school
Household characteristics (ISELA)	Perceptions of teachers (ISELA)	**High & Low**
	Perceptions of school safety (ISELA)	Interviews with high & low performers
	Teacher performance (ISELA)	

Social-Emotional Learning

Social-emotional learning (SEL) was assessed using the ISELA, an interview-based questionnaire. Interviews were administered on school grounds or in other convenient village locations and were, on average, 45 minutes in duration. The first round of interviews was conducted by 12 enumerators who were selected from the community. The questionnaire included items about a student's family, past school experiences, and other social and economic indicators. The questionnaire was administered on tablets or smartphones and was conducted in the language the child was most comfortable speaking (i.e., Kiswahili, Kinyarwanda, French). The questionnaire was translated into each language by professional translators in the DRC. SEL behaviors were assessed in Phases 1 and 2.

ADOLESCENT RESILIENCE

Leveraged to develop a holistic understanding of the learners in the study and the potential impact of well-being on academic outcomes, the CYRM features 25 questions on psychosocial well-being and resilience designed for learners aged 9 years and older. The CYRM is a multifaceted tool that assesses positive youth development across four primary resilience domains: individual (e.g., assertiveness, problem-solving ability), relational (e.g., social competence), community (e.g., rites of passage, safety, and security), and cultural (e.g., affiliation with a religious organization, a life philosophy; Ungar & Liebenberg, 2011). This tool has been widely used in over 20 languages and 150 research studies. For the purposes of the present research, the CYRM assessment was collected during Phase 3.

ACADEMIC OUTCOMES

The ASER is a formative assessment of academic learning (literacy and numeracy capacities) that has been used in a variety of contexts. It was selected by the AEP-implementing INGO and has been administered as part of their program monitoring. Research has demonstrated the ASER tool to be a reliable and valid assessment of academic learning (Vagh, 2012). For the purposes of the present research, the ASER assessment was collected during Phase 3.

CLASSROOM OBSERVATIONS

In Tanzania, teacher classroom observations (TCOs) were conducted over 4 days in November 2020 for 18 teachers (5 females, 13 males) by the Norwegian Refugee Council (NRC). A lesson observation tool was used to observe each teacher on their preparation, the quality of their teaching (i.e., learner engagement, time management), and their connection with students. After the lesson observation task, feedback was shared with the teachers to enhance their professional development in teaching. In the DRC, TCOs were conducted in June 2020 by the Division of Social Affairs (DIVAS). Over 5 days, a total of 64 teachers in nine villages were observed using a lesson observation tool. Reports were created for each teacher observation, including an assessment of the teacher's mastery of the content, inclusiveness of the classroom, and how they structure their lessons. In this phase of observation, particular attention was paid to teacher adaptation to home-lesson activities due to COVID-19 school closures.

Analytic Plan

The majority of the findings presented in this chapter were collected from qualitative methods and derived from preliminary thematic analysis of interviews with learners, parents, and teachers. This work was approached from the perspective that individual participants' perspectives are what is important, and therefore themes extracted from interviews were not quantified in all instances. Regarding quantitative data in both countries, student data was matched by student registration number; nonmatching cases were then forwarded to the team in country for further examination and manual matching. When matching was complete, in both countries, we performed an initial round of descriptive analyses (e.g., frequencies, correlations).

RESULTS

For the purposes of this chapter, the authors present findings and implications from the two AEPs currently being implemented by the INGO. These AEPs are implemented in community settings in the DRC for internally displaced populations and in subsidized-camp settings in Tanzania for Burundian refugees.

Findings are divided into four categories: learner profiles and demographics, education outcomes, classroom observations, and academic performance.

Learner Profiles and Demographics at Baseline

Student learners in the AEP in Tanzania left Burundi where years of civil wars between the Hutu and Tutsi ethnic groups have led to mass refugee migrations (Lischer, 2003). Although the community setting examined in this chapter is an internationally subsidized refugee camp, fear and intimidation continued to create a culture of fear and insecurity (United Nations, 2021). The AEPs there were also burdened by not being recognized by the official education system of Tanzania. Coupled with ambiguity surrounding their acceptance by the Burundi government, this further limited programmatic interventions and complicated the potential continuity of learning options for Burundi students. Limitations were also exacerbated by the fact that the Tanzanian government continues to limit refugee teacher salaries and wider opportunities in its civil society and economy.

Both conflicts have led to the INGO's implementation of AEPs in an effort to combat the ill effects of conflict and disruption on education. The mean age of learners in the Tanzania AEP is 12.9 years, and the mean age of learners in the DRC AEP is 12.6 years. Phase 1 data collection focused on student demographics and provides important insights on students' household and social continuity, household income, previous school experiences, and experiences with violence.

Household and Social Continuity

Household continuity, or the constancy of people living in a household[2], can have a profound impact on a child's emotional stability, affecting students both inside and outside of the classroom (Evans et al., 2005). Understanding factors such as separation from parents, caregivers, and communities can provide important insight into a child's household and social continuity. Of the 418 Burundian children, 72 (17.14%) had been separated from a parent or a primary caregiver at some point in their lives. Of these 72, 74% were separated from their parents permanently or for a minimum of 1 year. Approximately 37% of Burundian students also indicated having at least one positive relationship at the household level, contributing to an emotionally stable environment. Over 60% of Burundi students reported that they had friends from Burundi living in the same camp as them, suggesting that entire communities or towns may have moved together, enhancing social continuity for learners. Additionally, most learners indicated that they spent every day with childhood friends. This knowledge, in conjunction with the data on parent and caregiver

---

2. As defined for the parameters of this study.

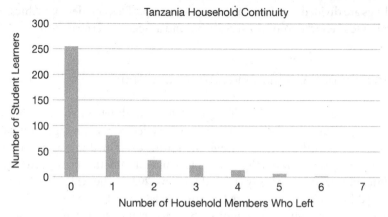

Figure 12.1a. Summary of Household Social Continuity for Learners in Tanzania.

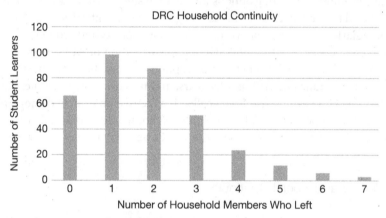

Figure 12.1b. Summary of Household Social Continuity for Learners in the DRC.

separation, suggests that although a number of children experienced social disruption, Burundian students in the AEP maintained an overall high degree of relationship continuity throughout the displacement period. See Figures 12.1a-b and 12.2a-b.

Household Income

In Tanzania, the type of house in which children live can be used as a proxy for family income. For the purposes of this study, the indicator used for family income was whether or not the household that a student lives in had a kitchen or a garden (Depenbusch et al., 2021; Ghirotti, 1992, World Bank, 2014). Ultimately, less than half (44.52%) of the student learners had a kitchen or a garden, suggesting that most of the children live in an economically challenged home. Additionally, about 25% of the Burundian students surveyed have held

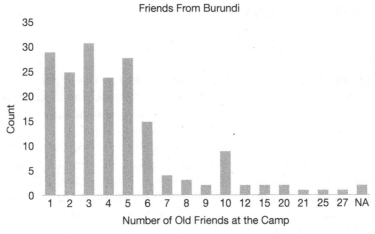

Figure 12.2a. Summary of Number of Friends for Learners in Tanzania.

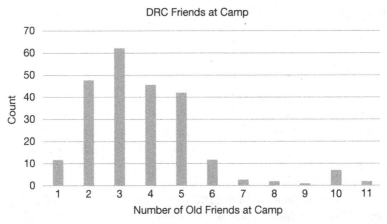

Figure 12.2b. Summary of Number of Friends for Learners in the DRC.

some kind of paid employment by this point in their lives, typically agriculture or tenant farming work, and roughly 34% of the Burundian students had to stop going to school at some point in time because of the financial burden on the household. Income generated through employment via INGOs inside the camp, including teaching positions, was limited to the equivalent of $2 USD per day for each earner.

Fifty percent of student learners from the DRC and the majority of learners' parents were working. Agriculture and sugarcane farming are the primary means of livelihood in the community. Only 11% of learners had access to beds and mattresses in their homes, and only 22% had chairs—key indicators of household income. Nearly 81% of students reported having missed a meal within a day because there was not sufficient food at home. Data collected from both contexts suggests that household income is a hardship for families.

Previous School Experiences

School absenteeism and dropout were other common experiences that student learners had. In both the DRC and Tanzania, most students left school in the lower grades. Of the 418 Burundian students, 389 had previously attended school, and of those 389 students, 58 of them reported prolonged absences from school. The most common reasons for prolonged absences were the same as for dropping out: illness, lack of supplies and lack of money for supplies, and helping with the household. Most students, however, had positive experiences at their previous schools in Burundi. They claimed that teachers treated them fairly and praised them for good work. While some students noted that teachers employed corporal punishment in classrooms and that peer bullying took place, the majority of students claimed that they never felt afraid. Of the 421 student learners in the DRC, 259 had previously attended school, the majority of whom had been out of school for 1 to 4 years before entering the AEP. The most common reasons for leaving school were lack of funds (59%), illness (27%), or the need to work in order to support the household (3%), suggesting a monetary barrier.

Experiences With Violence

Finally, exposure to violence can have a consequential impact on a child's mental health and psychosocial well-being; therefore, the research team also sought to understand the role of violence in students' lives. More than 20% of Burundian students knew a family member who was killed during conflict, and almost 10% knew someone who was injured. In the DRC, more than 25% of the students knew a family member who was killed during conflict, and 15% knew someone who was injured. Ultimately, in the DRC, research revealed that, adjusting for a measure of "bad" teaching, as well as for the number of positive relationships with family, friends, and community, students who know someone who was recruited to fight are more likely to be lost to follow-up at Phase 2. Furthermore, their odds of being lost to follow-up[3] are 84% higher than those of students who did not know anyone who was recruited to fight.

Education Outcomes

Although Phase 1 of the research was designed to develop a preliminary profile of learners, Phases 2 and 3 took a closer look at the extent to which AEPs reached and supported marginalized children and youth and the socioecological factors that enhanced or impeded academic achievement.

---

3. In this case, being lost to follow-up is the same as being out of school.

Table 12.2. STUDENT LEARNER STATUS BY COUNTRY

Student Learner Status	Democratic Republic of the Congo ($n = 421$)				Tanzania ($n = 418$)			
	2019		2020		2019		2020	
Enrolled but never started	42	10%	39	9.3%	166	39.8%	55	13.2%
In AEP	156	37.1%	65	15.4%	187	44.7%	88	21.1%
Transferred to formal school	25	5.9%	57	13.5%	8	1.9%	51	12.2%
Started—dropped out or could not be found	198	47.0%	260	61.8%	41	9.8%	184	44.0%
Repatriated	0	0%	0	0%	16	3.8%	40	9.60%
Total student learners	421		421		418		418	

Data collected identified the number of students from panel 1 who (a) enrolled in AEPs but never started, (b) remained in an AEP, (c) transferred to a formal school, (d) dropped out of an AEP, or (e) repatriated. The numbers provide an initial understanding of the reach and impact of AEPs (see Table 12.2).

At baseline in 2018, there were 421 student learners in the study in the DRC and 418 in Tanzania. Table 12.2 shows student learner status of the original cohort in the DRC and Tanzania in 2019 (after 1 year of the program) and in 2020 (after 2 years of the program). In 2019, 156 student learners (37%) remained in the program in the DRC, and 25 (5.9%) transitioned to formal school. In Tanzania, 187 student learners (44.7%) remained in the AEP, and 8 (1.9%) transitioned to formal school. By 2020, the number of student learners in formal school or refugee school rose to 13.5% in the DRC and 12.2% in Tanzania. A greater proportion of student learners (43% in Tanzania and 69% in the DRC) were missing in 2020 due to challenges in follow-up, exacerbated by the COVID-19 global pandemic.

Researchers leveraged in-depth qualitative interviews to understand the causal factors for the AEP outcomes outlined in Table 12.3.

For students who entered AEP programs and eventually dropped out, the main reasons across the two contexts were similar. Although percentages for each reason were not available, prevalent reasons for dropping out of the AEP programs were as follows: (a) the need to contribute to household income or chores (i.e., child labor), (b) illness (i.e., student learner illness and student learner caring for ill household members), (c) food insecurity and hunger, and (d) unmet school-related needs (e.g., soap, clothing, school supplies). In the DRC, fear of armed individuals and groups, fear of being raped for girls, and insecurity to and from school were cited as causal factors as well. In Tanzania, repatriation was another common reason for leaving education programs among student learners.

Interviews also revealed a series of additional trends and factors that contributed to students' decisions to drop out (see Table 12.3). Notably, less education was reported as a reason for many students who ultimately dropped out of the AEPs.

Table 12.3. ADDITIONAL TRENDS AND FACTORS (NONPRIMARY) FOR DROPPING OUT
BY CONTEXT

Tanzania

Reasons for Staying in AEPs	Reasons for Leaving AEPs
Previous Education: Students with positive perceptions of education and more years of experience in school	**Repatriation**: Returning to Burundi
Home Environment: Education is valued at home, and parents help student balance work and school	**Home Environment**: Verbal and physical abuse at home and less parental support for continuation
Individual Characteristics: Motivation and persistence	**School Environment**: Limitations of classroom environment and materials, concerns with school safety
Role of Teacher: Positive relationships with teachers and home visitations from teacher	**Role of Teacher**: Favoritism based on achievement
	Previous Education: Less education is an indicator of future dropout

Democratic Republic of the Congo

Reasons for Staying in AEPs	Reasons for Leaving AEPs
Previous Education: Positive perceptions of education and more years of experience	**Previous Education**: Less education is an indicator of future dropout
Home Environment: Education is valued at home, and parents help students balance school and work	**Home Environment**: Economic needs limit participation in schools
Individual Characteristics: Motivation and persistence	**School Environment**: Limitations of classroom environment and materials are obstacles
Role of Teacher: Positive relationships with teachers and home visitations from teachers	**Safety**: Concerns of getting to and from school safely

Additionally, in Tanzania, teacher preference for high achievers and neglect of low achievers were cited as a significant challenge by students. In both contexts, qualitative data revealed that large classroom sizes, poor classroom infrastructure, and an overall lack of school supplies contributed to decisions to drop out.

Although students who completed 1 or 2 years of a program faced similar challenges as their peers who dropped out, qualitative interviews revealed a series of factors that contributed to their ability to persist. Student learners who completed first-year AEP programs had more previous education than peers who dropped out. Additionally, student learners who remained in programs for 1 to 2 years reported fewer negative previous school experiences than their counterparts who dropped out. The role of the current AEP teacher also emerged as a key factor in students' persistence in the programs. Students who reported positive relationships with their teachers or who had teachers who leveraged home visitations to inquire about student absenteeism and offer tutoring and/or other forms of assistance were more likely to remain in a program.

Notably, in both contexts, a combination of factors outside the confines of the school also contributed to students' abilities to persist in the program: namely their home environment and individual characteristics. Student learners who completed 1 or 2 years of programs had parents who valued education and linked it to their child's future. These parents also reported taking an interest in their children's homework and visiting schools one or more times. Additionally, these students reported higher levels of motivation and persistence, as evidenced by their ability to navigate the need to work after school and on weekends while attending school and completing homework.

Classroom Observations and Parent, Teacher, and Student Interviews

Classroom observations and interviews with parents, teachers, and students were also utilized to further understand the realities of students' lives and their classroom environments as well as the causal factors behind high rates of AEP attrition. Interviews with learners and parents revealed that students faced a number of challenges in their home life. Especially in the DRC, learners reported being hungry often. When not in school, it was also common for learners to help their families with household tasks and income-generating activities. Salient needs outside of the classroom, in both contexts, included soap, clothing (e.g., school uniforms), school supplies, housing repairs, and financial income. The most commonly cited reason for missing school was sickness. In Tanzania, learners also missed school on camp food distribution days when they needed to be available to help their families.

Despite the high rates of absenteeism, parents of learners who remained in AEPs expressed high value and prioritization of education. They tended to view it as an investment in their children's and their futures. Indeed, many parents had visited their child's school for meetings with teachers, parent meetings, or community projects. Furthermore, parents saw education as a positive force for discipline and structure in their child's life. High-achieving students in particular attributed their classroom success to the quality and intentionality of their educators. Many of these parents and students gave anecdotes of teachers going above and beyond to follow up with students at home, especially if they had missed school or had been sick.

Although parents and learners alike expressed gratitude for being able to participate in the free AEP, there were challenges. Learners in both contexts reported fighting in some classrooms that disrupted learning and a few cases of corporal punishment from teachers that made them reconsider attending the program. In addition, parents and learners expressed trouble keeping up with the resources needed for school. Although books and pens are distributed within the program, there are no replacements if learners, for example, lose a pen. In Tanzania, there was also indication of boys receiving more assistance than girls, and in the DRC, learners shared that replacement school resources were preferentially given to high achievers more than low achievers.

Classroom observations further illustrated the realities of students' lives and AEP experiences. Observations, conducted in 2020, showed that even in the context of adapted classroom settings (due to the COVID-19 pandemic), teachers followed classroom pedagogy well. However, observation assessments also identified areas for improvement including additional teacher and supervisor training, increased classroom resources (e.g., textbooks in classrooms and water, sanitation, and hygiene [WASH] supplies, especially in light of COVID-19), and decreased preferential gender bias toward male learners. In Tanzania, although the majority of teachers had lesson plans, they could not clearly state lesson objectives to the assessors or give an accurate description of the lesson plan. Observations indicated there was room for improvement in terms of asking open-ended questions and responding to student learners in a positive, encouraging manner. In both contexts, in-depth interviews with teachers revealed that there were inconsistencies among teachers in training and programming preparation. In particular, teachers in Tanzania received less direct training, mentorship, and resources than teachers in the DRC.

Academic Performance

Finally, a key component of this research was tracking the academic performance of students in the AEPs in both contexts. ASER data, collected in Phase 3, showed an increase in measured learning achievement in both countries for panel 2 learners (see Figures 12.3 through 12.5). For the ASER math score, the percentage of students whose scores increased (or remained at the maximum value) was 87%

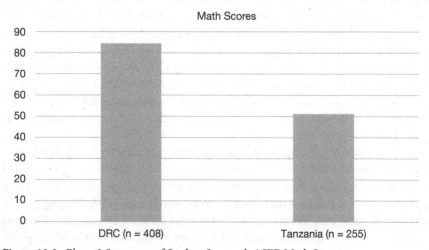

Figure 12.3. Phase 3 Summary of Student Learner's ASER Math Scores.

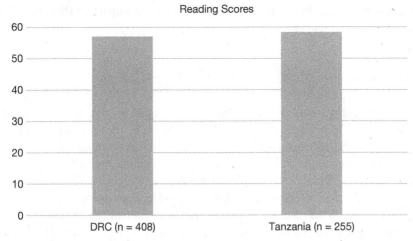

Figure 12.4. Phase 3 Summary of Student Learner's ASER Reading Scores.

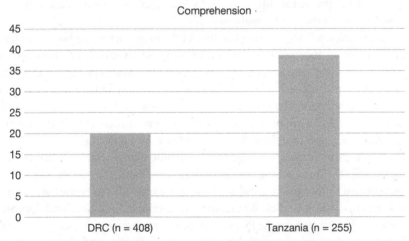

Figure 12.5. Phase 3 Summary of Student Learner's ASER Comprehension Scores.

in the DRC and 66% in Tanzania. In reading, 66% of DRC students' scores and 80% of Tanzania students' scores increased or remained at the maximum. The comprehension scores of students in the DRC increased in 12% of cases, while in Tanzania, 67% percent of students' scores increased or remained at the maximum. There was no significant association between gender and any of the scores. Importantly, ASER findings should be interpreted cautiously, as they are limited by a ceiling effect such that the majority of the scores were clustered toward the maximum possible values on the assessment.

Notably, the CYRM assessment, leveraged in order to understand any links between student learners' psychosocial well-being and their academic success, showed no correlation between the two. This suggests that students' previous experiences and psychosocial well-being may have less impact on their academic success than their current realities.

Implications

Upon examining these research findings in light of this study's primary questions—(a) *How successful are AEPs in integrating learners into formal education?* and (b) *To what extent are AEPs successful in reaching and supporting marginalized learners?*—a clear trend emerges. Ultimately, the AEPs in this study do not do a good job of keeping students in school or integrating them into formal education. However, the reasons behind this trend have less to do with the quality of education students receive and more with the harsh realities of students' lives. In both contexts, the primary reasons students gave for dropping out all occurred outside of the classroom: the need to contribute to household income or chores, illness, food insecurity and hunger, and unmet school-related needs. Indeed, it appears that the present reality of students' lives provides the greatest indication for whether or not they will remain in AEPs.

In fact, when students remained in the AEPs, they learned. In both countries, ASER revealed an increase in measured learning achievement. While classroom observations did indicate areas for teacher improvement and pedagogical reform, for the most part, teachers followed classroom pedagogy well, and students and parents expressed general approval of their teachers. Such findings then beg the question of how AEPs can be improved to retain more students and better support marginalized learners to ultimately integrate them into formal education.

This research indicates that a multisectoral approach may be in order. If AEPs are to be effective in reaching conflict-affected learners, they likely need to do more in regard to recognizing and addressing the immediate realities of students' lives (e.g., child labor, household income, etc.). Taking a multisectoral approach to addressing retention in AEPs necessitates focusing on the individual child and understanding relationships between a child's family, school, and community and the various factors at each level that impact this child's ability to stay in school. Figure 12.6 offers a visual overview of this study's findings and potential intervention points to better support and keep students in AEPs in these two contexts. While the classroom is an initial starting point for interventions, and this research indicates a number of valuable classroom intervention points (e.g., reducing gender and achievement biases), AEP designs need to move beyond the classroom and address a range of potential interventions at various levels of a learner's social ecology.

While an effective classroom is important, it is ultimately insufficient when it comes to keeping conflict-affected students enrolled, engaged, and learning. Therefore, AEP-implementing organizations would be wise to explore how they can bolster their academic programming and foster the resilience of their students through engaging with stakeholders in at least some of the intervention points, outlined in Figure 12.6, and equipping them with the tools necessary to support

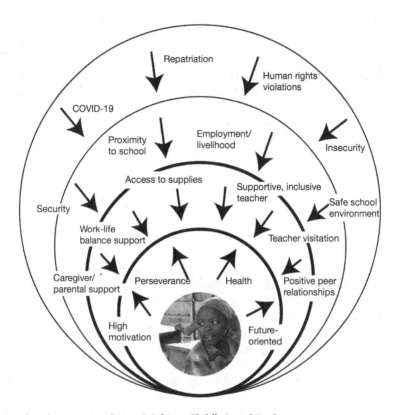

Figure 12.6. Intervention Points Within a Child's Social Ecology.

student learners. For example, while an AEP-implementing organization may take great care to ensure teachers follow a clear, well-organized curriculum, students will have limited academic success if they do not have a supportive household that encourages their education. Perhaps it is then necessary for implementing organizations to introduce programming for parents that addresses the role of the household and equips parents with the tools and skills necessary to support their learners. Similarly, if students continue to drop out of programs, citing learning-adjacent needs such as health and nutrition as key factors, implementing organizations must look beyond their academic programming and strategize around how to bolster student health or nutrition. This may take the form of partnering with another nongovernmental organization to provide basic health screenings to learners and families or developing a school feeding program. Depending on the circumstances and contexts, any one of these interventions would have a positive impact on student outcomes, and student success is not ultimately tied to addressing all the intervention points outlined in Figure 12.6. Indeed, until the primary factors that impede students from success and the ability to flourish in their unique context are addressed, catch-up and emergency education programming such as AEPs will remain fledgling pursuits in conflict-affected areas.

REFERENCES

Accelerated Education Working Group (AEWG). (2017). *Learning agenda*. https://inee.org/resources/accelerated-education-working-group-learning-agenda

Akresh, R., & de Walque, D. (2011). *Armed conflict and schooling: Evidence from the 1994 Rwandan genocide*. HiCN Working Paper 47. Households in Conflict Network. www.hicn.org.

Alderman, H., Hoddinott J., & Kinsey, B. (2006). Long term consequences of early childhood malnutrition. *Oxford Economic Papers, 58*(3), 450–474.

Alexander, J., Boothby, N., & Wessells, M. (2010). Education and protection of children and youth affected by armed conflict: An essential link. *Protecting education from attack: A state of the art review*, 55-67.

Baxter, P., Ramesh, A., Menendez, A., & North, L. (2016). *Accelerated education programs in crisis and conflict: Building evidence and learning*. United States Agency for International Development. https://www.edu-links.org/sites/default/files/media/file/AEP-Literature-Review-FINAL.pdf

Bronfenbrenner, U. (1977). Toward an experimental ecology of human development. *American Psychologist, 32*(7), 513–530.

Bronfenbrenner, U. (1979). *The ecology of human development: Experiments by nature and design*. Harvard University Press.

Bronfenbrenner, U. (1986). Ecology of the family as a context for human development: Research perspectives. *Developmental Psychology, 22*(6), 723–742. doi:10.1037/0012-1649.22.6.723

Bronfenbrenner, U. (1992). Ecological systems theory. In R. Vasta (Ed.), *Six theories of child development: Revised formulations and current issues* (pp. 187–249). Jessica Kingsley Publishers.

Chamarbagwala, R., & Morán, H. E. (2010). The human capital consequences of civil war: Evidence from Guatemala. *Journal of Development Economics, 94*(1), 41–61.

Depenbusch, L., Schreinemachers, P., Roothaert, R., Namazzi, S., Onyango, C., Bongole, S., & Mutebi, J. (2021). Impact of home garden interventions in East Africa: Results of three randomized controlled trials. *Food Policy, 104*, 102140.

Evans, G. W., Gonnella, C., Marcynyszyn, L. A., Gentile, L., & Salpekar, N. (2005). The role of chaos in poverty and children's socioemotional adjustment. *Psychological Science, 16*(7), 560–565.

Ghirotti, M. (1992). A simple method for scoring housing conditions as income proxy in Ethiopia. *RRA Notes, 15*, 43–47.

IASC Reference Group for Mental Health and Psychosocial Support in Emergency Settings. (2010). *Mental health and psychosocial support in humanitarian emergencies: What should humanitarian health actors know?* World Health Organization. https://www.who.int/mental_health/publications/what_should_humanitarian_health_actors_know/en/

International Federation for Human Rights. (2016). *Repression and genocidal dynamics in Burundi*. https://reliefweb.int/sites/reliefweb.int/files/resources/burundi_report_english-2.pdf

Justin, P., Leone, M., & Salardi, P. (2013). Short- and long-term impact of violence on education: The case of Timor Leste. *World Economic Review, 28*(22), 320–353. doi:10.1093/wber/lht007

Kolb, S. M. (2012). Grounded theory and the constant comparative method: Valid research strategies for educators. *Journal of Emerging Trends in Educational Research and Policy Studies*, 3(1), 83–86.

Lischer, S. K. (2003). Collateral damage: Humanitarian assistance as a cause of conflict. *International Security*, 28(1), 79–109.

Nicolai, S., Greenhill, R., d'Orey, M. J., Magee, A., Rogerson, A., Wild, L., & Wales, J. (2016). *Education cannot wait: Proposing a fund for education in emergencies.* Overseas Development Institute.

Rogers, H., Sabarwal, S., Avitabile, C., Lee, J., Miyamoto, K., Nellemann, S., & Venegas Marin, S. (2020). *The COVID-19 pandemic: Shocks to education and policy responses.* World Bank Group Education. https://openknowledge.worldbank.org/bitstream/handle/10986/33696/148198.pdf?sequence=4&isAllowed=y

Shemyakina, O. (2011). The effect of armed conflict on accumulation of schooling: Results from Tajikistan. *Journal of Development Economics, 95*(2), 186–200.

Ungar, M., & Liebenberg, L. (2011). Assessing resilience across cultures using mixed methods: Construction of the Child and Youth Resilience Measure. *Journal of Mixed Methods Research*, 5(2), 126–149. http://dx.doi.org/10.1177/1558689811400607

UNICEF. (2016). *The state of the world's children 2016: A fair chance for every child.* http://www.ununiceficef.org/publications/ files/UNICEF_SOWC_2016.pdf

United Nations. (2021, April 13). Burundi refugees in Tanzania living in fear: UN rights experts. *UN News.* https://www.scribbr.com/apa-examples/website/

United Nations Office for the Coordination of Humanitarian Affairs (OCHA). (2019). *Global humanitarian overview 2019.* https://www.unocha.org/sites/unocha/files/GHO2019.pdf

Vagh, S. B. (2012). *Validating the ASER testing tools: Comparisons with reading fluency measures and the Read India measures.* Unpublished report.

World Bank Group. (2014). *Measuring income and poverty using Proxy Means Tests.* https://olc.worldbank.org/sites/default/files/1.pdf

13

Addressing Violence Against Children in Low-Resource and Humanitarian Settings

Potential of Family-Based Approaches

EVE S. PUFFER, SAVANNAH L. JOHNSON, AND
AMANDA L. SIM ∎

Violence against children is a global problem of enormous scale, with a billion children estimated to have been victimized by violence worldwide in 2014 alone (Hillis et al., 2016). Experiences of violence are among the many adverse childhood experiences (ACEs) that can have devastating effects on children's physical and psychological health throughout development (Hillis et al., 2017). Some ACEs are one-time events, others are time limited, and still others, including family violence within households, are chronic and part of a child's daily life. At the family level, ACEs might include maltreatment—abuse or neglect—coupled with related family problems, such as domestic violence, divorce, or parental substance use (Felitti et al., 1998; Narayan et al., 2021).

While it is important to understand the effects of each discrete ACE, the harsh reality is that children rarely face just one. While robust ACE prevalence data from low- and middle-income countries (LMICs) is scarce, 51% of a young adult sample in South Africa (Manyema & Richter, 2019), 36% of a young adult sample from Vietnam (Tran et al., 2015), and over 10% of an adolescent Brazilian sample had experienced at least three ACEs (Soares et al., 2016). In the United States, over 60% of adults have experienced at least one ACE and over 15% have experienced four or more (Jones et al., 2020). Research consistently supports that this accumulation of stressors—both the number and severity—is a major risk factor for multiple negative outcomes, including mental health problems, substance use, and problems in relationships (Anda et al., 2010; Hughes et al., 2017). Addressing both ACEs themselves and these health consequences is of increasing interest among practitioners and researchers and fits within the Sustainable Development Goals (SDGs), providing motivation for the global community to respond; ending violence against children is stated as a goal in its own right within SDG 16, and SDG 3—achieving good health and well-being—encompasses both physical and mental health (Cratsley & Mackey, 2018).

Many children experiencing ACEs are also living in chronic poverty, with global evidence suggesting ACEs occur at higher rates in low-income communities (Blum et al., 2019). Some children experience poverty at the household level within high-resource contexts, while others live in very low-resource contexts where poverty is pervasive both within children's homes and in their broader communities. Either can have serious consequences for children's development, and some have proposed that poverty is an ACE in and of itself (Crouch et al., 2019). Regardless of geographical region, the associations between poverty and exposure to other adverse experiences are clear, and the interactive effects can compound, leading to poorer long-term outcomes (Alhowaymel et al., 2021; Cuartas et al., 2019; Rubenstein et al., 2020). Here, the SDGs again open the door for attention to these complex associations. Progress toward eradicating poverty—the first SDG—contributes to reducing ACEs and their consequences, while reducing ACEs supports children to reach their developmental potential, becoming productive, healthy adults to help achieve improvements in their own communities (UNICEF et al., 2018).

This chapter focuses primarily on the ACE of interpersonal violence and the ways in which poverty, and resource constraints more broadly, affects the experiences and consequences of this violence. At the center of these interacting risk factors is a child's household, making family-based interventions a promising avenue for reducing exposure to ACEs and to mitigating their harmful effects. Examples of family-level interventions in low-resource settings are presented, including a parenting intervention in Liberia, a family-strengthening intervention for Burmese migrant families living in Thailand, and a family therapy intervention in Kenya.

THE CONTEXT OF POVERTY

In low-resource settings—often conceptualized as lacking adequate funds to meet the needs of the population (e.g., health care)—children and their families face multiple, concurrent stressors. These range from unmet basic needs and crowding within households to broader concerns of poor access to health care or high-quality education. These challenges are pervasive in LMICs as well as humanitarian settings—places that have experienced conflict, complex political emergencies, or natural disasters (Sphere Project, 2011). However, they certainly exist within low-resource areas of high-income countries (HICs) as well. The experiences of poverty across settings have similarities, though contexts lead to important differences. For families experiencing poverty within an HIC, like the United States, complex health care systems are established, but significant disparities remain in *who* can access care (Kataoka et al., 2002). Co-occurring, systemic inequities—cutting across education, employment, insurance policies, housing, and criminal justice—leave many families and children without access to quality health services, especially for mental health needs (Wheeler & Bryant, 2017).

In LMIC or humanitarian settings—settings emphasized in this chapter's examples—there are certainly still large disparities between families, but the lack of resources in the broader community- and country-level contexts create a different experience for children and families. Educational and health care services—especially those needed for children and families requiring specialized support—are virtually nonexistent regardless of household-level resources. An analysis of 58 LMICs documented that 239,000 more mental health professionals would be needed to fill the gap to treat the top eight mental disorders prioritized by the World Health Organization (Bruckner et al., 2011). The services that are available are centralized in urban areas and can be costly, remaining inaccessible to most families. LMIC settings also offer few opportunities for training professionals in child and family treatments, leaving families who are struggling with stressors of poverty, disrupted relationships, and children's emotional, behavioral, and academic needs with few options for care (Patel et al., 2013). The pervasive pressures resulting from poverty in LMICs, conflict or disaster in humanitarian settings, and the dearth of available supports likely contribute to the apparent higher rates of violence against children in these settings (Beatriz & Salhi, 2019; Stark & Landis, 2016).

THEORETICAL FRAMEWORKS: ECONOMIC ADVERSITY, VIOLENCE, AND CHILD WELL-BEING

Two influential theoretical models are helpful in guiding thought about how economic adversity and lack of research influence exposure to violence, especially within families, and resulting consequences for children's development. First, the family stress model (FSM) developed by Conger and Donnellan (2007) puts a strong emphasis on the external stress—often economic—exerted on families as a function of their context. The FSM posits that external stress negatively influences caregiver mental health, in turn increasing the likelihood of various forms of interpersonal conflict in families: interparental relationship problems and intimate partner violence, as well as fewer positive and more frequent harsh parenting practices. Consistent with the broader literature, harsh parenting then increases risk among children for difficulties across domains of functioning, including increased risk for mental health problems (Neppl et al., 2016). While the FSM was developed to explain the pathway from economic disadvantage to adverse child outcomes in low-resource communities in the United States, this pathway has demonstrated consistency across geographic locations (Masarik & Conger,

2017), including Kenya (Kumar et al., 2018), South Africa (Meinck et al., 2017), and Ghana (Huang et al., 2018), as well as in humanitarian contexts such as the Syrian refugee crisis (Sim et al., 2018).

The toxic stress model (TSM) provides a complementary perspective on how a child's biological development is affected by a broad range of individual-, family-, and community-level risk factors. In their foundational work on the TSM, Shonkoff and colleagues (2012) describe the ways in which stressors, including ACEs, accumulate to affect children and their caregivers. The model includes poverty as one of the key stressors alongside other resource-related risk factors at the community and family levels, such as low-quality childcare and lack of health care access. Further, the model highlights how the experience of chronic stressors in a caregiving environment that lacks supportive, responsive adults leaves children vulnerable to toxic stress—the frequent, intense, and prolonged activation of the body's stress response systems. Chronic stressors affect caregivers as well, impacting their physical and mental health, stress responses, and executive functioning associated with planning and decision-making (McEwen & McEwen, 2017). Taken together, children in low-resource contexts may experience negative caregiving environments, both inside and outside of the home, sometimes characterized by neglect or harsh treatment. When experienced over time and early in life, effects on children can be dramatic and lasting, including problems in structural and functional brain development (Brisson et al., 2020).

RESILIENCE: BUFFERING CONSEQUENCES OF ADVERSITY IN LOW-RESOURCE SETTINGS

Understanding how low-resource contexts increase violence exposure and threaten children's well-being prompts the need to identify and strongly emphasize factors that can buffer the stresses of poverty (Ungar, 2011; Ungar & Theron, 2020). Resilience theory contributes by continuing to recognize individual-, family-, and community-level influences while flipping the focus to promotive and protective factors and processes (PPFPs) that contribute to positive adaptation in the face of adversity (Masten & Cicchetti, 2016; Ungar, 2019). Specific to understanding ACEs, researchers have expanded on concepts of resilience by studying "counter-ACEs"—positive experiences during childhood that may counteract the negative consequences of early adverse experiences (Crandall et al., 2019). Definitions of counter-ACEs vary but include experiences such as having people in a child's life who are safe and supportive (e.g., teachers, friends, family members), experiencing engagement and enjoyment in some activities (e.g., school), or having internal beliefs that are positive and comforting (Narayan et al., 2018). Relevant to children in low-resource contexts, some also include factors such as perceived high socioeconomic status or having residential stability (Slopen et al., 2017). Overall, findings from this work support the protective nature of positive experiences in reducing the long-term negative health consequences of adversity. Results from resilience research highlight the importance of promoting positive experiences for children to the extent possible, even within contexts where poverty and violence persist (Masten & Narayan, 2012; Tol et al., 2013). This needs to occur alongside the urgent work of reducing violence and increasing access to resources.

INTERVENTION GOALS: ADDRESSING THE CONTINUUM FROM PREVENTION TO TREATMENT

The evidence describing how poverty and violence affect children—paired with the evidence on protective factors that can mitigate harm—points to four major intervention goals for addressing violence and its psychological effects on children in low-resource settings: (a) violence prevention—preventing the initiation of violence, (b) violence reduction—decreasing ongoing violence against children, (c) promotion of protective factors—increasing positive individual and interpersonal experiences to reduce consequences of violence, and (d) treatment of consequences—directly treating children's mental health or developmental problems associated with violence.

These four goals can help identify *who* can benefit from an intervention, an intervention's *goals and measures* of outcomes, and the *core evidence-based content* needed to achieve those goals. However, the goals should not, and usually cannot, be addressed in isolation. Rather, programs should be designed to consider the continuum of risk, the continuum of violence experiences and behaviors, and the continuum of consequences. Programs designed with this broader perspective can then aim to reduce risk and increase protection at multiple steps in the pathways that move children from being at risk for violence to experiencing severe violence. Facilitating this is the fact that there are many commonalities across the core evidence-based components effective for achieving prevention, reduction, and promotion goals, several of which are presented within examples later in this chapter. These core components can form the foundation for an intervention that aims to achieve multiple goals, especially for groups of participants with varied needs.

In addition to targeting multiple goals, intervention strategies for reducing risk and increasing resilience—especially in low-resource contexts—need to consider multiple levels of influence: individuals, families, and communities. For each of the four goals described previously, change can be achieved through behavior change of individuals, often the adults in a child's life; change can be achieved through shifts in family interactions; and change can be achieved by activating community support and increasing access to resources. Considering all three levels, even if the intervention does not act directly on all three, is likely to be most effective.

While targeting a range of goals and multiple levels of influence broadens the scope of interventions, the reality is that most individuals, families, and communities come to an intervention with constellations of needs that do not fit cleanly into the categories for goals or levels of intervention. Consider a parent, perhaps with their own history of ACEs, who has recently begun using moderately harsh physical discipline after losing her job and noticing that her child has become more disruptive. If this parent presents to a program that addresses violence and child well-being, the primary goal may be to *reduce* violent discipline, but goals also include *preventing* escalation of severity, *promoting* positive coping and parenting skills, and perhaps providing *early behavioral intervention* for the child. For this parent, who is also coping with loss of resources, concurrent goals may be to support them in accessing community-based resources to meet physical needs and regain employment and to ensure that the program teaches skills that are feasible within their current circumstances.

ACHIEVING GOALS IN LOW-RESOURCE SETTINGS: IMPLEMENTATION CHALLENGES AND OPPORTUNITIES

It is important to think about *how* evidence-based interventions can be delivered effectively in low-resource contexts. As noted, many low-resource communities, and sometimes entire regions or countries in the case of LMICs, have very limited infrastructure for supporting the delivery of interventions, including mental health care and psychosocial support more broadly (Barnett et al., 2018; Hoeft et al., 2018; Jacob et al., 2007). With immense pressure on health and social service systems, little attention is given to public health efforts, including those related to violence and child well-being; prevention and promotion programs are rare and implementation barriers are many (Mejia et al., 2017). The lack of human resources is a central problem. In LMICs, there are inadequate numbers of professionals or paraprofessionals in fields related to these services (e.g., mental health care, social work, public health). Similarly, in HICs, the poorest communities, including rural areas, often have the poorest access to high-quality services (Singh et al., 2017). In either setting, nontraditional delivery strategies are needed to address the human resources gap and shrink the overall gap in access to care (Baumann et al., 2019).

Task Shifting

A primary strategy for shrinking the human resource gap is task shifting or task sharing—practices of training nonspecialists to provide services usually delivered by specialists. This increases the number of trained providers, allowing specialists to reserve limited time for training and more intensive levels of care (Eaton et al., 2011; Kakuma et al., 2011). In the field of global mental health, task shifting is a primary focus of research on and implementation of interventions in LMICs. Evidence is growing, with findings showing that nonspecialists can effectively provide evidence-based care for a range of disorders and interventions (Joshi et al., 2014). As examples, lay providers have delivered trauma-focused cognitive behavioral therapy to children in multiple countries in sub-Saharan Africa (Dorsey et al., 2020), as well as family-based group interventions to reduce violence and improve mental health in LMICs (Healy et al., 2018) and humanitarian settings (Jordans et al., 2013; Puffer et al., 2015, 2017). More intensive home-visiting family interventions also have been delivered by lay providers with promising results (Betancourt et al., 2011; Puffer et al., 2019). While tested more extensively in LMICs, task shifting is also gaining attention as a strategy for reaching underserved communities in HICs (Sashidharan et al., 2016). Two reviews documented that most task shifting for mental health in HICs involves community health workers or primary care providers as part of clinic-based collaborative care models (Barnett et al., 2018) and that task shifting is proving feasible, acceptable, and likely effective in the United States (Weaver & Lapidos, 2018).

Engaging Communities

In addition to the question of who delivers interventions, the location of delivery must overcome common barriers to access—the clear geographical and cost barriers for families living in poverty, as well as the invisible barriers of stigma and mistrust that are just beneath the surface. Providing services through community-based care, broadly defined, has helped address these barriers and move toward increasing access and engagement (Kohrt et al., 2018; Settipani et al., 2019). Community-based care can range from delivering an intervention within a clinic located in a community to embedding a mental health intervention into other community-based social structures and services, such as schools (Sanchez et al., 2018), religious institutions (Blank et al., 2002; Puffer et al., 2013), or existing community-based or nongovernmental organizations (NGOs) providing other support to individuals and families.

More deeply embedded community-based approaches may be particularly important for interventions addressing the potentially sensitive issues of violence against children and mental health, as stigma for seeking or participating in these programs may be high. Forming true collaborations with community partners from the beginning of implementation can facilitate greater feasibility, acceptability, and overall effectiveness (Collins et al., 2018); stakeholders within a community are best placed to advise on delivery strategies that will have the greatest reach (Puffer et al., 2016). Further, integrating interventions into existing community structures that have complementary values and goals could lead to packages of services that provide a more comprehensive, synergistic experience for participants. For example, one of the family interventions described below, Tuko Pamoja, has been implemented in Kenya within churches—trusted social settings that provide a wide range of instrumental and psychosocial support *and* have an explicit goal of supporting family relationships (Puffer et al., 2019). Building on existing sources of support can facilitate engagement and perhaps bolster effectiveness if programs meet multiple levels of need simultaneously (Puffer & Ayuku, 2022).

INTERVENTION APPROACHES

In the lowest resource settings globally, interventions addressing violence against children have commonly been implemented with (a) families experiencing interpersonal violence and (b) families exposed to war or other community violence in humanitarian settings. Research has identified important connections between the two, showing both elevated rates of family violence within conflict-affected contexts (Stark & Landis, 2016) and the protective effects of positive, nonviolent family relationships on children exposed to war (Miller & Jordans, 2016). This has led to a major focus on understanding and reducing family violence to maximize benefits for children.

Interventions for addressing family violence against children have included universal public health interventions, such as awareness-raising campaigns to provide information on the negative impacts of child maltreatment (Poole et al., 2014). International NGOs operating in LMICs or humanitarian contexts also hold community-based campaigns to raise awareness of the harms of abuse as part of their child protection efforts (Zuilkowski et al., 2019). Structural and policy-level interventions further attempt to reduce child maltreatment, including enacting mandatory reporting guidelines and providing legal pathways for accountability.

In addition to these broader interventions in low-resource communities, growing evidence across HICs and LMICs points to intervening directly at the family level as a very promising approach for addressing the four intervention goals listed earlier. Family interventions can often target goals simultaneously: prevention, reduction, promotion, and early treatment. The interventions described in later sections are examples of those that focus on reducing violence and improving interactions *within families*. They are designed to be implemented in communities with very little infrastructure for formal and professional services, including humanitarian settings. One overarching goal of these programs is to build resilience among children and caregivers often living through the chronic stressors of poverty, community disruption, and ongoing threat of violence.

Family-Level Interventions: Core Strategies and Adaptation Considerations

Evidence-based interventions that aim to prevent and reduce violence, alongside improving protective factors—positive interactions and relationship quality—share many of the same strategies and guiding principles (Berry et al., 2014; Pedersen et al., 2019). Interventions also have important differences, but it can be helpful to recognize some common elements when considering the development and adaptation of interventions for varied low-resource settings. Common strategies include behavioral skills training in nonviolent behavior management strategies (e.g., differential attention, brief time-out), positive attention and reinforcement strategies (e.g., praise, rewards), and communication skills—especially for programs involving adolescents or the whole family. Many interventions also include skills for caregivers to cope and manage their own emotional reactions. Skills training strategies often include modeling and in-session practice, as well as homework; these are consistent with social learning theory, which emphasizes the importance of observing and imitating the behaviors of others to achieve behavior change (Bandura & McClelland, 1977). Other behavior management strategies, including setting rules and routines, are also often incorporated, and nearly all interventions typically include psychoeducation based on goals and target population, ranging from information on child development to information related to stress responses and child or caregiver mental health.

Some established evidence-based interventions based on the aforementioned core components have proven effective for families in low-resource contexts within HICs. However, many families affected by poverty or living in low-resource communities differ in significant ways from the primary populations in which these interventions have been developed and tested. Some of these challenges relate directly to restricted resources (e.g., logistical barriers to care), while others are more complex: cultural differences among minority populations who may be overrepresented among families affected by poverty or cultural and contextual differences among families in LMICs receiving interventions transferred from HIC settings. These differences lead to the important issue of intervention adaptation: changes that may need to be made to improve the feasibility, relevance, and effectiveness of interventions across diverse populations and contexts. In thinking this through, it can be helpful to categorize adaptations into two categories: (a) content adaptations and (b) implementation adaptations.

Related to the core strategies described earlier, which span interventions across contexts, evidence suggests that many of the same basic principles can be applied across populations (Knerr et al., 2013). However, there is debate over the extent to which existing evidence-based interventions should be adapted for specific populations, cultures, and settings (Leijten et al., 2016; Mejia et al., 2017). Possibilities range from using established manualized interventions with very minimal surface adaptations (e.g., translation, changes in examples), to making substantive changes to an evidence-based program to improve fit with a population's context and culture, to developing new programs based on core strategies but highly tailored for a specific population (López-Zerón et al., 2020). Adaptations to implementation strategies are a bit less controversial. In low-resource contexts, these adaptations are likely to focus on increasing access and engagement (Lau, 2006). For example, this could include identifying providers who will be most appropriate and trusted or delivering an intervention in a new type of setting—both often outside of the health system. Some adaptations then fall in between content and implementation (e.g., switching written information to visual to increase feasibility and appropriateness for participants with less education).

Overall, each level of adaptation is important to consider, and clear pros and cons exist across approaches. Evidence is limited on the impacts of adaptation on efficacy, though some data from parenting programs suggest that adapted programs achieve equivalent results (Leijten et al., 2016) and that surface-level adaptations paired with implementation adaptations can improve engagement and outcomes (Kumpfer et al., 2002). Overall, the adaptation process requires a careful examination of how to balance fidelity (i.e., adhering to the hypothesized evidence basis for intervention effectiveness strategies) with fit (i.e., ensuring that the intervention is relevant and acceptable for a population; Lau, 2006). A participatory process including members of the target population and community partners can also facilitate adaptation efforts, grounding adaptations in population-specific data (Puffer et al., 2013).

Parenting and Family Interventions: Overview and Examples of Evidence-Based Programs

In the following sections, examples of parenting and family interventions that target one or more of the central goals in addressing violence and its impact on children are reviewed. Intervention research has documented effects of these programs on one or more of these key outcomes: (a) reducing family-level violence against children, (b) improving family-level protective factors that prevent violence and build resilience, and (c) improving child mental health outcomes. First, interventions that include only caregivers are described, followed by "whole family" interventions that include both caregivers and children. Within these categories, examples of specific interventions are provided, including their goals, content, implementation strategy, and outcomes. As described previously, task shifting and community engagement are core strategies illustrated here.

CAREGIVER-LEVEL INTERVENTIONS

Parenting interventions delivered to primary caregivers of children show promise for violence prevention and reduction in both HICs and LMICs (Desai et al., 2017; Efevbera et al., 2018; Knerr et al., 2013). A review of reviews, primarily from HICs, documented overall positive effects of parenting programs on violence outcomes ranging from self-reported violence discipline to rates of child injuries (Desai et al., 2017). Many parenting programs delivered in low-resource settings also have shown positive effects related to the emotional and behavioral health of children and adolescents (Efevbera et al., 2018; Mejia et al., 2012; Pedersen et al., 2019).

Within low-resource populations in HICs, for example, the Triple P program, with its public health approach, has shown population-level reductions in child maltreatment in low-income communities (Sanders et al., 2014). Incredible Years is another empirically supported program that has shown reductions in harsh parenting practices among low-income parents, including those with their own history of child maltreatment (Hurlburt et al., 2013). For prevention of child maltreatment among mothers of very young children in the United States, home visiting programs also have proven effective for high-risk, low-income populations (Levey et al., 2017). In LMICs, Parenting for Lifelong Health (PLH) is among the parenting programs with the strongest evidence; versions of PLH for both children and adolescents have been evaluated in multiple countries showing efficacy on multiple outcomes related to violent discipline and protective factors, including positive parenting, improved parent-child relationships, and improved child behavior (Ward et al., 2020). Parenting programs have demonstrated positive effects in humanitarian settings as well; Syrian refugees who participated in the Caregiver Support Intervention—a program targeting stress of the caregivers alongside positive parenting education—reduced harsh parenting and parental stress and increased parental warmth and responsiveness (Miller et al., 2020). Lastly, Parents Make the Difference (PMD) is an intervention delivered in the humanitarian setting of postconflict Liberia shown to reduce harsh discipline. We provide details of this intervention and its evaluation as an example of a caregiver-level intervention.

Parents Make the Difference: A Positive Parenting Program in Postconflict Liberia. Parents Make the Difference (PMD) is a 10-session group-based parenting intervention for caregivers of young children implemented by the International Rescue Committee in postconflict Liberia (Puffer et al., 2015). The primary goals of PMD were to reduce child maltreatment within families, especially harsh physical discipline, and to improve the quality of parent-child interactions—both through increasing use of positive parenting strategies. Figure 13.1 outlines the intervention's theory of change.

The sessions of PMD covered psychoeducation related to appropriate developmental expectations and the influence of nurturing versus harsh parenting on children's development; active behavioral skills training on positive parenting strategies, including effective and empathic communication with children, provision of positive attention, and praise; behavioral skills training on nonviolent

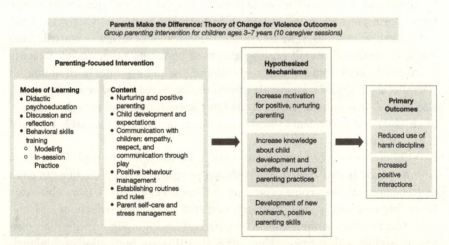

Figure 13.1. Parents Make the Difference: Theory of Change for Violence Outcomes.
NOTE: Secondary content included two sessions of caregiver training on activities to promote preacademic skills and a session on malaria prevention. Secondary outcomes included child cognitive abilities, child psychological well-being, and malaria prevention behaviors, with no significant findings.

discipline practices, including withdrawal of attention and time-out; instruction and discussion about setting routines and rules; and skills training on caregiver stress management. Material also included ideas for encouraging children's learning through simple academic games and health behavior information related to malaria prevention—a major health concern in the area at the time of implementation.

PMD sessions were highly interactive with an emphasis on discussion, modeling, and in-session skills practice through role play with other caregivers and coaching from facilitators. Approximately 25 caregivers attended together, meeting in central community locations. Lay facilitators with no previous experience related to parenting programs delivered PMD under the supervision of more highly trained staff (though also nonmental health professionals) and in consultation with mental health professionals in the United States as needed. In addition to the group sessions, one of the facilitators visited the home of each caregiver once during the program to discuss and reinforce skills.

Evaluation. A randomized controlled trial of PMD was conducted with a sample of 270 caregivers of children aged 3 to 7 years old. Caregivers were randomized to PMD or a waitlist control condition, and outcomes were measured via interviewer-administered surveys at baseline and 1 month after completion of the intervention. Results showed that PMD led to a 55.5% reduction in caregiver-reported use of harsh punishment practices ($p < 0.001$). Caregivers' positive behavior management strategies also increased, and caregiver-child interactions improved, with an average increase in positive interactions of 4.4%. After the 1-month follow-up period, PMD did not show a measurable downstream impact on child well-being, cognitive skills, or household adoption of malaria prevention behaviors based on survey data. Qualitative data also were collected to elucidate caregivers' perspectives on the changes and potential mechanisms of change (Giusto et al., 2017). Caregivers reported that the PMD sessions—especially those focused on empathy and child development—increased their identities as nurturers, protectors, and role models. This in turn drove their efforts to decrease harsh discipline, which reduced children's fear and led to more opportunities for positive interactions. (This study was preregistered at ClinicalTrials.gov [NCT01829815].)

Whole-Family Interventions

Interventions that include multiple members of the family as a central characteristic of the intervention remain less common than those focusing on caregivers as the main participant. However, especially for families with school-aged children or adolescents, these interventions can provide an opportunity for direct child intervention, positive shared family experiences, and real-world application of new communication and relationship-building skills during sessions. Perhaps unsurprisingly, these interventions tend to have stronger effects on increasing the protective outcomes and experiences hypothesized to prevent future violence or buffer the effects of past violence; they are less likely to directly target reductions in current child maltreatment, in some cases because a family approach is less appropriate in situations of ongoing violence. In a systematic review including 18 family-focused interventions in LMICs (Pedersen et al., 2019), results showed benefits of the majority of interventions on measures of family functioning, parenting, and/or child well-being. Within HICs, interventions delivered to multiple families together are backed by strong evidence for improving protective family- and child-level outcomes and have been implemented successfully in low-resource communities; some have also been adapted for use in LMICs. One example is 4Rs 2Ss for Strengthening Families, a multiple-family group intervention that has improved parenting stress and child behavior problems among families living in poverty in the United States (McKay et al., 2002); it has been adapted for implementation and evaluation in Uganda (Ssewamala et al., 2018). Another is the Strengthening Families Program (SFP), also group based, and developed in the United States for high-risk families. In numerous randomized controlled trials, the SFP has demonstrated positive impacts on both youths' behaviors and child maltreatment, and it has been adapted for 36 countries (Kumpfer & Magalhães, 2018). The following example is one of the SFP adaptations in a humanitarian setting.

Happy Families: A Family Strengthening Program for Burmese Migrant Families in Thailand. Happy Families is a 12-session, group-based intervention adapted from the Strengthening Families Program (SFP; Kumpfer et al., 2008). Happy Families was implemented by the International Rescue Committee with Burmese migrant families living in Thailand who had children ages 7 to 15, many who were experiencing stressors related to displacement, poverty, and security concerns. Proximal goals of the intervention included improving positive parenting and family interaction skills, to reach the primary outcomes of reducing child maltreatment and improving family functioning. The theory of change (Figure 13.2) then posited that these changes would contribute to improving the mental health of participating children. Happy Families was delivered in community spaces (e.g., schools) by pairs of lay facilitators—one staff member from the NGO and one community member. A family meal was provided for all sessions, as well as childcare for children too young to participate.

Sessions within Happy Families were divided, with some time spent in separate groups for children and caregivers and some time spent in a large session with all family members together. All content was highly interactive, including short didactic material followed by role plays and active practice. For the children in particular, material emphasized games and hands-on activities. When together, family members also completed in-session activities designed to facilitate skills practice. Specific session topics included psychoeducation on child development, behavioral skills training related to positive rewards, communication, and problem-solving, as well as setting goals, setting limits, and using behavior change plans. The effects of alcohol and drug use on the family were also covered.

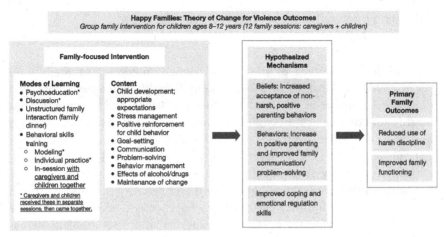

Figure 13.2. Happy Families: Theory of Change for Violence Outcomes.
NOTE: Secondary outcomes included improvements in children's physical, social, and emotional well-being.

Across topics, while the main focus was often on parent-child interactions and child behavior, there was discussion about applying skills throughout the family system. Teaching coping skills for caregivers' own well-being also was incorporated throughout.

Evaluation. A randomized controlled trial was conducted with 479 families who were randomly assigned to the intervention group or to a waitlist control condition (Annan et al., 2016; Puffer et al., 2017). One month after the intervention, the intervention group demonstrated improvements on overall family functioning; parent-child interactions, including reduced negative interactions; and parent-child relationship quality. Caregivers also reported reduced use of harsh discipline practices. For child outcomes, the interventions led to reductions in externalizing and attention problems, and child-reported prosocial behaviors; no impact was shown on internalizing problems. (This study was preregistered at ClinicalTrials.gov [NCT01829815].)

EMERGING OPPORTUNITIES AND FUTURE DIRECTIONS: BROADENING THE LENS

Given the growing body of evidence supporting individual interventions at the caregiver and family levels, valuable next steps could include combining and integrating intervention approaches that take on some of the broader factors that influence violence against children and the impacts that it has on their lives. There are many opportunities for integrated approaches, and innovation and research are already beginning in the three approaches discussed here.

Integrating Interventions to Prevent Violence Across the Family System

First, while the content of most family-based interventions focuses on parent-child relationships and child mental health outcomes, there is a growing recognition of the need to address violence prevention and relationship functioning at the couple and family systems levels as well, perhaps integrating strategies to prevent violence against both women and children (Bacchus et al., 2017). One approach to this—especially at a group level—is to develop family-strengthening interventions that include, within one manualized intervention, psychoeducation and behavioral skills specific to both parenting and intimate partnerships. Another is to take a more flexible and tailored approach, akin to family therapy, that addresses problems across the family system that are risk factors for violence, including couple's conflict and problems related to parenting. An example of this type of intervention, Tuko Pamoja, is described here, with pilot results in Kenya showing promising results.

Tuko Pamoja: A Family Therapy Intervention for Low-Resource Settings

Tuko Pamoja ("We Are Together" in Swahili) is an evidence-informed family therapy intervention designed for lay counselor delivery in low-resource settings (Puffer et al., 2019). Tuko Pamoja is a components-based family intervention that integrates multiple strategies from solution-focused and systems-based family therapies, as well as those from parenting skills training and cognitive behavioral therapies. This is an intervention for individual families, provided primarily in homes, by lay providers identified within the community as individuals already sought out for assistance with family conflict and related problems. The primary goal of Tuko Pamoja is to improve family functioning as a mechanism for preventing family violence and improving mental health of both children and caregivers. Tuko Pamoja is manualized, including five modules for different family relationships and presenting problems; each module has similar core steps, and families receive only the modules that they need. The intervention is not time limited; families may continue until they have reached their goals.

A mixed-methods pilot study of Tuko Pamoja in Kenya was conducted with 10 families (Puffer et al., 2020). Results showed pre-post improvements on the primary outcome—family functioning—as well as on the mental health of children and caregivers. Harsh discipline and harsh interactions between caregivers also decreased. With point estimates representing change of more than two standard deviations from baseline for the majority of primary outcomes, data are preliminary but provide encouraging pilot data to support a larger randomized trial of the intervention.

Integrating Violence Reduction and Direct Poverty Alleviation Interventions

Thinking back to the theoretical models guiding our understanding of violence in families within the context of poverty, a clear next direction is to combine violence reduction interventions with concrete poverty alleviation strategies (Zuilkowski et al., 2019). Multiple parenting and family interventions have included material related to economic problem-solving (Cluver et al., 2020; Puffer et al., 2016), and some interventions described previously have been delivered in collaboration with organizations that provide material support. However, far fewer approaches have truly integrated poverty alleviation strategies in ways that link to family-strengthening principles in meaningful ways. Two recent exceptions first include a combined women's economic support (i.e., livelihood development, seed grants) and family coaching intervention piloted in Burkina Faso that reduced harsh parenting and overall violence against children in homes (Ismayilova & Karimli, 2020). In Tanzania, the Skillful Parenting and Agribusiness Child Abuse Prevention Study also showed reduced child maltreatment following a combined agribusiness and parent management training intervention that intentionally engaged fathers through existing farmers' groups. The parenting intervention alone also showed benefits, but participants in the agribusiness-only intervention arm actually showed increases in child abuse indicators (Lachman et al., 2020). Taken together, this early evidence is encouraging, and future studies can elucidate types of poverty alleviation strategies that may act most synergistically with family-based interventions. Possibilities may include economic-strengthening strategies, including income-generating activities, that actively involve all members of the family in developmentally appropriate roles.

Integrating Violence Reduction and Policy-Level Interventions

Lastly, it is clear that structural and policy-level factors affect families' daily lives, creating and exacerbating poor economic conditions that contribute to stressors and downstream mental health concerns and family violence (Sim et al., 2018; Wahlbeck et al., 2017). It is therefore important to continue to strive to act on these broader societal levels alongside "bottom-up" community-driven and family-centered approaches (Wessells, 2015). There may be creative ways to integrate the efforts, or to at least connect the two in the context of advocacy and policy formation. Baumann and colleagues (2019) describe the need for this well, emphasizing the need for partnering with local policymakers to ensure sustainable implementation efforts through buy-in and resource allocation. On the global level, some progress has also been made, with the World Health Organization endorsing the Nurturing Care Framework that has responsive caregiving as a major element to be prioritized in policymaking and scaling up of intervention strategies to promote positive child development (UNICEF et al., 2018). Governments and stakeholders established multilevel national and global Nurturing Care milestones—including advocacy, workforce development, and research—to be reached by 2023. Across both smaller-scale local efforts and large-scale global initiatives, a very concrete step is engaging with policymakers for improving program reach and impacts. In future work, implementation strategies can be evaluated that involve engaging with these broader systems much earlier in the intervention implementation and evaluation process.

REFERENCES

Alhowaymel, F., Kalmakis, K., & Jacelon, C. (2021). Developing the concept of adverse childhood experiences: A global perspective. *Journal of Pediatric Nursing, 56*, 18–23. https://doi.org/10.1016/j.pedn.2020.10.004

Anda, R. F., Butchart, A., Felitti, V. J., & Brown, D. W. (2010). Building a framework for global surveillance of the public health implications of adverse childhood experiences. *American Journal of Preventive Medicine, 39*(1), 93–98. https://doi.org/10.1016/j.amepre.2010.03.015

Annan, J., Sim, A., Puffer, E. S., Salhi, C., & Betancourt, T. S. (2016). Improving mental health outcomes of Burmese migrant and displaced children in Thailand: A community-based randomized controlled trial of a parenting and family skills intervention. *Prevention Science, 18*(7), 793–803. https://doi.org/10.1007/s11121-016-0728-2

Bacchus, L. J., Colombini, M., Urbina, M. C., Howarth, E., Gardner, F., Annan, J., Ashburn, K., Madrid, B., Levtov, R., & Watts, C. (2017). Exploring opportunities for coordinated responses to intimate partner violence and child maltreatment in low and middle income countries: A scoping review. *Psychology, Health & Medicine, 22*(Suppl. 1), 135–165. https://doi.org/10.1080/13548506.2016.1274410

Bandura, A., & McClelland, D. C. (1977). *Social learning theory*. Prentice Hall.

Barnett, M. L., Gonzalez, A., Miranda, J., Chavira, D. A., & Lau, A. S. (2018). Mobilizing community health workers to address mental health disparities for underserved populations: A systematic review. *Administration and Policy in Mental Health, 45*(2), 195–211. https://doi.org/10.1007/s10488-017-0815-0

Baumann, A. A., Mejia, A., Lachman, J. M., Parra Cardona, J. R., López-Zerón, G., Amador Buenabad, N. G., Vargas, E., & Domenech Rodríguez, M. M. (2019). Parenting programs for underserved populations in low- and middle-income countries: Issues of scientific integrity and social justice. *Global Social Welfare: Research, Policy & Practice, 6*(3), 199–207. https://doi.org/10.1007/s40609-018-0121-0

Beatriz, E., & Salhi, C. (2019). Child discipline in low- and middle-income countries: Socioeconomic disparities at the household- and country-level. *Child Abuse & Neglect, 94*, 104023. https://doi.org/10.1016/j.chiabu.2019.104023

Berry, V., Blower, S., Axford, N., Little, M., & Kaoukji, D. (2014). The prevention of child maltreatment and neglect. In Jon R. Conte (Ed.), *Child abuse and neglect worldwide: Understanding, defining, and measuring child maltreatment; Global responses; Interventions and treatments* (Vols. 1–3, pp. 177–204). Praeger/ABC-CLIO.

Betancourt, T. S., Meyers-Ohki, S. E., Stevenson, A., Ingabire, C., Kanyanganzi, F., Munyana, M., Mushashi, C., Teta, S., Fayida, I., Cyamatare, F. R., Stulac, S., & Beardslee, W. R. (2011). Using mixed-methods research to adapt and evaluate a family strengthening intervention in Rwanda. *African Journal of Traumatic Stress*, *2*(1), 32–45.

Blank, M. B., Mahmood, M., Fox, J. C., & Guterbock, T. (2002). Alternative mental health services: The role of the Black church in the South. *American Journal of Public Health*, *92*(10), 1668–1672. https://doi.org/10.2105/AJPH.92.10.1668

Blum, R. W., Li, M., & Naranjo-Rivera, G. (2019). Measuring Adverse Child Experiences among young adolescents globally: Relationships with depressive symptoms and violence perpetration. *Journal of Adolescent Health*, *65*(1), 86–93. https://doi.org/10.1016/j.jadohealth.2019.01.020

Brisson, D., McCune, S., Wilson, J. H., Speer, S. R., McCrae, J. S., & Calhoun, K. H. (2020). A systematic review of the association between poverty and biomarkers of toxic stress. *Journal of Evidence-Based Social Work*, *17*(6), 696–713. https://doi.org/10.1080/26408066.2020.1769786

Bruckner, T. A., Scheffler, R. M., Shen, G., Yoon, J., Chisholm, D., Morris, J., Fulton, B. D., Dal Poz, M. R., & Saxena, S. (2011). The mental health workforce gap in low- and middle-income countries: A needs-based approach. *Bulletin of the World Health Organization*, *89*(3), 184–194. https://doi.org/10.2471/BLT.10.082784

Cluver, L., Shenderovich, Y., Meinck, F., Berezin, M. N., Doubt, J., Ward, C. L., Parra-Cardona, J., Lombard, C., Lachman, J. M., Wittesaele, C., Wessels, I., Gardner, F., & Steinert, J. I. (2020). Parenting, mental health and economic pathways to prevention of violence against children in South Africa. *Social Science & Medicine*, *262*, 113194. https://doi.org/10.1016/j.socscimed.2020.113194

Collins, S. E., Clifasefi, S. L., Stanton, J., Straits, K. J., Gil-Kashiwabara, E., Rodriguez Espinosa, P., . . . Wallerstein, N. (2018). Community-based participatory research (CBPR): Towards equitable involvement of community in psychology research. *American Psychologist*, *73*(7), 884–898. https://doi.org/10.1037/amp0000167

Conger, R. D., & Donnellan, M. B. (2007). An interactionist perspective on the socioeconomic context of human development. *Annual Review of Psychology*, *58*(1), 175–199. https://doi.org/10.1146/annurev.psych.58.110405.085551

Crandall, A., Miller, J. R., Cheung, A., Novilla, L. K., Glade, R., Novilla, M. L. B., Magnusson, B. M., Leavitt, B. L., Barnes, M. D., & Hanson, C. L. (2019). ACEs and counter-ACEs: How positive and negative childhood experiences influence adult health. *Child Abuse & Neglect*, *96*, 104089. https://doi.org/10.1016/j.chiabu.2019.104089

Cratsley, K., & Mackey, T. K. (2018). Health policy brief: Global mental health and the United Nations' sustainable development goals. *Families, Systems & Health: The Journal of Collaborative Family Healthcare*, *36*(2), 225–229. https://doi.org/10.1037/fsh0000329

Crouch, E., Probst, J. C., Radcliff, E., Bennett, K. J., & McKinney, S. H. (2019). Prevalence of adverse childhood experiences (ACEs) among US children. *Child Abuse & Neglect*, *92*, 209–218. https://doi.org/10.1016/j.chiabu.2019.04.010

Cuartas, J., Grogan-Kaylor, A., Ma, J., & Castillo, B. (2019). Civil conflict, domestic violence, and poverty as predictors of corporal punishment in Colombia. *Child Abuse & Neglect*, *90*, 108–119. https://doi.org/10.1016/j.chiabu.2019.02.003

Desai, C. C., Reece, J.-A., & Shakespeare-Pellington, S. (2017). The prevention of violence in childhood through parenting programmes: A global review. *Psychology, Health & Medicine, 22*(Suppl. 1), 166–186. https://doi.org/10.1080/13548506.2016.1271952

Dorsey, S., Lucid, L., Martin, P., King, K. M., O'Donnell, K., Murray, L. K., Wasonga, A. I., Itemba, D. K., Cohen, J. A., Manongi, R., & Whetten, K. (2020). Effectiveness of task-shifted trauma-focused cognitive behavioral therapy for children who experienced parental death and posttraumatic stress in Kenya and Tanzania: A randomized clinical trial. *JAMA Psychiatry, 77*(5), 464–473. https://doi.org/10.1001/jamapsychiatry.2019.4475

Eaton, J., McCay, L., Semrau, M., Chatterjee, S., Baingana, F., Araya, R., Ntulo, C., Thornicroft, G., & Saxena, S. (2011). Scale up of services for mental health in low-income and middle-income countries. *The Lancet, 378*(9802), 1592–1603. https://doi.org/10.1016/S0140-6736(11)60891-X

Efevbera, Y., McCoy, D. C., Wuermli, A. J., & Betancourt, T. S. (2018). Integrating early child development and violence prevention programs: A systematic review. *New Directions for Child and Adolescent Development, 2018*(159), 27–54. https://doi.org/10.1002/cad.20230

Felitti, V. J., Anda, R. F., Nordenberg, D., Williamson, D. F., Spitz, A. M., Edwards, V., Koss, M. P., & Marks, J. S. (1998). Relationship of childhood abuse and household dysfunction to many of the leading causes of death in adults: The Adverse Childhood Experiences (ACE) study. *American Journal of Preventive Medicine, 14*(4), 245–258. https://doi.org/10.1016/S0749-3797(98)00017-8

Giusto, A., Friis, E., Sim, A. L., Chase, R. M., Zayzay, J. O., Green, E., & Puffer, E. (2017). A qualitative study of mechanisms underlying effects of a parenting intervention in rural Liberia. *European Journal of Development Research, 29*(5), 964–982.

Healy, E. A., Kaiser, B. N., & Puffer, E. S. (2018). Family-based youth mental health interventions delivered by nonspecialist providers in low- and middle-income countries: A systematic review. *Families, Systems & Health: The Journal of Collaborative Family Healthcare, 36*(2), 182–197. https://doi.org/10.1037/fsh0000334

Hillis, S., Mercy, J., Amobi, A., & Kress, H. (2016). Global prevalence of past-year violence against children: A systematic review and minimum estimates. *Pediatrics, 137*(3), e20154079. https://doi.org/10.1542/peds.2015-4079

Hillis, S. D., Mercy, J. A., & Saul, J. R. (2017). The enduring impact of violence against children. *Psychology, Health & Medicine, 22*(4), 393–405. https://doi.org/10.1080/13548506.2016.1153679

Hoeft, T. J., Fortney, J. C., Patel, V., & Unützer, J. (2018). Task-sharing approaches to improve mental health care in rural and other low-resource settings: A systematic review. *Journal of Rural Health, 34*(1), 48–62. https://doi.org/10.1111/jrh.12229

Huang, K.-Y., Bornheimer, L. A., Dankyi, E., & de-Graft Aikins, A. (2018). Parental wellbeing, parenting and child development in Ghanaian families with young children. *Child Psychiatry & Human Development, 49*(5), 833–841. https://doi.org/10.1007/s10578-018-0799-3

Hughes, K., Bellis, M. A., Hardcastle, K. A., Sethi, D., Butchart, A., Mikton, C., Jones, L., & Dunne, M. P. (2017). The effect of multiple adverse childhood experiences on health: A systematic review and meta-analysis. *Lancet Public Health, 2*(8), e356–e366. https://doi.org/10.1016/S2468-2667(17)30118-4

Hurlburt, M. S., Nguyen, K., Reid, J., Webster-Stratton, C., & Zhang, J. (2013). Efficacy of the Incredible Years group parent program with families in Head Start who self-reported a history of child maltreatment. *Child Abuse & Neglect, 37*(8), 531–543. https://doi.org/10.1016/j.chiabu.2012.10.008

Ismayilova, L., & Karimli, L. (2020). Harsh parenting and violence against children: A trial with ultrapoor families in Francophone West Africa. *Journal of Clinical Child & Adolescent Psychology, 49*(1), 18–35. https://doi.org/10.1080/15374416.2018.1485103

Jacob, K., Sharan, P., Mirza, I., Garrido-Cumbrera, M., Seedat, S., Mari, J., Sreenivas, V., & Saxena, S. (2007). Mental health systems in countries: Where are we now? *The Lancet, 370*(9592), 1061–1077. https://doi.org/10.1016/S0140-6736(07)61241-0

Jones, C. M., Merrick, M. T., & Houry, D. E. (2020). Identifying and preventing adverse childhood experiences: Implications for clinical practice. *JAMA, 323*(1), 25. https://doi.org/10.1001/jama.2019.18499

Jordans, M. J. D., Tol, W. A., Susanty, D., Ntamatumba, P., Luitel, N. P., Komproe, I. H., & de Jong, J. T. V. M. (2013). Implementation of a mental health care package for children in areas of armed conflict: A case study from Burundi, Indonesia, Nepal, Sri Lanka, and Sudan. *PLoS Medicine, 10*(1), e1001371. https://doi.org/10.1371/journal.pmed.1001371

Joshi, R., Alim, M., Kengne, A. P., Jan, S., Maulik, P. K., Peiris, D., & Patel, A. A. (2014). Task shifting for non-communicable disease management in low and middle income countries—A systematic review. *PLoS One, 9*(8), e103754. https://doi.org/10.1371/journal.pone.0103754

Kakuma, R., Minas, H., van Ginneken, N., Dal Poz, M. R., Desiraju, K., Morris, J. E., Saxena, S., & Scheffler, R. M. (2011). Human resources for mental health care: Current situation and strategies for action. *The Lancet, 378*(9803), 1654–1663. https://doi.org/10.1016/S0140-6736(11)61093-3

Kataoka, S. H., Zhang, L., & Wells, K. B. (2002). Unmet need for mental health care among US children: Variation by ethnicity and insurance status. *American Journal of Psychiatry, 159*(9), 1548–1555. https://doi.org/10.1176/appi.ajp.159.9.1548

Knerr, W., Gardner, F., & Cluver, L. (2013). Improving positive parenting skills and reducing harsh and abusive parenting in low- and middle-Income countries: A systematic review. *Prevention Science, 14*(4), 352–363. https://doi.org/10.1007/s11121-012-0314-1

Kohrt, B. A., Asher, L., Bhardwaj, A., Fazel, M., Jordans, M. J. D., Mutamba, B. B., Nadkarni, A., Pedersen, G. A., Singla, D. R., & Patel, V. (2018). The role of communities in mental health care in low- and middle-income countries: A meta-review of components and competencies. *International Journal of Environmental Research and Public Health, 15*(6). https://doi.org/10.3390/ijerph15061279

Kumar, M., Amugune, B., Madeghe, B., Wambua, G. N., Osok, J., Polkonikova-Wamoto, A., Bukusi, D., Were, F., & Huang, K.-Y. (2018). Mechanisms associated with maternal adverse childhood experiences on offspring's mental health in Nairobi informal settlements: A mediational model testing approach. *BMC Psychiatry, 18*(1), 381. https://doi.org/10.1186/s12888-018-1953-y

Kumpfer, K. L., Alvarado, R., Smith, P., & Bellamy, N. (2002). Cultural sensitivity and adaptation in family-based prevention interventions. *Prevention Science: The Official*

Journal of the Society for Prevention Research, 3(3), 241–246. https://doi.org/10.1023/a:1019902902119

Kumpfer, K. L., & Magalhães, C. (2018). Strengthening Families Program: An evidence-based family intervention for parents of high-risk children and adolescents. *Journal of Child & Adolescent Substance Abuse, 27*(3), 174–179. https://doi.org/10.1080/1067828X.2018.1443048

Kumpfer, K. L., Pinyuchon, M., Teixeira de Melo, A., & Whiteside, H. O. (2008). Cultural adaptation process for international dissemination of the strengthening families program. *Evaluation & the Health Professions, 31*(2), 226–239. https://doi.org/10.1177/0163278708315926

Lachman, J., Wamoyi, J., Spreckelsen, T., Wight, D., Maganga, J., & Gardner, F. (2020). Combining parenting and economic strengthening programmes to reduce violence against children: A cluster randomised controlled trial with predominantly male caregivers in rural Tanzania. *BMJ Global Health, 5*(7), 1–9. https://doi.org/10.1136/bmjgh-2020-002349

Lau, A. S. (2006). Making the case for selective and directed cultural adaptations of evidence-based treatments: Examples from parent training. *Clinical Psychology: Science and Practice, 13*(4), 295–310. https://doi.org/10.1111/j.1468-2850.2006.00042.x

Leijten, P., Melendez-Torres, G. J., Knerr, W., & Gardner, F. (2016). Transported versus homegrown parenting interventions for reducing disruptive child behavior: A multilevel meta-regression study. *Journal of the American Academy of Child & Adolescent Psychiatry, 55*(7), 610–617. https://doi.org/10.1016/j.jaac.2016.05.003

Levey, E. J., Gelaye, B., Bain, P., Rondon, M. B., Borba, C. P. C., Henderson, D. C., & Williams, M. A. (2017). A systematic review of randomized controlled trials of interventions designed to decrease child abuse in high-risk families. *Child Abuse & Neglect, 65*, 48–57. https://doi.org/10.1016/j.chiabu.2017.01.004

López-Zerón, G., Parra-Cardona, J. R., & Yeh, H.-H. (2020). Addressing immigration-related stress in a culturally adapted parenting intervention for Mexican-origin immigrants: Initial positive effects and key areas of improvement. *Family Process, 59*(3), 1094–1112. https://doi.org/10.1111/famp.12481

Manyema, M., & Richter, L. M. (2019). Adverse childhood experiences: Prevalence and associated factors among South African young adults. *Heliyon, 5*(12). https://doi.org/10.1016/j.heliyon.2019.e03003

Masarik, A. S., & Conger, R. D. (2017). Stress and child development: A review of the Family Stress Model. *Current Opinion in Psychology, 13*, 85–90. https://doi.org/10.1016/j.copsyc.2016.05.008

Masten, A. S., & Cicchetti, D. (2016). Resilience in development: Progress and transformation. In D. Cicchetti (Ed.), *Developmental psychopathology: Risk, resilience, and intervention* (pp. 271–333). John Wiley & Sons, Inc. https://doi.org/10.1002/9781119125556.devpsy406

Masten, A. S., & Narayan, A. J. (2012). Child development in the context of disaster, war, and terrorism: Pathways of risk and resilience. *Annual Review of Psychology, 63*(1), 227–257. https://doi.org/10.1146/annurev-psych-120710-100356

McEwen, C. A., & McEwen, B. S. (2017). Social structure, adversity, toxic stress, and intergenerational poverty: An early childhood model. *Annual Review of Sociology, 43*(1), 445–472. https://doi.org/10.1146/annurev-soc-060116-053252

McKay, M. M., Harrison, M. E., Gonzales, J., Kim, L., & Quintana, E. (2002). Multiple-family groups for urban children with conduct difficulties and their families. *Psychiatric Services (Washington, D.C.)*, *53*(11), 1467–1468. https://doi.org/10.1176/appi.ps.53.11.1467

Meinck, F., Cluver, L. D., Orkin, F. M., Kuo, C., Sharma, A. D., Hensels, I. S., & Sherr, L. (2017). Pathways from family disadvantage via abusive parenting and caregiver mental health to adolescent health risks in South Africa. *Journal of Adolescent Health*, *60*(1), 57–64. https://doi.org/10.1016/j.jadohealth.2016.08.016

Mejia, A., Calam, R., & Sanders, M. R. (2012). A review of parenting programs in developing countries: Opportunities and challenges for preventing emotional and behavioral difficulties in children. *Clinical Child and Family Psychology Review*, *15*(2), 163–175. https://doi.org/10.1007/s10567-012-0116-9

Mejia, A., Haslam, D., Sanders, M. R., & Penman, N. (2017). Protecting children in low- and middle-income countries from abuse and neglect: Critical challenges for successful implementation of parenting programmes. *European Journal of Development Research*, *29*(5), 1038–1052. https://doi.org/10.1057/s41287-017-0105-4

Miller, K. E., & Jordans, M. J. D. (2016). Determinants of children's mental health in war-torn settings: Translating research into action. *Current Psychiatry Reports*, *18*(6), 58. https://doi.org/10.1007/s11920-016-0692-3

Miller, K. E., Koppenol-Gonzalez, G. V., Arnous, M., Tossyeh, F., Chen, A., Nahas, N., & Jordans, M. J. D. (2020). Supporting Syrian families displaced by armed conflict: A pilot randomized controlled trial of the Caregiver Support Intervention. *Child Abuse & Neglect*, *106*, 104512. https://doi.org/10.1016/j.chiabu.2020.104512

Narayan, A. J., Lieberman, A. F., & Masten, A. S. (2021). Intergenerational transmission and prevention of adverse childhood experiences (ACEs). *Clinical Psychology Review*, *85*, 101997. https://doi.org/10.1016/j.cpr.2021.101997

Narayan, A. J., Rivera, L. M., Bernstein, R. E., Harris, W. W., & Lieberman, A. F. (2018). Positive childhood experiences predict less psychopathology and stress in pregnant women with childhood adversity: A pilot study of the benevolent childhood experiences (BCEs) scale. *Child Abuse & Neglect*, *78*, 19–30. https://doi.org/10.1016/j.chiabu.2017.09.022

Neppl, T. K., Senia, J. M., & Donnellan, M. B. (2016). Effects of economic hardship: Testing the family stress model over time. *Journal of Family Psychology*, *30*(1), 12–21. https://doi.org/10.1037/fam0000168

Patel, V., Kieling, C., Maulik, P. K., & Divan, G. (2013). Improving access to care for children with mental disorders: A global perspective. *Archives of Disease in Childhood*, *98*(5), 323–327. https://doi.org/10.1136/archdischild-2012-302079

Pedersen, G. A., Smallegange, E., Coetzee, A., Hartog, K., Turner, J., Jordans, M. J. D., & Brown, F. L. (2019). A systematic review of the evidence for family and parenting interventions in low- and middle-income countries: Child and youth mental health outcomes. *Journal of Child and Family Studies*, *28*(8), 2036–2055. https://doi.org/10.1007/s10826-019-01399-4

Poole, M. K., Seal, D. W., & Taylor, C. A. (2014). A systematic review of universal campaigns targeting child physical abuse prevention. *Health Education Research*, *29*(3), 388–432. Scopus. https://doi.org/10.1093/her/cyu012

Puffer, E. S., Annan, J., Sim, A. L., Salhi, C., & Betancourt, T. S. (2017). The impact of a family skills training intervention among Burmese migrant families in Thailand: A randomized controlled trial. *PLoS One, 12*(3), e0172611. https://doi.org/10.1371/journal.pone.0172611

Puffer, E. S., & Ayuku, D. (2022). A community-embedded implementation model for mental-health interventions: Reaching the hardest to reach. *Perspectives on Psychological Science*, 17456916211049362.

Puffer, E. S., Friis-Healy, E. A., Giusto, A., Stafford, S., & Ayuku, D. (2019). Development and implementation of a family therapy intervention in Kenya: A community-embedded lay provider model. *Global Social Welfare, 8*, 11–28. https://doi.org/10.1007/s40609-019-00151-6

Puffer, E. S., Green, E. P., Chase, R. M., Sim, A. L., Zayzay, J., Friis, E., Garcia-Rolland, E., & Boone, L. (2015). Parents make the difference: A randomized-controlled trial of a parenting intervention in Liberia. *Global Mental Health, 2*, e15. https://doi.org/10.1017/gmh.2015.12

Puffer, E. S., Green, E. P., Sikkema, K. J., Broverman, S. A., Ogwang-Odhiambo, R. A., & Pian, J. (2016). A church-based intervention for families to promote mental health and prevent HIV among adolescents in rural Kenya: Results of a randomized trial. *Journal of Consulting and Clinical Psychology, 84*(6), 511–525. https://doi.org/10.1037/ccp0000076

Puffer, E. S., Healy, E. F., Green, E. P., Giusto, A. M., Kaiser, B. N., Patel, P., & Ayuku, D. (2020). Family functioning and mental health changes following a family therapy intervention in Kenya: A pilot trial. *Journal of Child and Family Studies, 29*(12), 3493–3508.

Puffer, E. S., Pian, J., Sikkema, K. J., Ogwang-Odhiambo, R. A., & Broverman, S. A. (2013). Developing a family-based HIV prevention intervention in rural Kenya: Challenges in conducting community-based participatory research. *Journal of Empirical Research on Human Research Ethics, 8*(2), 119–128. https://doi.org/10.1525/jer.2013.8.2.119

Rubenstein, B. L., Lu, L. Z. N., MacFarlane, M., & Stark, L. (2020). Predictors of interpersonal violence in the household in humanitarian settings: A systematic review. *Trauma, Violence, & Abuse, 21*(1), 31–44. https://doi.org/10.1177/1524838017738724

Sanchez, A. L., Cornacchio, D., Poznanski, B., Golik, A. M., Chou, T., & Comer, J. S. (2018). The effectiveness of school-based mental health services for elementary-aged children: A meta-analysis. *Journal of the American Academy of Child & Adolescent Psychiatry, 57*(3), 153–165. https://doi.org/10.1016/j.jaac.2017.11.022

Sanders, M. R., Kirby, J. N., Tellegen, C. L., & Day, J. J. (2014). The Triple P-Positive Parenting Program: A systematic review and meta-analysis of a multi-level system of parenting support. *Clinical Psychology Review, 34*(4), 337–357. https://doi.org/10.1016/j.cpr.2014.04.003

Sashidharan, S. P., White, R., Mezzina, R., Jansen, S., & Gishoma, D. (2016). Global mental health in high-income countries. *British Journal of Psychiatry, 209*(1), 3–5. https://doi.org/10.1192/bjp.bp.115.179556

Settipani, C. A., Hawke, L. D., Cleverley, K., Chaim, G., Cheung, A., Mehra, K., Rice, M., Szatmari, P., & Henderson, J. (2019). Key attributes of integrated community-based youth service hubs for mental health: A scoping review. *International Journal of Mental Health Systems, 13*(1), 1–26. https://doi.org/10.1186/s13033-019-0306-7

Shonkoff, J. P., Garner, A. S., The Committee on Psychosocial Aspects of Child and Family Health, Committee on Early Childhood Adoption, and Dependent Care, and Section on Developmental and Behavioral Pediatrics, Siegel, B. S., Dobbins, M. I., Earls, M. F., Garner, A. S., McGuinn, L., Pascoe, J., & Wood, D. L. (2012). The lifelong effects of early childhood adversity and toxic stress. *Pediatrics, 129*(1), e232–e246. https://doi.org/10.1542/peds.2011-2663

Sim, A., Fazel, M., Bowes, L., & Gardner, F. (2018). Pathways linking war and displacement to parenting and child adjustment: A qualitative study with Syrian refugees in Lebanon. *Social Science & Medicine, 200,* 19–26. https://doi.org/10.1016/j.socscimed.2018.01.009

Singh, G. K., Daus, G. P., Allender, M., Ramey, C. T., Martin, E. K., Perry, C., Reyes, A. A. D. L., & Vedamuthu, I. P. (2017). Social determinants of health in the United States: Addressing major health inequality trends for the nation, 1935–2016. *International Journal of MCH and AIDS, 6*(2), 139–164. https://doi.org/10.21106/ijma.236

Slopen, N., Chen, Y., Guida, J. L., Albert, M. A., & Williams, D. R. (2017). Positive childhood experiences and ideal cardiovascular health in midlife: Associations and mediators. *Preventive Medicine, 97,* 72–79. https://doi.org/10.1016/j.ypmed.2017.01.002

Soares, A. L. G., Howe, L. D., Matijasevich, A., Wehrmeister, F. C., Menezes, A. M. B., & Gonçalves, H. (2016). Adverse childhood experiences: Prevalence and related factors in adolescents of a Brazilian birth cohort. *Child Abuse & Neglect, 51,* 21–30. https://doi.org/10.1016/j.chiabu.2015.11.017

Sphere Project. (2011). *Humanitarian charter and minimum standards in humanitarian Response: The Sphere Handbook.* https://doi.org/10.3362/9781908176202

Ssewamala, F. M., Bahar, O. S., McKay, M. M., Hoagwood, K., Huang, K.-Y., & Pringle, B. (2018). Strengthening mental health and research training in Sub-Saharan Africa (SMART Africa): Uganda study protocol. *Trials, 19*(1), 1–19. https://doi.org/10.1186/s13063-018-2751-z

Stark, L., & Landis, D. (2016). Violence against children in humanitarian settings: A literature review of population-based approaches. *Social Science & Medicine, 152,* 125–137. https://doi.org/10.1016/j.socscimed.2016.01.052

Tol, W. A., Song, S., & Jordans, M. J. D. (2013). Annual research review: Resilience and mental health in children and adolescents living in areas of armed conflict—A systematic review of findings in low- and middle-income countries. *Journal of Child Psychology and Psychiatry, 54*(4), 445–460. https://doi.org/10.1111/jcpp.12053

Tran, Q. A., Dunne, M. P., Vo, T. V., & Luu, N. H. (2015). Adverse childhood experiences and the health of university students in eight provinces of Vietnam. *Asia Pacific Journal of Public Health, 27*(8 Suppl.), 26S–32S. https://doi.org/10.1177/1010539515589812

Ungar, M. (2011). The social ecology of resilience: Addressing contextual and cultural ambiguity of a nascent construct. *American Journal of Orthopsychiatry, 81*(1), 1–17. https://doi.org/10.1111/j.1939-0025.2010.01067.x

Ungar, M. (2019). Designing resilience research: Using multiple methods to investigate risk exposure, promotive and protective processes, and contextually relevant outcomes for children and youth. *Child Abuse & Neglect, 96,* 104098. https://doi.org/10.1016/j.chiabu.2019.104098

Ungar, M., & Theron, L. (2020). Resilience and mental health: How multisystemic processes contribute to positive outcomes. *Lancet Psychiatry, 7*(5), 441–448. https://doi.org/10.1016/S2215-0366(19)30434-1

UNICEF, World Bank, & World Health Organization. (2018). *Nurturing care for early childhood development: A framework for helping children survive and thrive to transform health and human potential*. World Health Organization. https://apps.who.int/iris/bitstream/handle/10665/272603/9789241514064-eng.pdf

Wahlbeck, K., Cresswell-Smith, J., Haaramo, P., & Parkkonen, J. (2017). Interventions to mitigate the effects of poverty and inequality on mental health. *Social Psychiatry and Psychiatric Epidemiology, 52*(5), 505–514. https://doi.org/10.1007/s00127-017-1370-4

Ward, C. L., Wessels, I. M., Lachman, J. M., Hutchings, J., Cluver, L. D., Kassanjee, R., Nhapi, R., Little, F., & Gardner, F. (2020). Parenting for Lifelong Health for Young Children: A randomized controlled trial of a parenting program in South Africa to prevent harsh parenting and child conduct problems. *Journal of Child Psychology and Psychiatry, 61*(4), 503–512. https://doi.org/10.1111/jcpp.13129

Weaver, A., & Lapidos, A. (2018). Mental health interventions with community health workers in the United States: A systematic review. *Journal of Health Care for the Poor and Underserved, 29*(1), 159–180. https://doi.org/10.1353/hpu.2018.0011

Wessells, M. G. (2015). Bottom-up approaches to strengthening child protection systems: Placing children, families, and communities at the center. *Child Abuse & Neglect, 43*, 8–21. https://doi.org/10.1016/j.chiabu.2015.04.006

Wheeler, S. M., & Bryant, A. S. (2017). Racial and ethnic disparities in health and health care. *Obstetrics and Gynecology Clinics of North America, 44*(1), 1–11. https://doi.org/10.1016/j.ogc.2016.10.001

Zuilkowski, S. S., Thulin, E. J., McLean, K., Rogers, T. M., Akinsulure-Smith, A. M., & Betancourt, T. S. (2019). Parenting and discipline in post-conflict Sierra Leone. *Child Abuse & Neglect, 97*, 104138. https://doi.org/10.1016/j.chiabu.2019.104138

14

Formal and Informal Social Control of Family Violence

A Comparison of Protective and Punitive Approaches With Respect to Family Heterogeneity

CLIFTON R. EMERY AND ALHASSAN ABDULLAH ■

Globally, one in every three women has experienced intimate partner violence (IPV) in their lives (World Health Organization, 2021), and between 8% and 25% and 10% and 39% of children in high-income and middle-income countries, respectively, witness IPV in their homes (Fang et al., 2015; Gilbert et al., 2009; Kieselbach et al., 2021). Prevalence estimates from countries across the globe show that IPV is common (Australia, 27%; Denmark, 22%; and Mozambique, 40%; H. Johnson et al., 2007). Records from the Global Burden of Disease (GBD) in 2010 ranked IPV the 23rd highest risk worldwide in terms of its effects on disability-adjusted life-years (DALYs) among women (Lim et al., 2012), with an estimated country-specific lifetime cost of $3.6 trillion USD in the United States alone (Peterson et al., 2018). Family violence is a significant public health challenge and disproportionately affects women and children. One mechanism of reducing family violence is the social control of behavior via formal or informal channels. Efforts to address and control family violence through formal social control (e.g., by government agents) and informal social control (e.g., by ordinary citizens) have increased in recent years, as has the growing awareness of family violence and its consequences. Reviews of the research have highlighted two modes of intervention related to formal and informal social control—protective and punitive (cf. Emery, Trung, et al., 2015; Gelles & Straus, 1979; Hirschi, 1969/2002; Messing, 2011). Protective social control denotes acts of intervention that protect the victim and use a communicative approach to deter the perpetrator (Emery, Trung, et al., 2015). Punitive intervention, alternatively, involves acts that control family violence by punishing the perpetrator. Research on the efficacy of each intervention approach has been the growing focus of recent literature on family violence, particularly research on informal social control (Emery, Thapa, et al., 2015; Emery, Trung, et al., 2015; Emery, Yang, et al., 2017; Emery, Wu, Yang, et al., 2019). How family-level heterogeneity (diversity) impacts the relative effectiveness of protective and punitive forms of social control, however, has not been well studied. This chapter first investigates, through analysis of evidence on formal social control policies and findings on informal social control of IPV, the relative efficacy of protective and punitive interventions, including impacts on children. In addition, it examines how family-level factors contribute, particularly how the concepts of order and power matter when thinking about how to intervene against family violence (Emery, 2011).

FORMAL AND INFORMAL SOCIAL CONTROL OF FAMILY VIOLENCE

Social control, in general, underscores the mechanisms to ensure conformity to norms and standards using formal and informal measures (cf. Gelles & Straus, 1979; Horwitz, 1990; Janowitz, 1975). Horwitz (1990) argued in *The Logic of Social Control* that social control is the aspect of society that protects social order. Hence, studies of social control concern themselves with the study of variations in responses to acts that disturb the normative order, such as family violence (Gelles & Straus, 1979). The theoretical rationale for both formal and informal social control is premised on a rational deterrence framework (Hirschi, 1969/2002). This framework assumes that individuals will respond rationally to costs associated with formal and informal social control intervention (see Emery, Thapa, et al., 2015; Iyengar, 2009; Sherman & Berk, 1984). For example, child abuse and IPV perpetrators who are punished by formal control agents, such as the police, are—in theory—deterred from similar maltreatment behaviors. In a similar vein, acts of informal social control by neighbors, such as issuing threats against perpetrators of child abuse and IPV, should deter family violence. Thus, whether protective or punitive, formal and informal social control should trigger deterrence responses from perpetrators of family violence.

In the language of systems frameworks (*cf.* Payne, 2005/2021), formal social control could be considered as located at the macro level, while informal social control might be located at the micro level. The justification for considering formal social control at the macro level is based on the fact that intervention efforts are often standardized procedures outlined in state policies (Hoppe et al., 2020; Ryan et al., 2021). Hence, intervention approaches by agents of formal social control are predetermined based on the dictates of the policy. Common examples of formal social control of IPV are mandatory arrest policies (cf. Bridgett, 2020; Iyengar, 2009; Sherman & Berk, 1984) and protection orders (cf. Dowling et al., 2018; Holt et al., 2003). Independent assessment of the efficacy of these formal control measures has appeared in the research literature (Dowling et al., 2018; Hoppe et al., 2020), but mixed and contrary findings undermine confidence in the efficacy of these approaches to informing policy decisions on police and law enforcement intervention in IPV.

Informal social control, which involves actions by ordinary citizens who are not acting in a professional capacity, is carried out by individuals within the social microsystem. Examples of acts of informal social control include individual efforts to intervene and save the victim, calm the perpetrator by talking, and threaten or call the police to arrest the perpetrator.

PROTECTIVE AND PUNITIVE FORMAL SOCIAL CONTROL OF IPV

A recent introduction of punitive and protective approaches within the social control literature introduces a theoretical lens to systematically examine the effectiveness of formal control measures based on analysis of the approach used by the control agent to correct the behavior (Emery, Trung, et al., 2015). Protective social control involves formal control measures that primarily protect victims of child abuse and IPV. Protective actions carried out by social control agents include getting in to safeguard victims of abuse or IPV and initiating dialogue or engagements to ensure that perpetrators desist from the abuse and IPV. Perpetrators are theorized to learn accepted and normatively sanctioned behaviors through the protective control efforts from the neighbor or other agents of control (Emery, Trung, et al., 2015). However, punitive formal social control prioritizes actions to punish the perpetrator and seeks to evoke deterrence through punishment. It can therefore be deduced (on the surface) that protective social control focuses on victim protection, while punitive intervention highlights perpetrator punishment. A further analysis, however, indicates restorative justice—an approach that attends to the needs of both the victim and the perpetrator—as an extended dimension of protective social control.

Outcomes from studies of formal social control, such as those on protection orders and mandatory arrest, have provided significant insights into violence control measures. Such research has informed interventions to boost formal control of IPV and has enhanced policy responses to IPV (Gelles & Straus, 1979). Mandatory arrest policies (Hoppe et al., 2020; Iyengar, 2009) and civil protection orders (Dowling et al., 2018) are common and widely recognized legal and formal responses to IPV. They also fall within the protective (protection orders) and punitive (mandatory arrest) classification.

Protection Order as Protective Formal Social Control of IPV

For several decades, the primary international protective legal response to IPV has been the institution of civil laws allowing orders of protection (Cordier et al., 2019). Further, legislation strengthening the ability of child protection services

(CPS) to remove children from abusive and violent family settings has been widely recognized as an instrumental protective measure[1] (Crawford & Bradley, 2016; Milani et al., 2020). Domestic violence civil protection orders are ratified in all 50 states in the United States as well as in most nations, including Canada, Australia, and the United Kingdom. Protection orders describe measures undertaken by the court (court order) to ensure the protection of victims of IPV against future victimization while providing restrictions on the offenders and their behavior. Similarly, child protection legislation that underlies the CPS removal of children enables child protection practitioners to safeguard children from adverse outcomes of witnessing IPV and experiences of abuse (Milani et al., 2020). However, removing children from violent homes into alternative care could also heighten other risk factors and negative outcomes, such as attachment problems (Dozier et al., 2001), juvenile delinquency, and abuse (Doyle, 2007), suggesting that child removal into alternative care might not be effective in ensuring child well-being in all cases.

In some cases, after establishing reasonable proof of violence or apparent risk of violence, the justice system may grant a protection order to applicants that imposes restraints between them and their abusers. Such measures have indirect positive and negative ripple effects on children. On the positive side, restraining orders could protect children from witnessing IPV in the family. However, it can also expose children to the risk of child poverty due to inequities in parental separation (Cancian & Meyer, 2018). Living with separated lone parents is associated with elevated risk of low educational attainment (Amato et al., 2015), child involvement in delinquent behaviors (Kroese et al., 2021), and attachment difficulties (Nicholson et al., 2014). Practitioners should be aware of the possible outcomes for children when implementing restraining orders in family violence. Protective orders are classified into (a) those that require parties to separate and (b) others that do not mandate separation between parties (Goldfarb, 2007). Separating partners under civil protection orders is the most common form of protective order (Dowling et al., 2018; Goldfarb, 2007), and breaches of such protective orders are expected to be treated as criminal offenses (Dowling et al., 2018). Common benefits that may accompany protection orders include stopping the perpetrator from making contact with the victim, restraining the perpetrator from frequenting places where the victim is present, ensuring the perpetrator does not share a common apartment with the victim, and prohibiting the possession of firearms and weapons (Fagan, 1996). In some cases, protection orders are tied to divorce and can include child custody, arrangements for child access, spouse and child support measures, and financial compensation (Fagan, 1996). Protection orders are, in theory, deemed to provide perpetrators of IPV with some space to reflect on their behaviors and refrain from their violent conduct.

---

1. Removing children from birth parents might not be all that fruitful in promoting better outcomes for children. Evidence on alternative care, including foster care, kinship, and residential care, continues to examine the efficacy of child removal and well-being in alternative care settings.

Research on the effectiveness of protection orders has expanded over the last decades, with over 12 systematic reviews and meta-analytic studies on the subject. Rates of reoffense and extent of the violations of protection orders are the common criteria to establish the effectiveness of protection orders (Benitez et al., 2010; Cordier et al., 2019; Dowling et al., 2018; Jordan, 2004; Russell, 2012; Shannon et al., 2007; Spitzberg, 2002). For example, Spitzberg (2002) reports that a total of 40% of protection orders were violated following a review of reports from 32 studies globally, while Shannon et al. (2007) found as few as 17.4% of violations of protection orders based on victim reports in the United States. Compared to the 17.4% violation rate reported in the Shannon et al. (2007) review, Brame et al. (2015) reported a 38.8% violation rate based on data from both police reports and victims. Differences in the violation rates are likely attributable to victims' willingness to report violations of protection orders. Goldfarb's (2007) findings indicate that women of color and immigrants may be especially unwilling to report violations of protection orders due to the fear of resulting incarceration of perpetrators. Benitez and colleagues' (2010) review of 15 studies showed that most of these infractions happen in the first 3 months under the protection order. These breaches notwithstanding, analysis of the violation rates still suggests that protection orders are effective in reducing the risk of reoffense.

Similarly, reports from some studies suggest protective orders may be effective in reducing IPV, as reported by victims. Holt et al. (2003) found a 70% reduction in rates of IPV for women who secured protection orders. Russell's (2012) literature review identified protection orders as significantly reducing risks of physical and psychological abuse, and evidence from a systematic meta-analysis showed that victims who received protection orders were significantly less likely to face revictimization (Dowling et al., 2018). The evidence reinforces the notion that protection orders are effective mechanisms to address IPV. Studies of victims show that they are satisfied with protection orders and feel safer when their protection order applications are granted (Logan et al., 2007; Logan & Walker, 2009).

Mandatory Arrest as Punitive Formal Social Control of IPV

Mandatory arrest laws also highlight another landmark movement by states in response to IPV and family violence. These laws mandate that police arrest perpetrators of IPV—including warrantless arrest—when they receive reports of IPV or witness cases of IPV (Iyengar, 2009; Sherman & Berk, 1984). Arrest becomes the predominant response for the police when they receive reports of IPV. Mandatory arrest laws were a timely response to the growing demands from feminist movements that states be involved in IPV and family violence by holding perpetrators accountable (Ryan et al., 2021). Before then, IPV and family violence were considered private matters of individual families that required familial arrangements and intervention measures (Durfee & Fetzer, 2016). Laws on mandatory arrest criminalize IPV and provide standardized formal responses to the problem of IPV. The aim of mandatory arrest policies is to (a) protect victims of

IPV, (b) increase deterrence, and (c) hold perpetrators accountable (Hoppe et al., 2020; Sherman & Berk, 1984).

Mandatory arrest laws received considerable attention in the United States and across the globe following the landmark experiment by Sherman and Berk (1984) in the early 1980s, known as the Minneapolis Domestic Violence Experiment. The experiment found that perpetrators of IPV who were arrested had the least proportion of reoffense (19%) compared to 37% for those who received advice and 33% for those who were separated from their partners (Iyengar, 2009; Sherman & Berk, 1984). Sherman and Berk's (1984) study provided landmark findings that increased the formulation and enforcement of mandatory arrest laws in several states in the United States (from 15 to 28 states as of 2018) and the world (Durfee & Fetzer, 2016; Sherman & Berk, 1984). During the same period, following the Minneapolis experiment, Canada implemented pro-arrest, pro-charge, and pro-prosecution policies as measures to increase the criminal justice system's involvement in IPV issues (Barata & Schneider, 2004).

Research studies replicating the Minneapolis experiment (in several parts of the United States and the world) have strongly contrasting findings on the efficacy and deterrent effects from police arrest (Dunford et al., 1990; Sherman, Schmidt, et al., 1992; Sherman, Smith, et al., 1992), including follow-up studies from Sherman (Sherman, Schmidt, et al., 1992; Sherman, Smith, et al., 1992). Soon after the publication of the Minneapolis experiment, other studies (Sherman, Schmidt, et al., 1992; Sherman, Smith, et al., 1992) found arrest in the short term to be *positively* correlated with reoffense. A recent meta-analytic synthesis of 11 studies found that arrest of IPV offenders did not reduce rates of revictimization (Hoppe et al., 2020) and thus did not have a deterrent effect. Further, a review on pro-arrest and pro-prosecution policies in Canada showed a general consensus of studies on the ineffectiveness of mandatory arrest programs (Ryan et al., 2021).

Discussions on mandatory arrest and the associated consequences require serious reconsideration as implementation of mandatory arrest laws have also been positively associated with increased IPV-related homicide (Iyengar, 2009), while more recent corrections find there is no effect of mandatory or preferred arrest on IPV-related homicide (Chin & Cunningham, 2019). Rather, discretionary arrest statutes appear to be associated with less IPV homicide (ibid). In addition to risk for reoffense, factors including police frustration with IPV offenders, police difficulty in establishing the predominant aggressor, and the inability to address sustained IPV victimization (Ryan et al., 2021) notably undermine the logic of mandatory arrest as an effective IPV intervention measure. Police difficulty in establishing the predominant aggressor often leads to dual arrests (Ryan et al., 2021). About 20% of female victims of IPV get arrested together with their abusers (Iyengar, 2009). In fact, the odds for dual arrest are 3 times higher when the victims are women (Bridgett, 2020). The evidence suggests that the likelihood of dual arrest is lower when men are victimized. Incidence of dual arrest and countercharging are core elements of revictimization experiences for survivors (Ryan et al., 2021), which may inhibit victims from seeking help. This has far-reaching impact on the effectiveness of mandatory arrest laws. Many have questioned the operational logic of mandatory arrest policies due to the lack of primary emphasis on victim safety, protection, and needs (Ryan et al., 2021). Similarly, if, as research suggests, the type of IPV moderates the effect of social control (Johnson, 2008; Emery, 2011), mandatory arrest represents a one-size-fits-all approach to a markedly heterogeneous problem.

Restorative Justice Interventions for IPV

Restorative justice is both a philosophy and practice approach to control crime and, recently, family violence (cf. Johnstone, 2003). In restorative justice interventions, victims and offenders are brought together to dialogue and discuss the harm caused by the violence (physical, psychological, and relational), identify the needs of the victim (Cheon & Regehr, 2006), and develop ways to repair the harm (Umbreit, 1999). Restorative justice meetings focus on preventing further harm to the victim by developing sustainable practices that will benefit the victim and the perpetrator (Johnstone, 2003). Victim-offender mediation (VOM), family case conferencing, sentencing circles, and peacemaking are common restorative justice techniques (Cheon & Regehr, 2006) that are widely practiced in many countries including New Zealand, Norway, South Africa, and Australia (Barocas et al., 2016; Pennell & Burford, 2000). Targeted restorative justice programs (such as Circles of Peace, Community Holistic Circle Healing Process, etc.) have been developed in some of these countries to combat crime and IPV (Cheon & Regehr, 2006).

Victims in restorative justice interventions gain the opportunity to know offenders' motives, share the effects of the offenders' actions, and contribute to decisions and sanctions required to restore justice (Cheon & Regehr, 2006). Offenders have the opportunity to repair the social harm caused by the violence by showing remorse. Offenders' show of remorse enhances victims' healing processes (Cheon & Regehr, 2006). The repair motive in restorative justice interventions helps to achieve the objectives of deterrence and to develop sustained protective measures against the reoccurrence of IPV.

From a systems perspective, restorative justice control measures help to ensure family stability, in contrast with interventions that promote separation. Children are thus protected from the risks of experiencing divorce and challenges of staying with single parents when IPV intervention measures focus on maintaining the relationship, repairing harm, and developing sustained protective measures. That said, the success of restorative justice interventions, especially their impact on children, could backfire when the abuser reoffends against the victim or attempts to use the restorative justice process to manipulate the victim. Thus, assessment of the risk of recidivism and IPV type should be carefully considered when implementing restorative justice interventions. Braithwaite (2000) argues that the shame associated with restorative justice processes theoretically increases deterrence of IPV perpetration.

Restorative justice interventions are commonly used in crime and among juvenile offenders, as some meta-analytic studies have reported program efficacy against crime (Sherman et al., 2015) and among juvenile offenders (Latimer et al., 2005). However, restorative justice is relatively underdeveloped and underutilized in family violence interventions. Hence, its efficacy for IPV and other forms of family violence has not been extensively explored or established. The limited available research on the efficacy of restorative justice interventions, however, is promising. A combination of restorative justice interventions—Circle of Peace and Batterer Intervention programs—helped to reduce arrest rates and crime severity for all offenses including IPV (Mills et al., 2019). Victims and offenders of IPV who engaged in IPV restorative justice mediation in South Africa felt an improved sense of safety (especially the victims) and confidence (through talking freely with the offender) and felt that they had options to discuss their matters in private while receiving support (Edwards & Sharpe, 2004). Pennell and Burford s' (2002) study on participants of the Community Holistic Circle Healing Process found that rates of IPV among the participants decreased significantly after the program.

The central approach of using a communicative approach to control violence makes restorative justice another dimension of formal control that is significantly congruent with the protective approach. Control that is initially protective (in the immediate incident) may be more likely to extend to restorative measures. In fact, Sherman (2000) suggests that restorative justice interventions should adopt a holistic community care approach and emphasize informal social control measures that protect the victim. Social learning–oriented modules that are practiced during restorative justice intervention programs/meetings echo the orientation of protective intervention, as they seek to correct wrongs and deter family violence through social learning (Emery, Trung, et al., 2015). Hence, restorative justice interventions (within the modern classification of social control) could be classified as a third dimension of social control under the name *restitute social control*. That is, such control is extended to ensure that harms (physical, emotional, and social) that are caused by violence are removed. Restitute social control may have an added advantage of ensuring sustained protection against IPV and family violence. Also, restorative justice techniques and other protective social control measures impact positively on the mental health and well-being of children (Thomas et al., 2019). Curtailing violence through social control measures supports the possibility of secure family environments that promote children's positive development (Child Welfare Information Gateway, 2015). Compared to severe punitive social control measures, such as victim or offender arrest, restorative justice intervention may ensure family stability and relationship maintenance, which may impact positively on childcare and well-being in intact families.

The limited attention to restorative justice techniques in IPV and family violence may be attributed to the criticisms levied against it. It is suggested that restorative justice interventions may reify power differentials among partners and families (Cheon & Regehr, 2006; Mills et al., 2019). Arguments on the potential impact of power and the nature of order within families reinforce the position of this chapter, which is to highlight the vital importance of family heterogeneity in determining appropriate social control interventions for family violence.

PUNITIVE AND PROTECTIVE INFORMAL SOCIAL CONTROL OF IPV

Informal social control has its roots in Shaw and McKay's (1942) social disorganization theory (Sampson et al., 1997). It describes actions from neighborhood residents, who are nonprofessionals, to deter violent crimes and achieve social order. Hirschi (1969/2002) identified the extent of social bonds (attachment), the rational cost for committing deviance (commitment), involvement in conventional neighborhood activities, and beliefs as variables that account for the strength of informal social control. Sampson et al. (1997) shifted the explanation away from social bonds toward whether neighbors intervene to correct undesirable behaviors in their explanation of neighborhood collective efficacy.

Research in the field of IPV began to examine its relationship with neighborhood informal social control (Browning, 2002; Dekeseredy et al., 2003; Emery et al., 2011; Jain et al., 2010) under the auspices of social disorganization theory and the implied theoretical position of rational choice deterrence (Matsueda et al., 2006). Acts of informal social control are conceived of as increasing the cost of violence, including family violence, which then deters perpetrators from further violence. However, empirical IPV research using Sampson and colleagues' (1997) collective efficacy measure has been mixed. For example, while Browning's (2002) study in the United States found a negative association between collective efficacy and IPV, studies with samples drawn from the United States and Canada (Dekeseredy et al., 2003; Jain et al., 2010) found no association between the collective efficacy measure of informal social control and IPV. Similarly, Emery et al. (2011) found no significant association between IPV desistance and neighborhood informal social control.

Emery, Thapa, et al. (2015) attributed the null findings between IPV and informal social control to (a) measurement error and (b) limited theoretical adaptation of informal social control in family violence. In response, Emery and colleagues developed a context-based scale for informal social control of IPV (ISC-IPV scale, cf. Emery, Wu, et al., 2017) and child maltreatment (ISC-CM scale, cf. Emery, Trung, et al., 2015) that measures informal social control based on *how* and *what* actions are carried out to correct the undesirable behavior. The ISC-IPV or ISC-CM scale classified informal social control into two approaches of intervention: protective (i.e., an approach that aims to protect the victim) and punitive (i.e., an approach that aims to punish the perpetrator).

Empirical research from several countries, mostly in Asia, on informal social control of IPV and child maltreatment has found significant support for the logic and relevance of the protective/punitive distinction in informal social control (cf. Emery, Eremina, et al., 2015; Emery, Thapa, et al., 2015; Emery, Trung, et al., 2015; Emery, Wu, et al., 2015; Emery, Wu, et al., 2017). Specifically, protective informal social control by adult family members has been found to be negatively associated with husband-perpetrated IPV and IPV abuse severity in a sample from Beijing (Emery, Wu, et al., 2017). Emery, Wu, et al. (2015) also found protective informal social control to be associated with less likelihood of IPV injury. Further, findings from a sample of 300 families in Kathmandu revealed that protective informal social control is associated with lower abuse severity (Emery, Thapa, et al., 2015). However, neither study found a significant association between punitive informal social control and IPV or IPV-related injury.

Evidence on the null findings from punitive informal social control paves the way for us to critically analyze informal social control within the context of family heterogeneity. Understanding the heterogeneity of families, specifically in terms of power and order, may help us to target and tailor protective and punitive control efforts to those family contexts in which each type is most likely to be efficacious.

IPV HETEROGENEITY AND FORMAL AND INFORMAL SOCIAL CONTROL OF IPV

Family heterogeneity is defined here as diversity in terms of cultural norms and systematic differences in socioeconomic, race, gender, and sexuality experiences. The efficacy of informal social control is theorized to be high in collectivist cultural context, particularly where acts of informal social control are culturally sanctioned (Abdullah et al., 2021), compared to individualistic societies. Such differences are vitally important in understanding both the meaning and efficacy of social control of IPV. We argue that much of the impact of the family differences is mediated via the sociocultural implications of the distribution of power within families. The distribution of power in the family is considered to be one of the most theoretically important aspects of understanding and controlling IPV (Dobash, 1979; Emery, 2011; M. P. Johnson, 2008; Stark, 2007).

Emery (2011) first distinguished between IPV in families in which no normative order exists (anarchic-type IPV) versus all other types. The power distribution is important in classification of all other types of IPV. Weber (1922/1978) defines power as a group or individual's ability to "realize their own will in a social action even against the resistance of others who are participating in the action" (p. 926). If power is shared, IPV is classified as violent conflict (Emery, 2011), which is similar to M. P. Johnson's (1995) conceptualization of common couple violence. When power is systematically unequal, IPV is classified as either tolerant dictatorship (no violence by the superordinate partner), despotic dictatorship (violent acts by the superordinate partner are acts of inconsistent control—violating the norms that support the superordinate partner's authority), or totalitarian dictatorship type (violent acts by the superordinate partner are acts of consistent control—supporting the norms that support the superordinate partner's authority; Emery, 2011). The totalitarian dictatorship type of IPV bears a resemblance to M. P. Johnson's (2008) intimate terrorist type but avoids the problem of

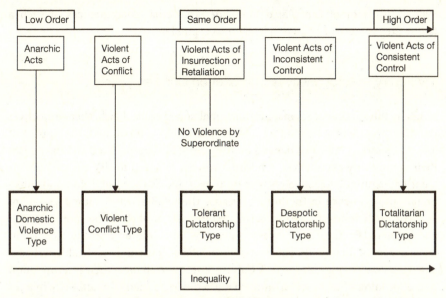

Figure 14.1. Typologies of Intimate Partner Violence (IPV).

intimate terrorists who attempt to use violence to control the victim but systematically fail to achieve control. Figure 14.1 shows the IPV typologies.

Heterogeneity with respect to IPV type is of vital importance to inform formal/informal and protective/punitive approaches to intervention. For example, interventions that target the totalitarian IPV type for increased surveillance and pretrial arrest of perpetrators and frequent victim contact and follow-up appear to be associated with decreases in IPV homicide rates (Snyder, 2013). Similarly, interventions that enlist front-line officers to screen for high homicide risk appear to decrease violent victimization and increase victim self-protective behavior (Messing, 2011). Social control that is more formal and more punitive may be more necessary when power differences are extreme, totalitarian style partner control is apparent (Emery et al., 2018), and physical violence is more frequent and severe. However, informal, protective, and restorative justice–type approaches may be problematic for situations in which the perpetrator is likely to systematically exploit power differentials with the victim to deceive the community and agents of control with respect to both the perpetrator's true intentions and the severity of the violence (Emery, 2011; Messing, 2011; Snyder, 2013; Stark, 2007). Hence, screening and analyzing the implications for any type of social control intervention in terms of family heterogeneity is vitally important in all circumstances. The macro-systemic environment is also vitally important to consider in targeting social control when prevailing social conditions (e.g., racism) merit strong community distrust of formal social control (exemplified by Black communities in the United States; Kwak et al., 2019). Failure to make social control decisions with reference to family heterogeneity or applying a simple "one-size-fits-all" approach may result in increased IPV homicide (Iyengar, 2009; Chin & Cunningham, 2019;

Synder, 2013) or officer-related homicide. The lethal consequences of such a failure are predictable and completely unacceptable.

IPV Family Heterogeneity and Impact on Children

Much as the success of formal and informal social control (whether protective/ punitive) would vary depending on the type of IPV perpetrated, the impact of IPV on children could also depend on the type of IPV perpetrated and the racism their community experiences. Children who are exposed to IPV process the violent happenings subjectively based on how it affects their cognition and interpretation of violence in the home. Because the totalitarian dictatorship type of IPV (or M. P. Johnson's [2008] intimate terrorist) is likely to be more physical and frequent (Emery, 2011), its associated effect on children worsens. Consistent exposure to totalitarian dictatorship type of IPV affects children's health and psychological well-being (Izaguirre & Calvete, 2015) and changes their interpretation of the meaning of relationship and what it requires to maintain authority in a relationship. Their worldview on violence as the means to maintain a superordinate position in a relationship would be reinforced, hence strengthening the intergenerational link of family IPV (Wood & Sommers, 2011). Exposure to other types of IPV, such as violent conflict, would have no or less impact on children's interpretation of using power or inequality as the norm in a relationship. Essentially, the impact of IPV on child witnesses varies based on the IPV type witnessed. Some IPV types would have weaker effects on children's health and well-being and the intergenerational perpetration of IPV (e.g., violent conflict type), while others may have exacerbated effects (totalitarian dictatorship type of IPV). Formal and informal social control interventions would be useful in addressing the negative consequences from children witnessing IPV and important in breaking the intergenerational link of family IPV.

IMPLICATIONS FOR PRACTICE

Systematic differences between families have consequences for the efficacy of formal or informal social control interventions for IPV. Such differences determine whether victims, perpetrators, and bystanders will be receptive to control efforts or repel them. Violence in families could escalate and even lead to homicide, and control efforts could be rendered ineffective if family heterogeneity is not carefully considered with respect to social control measures. The choice of the control intervention (protective or punitive approach, informal or formal approach) should be informed by knowledge of power dynamics within the family and between the family and the community. We show in this chapter the need for control agents, both formal and informal, in IPV problems to have reasonable knowledge of the power and order within families. Programs to boost informal social control should include aspects that educate control agents (neighbors, friends and families, and representatives of the criminal justice system) about diversity in families (based on power and order) and the choice of IPV intervention necessary to achieve success. Practitioners should develop frameworks to assess the levels of power and norms within families so as to guide the criminal justice system and family courts on the most efficacious type of intervention to be adopted: civil protection orders, mandatory arrests, and/or restorative justice interventions. For example, mandatory arrest programs, intensive monitoring of both perpetrator and victim, and pretrial incarceration should be considered for families with extreme power differentials and totalitarian-style partner control problems, and with high frequency and severity of physical violence. On the other hand, restorative justice interventions should be prioritized in families with smaller power differences, stronger commitments to community norms, and less severe IPV. Restorative justice interventions should also be considered for communities in which a history of racialized policing and procedural injustice has undermined the efficacy of formal social control (Kwak et al., 2019).

IMPLICATIONS FOR RESEARCH

The argument in this chapter on the usefulness of distinctions based on family heterogeneity and formal and informal social control approaches (protective and punitive) is partially supported by Emery's (2011) IPV typology as well as M. P. Johnson's (2008) and Stark's (2007) typologies of IPV. However, research on the emerging hypothesis from this chapter is needed to advance theoretical knowledge of formal and informal social control of IPV, specifically taking into account heterogeneity in families. Studies examining the efficacy of protective formal and informal social control measures and punitive formal and informal social control interventions among the different IPV-informed elements of family heterogeneity (order, power) is needed to inform theory development. Additionally, examining the elements of family dynamics (order and power) as mediators or moderators of the relationship between IPV frequency/severity and any of the formal or informal social control measures would be useful to reveal nuances that could inform theory and policy decisions. For example, families with totalitarian-type IPV characterized by high levels of order and power disparity (in which the violent acts of the perpetrator consistently support the relationship norms that maintain order and power disparity) may be able to better mobilize resources and family members to conceal and minimize severe violence. If empirical research confirms that IPV in such families is harder to detect, then policy can be designed specifically to target such families. Research is also needed to examine the degree to which life-threatening violence varies across these types. Such research could make use of existing IPV-informed measures of power and order (cf. Emery, 2011; Emery, Thapa, et al., 2015, Emery, Thapa, et al., 2017). Longitudinal and controlled experimental studies are desirable to substantiate the rigor of the potential findings that could emerge from cross-sectional studies. We advocate for research attention to restorative justice interventions for IPV. Within informal social control specifically, we call for research that examines the hypothesized logical connection between protective informal social control and restitute informal social control. For this to be achieved, measures of restitute informal social control of IPV need to be developed to support research. Further, research examining the impact of the various IPV typologies (as elements of family heterogeneity) on child witnesses would be useful. Qualitative studies that explore children's experiences of witnessing the different IPV types would be particularly important in efforts to gain deeper insight into the connection between IPV type and impact on child witnesses. Such evidence would collectively inform theory development in the field of IPV and child witnesses of family violence.

REFERENCES

Abdullah, A., Cudjoe, E., Ryu, W., & Emery, C. R. (2021). During and beyond the frequent lockdowns: Addressing the pandemic (COVID-19)–related family violence through informal social control. *Developmental Child Welfare*, *3*(3), 225–234. 25161032211046410. https://doi.org/10.1177/25161032211046409

Abdullah, A., Emery, C. R., & Jordan, L. P. (2020). Neighbourhood collective efficacy and protective effects on child maltreatment: A systematic literature review. *Health & Social Care in the Community*, *28*(6), 1863–1883. https://doi.org/10.1111/hsc.13047

Amato, P. R., Patterson, S., & Beattie, B. (2015). Single-parent households and children's educational achievement: A state-level analysis. *Social Science Research*, *53*, 191–202. https://doi.org/10.1016/j.ssresearch.2015.05.012

Barata, P. C., & Schneider, F. (2004). Battered women add their voices to the debate about the merits of mandatory arrest. *Women's Studies Quarterly*, *32*(3/4), 148–163.

Barocas, B., Emery, D., & Mills, L. G. (2016). Changing the domestic violence narrative: Aligning definitions and standards. *Journal of Family Violence*, *31*(8), 941–947. https://doi.org/10.1007/s10896-016-9885-0

Benitez, C. T., McNiel, D. E., & Binder, R. L. (2010). Do protection orders protect? *Journal of the American Academy of Psychiatry and the Law*, *38*(3), 376–385.

Braithwaite, J. (2000). Shame and criminal justice. *Canadian Journal of Criminology*, *42*(3), 281–298. https://doi.org/10.3138/cjcrim.42.3.281

Brame, R., Kaukinen, C., Gover, A. R., & Lattimore, P. K. (2015). No-contact orders, victim safety, and offender recidivism in cases of misdemeanor criminal domestic violence: A randomized experiment. *American Journal of Criminal Justice*, *40*(2), 225–249. https://doi.org/10.1007/s12103-014-9242-x

Bridgett, A. (2020). Mandatory-arrest laws and domestic violence: How mandatory-arrest laws hurt survivors of domestic violence rather than help them. *Health Matrix: The Journal of Law-Medicine*, *30*(1), 437.

Browning, C. R. (2002). The span of collective efficacy: Extending social disorganization theory to partner violence. *Journal of Marriage and Family*, *64*(4), 833–850. https://doi.org/10.1111/j.1741-3737.2002.00833.x

Cancian, M., & Meyer, D. R. (2018). Reforming policy for single-parent families to reduce child poverty. *RSF: The Russell Sage Foundation Journal of the Social Sciences*, *4*(2), 91–112. https://doi.org/10.7758/RSF.2018.4.2.05

Cheon, A., & Regehr, C. (2006). Restorative justice models in cases of intimate partner violence: Reviewing the evidence. *Victims & Offenders*, *1*(4), 369–394. https://doi. org/10.1080/15564880600934138

Child Welfare Information Gateway. (2015). *Acts of omission. An overview of child neglect?* Retrieved from: https://www.childwelfare.gov/pubs/focus/acts/

Chin, Y. M., & Cunningham, S. (2019). Revisiting the effect of warrantless domestic violence arrest laws on intimate partner homicides. *Journal of Public Economics*, *179*, 104072.

Cordier, R., Chung, D., Wilkes-Gillan, S., & Speyer, R. (2019). The effectiveness of protection orders in reducing recidivism in domestic violence: A systematic review and meta-analysis. *Trauma, Violence, & Abuse*, *22*(4), 804–828. 1524838019882361. https://doi.org/10.1177/1524838019882361

Crawford, B., & Bradley, M. S. (2016). Parent gender and child removal in physical abuse and neglect cases. *Children and Youth Services Review*, *65*, 224–230. https://doi.org/10.1016/j.childyouth.2016.04.013

Dekeseredy, W. S., Schwartz, M. D., Alvi, S., & Tomaszewski, E. A. (2003). Perceived collective efficacy and women's victimization in public housing. *Criminal Justice: International Journal of Policy and Practice*, *3*(1), 5–27. https://doi.org/10.1177/1466802503003001453

Dobash, R. E. (1979). *Violence against wives. A case against the patriarchy* (pp. 179–206). New York: Free Press.

Dowling, C., Morgan, A., Hulme, S., Manning, M., & Wong, G. (2018). Protection orders for domestic violence: A systematic review. *Trends and Issues in Crime and Criminal Justice*, *551*, 1–19. https://search.informit.org/doi/abs/10.3316/INFORMIT.7242 37717404777

Doyle, J. J. (2007). Child protection and child outcomes: Measuring the effects of foster care. *American Economic Review*, *97*(5), 1583–1610. https://doi.org/10.1257/aer.97.5.1583

Dozier, M., Stoval, K. C., Albus, K. E., & Bates, B. (2001). Attachment for infants in foster care: The role of caregiver state of mind. *Child Development*, *72*(5), 1467–1477. https://doi.org/10.1111/1467-8624.00360

Dunford, F. W., Huizinga, D., & Elliott, D. S. (1990). The role of arrest in domestic assault: The Omaha police experiment. *Criminology*, *28*(2), 183–206. https://doi.org/10.1111/j.1745-9125.1990.tb01323.x

Durfee, A., & Fetzer, M. D. (2016). Offense type and the arrest decision in cases of intimate partner violence. *Crime & Delinquency*, *62*(7), 954–977. https://doi.org/10.1177/0011128714540277

Edwards, A., & Sharpe, S. (2004). *Restorative justice in the context of domestic violence: A literature review*. Edmonton, Alberta: Mediation and Restorative Justice Centre, forthcoming at www.mrjc.ca

Emery, C. R. (2011). Disorder or deviant order? Re-theorizing domestic violence in terms of order, power and legitimacy: A typology. *Aggression and Violent Behavior*, *16*(6), 525–540. https://doi.org/10.1016/j.avb.2011.07.001

Emery, C. R., Eremina, T., Yang, H. L., Yoo, C., Yoo, J., & Jang, J. K. (2015). Protective informal social control of child maltreatment and child abuse injury in Seoul. *Journal of Interpersonal Violence*, *30*(18), 3324–3339. https://doi.org/10.1177/088626051 4554422

Emery, C. R., Jolley, J. M., & Wu, S. (2011). Desistance from intimate partner violence: The role of legal cynicism, collective efficacy, and social disorganization in
Chicago neighborhoods. *American Journal of Community Psychology*, *48*(3–4), 373–
383. https://doi.org/10.1007/s10464-010-9362-5

Emery, C. R., Thapa, S., Do, M. H., & Chan, K. L. (2015). Do family order and neighbor
intervention against intimate partner violence protect children from abuse? Findings
from Kathmandu. *Child Abuse & Neglect, 41*, 170–181. https://doi.org/10.1016/j.chi
abu.2014.10.001

Emery, C. R., Thapa, S., & Wu, S. (2017). Power and control in Kathmandu: A comparison of attempted power, actual power, and achieved power. *Violence Against
Women*, *23*(4), 482–502. https://doi.org/10.1177/1077801216644993

Emery, C. R., Trung, H. N., & Wu, S. (2015). Neighborhood informal social control
and child maltreatment: A comparison of protective and punitive approaches. *Child
Abuse & Neglect, 41*, 158–169. https://doi.org/10.1016/j.chiabu.2013.05.002

Emery, C., Wu, S., & Chan, K. L. (2018). A comparative study of totalitarian style partner
control in Seoul and Beijing: Confucian sex role norms, secrecy, and missing
data. *Journal of Interpersonal Violence*, *36*(7-8), NP4443–NP4467. https://doi.org/
10.1177/0886260518787208.

Emery, C. R., Wu, S., Eremina, T., Yoon, Y., Kim, S., & Yang, H. (2019). Does informal
social control deter child abuse? A comparative study of Koreans and Russians.
International Journal on Child Maltreatment: Research, Policy and Practice, *2*(1), 37–
54. https://doi.org/10.1007/s42448-019-00017-6

Emery, C. R., Wu, S., Kim, O., Pyun, C., & Chin, W. W. (2017). Protective family informal social control of intimate partner violence in Beijing. *Psychology of Violence*,
7(4), 553–562. https://doi.org/10.1037/vio0000063

Emery, C. R., Wu, S., & Raghavan, R. (2015). The Hutong effect: Informal social control
and community psychology in Beijing. *Injury Prevention*, *21*(2), 121–125. https://
doi.org/10.1136/injuryprev-2013-041117

Emery, C. R., Wu, S., Yang, H., Lee, H., Kim, J., & Chan, K. L. (2019). Informal control by family and risk markers for alcohol abuse/dependence in Seoul. *Journal
of Interpersonal Violence*, *34*(5), 1000–1020. https://doi.org/10.1177/088626051
6647003

Emery, C. R., Yang, H., Kim, O., Arenas, C., & Astray, A. (2017). What would your
neighbor do? An experimental approach to the study of informal social control of
intimate partner violence in South Korea. *Journal of Community Psychology*, *45*(5),
617–629. https://doi.org/10.1002/jcop.21882

Fagan, J. (1996). *The criminalization of domestic violence: Promises and limits*. United
States Department of Justice, Office of Justice Programs, National Institute of Justice,
Books. https://scholarship.law.columbia.edu/books/301

Fang, X., Fry, D. A., Brown, D. S., Mercy, J. A., Dunne, M. P., Butchart, A. R., Corso, P.
S., Maynzyuk, K., Dzhygyr, Y., Chen, Y., McCoy, A., & Swales, D. M. (2015). The
burden of child maltreatment in the East Asia and Pacific region. *Child Abuse &
Neglect, 42*, 146–162. https://doi.org/10.1016/j.chiabu.2015.02.012

Gelles, R. J., & Straus, M. A. (1979). Violence in the American family. *Journal of Social
Issues*, *35*(2), 15–39. https://doi.org/10.1111/j.1540-4560.1979.tb00799.x

Gilbert, R., Widom, C. S., Browne, K., Fergusson, D., Webb, E., & Janson, S. (2009). Burden and consequences of child maltreatment in high-income countries. *Lancet (London, England)*, *373*(9657), 68–81. https://doi.org/10.1016/S0140-6736(08)61706-7

Goldfarb, S. F. (2007). Reconceiving civil protection orders for domestic violence: Can law help end the abuse without ending the relationship. *Cardozo Law Review*, *29*, 1487.

Hirschi, T. (1969/2002). *Causes of delinquency*. Routledge.

Holt, V. L., Kernic, M. A., Wolf, M. E., & Rivara, F. P. (2003). Do protection orders affect the likelihood of future partner violence and injury? *American Journal of Preventive Medicine*, *24*(1), 16–21. https://doi.org/10.1016/S0749-3797(02)00576-7

Hoppe, S. J., Zhang, Y., Hayes, B. E., & Bills, M. A. (2020). Mandatory arrest for domestic violence and repeat offending: A meta-analysis. *Aggression and Violent Behavior*, *53*, 101430. https://doi.org/10.1016/j.avb.2020.101430

Horwitz, A. V. (1990). *The logic of social control*. Springer.

Iyengar, R. (2009). Does the certainty of arrest reduce domestic violence? Evidence from mandatory and recommended arrest laws. *Journal of Public Economics*, *93*(1), 85–98. https://doi.org/10.1016/j.jpubeco.2008.09.006

Izaguirre, A., & Calvete, E. (2015). Children who are exposed to intimate partner violence: Interviewing mothers to understand its impact on children. *Child Abuse & Neglect*, *48*, 58–67. https://doi.org/10.1016/j.chiabu.2015.05.002

Jain, S., Buka, S. L., Subramanian, S. V., & Molnar, B. E. (2010). Neighborhood predictors of dating violence victimization and perpetration in young adulthood: A multilevel study. *American Journal of Public Health*, *100*(9), 1737–1744. https://doi.org/10.2105/AJPH.2009.169730

Janowitz, M. (1975). Sociological theory and social control. *American Journal of Sociology*, *81*(1), 82–108.

Johnson, H., Ollus, N., & Nevala, S. (2007). *Violence against women: An international perspective*. Springer.

Johnson, M. P. (1995). Patriarchal terrorism and common couple violence: Two forms of violence against women. *Journal of Marriage and Family*, *57*(2), 283–294. https://doi.org/10.2307/353683

Johnson, M. P. (2008). *A typology of domestic violence: Intimate terrorism, violent resistance, and situational couple violence*. Northeastern University Press.

Johnstone, G. (Ed.). (2003). *A restorative justice reader*. Willan.

Jordan, C. E. (2004). Intimate partner violence and the justice system: An examination of the interface. *Journal of Interpersonal Violence*, *19*(12), 1412–1434. https://doi.org/10.1177/0886260504269697

Kieselbach, B., Kress, H., MacMillan, H., & Perneger, T. (2021). Prevalence of childhood exposure to intimate partner violence and associations with mental distress in Cambodia, Malawi and Nigeria: A cross-sectional study. *Child Abuse & Neglect*, *111*, 104807. https://doi.org/10.1016/j.chiabu.2020.104807

Kroese, J., Bernasco, W., Liefbroer, A. C., & Rouwendal, J. (2021). Growing up in single-parent families and the criminal involvement of adolescents: A systematic review. *Psychology, Crime & Law*, *27*(1), 61–75. https://doi.org/10.1080/1068316X.2020.1774589

Kwak, H., Dierenfeldt, R., & McNeeley, S. (2019). The code of the street and cooperation with the police: Do codes of violence, procedural injustice, and police ineffectiveness discourage reporting violent victimization to the police. *Journal of Criminal Justice, 60,* 25–34. https://doi.org/10.1016/j.jcrimjus.2018.11.001

Latimer, J., Dowden, C., & Muise, D. (2005). The effectiveness of restorative justice practices: A meta-analysis. *Prison Journal, 85*(2), 127–144. https://doi.org/10.1177/0032885505276969

Lim, S. S., Vos, T., Flaxman, A. D., Danaei, G., Shibuya, K., Adair-Rohani, H., Amann, M., Anderson, H. R., Andrews, K. G., Aryee, M., Atkinson, C., Bacchus, L. J., Bahalim, A. N., Balakrishnan, K., Balmes, J., Barker-Collo, S., Baxter, A., Bell, M. L., Blore, J. D., . . . Memish, Z. A. (2012). A comparative risk assessment of burden of disease and injury attributable to 67 risk factors and risk factor clusters in 21 regions, 1990-2010: A systematic analysis for the Global Burden of Disease Study 2010. *The Lancet, 380*(9859), 2224–2260. https://doi.org/10.1016/S0140-6736(12)61766-8

Logan, T., Cole, J., Shannon, L., & Walker, R. (2007). Relationship characteristics and protective orders among a diverse sample of women. *Journal of Family Violence, 22*(4), 237–246. https://doi.org/10.1007/s10896-007-9077-z

Logan, T., & Walker, R. (2009). Civil protective order outcomes: Violations and perceptions of effectiveness. *Journal of Interpersonal Violence, 24*(4), 675–692. https://doi.org/10.1177/0886260508317186

Matsueda, R. L., Kreager, D. A., & Huizinga, D. (2006). Deterring delinquents: A rational choice model of theft and violence. *American Sociological Review, 77*(1), 95–122. https://doi.org/10.1177/000312240607100105

Messing, J. T. (2011). The social control of family violence. *Affilia, 26*(2), 154–168. https://doi.org/10.1177/0886109911405492

Milani, L., Grumi, S., Camisasca, E., Miragoli, S., Traficante, D., & Di Blasio, P. (2020). Familial risk and protective factors affecting CPS professionals' child removal decision: A decision tree analysis study. *Children and Youth Services Review, 109,* 104687. https://doi.org/10.1016/j.childyouth.2019.104687

Mills, L. G., Barocas, B., Butters, R. P., & Ariel, B. (2019). A randomized controlled trial of restorative justice-informed treatment for domestic violence crimes. *Nature Human Behaviour, 3*(12), 1284–1294. https://doi.org/10.1038/s41562-019-0724-1

Nicholson, J. M., D'Esposito, F., Lucas, N., & Westrupp, E. M. (2014). Raising children in single-parent families. In Angela Abela and Janet Walker (Eds.), *Contemporary issues in family studies: Global perspectives on partnerships, parenting and support in a changing world* (pp. 166–188). Wiley-Blackwell.

Payne, M. (2005/2021). *Modern social work theory* (3rd ed.). Lyceum Books.

Pennell, J., & Burford, G. (2000). Family group decision making: Protecting children and women. *Child Welfare, 79*(2), 131–158.

Pennell, J., & Burford, G. (2002). Feminist praxis: Making family group conferencing work. In H. Strang & J. Braithwaite (Eds.), *Restorative justice and family violence* (pp. 108–127). New York: Cambridge University Press.

Peterson, C., Kearns, M., McIntosh, W., Estefan, L., Nicolaidis, C., McCollister, K., Gordon, A., & Florence, C. (2018). Lifetime economic burden of intimate partner violence among U.S. adults. *American Journal of Preventive Medicine, 55*(4), 433–444.

Russell, B. (2012). Effectiveness, victim safety, characteristics, and enforcement of protective orders. *Partner Abuse, 3*(4), 531–552. https://doi.org/10.1891/1946-6560.3.4.531

Ryan, C., Silvio, D., Borden, T., & Ross, N. M. (2021). A review of pro-arrest, pro-charge, and pro-prosecution policies as a response to domestic violence. *Journal of Social*

Work, 22(1), 211–238. 1468017320979956. https://doi.org/10.1177/146801732 0979956

Sampson, R. J., Raudenbush, S. W., & Earls, F. (1997). Neighborhoods and violent crime: A multilevel study of collective efficacy. *Science, 277*(5328), 918–924. https://doi.org/10.1126/science.277.5328.918

Shannon, L., Logan, T. K., & Cole, J. (2007). Intimate partner violence, relationship status, and protective orders: Does "living in sin" entail a different experience? *Journal of Interpersonal Violence, 22*(9), 1114–1130. https://doi.org/10.1177/08862 60507302880

Shaw, C. R., & McKay, H. D. (1942). *Juvenile delinquency and urban areas.* University of Chicago Press.

Sherman, L., Schmidt, J., Rogan, D., & Smith, D. (1992). The variable effects of arrest on criminal careers: The Milwaukee domestic violence experiment. *Journal of Criminal Law and Criminology, 83*(1), 137.

Sherman, L. W. (2000). Domestic violence and restorative justice: Answering key questions. *Virginia Journal of Social Policy & the Law, 8,* 263.

Sherman, L. W., & Berk, R. A. (1984). The specific deterrent effects of arrest for domestic assault. *American Sociological Review, 49*(2), 261–272. https://doi.org/10.2307/ 2095575

Sherman, L. W., Smith, D. A., Schmidt, J. D., & Rogan, D. P. (1992). Crime, punishment, and stake in conformity: Legal and informal control of domestic violence. *American Sociological Review, 57*(5), 680–690. https://doi.org/10.2307/2095921

Sherman, L. W., Strang, H., Mayo-Wilson, E., Woods, D. J., & Ariel, B. (2015). Are restorative justice conferences effective in reducing repeat offending? Findings from a Campbell systematic review. *Journal of Quantitative Criminology, 31*(1), 1–24. https://doi.org/10.1007/s10940-014-9222-9

Snyder, R. L. (2013, July 15). A raised hand: Can a new approach curb domestic homicide? *New Yorker.* https://www.newyorker.com/magazine/2013/07/22/a-raised-hand

Spitzberg, B. H. (2002). The tactical topography of stalking victimization and management. *Trauma, Violence, & Abuse, 3*(4), 261–288. https://doi.org/10.1177/15248 38002237330

Stark, E. (2007). *Coercive control: How men entrap women in personal life.* Oxford University Press.

Thomas, E. C., Bilger, A., Wilson, A. B., & Draine, J. (2019). Conceptualizing restorative justice for people with mental illnesses leaving prison or jail. *American Journal of Orthopsychiatry, 89*(6), 693–703. https://doi.org/10.1037/ort0000316

Umbreit, M. S. (1999). Victim-offender mediation in Canada: The impact of an emerging social work intervention. *International Social Work, 42*(2), 215–227. https://doi.org/ 10.1177/002087289904200209

Weber, M. (1978). *Economy and society: A new translation* (K. Tribe, Trans.). Harvard University Press.

Wood, S. L., & Sommers, M. S. (2011). Consequences of intimate partner violence on child witnesses: A systematic review of the literature. *Journal of Child and Adolescent Psychiatric Nursing, 24*(4), 223–236. https://doi.org/10.1111/ j.1744-6171.2011.00302.x

World Health Organization. (2021). Violence against women prevalence estimates. https://www.who.int/publications-detail-redirect/9789240022256

15

Psychosocial Support for Syrian Refugee Youth

Comparing Delivery Modes of a Digital Mental Health Game

DANA TOWNSEND, SOLFRID RAKNES, AND
MAHMOUD HAMMOUD ■

Over the past decade, Syrians have become the largest forcibly displaced population in the world, with roughly 2.5 million children and adolescents living in surrounding countries (United Nations High Commissioner for Refugees [UNHCR], 2021). Since the Syrian war began in 2011, they have endured immeasurable losses and continue to withstand adversity. The destruction of their nation, communities, homes, and cultural heritage has forever shifted the way that they make sense of their identity (Gibbons, 2017). On top of the grief and trauma associated with this loss of place and loved ones, many also face ongoing violence, harsh living conditions, poor nutrition, and uncertainty about the future (Cratsley et al., 2021). Children and adolescents have been disproportionately affected, as these rifts have taken place during the years that are most critical for establishing a strong foundation for healthy development.

One of the key strategies for promoting well-being and either preventing or attenuating mental health conditions among youth is the provision of psychosocial support services (World Health Organization [WHO], 2021). These services can be effective for young refugees because they address not only cognitive and emotional challenges but also the broader social and environmental factors that interrelate with their well-being—such as peer relationships, family and community dynamics, cultural traditions, education, and living situations (Inter-Agency Standing Committee, 2007). The gap between the number of displaced adolescents who could potentially benefit from evidence-based psychosocial support and the number who actually receive it is substantial. This is particularly the case for adolescents living under the poverty line or in countries beset by economic crises, such as those in eastern Lebanon (UNICEF, 2021).

Numerous barriers prevent refugee youth from accessing support—most notably the prohibitively high cost of traditional mental health care and the sociocultural stigma toward mental illness (Bär et al., 2021; Hendrickx et al., 2020). Interventions that can be scaled up without relying on specialized therapists are of particular interest (Bennett-Levy, 2010). In an evolving digital age, the interest in technology for mental health interventions has increased (Eichenberg & Schott, 2017; Zayeni et al., 2020). Tools such as games, virtual reality, and smartphone applications are increasingly explored for their capacity to enhance learning, motivation, cognitive and behavioral change, and empowerment (Khazaal et al., 2018). Digital tools can be especially relevant for youth who have grown up under the influence of these technologies (Patel et al., 2018), and digital games in particular align with recommendations that mental health interventions for children should provide an engaging, client-centered experience (Coyle & Doherty, 2009). So-called serious games have a purpose other than pure entertainment, such as education, skill enhancement, or behavioral change (Carlier et al., 2020). Research on the use of serious games in mental health interventions has shown that they were especially well received by children and teenagers, and dropout rates were low (Coyle & Doherty, 2009; Zayeni et al., 2020). In this chapter, we explore the role that digital games can play in promoting well-being and preventing mental disorders, and we assess the effectiveness of a digital, cognitive behavioral therapy (CBT)-based intervention called the Helping Hand, which was implemented for Syrian refugee adolescents in Lebanon.

THE SYRIAN REFUGEE CRISIS

The Syrian war began as a surge of popular protests in March 2011, which were violently suppressed by the Syrian government. Several opposition groups mobilized in response, and the conflict quickly escalated. Fighting, airstrikes, sieges, and other operations intensified throughout the country, and foreign coalitions became involved both logistically and militarily. As infrastructure was increasingly decimated and the number of casualties climbed, many Syrians were forced to flee the country in a series of waves that continued over the next decade. The most recent figures from the UNHCR (2021) estimate that 5.6 million Syrians are currently living as refugees in surrounding countries, and roughly 45% are children and adolescents who have spent most of their lives in displacement. The majority have found safety in the neighboring countries of Turkey (3.6 million), Lebanon (1.5 million), and Jordan (1.3 million), though this influx has placed a heavy strain on host countries and their capacity to provide adequate services. Most refugees live in challenging conditions without access to financial resources, and a large number remain unregistered, further limiting their access to assistance (Cratsley et al., 2021). They have experienced trauma, loss of loved ones, and a total collapse of their social systems and networks.

In addition to facing postsettlement stressors and heightened levels of psycho-social distress (Dalgaard & Montgomery, 2017), displaced adolescents and those without secure residency status face financial, legal, procedural, lingual, and cultural challenges that prevent them from accessing the quality of mental health care that they need (Shannon et al., 2015). Though studies have found that many Syrian youth show immense resilience in the face of these obstacles (Hassan et al., 2016; Panter-Brick et al., 2018), there is still a large proportion struggling with mental distress (Yayan et al., 2019). Generally, conflict-affected youth are at a much higher risk for developing psychopathology than those in other populations (Charlson et al., 2019). Research has suggested that some of these risks have been passed to Syrian youth intergenerationally as they learn maladaptive behaviors from psychologically distressed parents (Sim et al., 2018). The lack of access to education among many Syrian youth is an additional risk, which can hamper their development and increase the chance for negative outcomes (Kim et al., 2020).

The utilization of mental health services among Syrian refugees is typically low despite the high prevalence of disorders (Hendrickx et al., 2020). Though there are a few reasons for this, the most frequently cited is the continued association of mental illness with shame and fear. Religious leaders are often considered the first line of support for distress, as they are more culturally acceptable and less stigmatizing than mental health professionals (Al Laham et al., 2020). Importantly, this stigma is not limited to fears of judgment from others in the community but also includes internalized stigma and a reluctance to admit that outside support is needed. This self-stigma is especially prevalent among Syrian youth and is often associated with comorbidities (Bär et al., 2021). Low mental health literacy has been identified as one of the primary reasons for this stigma (Miles et al., 2020), suggesting that psychoeducation efforts may help address the problem. Some Syrian refugees have also avoided seeking support due to the view that distress is a normal, shared reaction to adversity rather than a symptom of mental illness (Kerbage et al., 2020). In contexts like this where mental health problems are contentious, anti-stigma work is needed to normalize conversations about these topics (Dardas & Simmons, 2015), as well as community interventions that emphasize the collective nature of refugee experiences (Al Laham et al., 2020).

The Lebanese Context

The program assessed in this chapter was implemented in Lebanon, which currently hosts the largest concentration of refugees per capita in the world (UNHCR, 2021). Of the more than 800,000 Syrian children and adolescents in Lebanon, most live in informal tented settlements in the Beqaa Valley—an agricultural region in the east of the country. The Lebanese government does not permit the establishment of formal refugee camps, so these settlements have become the default option for displaced Syrians who are unable to afford regular housing. Since they are unofficial, they fall outside many domains of humanitarian response, and their inhabitants are not guaranteed access to shelter, food, water, sanitation, health, education, and other essential services (REACH, 2014). There is emerging evidence that these substandard living conditions have contributed to mental health difficulties among refugee youth (Habib et al., 2020).

At the time of this writing, refugee adolescents in Lebanon face a heightened level of adversity due to combined pressures from the global COVID-19 pandemic, an economic collapse in Lebanon described as one of the world's worst since the mid-19th century, and the aftermath of the Port of Beirut explosion that damaged much of the capital and left more than 300,000 people homeless (Brun et al., 2021; World Bank, 2021). Unemployment rates have increased dramatically—especially among refugee youth, which is associated with higher risks for substance use and antisocial behavior (Sleem & Dixon, 2018). Systems that were formally in place to normalize the lives of refugees have largely been suspended due to the COVID-19 pandemic, and the lack of access to education, health, and food are cited as the highest drivers of refugee distress along with financial difficulties (Lebanon Crisis Response Plan, 2021). Though there is a large network of mental health providers in Lebanon, there are few available in the Beqaa Valley, and the services that do exist are privatized. The cost of treatment is often cited as a major barrier for Syrians living below the poverty line (Blanchet et al., 2016). In addition to the lack of qualified professionals and high cost of treatment, youth mental health programs receive only 0.1% of assistance from global health-related initiatives (Frankish et al., 2018), further reducing the feasibility of organizing traditional, face-to-face services. Given these constraints, understanding how to better support mental health and development among refugee adolescents is critical (Dalgaard & Montgomery, 2017; Nolas et al., 2020).

PSYCHOSOCIAL SUPPORT FOR SYRIAN YOUTH

One way to increase access to mental health care on a larger scale is through the facilitation of community-based psychosocial support activities and other health-promoting interventions. These can be implemented efficiently in large groups, increase mental health literacy, and avoid or reduce the stigma associated with help seeking (Hassan et al., 2016). High-quality, low-cost interventions are crucial for increasing access to mental health services among people in extreme poverty. Prevention in childhood may cascade over the life course, and even small preventative effects may have substantial population impact (Mendelson, 2018). When designed well, psychosocial interventions can impact the adolescents involved but also their families and the group facilitators that receive training on the material.

Many challenges persist regarding the development of effective interventions, including a multitude of guideposts that often contradict. Program developers are expected to balance the technical generalizability of the intervention with sociocultural adaptation, to choose between pressures to alleviate immediate suffering or work toward long-term change, and to decide whether to prioritize targeted interventions or locally owned projects that promote community engagement and agency (Arakelyan & Ager, 2021). Many of these challenges do not have clear answers, and the development of interventions is an ongoing process of testing and refining. Keeping these tensions in mind, the existing gaps in refugee mental health support can be addressed through exploration of the following strategies: (a) development of brief, evidence-based therapies or low-intensity interventions that do not require specialists; (b) promotion of transdiagnostic approaches in which practitioners are trained in a single protocol that can be applied to treat a variety of mental health problems; and (c) the dissemination of technology that improves access to support in underserved and hard-to-reach areas (Bockting et al., 2016). It is essential to develop tools that assist youth in developing adaptive coping skills under displacement conditions while also supporting practitioners to deliver evidence-based and culturally competent support (UNICEF, 2021).

Digitalized Psychosocial Support

Many governance structures are exploring strategies for digitalizing humanitarian assistance as a way to ensure that developing countries can access and benefit from programs even when local infrastructure or specialized personnel are lacking (e.g., Meld. St. 11, 2019–2020; United Nations General Assembly [UNGA], 2020). Such digitalization can create new opportunities for innovative mental health tools and psychosocial programs, which can be adapted for use in different contexts (Burrows et al., 2019). The use of digital health tools, however, does not ensure positive outcomes for youth, and careful attention should be paid to the design and implementation of these tools (Sittig et al., 2020). In addition to ensuring that tools are actually effective, it is critical that aid workers pay close attention to the risks that digitalization can bring, such as cyber threats, mismanaged data, and exploitation of vulnerabilities (Akhmatova & Akhmatova, 2020). It is also important to apply a gender analysis when considering the use of digital tools, as previous research has shown that girls growing up in poverty are more at risk for missing out on the benefits of e-health interventions than girls with socioeconomic privilege (Andermann & CLEAR Collaboration, 2016). On average, women are 26% less likely than men to have a smartphone, and the adherence to traditional gender expectations prevents many from gaining digital skills (Organisation for Economic Co-operation and Development, 2018). Supporting girls to enhance their technological skills and take advantage of digital opportunities can help them access these interventions (Shermer & Fenner, 2018).

Positive outcomes from digital health tools can vary based on a number of factors, including but not limited to the specific target population, access to technology, relevance of the content, training in how to use the tool, and pedagogical approaches. When the right conditions are met, these programs have been shown to positively enhance cognitive, skill-based, and affective learning among youth (Clark et al., 2016). The ability to gain mental health literacy through technology can have a far-reaching impact. Beyond enhancing learning at the individual level, the spread of these technologies may also decrease the stigma associated with mental illness by helping to normalize these topics (Stuart, 2016). This has been found to be the case among Syrian refugees, as mental e-health interventions have been shown to increase the number of individuals treated by avoiding the typical barriers created by stigma and lack of infrastructure (Sijbrandij et al., 2017). These applications complement clinic-based care and help to bolster system capacity (Ashfaq et al., 2020). It is also an appropriate medium for the population, as the use of digital technologies among Syrian refugees is widespread. Though internet access can be unstable in many locations where they live, most are able to access digital e-health programs through their smartphones (Burchert et al, 2019). Developing programs that can be played entirely or partially offline can circumvent this challenge. Technology-based learning for mental health prevention is still a new and growing field, and sharing these experiences is crucial for refining knowledge and ensuring good investments.

Social and Emotional Learning Through Digital Games

Psychosocial support initiatives often take a comprehensive approach to youth mental health by going beyond the physical and psychological to also consider dynamics in the family, community, and society at large. One type of psychosocial support, social and emotional learning (SEL), aims to help youth learn how to build and apply the knowledge, skills, and attitudes necessary for managing their emotions, setting and achieving goals, empathizing with others, establishing and maintaining positive relationships, and making responsible decisions. SEL initiatives are especially critical in countries affected by violent conflict, as they can support healthy development, help youth break cycles of violence, and move society toward healing and reconciliation (Clarke-Habibi, 2019). SEL is also a core element of the UN Sustainable Development Goals—particularly target 4.7, which promotes human rights, gender equality, the promotion of cultures of peace and nonviolence, and global citizenship (Benavot et al., 2019).

Although it is agreed that SEL is important for youth, teachers typically report a lack of knowledge or professional skills in SEL delivery, and schools rarely provide resources (e.g., instruction materials, specific courses) or create conditions (e.g., teacher trainings, devoting teaching hours) that would promote teachers' instruction of SEL (Schiepe-Tiska et al., 2021). One way to teach SEL is to include experience-based learning tools like digital games. Digital games can be used to provide a forum for developing the skillsets, attitudes, and values that build resilience and maintain mental health (Hromek & Roffey, 2009). Digital psychoeducation games can foster healthy development in multiple ways, such as giving users the opportunity to experience learning in a multisensory, active, and experimental environment (Adachi & Willoughby, 2013). Studies have showed that game-based learning interventions offer the potential for increasing engagement and motivation, which have natural ties to learning (Sun-Lin & Chiou, 2019; Werner-Seidler et al., 2017).

Cognitive Behavioral Interventions Go Digital

Most of the existing mental e-health programs that are backed by research are based on CBT (Shams et al., 2021). A central principle of CBT stipulates that one's thoughts, behaviors, and emotions are inherently interconnected and mutually influence one another (Beck, 2011). CBT-based interventions typically focus on challenging and changing unhelpful cognitive distortions and behaviors, improving emotion regulation, and developing positive coping skills to solve existing problems in a constructive way. The basis of this theory is that maladaptive thoughts, including the individual's general beliefs about self, the world, and the future, can perpetuate their psychological distress and behavioral difficulties (Beck, 2011). Replacing them with alternative thoughts can lead to a change in emotions and behavior. The effect of CBT-based interventions, however, varies not only according to the tool and program itself but also by the methods of program implementation (Fixsen et al., 2013), who is delivering the program (Bennett-Levy, 2010), and broader procedures such as training, support, and workload (Pfadenhauer et al., 2017). Each of these should be considered when developing CBT-based digital tools.

THE HELPING HAND INTERVENTION

The Helping Hand (HH) application is a digital game grounded in CBT that was developed to help Arab adolescents improve their mental well-being. The overall concept is based on the Psychological First Aid Kit (Raknes, 2010), an analog self-help tool developed in Norway that has been found to effectively reduce anxiety and depression in adolescents (Haugland et al., 2020). One of its core elements is the "Helping Hand" problem-solving system. This system assigns a different question to each part of the hand, and the user answers these questions in a specific order to describe the situation and identify their emotions, cognitive distortions (red thoughts), useful perspectives (green thoughts), action steps, and support networks (see Table 15.1).

Form and Content of the Helping Hand Game

Digital games come in a variety of formats, from turn-taking games to more complex games where players require a fair degree of social and cognitive sophistication to play. Many use strategies such as discussion, role play, and problem-solving to engage players in solving social dilemmas while practicing social and emotional skills (Hromek & Roffey, 2009). The goal of the HH game is to support the main characters through a set of difficulties. It consists of two parts: a variety of *mini-games* and *dialogue* between the main characters. The mini games include tasks where the player has to identify different emotions and red and green thoughts;

Table 15.1. The Helping Hand System

The Hand	Focus	Explanation
Thumb	What's going on?	Identify the problem. Try to describe the situation in a neutral and precise way.
Index Finger	How do I feel?	Rate the intensity of the emotion(s) on a scale from 1 to 10. Describe where this feeling is located in the body.
Middle Finger	What are my red thoughts?	Recognize any unhelpful thoughts that make the situation more difficult to deal with.
Ring Finger	What are my green thoughts?	Identify thoughts and perspectives that are helpful and make it easier to cope with the situation.
Little Finger	What can I do?	Brainstorm ideas for responding to the situation in a way that will make you feel better and more confident in the long term. Think of advice that you would you give to a friend in the same situation.
Palm	Who can help me?	Seek out family members, friends, or other adults who can listen and provide support.

answer quiz questions about self-confidence, relationships, bullying, anxiety, and depression; recognize symptoms of suicidal ideation; and sort elements in the HH problem-solving system. In the dialogues, the player chooses how to respond as the main character talks about their challenges. The player will typically choose between responses that are empathetic and attentive, neutral, or lacking an appropriate level of support. The player then receives feedback based on their response and can earn points from successfully supporting the main character. Through participating in these virtual dialogues, the player strengthens their vocabulary for how to talk about feelings and mental health issues, which is important for gaining mental health literacy, decreasing stigma, and facilitating help seeking. For players who are facing posttraumatic difficulties and/or anxiety symptoms, these experiences can also be important first steps in gradual exposure.

During the development phase of the game, adolescents in Lebanon ($n = 90$) were presented with 15 different game scenarios and voted for the 10 that they would like to appear in the game. Lebanese, Palestinian, and Syrian adolescents selected settings for the game, the visual design, and the main challenges of the main characters. All of the characters speak Arabic, and their backstories are common among Arabic adolescents in Lebanon. Some of the main characters are Syrian refugees living in the tented settlements, while others are Lebanese youth living in nearby communities, and among the female characters are girls both with and without hijab. The 10 scenarios in the game focus on the following challenges:

1. *Presentation Anxiety.* Youth learn to identify the root of their fears when giving classroom presentations or speaking in public and explore options for minimizing anxiety.

2. *Criticism*. Youth learn how to receive constructive criticism and increase their awareness around negative reactions to feedback. They are encouraged to understand the intention behind others' criticism and to choose their words carefully when providing feedback for others.

3. *Social Rejection*. This scenario helps youth to cope with situations where they are excluded or rejected by their peers. They are encouraged to practice positive self-affirmations and understand that it is not only okay but also normal if they are not liked by everyone.

4. *Parents' Mental Illness*. Youth learn that their parents' mental health struggles are not their fault. They are encouraged to speak openly with trusted family members and friends about their difficulties in dealing with parents' behavior.

5. *Heartbreak*. This scenario helps youth explore the concept of love and feelings of heartbreak after losing a relationship. They are encouraged to talk with someone when they feel sad but to also stay active and social to help cope with the situation.

6. *Body Acceptance*. Youth learn how to deal with social comparison, body image struggles, and the importance of self-acceptance. They focus on identifying characteristics that they like about themselves.

7. *Suicidal Ideation*. This scenario helps youth to discuss the difficult topic of suicide. They learn the importance of taking their own and others' suicidal thoughts seriously and how to seek help before the situation worsens.

8. *Bullying and Racism*. Youth discuss the harmful effects of bullying and racism. They explore ways to confide in an adult and set personal boundaries to create safe spaces.

9. *Self-Assertiveness*. Youth gain awareness about their values, the importance of standing up for their beliefs, and sharing their opinions honestly. They are encouraged to have difficult conversations with people they trust.

10. *Traumatic Memories*. Youth learn how painful memories from the past can be triggered by what is happening in the present, and what those emotions can feel like. They discuss ways that they can cope with these emotions and how to seek help when needed.

Theoretical Foundations of the Helping Hand Game

The HH program includes several standard elements for increasing mental health literacy, such as psychoeducation about depression, anxiety, suicidal thoughts, and posttraumatic problems, and how our inner dialogue can influence feelings, motivation, and coping in challenging situations. The player learns general psychological principles that can be helpful for increasing self-confidence, improving relationships, and reducing anxiety and depression symptoms. The game also utilizes a CBT-based problem-solving system that the player learns and practices through the dialogues and mini games, thus training them to validate emotions, identify and restructure distorted thoughts, and look for coping behaviors that are helpful and intentional. Both psychoeducation and improved problem-solving skills can enhance the future safety of adolescents by teaching them skills to recognize maltreatment, harassment, and bullying and providing them with the language to tell others about potentially traumatic or abusive experiences (Endendijk et al., 2021).

The role plays used in the HH program were designed to be as realistic as possible, as this has been shown to predict the utility of role playing in interventions (Van Hasselt & Romano, 2004). In particular, virtual role plays have been perceived as more realistic and more effective than in-person role plays when it comes to learning self-protection skills for challenging situations, such as assertive refusal (Jouriles et al., 2011). In addition, role playing with avatars in a virtual environment has been associated with improvements in critical social skills such as emotion management, as well as less anxiety and more enjoyment than in-person role playing (Vallance et al., 2014).

The Helping Hand as a Blended Learning Program

A recent review suggests that digital teaching aids are most effective when they include some form of human interaction, such as a collaboration between users of the game or guidance from a facilitator (Lawrence et al., 2020). The current study builds on this finding by testing the HH program in the context of a 10-session facilitated group program with Syrian refugee adolescents in Lebanon (Raknes, 2021). Each session was an hour long and focused on one of the scenarios described previously. They were led by a facilitator whose role was to create a safe and welcoming atmosphere for the youth, oversee the gameplay, and lead group discussions and activities. The goal was to create a low-pressure, high-support environment for youth to learn healthy coping strategies while also expanding their social support networks through peer connections. The HH program was tested at two different time points using slightly different facilitation methods (e.g., using teachers and a short facilitator training during the school year vs. psychosocial workers and an extensive facilitator training during the summer). The two cases are assessed and compared to determine the feasibility of implementation with the target population, the preliminary effectiveness of the program for improving adolescents' well-being, and lessons learned from the different modes of facilitation.

METHOD

This study used an ecological, natural experimental approach (Card et al., 2021) in which the HH blended learning program was implemented among two samples of adolescents in Lebanon during spring 2021 (Trial 1) and summer 2021 (Trial 2). For Trial 1, the group facilitators were available for a half day of digital training only, while the Trial 2 group facilitators received 3 full days of face-to-face training, as well as weekly digital supervision during the implementation period. Quantitative and qualitative data were collected to assess changes to the adolescents' well-being and mental health, to solicit their input on the program and experience, and to compare procedures for implementing the program.

Participants

The program participants were recruited among Syrian adolescents between the ages of 13 and 17 living in informal tented settlements in either the Beqaa Valley or Arsal ($N = 372$). All of the participating adolescents were displaced as a result of the war in Syria, and many had directly witnessed violence or experienced the death of friends and family members. To combat the stigma toward mental illness that continues to persist in the region, a universal strategy was applied wherein all adolescents were invited to participate in the program regardless of their mental symptoms or coping skills. One hundred and two adolescents participated in Trial 1 (50% girls, 50% boys, M_{age} = 13.92), and 270 adolescents participated in Trial 2 (52.6% girls, 47.4% boys, M_{age} = 14.71).

Procedures

Both cases were implemented within the settlements at Beqaa and Arsal, Lebanon. The HH program developer was able to access these areas through collaboration with local humanitarian organizations that were already well established in the region and had strong connections with the refugee populations there. Trial 1 implementation was coordinated by Multi Aid Programs (MAPS), a refugee-led nongovernmental organization that supports community development programming in eastern Lebanon. Trial 2 implementation was coordinated by the Syrian American Medical Society (SAMS) Foundation, a nonprofit that works throughout the region to provide medical and mental health support for displaced Syrians and host communities.

The structure and delivery of the program shared a number of similarities for both cases. All participating adolescents met in small groups (10 to 18 per group) that were led by a facilitator who used a combination of role plays, group presentations, visual aids, and worksheets to enhance learning. After providing an overview on the topic at the beginning of each session, the students were invited to play the game using a digital device that was provided for them (i.e., tablet or phone). After they finished playing, the group discussed the topic and how the scenario related to their lives. All of the facilitators ($N = 15$) were Syrian adults living in Lebanon who shared the challenges associated with displacement. All had excellent writing and reading skills, and many had 1 to 3 years of education from a Syrian university. Each expressed an interest to participate in the project as group facilitators and take part in a training prior to beginning the group sessions.

Implementation of the two trials also differed in some notable ways. In Trial 1, the program was implemented at informal schools within the settlements by the adolescents' teachers. Each teacher participated in a remote, half-day digital training before delivering a 10-session program to students in their classrooms. Two of the 10 scenarios in the game were omitted—heartbreak and body image—because the facilitators felt that the themes and language were culturally challenging to deal with. The full Trial 1 program was completed over the course of 2 weeks, and all sessions were conducted face to face. After the initial facilitator training, the teachers did not receive any additional training or outside support during implementation.

In Trial 2, the program was implemented in settlement community centers by individuals whose primary work is in the field of psychosocial support. Before starting their groups, the facilitators participated in 3 full days of in-person training about the program and its theoretical framework, and also completed practice sessions with their colleagues and at least one adolescent to familiarize themselves with the content. Following the training, they delivered a 10-session program over the course of 10 weeks. Nine of the sessions were conducted face to face, and one of the sessions was remote online. Throughout implementation, the facilitators received weekly digital supervision from the HH developer as well as outside support from the project team, when needed (see Table 15.2 for details).

Table 15.2. COMPARISON OF TWO CASES OF HELPING HAND IMPLEMENTATION

	Trial 1	Trial 2
Time of Implementation	Spring 2021	Summer 2021
Location of Implementation	Beqaa Valley/Arsal	Beqaa Valley/Arsal
Background of Facilitators	Teachers (Syrian)	Psychosocial workers (Syrian)
Number of Facilitators	10 facilitators	5 facilitators
Groups per Facilitator	1 per facilitator	4–5 per facilitator
Group Size	10–11 per group	10–12 per group
Number of Sessions	8 sessions	10 sessions
Session Structure	All F2F	9 F2F, 1 digital
Program Duration	2 weeks	10 weeks
Facilitator Training	Digital, half-day	F2F, 3 days
Practice Sessions	No	Yes
Total Participants	102	270
Age (Mean)	13.92	14.71

NOTE: F2F = face-to-face. All facilitator trainings were led by Dr. Solfrid Raknes, Helping Hand developer.

Measures

The data for this project come from pre- and postprogram questionnaires completed by the participating adolescents. The questionnaires for Trials 1 and 2 both assessed the adolescents' well-being at baseline and after completion of the program. The Trial 1 questionnaire also included open-ended questions about the adolescents' attitudes toward the program, and the Trial 2 questionnaire also assessed the adolescents' anxiety and depression before and after the program.

PROGRAM FEEDBACK (TRIAL 1 ONLY)

In Trial 1, the postprogram questionnaires included open-ended questions to qualitatively assess learning points from the game and to get input from the adolescents and group facilitators about ideas for improvement. Participants were asked the following: (a) *What have you learned from the program?* (b) *What did you like least about the game?* and (c) *Do you have any tips on how the program could be used or how it could be improved?*

WELL-BEING (TRIAL 1 + TRIAL 2)

Adolescent well-being was measured using the Arabic version of the WHO's 5-item Well-Being Index (WHO-5). This questionnaire assessed the individual's well-being over the previous 2 weeks through positively phrased questions that avoid symptom-related language. For example, items include "*I have felt calm and relaxed,*" "*I have felt active and vigorous,*" and "*My daily life has been filled with things that interest me.*" Items are scored on a 6-point Likert scale from 0 = *At no time* to 5 = *All of the time.* WHO-5 has shown good reliability ($\alpha = .90$) as well as convergent and factorial validity (Halliday et al., 2017). The Arabic version of the WHO-5 has been validated in Lebanon and also showed acceptable reliability ($\alpha = .80$; Sibai et al., 2009).

ANXIETY AND DEPRESSION (TRIAL 2 ONLY)

In Trial 2, symptoms of anxiety and depression were measured using a 25-item version of the Revised Children's Anxiety and Depression Scale (RCADS-25). This shortened version of the 47-item self-report questionnaire was developed to reduce the burden on the participant and includes subscales on depression and a broad anxiety dimension (Ebesutani et al., 2012). The depression subscale includes 10 items ($\alpha = .80$), such as "*I feel sad or empty,*" "*I am tired a lot,*" and "*I have problems with my appetite.*" The anxiety subscale includes 15 items ($\alpha = .79$), such as "*I am restless,*" "*I worry what other people will think of me,*" and "*I suddenly start to tremble or shake when there is no reason for this.*" All items are scored on a 4-point Likert scale from 0 = *Never* to 3 = *Always.* A cut-off score of 27 has been found to correctly identify 87% of youth who are at risk for comorbid internalizing disorders (Loades et al., 2021), and youth scoring at or above this threshold were referred to external mental health services. The Arabic version of the RCADS-25 has been validated for use with Syrian youth and found to have acceptable reliability for total internalizing problems (α = .85) as well as the depression (α = .71) and anxiety (α = .76) subscales (Perkins & Alos, in press).

RESULTS

Qualitative Results

During Trial 1, students were asked what they learned from the game. Many adolescents reported similar learning points, which were grouped into the following themes: (a) supporting others, (b) solving problems, (c) becoming aware of thoughts, (d) regulating emotions, and (e) learning how to live in a more virtuous way by accessing their positive qualities and behaviors (see Table 15.3 for details).

A number of students reported that they did not like the scenario on suicidal ideation or feel that it was appropriate for their age. Others commented on "bad" words that were used in a couple scenarios and should be removed. A couple participants reported that the trauma scenario brought up some painful memories for them, which reinforces the importance of debriefing and discussing ways to cope with those memories. To improve the program, many students suggested creating more scenarios with additional topics that they can learn about. Others suggested making it part of the school curriculum so that all students can benefit or using the game with family so that parents can support their children through the lessons.

Quantitative Results

At Trial 1 baseline, 19.8% of adolescents indicated poor well-being as measured by the WHO-5 questionnaire (M_{pre} = 17.79, SD_{pre} = 5.05), while only 7.8% indicated poor well-being after completion of the program (M_{post} = 18.62, SD_{post} = 4.38). This suggests that a number of adolescents improved throughout the program, though a paired t-test showed that overall improvements in well-being were nonsignificant, $t(101)$ = 1.28, p = .20. When assessing girls and boys separately, however, the results were different. Boys showed no increase to their well-being from pre- to posttest (M_{pre} = 18.35, SD_{pre} = 4.71, M_{post} = 18.16, SD_{post} = 4.55), $t(50)$ = .22, p = .83, while girls did show significant improvements to well-being (M_{pre} = 17.24, SD_{pre} = 5.35, M_{post} = 19.08, SD_{post} = 4.20), $t(50)$ = 2.03, p = .047.

At Trial 2 baseline, 27.4% of adolescents indicated poor well-being as measured by the WHO-5 questionnaire (M_{pre} = 16.08, SD_{pre} = 5.83), while only 4.5% of adolescents indicated poor well-being after completion of the program (M_{post} = 21.16, $SD_{po}{}^{st}$ = 3.57). A paired t-test showed that overall improvements to well-being were significant, $t(245)$ = 13.71, $p < .001$. Regarding internalizing symptoms at Trial 2, 33% of adolescents indicated symptoms of anxiety and depression at baseline that exceeded the RCADS-25 cut-off (M_{pre} = 22.02, SD_{pre} = 11.68).

Table 15.3. LEARNING POINTS FROM THE PSS PROGRAM (TRIAL 1 ONLY)

Theme	Direct Responses
Supporting Others	Dealing with people better
	Helping other people
	To help others instead of bullying
	Helping and comforting someone
	Useful things like helping friends
	Giving advice to friends and parents
	Dealing with bullying
Problem-solving	Facing challenges/dealing with problems
	Being wise with problems/solving problems
	Making good decisions
	Not to withdraw
	Logical thinking before doing anything; not being in a hurry
	Thinking before actions
	How to solve my problems myself or consult an adult or friend
Awareness of Thoughts	How to think positively
	Using green thoughts
	Promoting green thoughts
	Mindfulness
	Red thoughts for the wrong way; green thoughts for the right way
	How to use my mind to be a good thinker
	Understanding the difference between thoughts and emotions
Emotion Regulation	How to control my feelings
	Controlling my emotions
	Not allowing red thoughts to affect me
	How to reduce my fears
	How to deal with sad thoughts
Virtuous Behavior	Confidence/Self-reliance
	Courage/Strength
	Altruism/Good actions
	Love/Compassion
	Patience
	Optimism/Positivity

After completion of the program, only 5% indicated symptoms (M_{post} = 9.58, SD_{post} = 8.34), which was a significant decrease, $t(245)$ = 15.68, $p < .001$ (see Table 15.4). There was no difference between girls and boys for either indicator.

Of the 270 participants at Trial 2, 24 dropped out of the program (6 girls, 18 boys). The majority of adolescents who dropped out of the program (54%) reported that the reason was due to full-time work responsibilities to assist their parents in covering family expenses. This may explain why a higher percentage of boys dropped out of the program than girls. Other explanations for attrition

Table 15.4. CHANGES IN WELL-BEING AND INTERNALIZING BEHAVIOR FROM PRE- TO POSTTEST

Measure	Pretest		Posttest		Mean Difference	t value	df	95% CI	Cohen's d
	M	SD	M	SD					
T1 Well-being	17.79	5.05	18.62	4.38	-.82	1.28 (n.s.)	101	-2.10, 0.45	.13
T2 Well-being	16.08	5.83	21.16	3.57	-5.08	13.71***	245	-5.81, -4.35	.85
T2 Depression	9.78	5.60	4.75	4.02	5.03	13.23***	245	4.28, 5.78	.84
T2 Anxiety	12.22	7.48	4.83	4.98	7.39	14.69***	245	6.40, 8.38	.94
T2 Depression + Anxiety	22.02	11.68	9.58	8.34	12.44	15.68***	245	10.88, 14.01	1.00

NOTE: ***p < .001, n.s. = nonsignificant, *M* = mean, *SD* = standard deviation, *df* = degrees of freedom, CI = confidence interval, T1 = Trial 1, T2 = Trial 2. The well-being scores come from the WHO-5 measure. The depression, anxiety, and combined scores come from the RCADS-25.

include moving to another area (29%), removal from the program after missing more than three sessions (8%), completing their education at another place (4%), and engagement (4%).

DISCUSSION

Overall, implementation of a CBT-based intervention for Syrian refugee adolescents in Lebanon showed positive results across both trials. The percentage of adolescents with mental health problems was reduced in all settings, though the effectiveness of the intervention varied based on the different implementation methods that were used.

The qualitative data suggest that adolescents and group facilitators alike found the game to be appropriate for Syrian refugee youth in Lebanon. Many of the participating adolescents expressed that this game was an accurate reflection of reality and the kind of issues they face, and that increasing access to the program could be beneficial to many. They commented that the digital game was a new and unique way for them participate interactively and creatively and found that they learned important skills in a way they enjoyed. In particular, youth noted that they learned useful information about how to support others, regulate emotions, solve problems, become aware of their thoughts, and get in touch with positive qualities like compassion, self-confidence, courage, and patience. These findings are in line with other studies on serious games that have demonstrated how they can lead to important learning and changes in attitudes and behavior (Coyle & Doherty, 2009; Zayeni et al., 2020). The youth's positive attitudes toward the game and acknowledgment of increased skills for help seeking and talking about emotional issues can be interpreted as a step toward normalization and decrease of stigma. If using a digital game reduces mental health stigma in adolescents, families, schools, and communities while also increasing awareness on the value of mental health and help seeking, then the potential benefits of such games can be extensive (Dardas & Simmons, 2015; Al Laham et al., 2020).

Quantitatively, the effectiveness of this intervention varied with the implementation method used. The adolescents' well-being did not significantly improve for groups during Trial 1, but adolescents in Trial 2 showed significant improvements to well-being, depression, and anxiety with large effect sizes. Since all the participants and group facilitators were Syrian refugees living in the Beqaa Valley and Arsal in Lebanon, the differences in program effectiveness are most likely a result of implementation procedures and timing. Regarding procedures, the Trial 2 facilitators underwent a much more extensive training in the program's core elements and theoretical foundations than Trial 1 facilitators. They also spent more time in practice sessions and received support and supervision from the program developer and outside staff. One takeaway is that the implementation frames provided for SEL group facilitators might be just as important as the content of the intervention itself. These results are in line with previous research showing that the facilitators' background and training, as well as their workload, can influence the program's impact (Bennett-Levy, 2010; Fixsen et al., 2013; Pfadenhauer et al., 2017; Sittig et al., 2020).

Recruiting psychosocial workers to serve as facilitators and providing them with extensive training and support seems to be beneficial, though there are also challenges to structuring SEL programs in this way. First, the dropout rate was higher when the program was not included in the classroom as part of an extended education program. Second, it takes more time and resources to create these conditions and build a strong facilitation team that understands the theoretical concepts well enough to explain them in a culturally relevant and engaging way. This can be difficult when funds are limited. A primary benefit of digitalizing interventions is that they tend to be more cost-effective, can be implemented in low-resource and hard-to-reach areas, and are easier to up-scale. If high-quality facilitation is required in order for the tools to be effective, however, then that reduces the potential scalability of the approach. Program staff will need to pay careful attention to these trade-offs. Third, the receptivity of adolescents to the program may depend in large part on the particular group dynamics—the facilitators' background, knowledge, and enthusiasm toward the content, and the adolescents' level of comfort with others in the group. These details can vary considerably from one setting to another, and it raises questions about how much of the improvements comes from the game and how much comes from the group atmosphere.

Another possible explanation for the differences in program effectiveness between Trials 1 and 2 is the shifting sociopolitical backdrop. Though these projects were implemented within months of each other, there were still some macro-level changes that took place during the study period. Even though the urgent financial crisis in Lebanon has been ongoing for years, the second implementation period coincided with a steep economic deterioration that included a crippling gasoline shortage, daily power outages, widespread food poisoning, and food insecurity. This context may have resulted in a greater need for support among adolescents. Perhaps even more relevant, during the first implementation, students were attending school and participating in other face-to-face group activities that were happening in parallel with the intervention program. This could have created a ceiling effect where improvements to well-being were less noticeable. Short-term interventions cannot compete with long-term education when it comes to the promotion of well-being and health for adolescents in poverty (Bergstrom & Ozler, 2021). In contrast, during the second implementation, the intervention program was the adolescents' primary means of interpersonal contact, "a window to the world" during a difficult period, and thus more meaningful to them. Opportunities to connect with peers and discuss mental health could have had a deeper impact during that time.

It also merits discussion that the group facilitators in Trial 2 included all of the 10 scenarios, while the facilitators in Trial 1 omitted the heartbreak and body acceptance scenarios due to their perception that the topics and language were not culturally acceptable. The Trial 2 facilitators disagreed and argued that these scenarios were indeed culturally relevant and valuable for the adolescents. They adjusted some of the language used to introduce each scenario in the game so that it could be discussed appropriately. For instance, the Trial 2 facilitators used the heartbreak scenario to focus on the importance of loving relationships and the pain of losing someone, and they used the body acceptance scenario to discuss positive self-talk and the importance of both body and soul for well-being. These facilitators also discussed the main elements of the program with parents, arguing that "Not including the mothers in SEL is like clapping with one hand." We do not know if these differences between Trial 1 and 2 were caused by the facilitators' training and supervision, their professional background, their investment in the program's elements, or other implementation factors. Considering that all group facilitators were Syrian refugees living in the same communities, their contrasting attitudes are likely a result of implementation frames more than culture. This highlights how local partners may disagree about the ways in which digital tools are adapted for the language and culture and shows the flexibility that can be brought to the content and its introduction.

There are some limitations to the study design that need to be considered when interpreting results. First, there have not been any subsequent assessments with the adolescents, so it is not yet clear how long the improvements will last. The potential long-term effects of digital interventions for at-risk youth in developing countries should be a focus of future research (Bergstrom & Ozler, 2021). Second, there was no control group at each time point, making it impossible to discern whether the differences in group-level change over time derive from sociopolitical changes or from alterations to the implementation procedure. In addition, a single-group design precludes clear causal inferences about the role of the intervention. A randomized controlled trial would be useful for clarifying the effectiveness of the program, and the pilot data suggest that this approach is sufficiently promising to merit further evaluation. Further, our results indicate that some youth had difficulty accessing electronic devices, which hindered their use of the application between group sessions and served as a barrier to their experience of the game. Project staff should pay close attention to any inequality in access that exists among the population they are working with so they can explore ways to minimize this barrier. Lastly, the program developer's involvement in the study may create some bias, as she has a stake in the game's success. To reduce this, the data were collected, analyzed, and discussed by members of the team who do not have a personal investment in the game.

Despite these limitations, the game also exhibited important strengths that likely played a role in the receptivity among participants. Arab adolescents—including Syrian refugees—were involved in multiple phases of the game's design and implementation. Their input on the characters, locations, and scenarios ensured that the game was culturally relevant from the start. In addition to this, both trials included a large number of adolescents and facilitators, which made it easier to assess program effectiveness and detect differences. Both of the measures—WHO-5 and RCADS-25—are high-quality assessments that have been validated in numerous contexts worldwide. The Arabic versions have been evaluated and refined through multiple studies, thus underscoring the credibility of the results.

Innovation is needed to improve digital health tools and programs (Meld. St. 11, 2019–2020; UNGA, 2020) and to create accessible services with a higher positive impact for Syrian refugees. For successful implementation of game-based mental health interventions, materials should be culturally and contextually relevant. This requires a collaborative approach that directly involves adolescents, group facilitators, and other community members in the development of the program content to ensure that it reflects local needs, values, and norms. In line with other studies on CBT-based serious mental health games, these results are promising with regard to adolescent engagement, program retention, increased well-being, and reduction of mental health symptoms (Carlier et al., 2020; Hromek & Roffey, 2009, Sun-Lin & Chiou, 2019; Werner-Seidler et al., 2017). The results indicate that digital mental health games, specifically the Helping Hand, can improve well-being and mental health for Syrian refugees when accompanied by group discussions. Developing and implementing psychosocial support interventions in general, and e-health technology in particular, is a continuous process of improvement and adaptation. Our results contribute to the accumulating evidence on digital health interventions and the efforts to develop tools that support well-being for all.

DISCLOSURE

I, Dr. Solfrid Raknes, have the following commercial relationship to disclose: Happy Helping Hand is a self-help material I have commercial interests in, in accordance with the standard sharing rules for innovation in the public and private health sector in Norway.

ACKNOWLEDGMENTS

Development of the Helping Hand program and proof-of-concept studies were supported by Innovation Norway, The Norwegian Research Council—Vision 2030, and Grand Challenges Canada. Thanks to Midsund Rotary Klubb Norway and Multi Aid Programs Lebanon for their support implementing the first trial, and to Syrian American Medical Society (SAMS) Foundation for their support implementing the second trial—particularly Mouhamad Harba, Charbel Ghostine, Eli Lebbos, and Mireille Dika. Thank you especially to the adolescents who participated in this program for making the study possible.

REFERENCES

Adachi, P. J., & Willoughby, T. (2013). More than just fun and games: The longitudinal relationships between strategic video games, self-reported problem-solving skills, and academic grades. *Journal of Youth and Adolescence, 42*(7), 1041–1052. https://doi.org/10.1007/s10964-013-9913-9

Akhmatova, D. M., Akhmatova, M. S. (2020). Promoting digital humanitarian action in protecting human rights: Hope or hype. *International Journal of Humanitarian Action, 5*(6), 1–7. https://doi.org/10.1186/s41018-020-00076-2

Al Laham, D., Ali, E., Mousally, K., Nahas, N., Alameddine, A., & Venables, E. (2020). Perceptions and health-seeking behaviour for mental illness among Syrian refugees and Lebanese community members in Wadi Khaled, North Lebanon: A qualitative study. *Community Mental Health Journal, 56*(5), 875–884. https://doi.org/10.1007/s10597-020-00551-5

Andermann, A., & CLEAR Collaboration. (2016). Taking action on the social determinants of health in clinical practice: A framework for health professionals. *CMAJ: Canadian Medical Association Journal (Journal de l'Association Medicale Canadienne), 188*(17–18), E474–E483. https://doi.org/10.1503/cmaj.160177

Arakelyan, S., & Ager, A. (2021). Annual research review: A multilevel bioecological analysis of factors influencing the mental health and psychosocial well-being of refugee children. *Journal of Child Psychology and Psychiatry, 62*, 484–509. https://doi.org/10.1111/jcpp.13424

Ashfaq, A., Esmaili, S., Najjar, M., Batool, F., Mukatash, T., Al-Ani, H. A., & Koga, P. M. (2020). Utilization of mobile mental health services among Syrian refugees and other vulnerable Arab populations—A systematic review. *International Journal of Environmental Research and Public Health, 17*(4), 1295. https://doi.org/10.3390/ijerph17041295

Bär, J., Pabst, A., Röhr, S., Luppa, M., Renner, A., Nagl, M., Dams, J., Grochtdreis, T., Kersting, A., König, H. H., & Riedel-Heller, S. G. (2021). Mental health self-stigma of Syrian refugees with posttraumatic stress symptoms: Investigating sociodemographic and psychopathological correlates. *Frontiers in Psychiatry, 12*, 642618. https://doi.org/10.3389/fpsyt.2021.642618

Beck, A. T. (2011). *Cognitive behavior therapy: Basics and beyond* (2nd ed.). Guilford Press.

Benavot, A., Chabbott, C., Sinclair, M., Williams, J., Bernard, J., Russel, S. G., & Smart, A. (2019). Introductory overview. In A. Benavot, C. Chabbott, M. Sinclair, J. Williams, J. Bernard, S. G. Russel, & A. Smart (Eds.), *NISSEM Global Briefs: Educating for the social, the emotional and the sustainable*. NISSEM.

Bennett-Levy, J., Richards, D., Farrand, P., Christensen, H., & Griffiths, K. (2010). *Oxford guide to low intensity CBT interventions*. Oxford University Press.

Bergstrom, K. A., & Ozler, B. (2021). *Improving the well-being of adolescent girls in developing countries (English)*. Policy Research Working Paper, no. WPS 9827. World Bank Group. http://documents.worldbank.org/curated/en/127361635787281327/Improving-the-Well-Being-of-Adolescent-Girls-in-Developing-Countries

Blanchet, K., Fouad, F. M., & Pherali, T. (2016). Syrian refugees in Lebanon: The search for universal health coverage. *Conflict and Health, 10*(12), 1–5. https://doi.org/10.1186/s13031-016-0079-4

Bockting, C., Williams, A. D., Carswell, K., & Grech, A. E. (2016). The potential of low-intensity and online interventions for depression in low- and middle-income countries. *Global Mental Health (Cambridge, England), 3*, e25. https://doi.org/10.1017/gmh.2016.21

Brun, C., Fakih, A., Shuayb, M., & Hammoud, M. (2021). *The economic impact of the Syrian refugee crisis in Lebanon.* World Refugee & Migration Council Research Report. https://wrmcouncil.org/wp-content/uploads/2021/09/Lebanon-Syrian-Refugees-WRMC.pdf

Burchert, S., Alkneme, M. S., Bird, M., Carswell, K., Cuijpers, P., Hansen, P., Heim, E., Harper Shehadeh, M., Sijbrandij, M., Van't Hof, E., & Knaevelsrud, C. (2019). User-centered app adaptation of a low-intensity e-mental health intervention for Syrian refugees. *Frontiers in Psychiatry, 9*, 663. https://doi.org/10.3389/fpsyt.2018.00663

Burrows, A., Meller, B., Craddock, I., Hyland, F., & Gooberman-Hill, R. (2019). User involvement in digital health: Working together to design smart home health technology. *Health Expectations: An International Journal of Public Participation in Health Care and Health Policy, 22*(1), 65–73. https://doi.org/10.1111/hex.12831

Card, D., Angrist, J. D., & Imbens, G. W. (2021). *Natural experiments help answer important questions.* The Sveriges Riksbank Prize in Economic Sciences in Memory of Alfred Nobel 2021. https://www.nobelprize.org/prizes/economic-sciences/2021/popular-information/

Carlier, S., Van der Paelt, S., Ongenae, F., De Backere, F., & De Turck, F. (2020). Empowering children with ASD and their parents: Design of a serious game for anxiety and stress reduction. *Sensors, 20*(4), 966. http://dx.doi.org/10.3390/s20040966

Charlson, F., van Ommeren, M., Flaxman, A., Cornett, J., Whiteford, H., & Saxena, S. (2019). New WHO prevalence estimates of mental disorders in conflict settings: A systematic review and meta-analysis. *The Lancet, 394*(10194), P240–P248. https://doi.org/10.1016/S0140-6736(19)30934-1

Clark, D. B., Tanner-Smith, E. E., & Killingsworth, S. S. (2016). Digital games, design, and learning: A systematic review and meta-analysis. *Review of Educational Research, 86*(1), 79–122.

Clarke-Habibi, S. (2019). Adolescent social and emotional learning in contexts of conflict, fragility and peacebuilding. In A. Smart, M. Sinclair, A. Benavot, J. Bernard, C. Chabbott, S. G. Russell, & J. Williams (Eds.), *NISSEM Global Briefs: Educating for the social, the emotional and the sustainable* (pp. 228–249). NISSEM. https://www.scribd.com/document/424176469/NISSEM-Global-Briefs

Coyle, D., & Doherty, G. (2009). Clinical evaluations and collaborative design: Developing new technologies for mental healthcare interventions. In *Proceedings of the SIGCHI Conference on Human Factors in Computing Systems (CHI '09)* (pp. 2051–2060). Association for Computing Machinery. https://doi.org/10.1145/1518701.1519013

Cratsley, K., Brooks, M. A., & Mackey, T. K. (2021). Refugee mental health, global health policy, and the Syrian crisis. *Frontiers in Public Health, 9*, 676000. https://dx.doi.org/10.3389%2Ffpubh.2021.676000

Dalgaard, N. T., Montgomery, E. (2017). The transgenerational transmission of refugee trauma: Family functioning and children's psychosocial adjustment. *International Journal of Migration, Health and Social Care, 13*(3), 289–301.

Dardas, L., & Simmons, L. A. (2015). The stigma of mental illness in Arab families: A concept analysis. *Journal of Psychiatric and Mental Health Nursing, 22*(9), 668–679.

Ebesutani, C., Reise, S. P., Chorpita, B. F., Ale, C., Regan, J., Young, J., Higa-McMillan, C., & Weisz, J. R. (2012). The Revised Child Anxiety and Depression Scale—Short Version: Scale reduction via exploratory bifactor modeling of the broad anxiety factor. *Psychological Assessment, 24*(4), 833–845. https://doi.org/10.1037/a0027283

Eichenberg, C., & Schott, M. (2017). Serious games for psychotherapy: A systematic review. *Games for Health Journal*, 6(3), 127–135. http://doi.org/10.1089/g4h.2016.0068

Endendijk, J. J., Tichelaar, H. K., Deen, M., & Deković, M. (2021). Vil Du?! Incorporation of a serious game in therapy for sexually abused children and adolescents. *Child & Adolescent Psychiatry & Mental Health*, 15(1), 1–13. https://doi.org/10.1186/s13 034-021-00377-3

Fixsen, D., Blasé, K., Naoom, S., & Duda, M. (2013). *Implementation drivers: Assessing best practices*. University of North Carolina at Chapel Hill.

Frankish, H., Boyce, N., & Horton, R. (2018). Mental health for all: A global goal. *The Lancet*, 392(10157), 1493–1494. https://doi.org/10.1016/S0140-6736(18)32271-2

Gibbons, E. (2017). The Syrian crisis and cultural memory. *Global Societies Journal*, 5, 59–69.

Habib, R. R., Ziadee, M., Abi Younes, E., El Asmar, K., & Jawad, M. (2020). The association between living conditions and health among Syrian refugee children in informal tented settlements in Lebanon. *Journal of Public Health*, 42(3), e323–e333. https://doi.org/10.1093/pubmed/fdz108

Halliday, J. A., Hendrieckx, C., Busija, L., Browne, J. L., Nefs, G., Pouwer, F., & Speight, J. (2017). Validation of the WHO-5 as a first step screening instrument for depression in adults with diabetes: Results from Diabetes MILES—Australia. *Diabetes Research and Clinical Practice*, 132, 27–35.

Hassan, G., Ventevogel, P., Jefee-Bahloul, H., Barkil-Oteo, A., & Kirmayer, L. J. (2016). Mental health and psychosocial wellbeing of Syrians affected by armed conflict. *Epidemiology and Psychiatric Sciences*, 25(2), 129–141. https://doi.org/10.1017/S2045796016000044

Haugland, B. S. M., Haaland, Å. T., Baste, V., Bjaastad, J. F., Hoffart, A., Rapee, R. M., Raknes, S., Himle, J. A., Husabø, E., & Wergeland, G. J. . (2020). Effectiveness of brief and standard school-based cognitive-behavioral interventions for adolescents with anxiety: A randomized noninferiority study. *Journal of the American Academy of Child & Adolescent Psychiatry*, 59(4), 552–564. https://doi.org/10.1016/j.jaac.2019.12.003

Hendrickx, M., Woodward, A., Fuhr, D. C., Sondorp, E., & Roberts, B. (2020). The burden of mental disorders and access to mental health and psychosocial support services in Syria and among Syrian refugees in neighboring countries: A systematic review. *Journal of Public Health*, 42(3), e299–e310. https://doi.org/10.1093/pubmed/fdz097

Hromek, R., & Roffey, S. (2009). Promoting social and emotional learning with games: "It's fun and we learn things." *Simulation & Gaming*, 40, 626–644.

Inter-Agency Standing Committee. (2007). *IASC guidelines on mental health and psychosocial support in emergency settings*.

Jouriles, E. N., Rowe, L. S., McDonald, R., Platt, C. G., & Gomez, G. S. (2011). Assessing women's responses to sexual threat: Validity of a virtual role-play procedure. *Behavior Therapy*, 42, 475–484. https://doi.org/10.1016/j.beth.2010.11.005

Kerbage, H., Marranconi, F., Chamoun, Y., Brunet, A., Richa, S., & Zaman, S. (2020). Mental health services for Syrian refugees in Lebanon: Perceptions and experiences of professionals and refugees. *Qualitative Health Research*, 30(6), 849–864. https://doi.org/10.1177/1049732319895241

Khazaal, Y., Favrod, J., Sort, A., Borgeat, F., & Bouchard, S. (2018). Editorial: Computers and games for mental health and well-being. *Frontiers in Psychiatry, 9*, 141. https://doi.org/10.3389/fpsyt.2018.00141

Kim, H. Y., Brown, L., Tubbs Dolan, C., Sheridan, M., & Aber, J. L. (2020). Post-migration risks, developmental processes, and learning among Syrian refugee children in Lebanon. *Journal of Applied Developmental Psychology, 69*, 101142. https://doi.org/10.1016/j.appdev.2020.101142

Lawrence, G., Ahmed, F., Cole, C., & Johnston, K. P. (2020). Not more technology but more effective technology: Examining the state of technology integration in EAP programmes. *RELC Journal, 51*(1), 101–116. https://doi.org/10.1177%2F0033688220907199

Lebanon Crisis Response Plan. (2021). *Lebanon crisis response plan: 2017–2021.* Government of Lebanon and the United Nations. https://reliefweb.int/sites/reliefweb.int/files/resources/LCRP_2021FINAL_v1.pdf

Loades, M., Stallard, P., Kessler, D. S., & Crawley, E. M. (2021). Mental health screening in adolescents with CFS/ME. *European Child and Adolescent Psychiatry, 31*, 1003–1005. https://doi.org/10.1007/s00787-021-01734-5

Mendelson, E. (2018). Recent advances in the prevention of mental disorders. *Social Psychiatry and Psychiatric Epidemiology, 53*(4), 325–339.

Miles, R., Rabin, L., Krishnan, A., et al. (2020). Mental health literacy in a diverse sample of undergraduate students: Demographic, psychological, and academic correlates. *BMC Public Health, 20*, 1699. https://doi.org/10.1186/s12889-020-09696-0

Nolas, S. M., Watters, C., Pratt-Boyden, K., & Maglajlic, R. A. (2020). Place, mobility and social support in refugee mental health. *International Journal of Migration, Health and Social Care, 16*(4), 333–348. https://doi.org/10.1108/IJMHSC-03-2019-0040

Organisation for Economic Co-operation and Development. (2018). *Bridging the digital gender divide: Include, upskill, innovate.* OECD Report. https://documentcloud.adobe.com/link/review?uri=urn:aaid:scds:US:711a3591-bd72-4b33-8f6d-a4c990f69dc1

Panter-Brick, C., Hadfield, K., Dajani, R., Eggerman, M., Ager, A., & Ungar, M. (2018). Resilience in context: A brief and culturally grounded measure for Syrian refugee and Jordanian host-community adolescents. *Child Development, 89*(5), 1803–1820. https://doi.org/10.1111/cdev.12868

Patel, V., Saxena, S., Lund, C., Thornicroft, G., Baingana, F., Bolton, P., Chisholm, D., Collins, P. Y., Cooper, J. L., Eaton, J., Herrman, H., Herzallah, M. M., Huang, Y., Jordans, M., Kleinman, A., Medina-Mora, M. E., Morgan, E., Niaz, U., Omigbodun, O., Prince, M., . . . Unützer, J. (2018). The Lancet Commission on global mental health and sustainable development. *The Lancet, 392*(10157), 1553–1598. https://doi.org/10.1016/S0140-6736(18)31612-X

Perkins, J., & Alos, J. (2021). Rapid mental health screening in conflict zones: A translation and cross-cultural adaptation into Arabic of the shortened Revised Child Anxiety and Depression scale (RCADS-25). *Conflict and Health, 15*(1), 51. https://doi.org/10.1186/s13031-021-00386-1

Pfadenhauer, L. M., Gerhardus, A., Mozygemba, K., et al. (2017). Making sense of complexity in context and implementation: The context and implementation of complex interventions (CICI) framework. *Implementation Science, 12*, 21. https://doi.org/10.1186/s13012-017-0552-5

Raknes, S. (2010). *Psykologisk førstehjelp for ungdom*. Gyldendal Akademisk.

Raknes, S. (2021). *A guide to using The Helping Hand in a psychological support group*. http://solfridraknes.no/ar/17-13/

REACH. (2014, October 2). *Syrian refugees staying in informal tented settlements in Jordan: Multi-sector needs assessment, August 2014*. https://reliefweb.int/sites/relief web.int/files/resources/REACH_UNICEF_ITS_MS_AUGUST2014_FINAL.PDF

Schiepe-Tiska, A., Dzhaparkulova, A., & Ziernwald, L. (2021). A mixed-methods approach to investigating social and emotional learning at schools: Teachers' familiarity, beliefs, training, and perceived school culture. *Frontiers in Psychology*, *12*, 518634. https://doi.org/10.3389/fpsyg.2021.518634

Shams, F., Wong, J., Nikoo, M., Outadi, A., Moazen-Zadeh, E., Kamel, M. M., Song, M. J., Jang, K. L., & Krausz, R. M. (2021). Understanding eHealth cognitive behavioral therapy targeting substance use: Realist review. *Journal of Medical Internet Research*, *23*(1). https://doi.org/10.2196/20557

Shannon, P., Wieling, E., Simmelink-McCleary, J., & Becher, E. (2015). Beyond stigma: Barriers to discussing mental health in refugee populations. *Journal of Loss and Trauma*, *20*(3), 281–296. https://doi.org/10.1080/15325024.2014.934629

Shermer, N. K., & Fenner, D. (2018). *Bridging cultures: Issues and strategies—A guide for schools*. Middle East Center, University of Washington. https://documentcloud. adobe.com/link/review?uri=urn:aaid:scds:US:22e03c1a-ab7d-4c79-813e-5c5d1 215d0cc

Sibai, A. M., Chaaya, M., Tohme, R. A., Mahfoud, Z., & AlAmin, H. (2009). Validation of the Arabic version of the 5-item WHO Well Being Index in elderly population. *International Journal of Geriatric Psychiatry*, *24*(1), 106–107. https://doi.org/ 10.1002/gps.2079

Sijbrandij, M., Acarturk, C., Bird, M., Bryant, R. A., Burchert, S., Carswell, K., de Jong, J., Dinesen, C., Dawson, K. S., El Chammay, R., van Ittersum, L., Jordans, M., Knaevelsrud, C., McDaid, D., Miller, K., Morina, N., Park, A. L., Roberts, B., van Son, Y., Sondorp, E., . . . Cuijpers, P. (2017). Strengthening mental health care systems for Syrian refugees in Europe and the Middle East: Integrating scalable psychological interventions in eight countries. *European Journal of Psychotraumatology*, *8*(Suppl. 2), 1388102. https://doi.org/10.1080/20008198.2017.1388102

Sim, A., Bowes, L., & Gardner, F. (2018). Modeling effects of ward exposure and daily stressors on maternal mental health, parenting, and child psychological adjustment: A cross-sectional study with Syrian refugees in Lebanon. *Global Mental Health*, *5*(40). https://dx.doi.org/10.1017%2Fgmh.2018.33

Sittig, D. F., Wright, A., Coiera, E., Magrabi, F., Ratwani, R., Bates, D. W., & Singh, H. (2020). Current challenges in health information technology–related patient safety. *Health Informatics Journal*, 181–189. https://doi.org/10.1177/1460458218814893

Sleem, H. N., & Dixon, J. (2018). Child poverty and youth unemployment in Lebanon. *Poverty and Public Policy*, *10*(3), 338–353. https://doi.org/10.1002/pop4.223

Meld. St. 11. (2019–2020). *Report to the Storting: Digital transformation and development policy* (white paper). Royal Norwegian Ministry of Foreign Affairs. https://www.regj eringen.no/en/dokumenter/meldst11_summary/id2699502/?ch=1

Stuart, H. (2016). Reducing the stigma of mental illness. *Global Mental Health*, *3*(17). https://doi.org/10.1017/gmh.2016.11

Sun-Lin, H.-Z., & Chiou, G.-F. (2019). Effects of gamified comparison on sixth graders' algebra word problem solving and learning attitude. *Journal of Educational Technology & Society, 22*(1), 120–130.

UNICEF. (2021). *On my mind: Promoting, protecting and caring for children's mental health. The state of the world's children, 2021.*

United Nations General Assembly (UNGA). (2020, May 29). *Road map for digital cooperation: Implementation of the recommendations of the High-Level Panel on Digital Cooperation.* UNGA, Report of the Secretary General. https://undocs.org/A/74/821

United Nations High Commissioner for Refugees (UNHCR). (2021). *Refugee data finder.* Retrieved on October 16, 2021, from https://www.unhcr.org/refugee-statist ics/download/

Vallance, A. K., Hemani, A., Fernandez, V., Livingstone, D., McCusker, K., & Toro-Troconis, M (2014). Using virtual worlds for role play simulation in child and adolescent psychiatry: An evaluation study. *Psychiatric Bulletin, 38,* 204–210. https://doi.org/10.1192/pb.bp.113.044396.

Van Hasselt, V. B., & Romano, S. J. (2004). Role-playing: A vital tool in crisis negotiation skills training. *FBI Law Enforcement Bulletin, 73,* 12–17.

Werner-Seidler, A., Perry, Y., Calear, A. L., Newby, J. M., & Christensen, H. (2017). School-based depression and anxiety prevention programs for young people: A systematic review and meta-analysis. *Clinical Psychology Review, 51,* 30–47. https://doi.org/10.1016/j.cpr.2016.10.005

World Bank. (2021, June 1). *Lebanon sinking into one of the most severe global crises episodes, amidst deliberate inaction.* https://openknowledge.worldbank.org/handle/10986/31205

World Health Organization (WHO). (2021). *Comprehensive mental health action plan: 2013–2030.* WHO Mental Health and Substance Use Team. https://www.who.int/publications/i/item/9789240031029

Yayan, E. H., Düken, M. E., Ozdemir, A. A., & Çelebioglu, A. (2019). Mental health problems of Syrian refugee children: Post-traumatic stress, depression, and anxiety. *Journal of Pediatric Nursing, 51,* 27–32. https://doi.org/10.1016/j.pedn.2019.06.012

Zayeni, D., Raynaud, J. P., & Revet, A. (2020). Therapeutic and preventive use of video games in child and adolescent psychiatry: A systematic review. *Frontiers in Psychiatry, 11,* 36. https://doi.org/10.3389/fpsyt.2020.00036.

Conclusions

16

Preventing and Responding to Violence Against Children

Implications for Researchers, Practitioners, and Policymakers

LAURA E. MILLER-GRAFF, SCOTT L. MOESCHBERGER, AND CATHERINE A. MALONEY ∎

AUTHOR NOTE

The development of this work was supported by the Kroc Institute for International Peace Studies via the Visiting Fellows program. Dr. Moeschberger was in residence as a visiting fellow during fall 2019.

The work in this edited volume provides an overview of contemporary research on violence against children (VAC) in multiple global settings. Viewed together, this volume underscores the inextricable connections between multiple types of VAC, including direct, structural, and cultural forms of violence. Although psychologists have often focused on the assessment of direct violence, this volume urges researchers, practitioners, and policymakers to consider how this narrow definition of violence results in an incomplete picture of what is at stake, compromising our ability to effectively understand and respond to the holistic needs of children. As we work together as a global community, rooted in our local contexts, mutual exchange of learnings should continue to inform ways in which we can better support the development and flourishing of young children, advancing a vision of child protection that emphasizes children's right to have lives free from violence in all its forms.

CROSS-CUTTING THEMES AND FUTURE DIRECTIONS: RESEARCH

Advancing Conceptualization and Measurement of Violence Against Children

Central to identifying the effects of VAC and building the evidence base for practice and policy is effective conceptualization and measurement. This volume provides key insights for the effective measurement of VAC. First, several of our authors highlight how children's experiences of violence shift across time, relative to their interaction with social systems, including variations in the manifestation of sociopolitical violence and shifts in their physical location that place them at risk for exposure to different types of violence across social macrosystems. Velez and colleagues (Chapter 3), for example, detail how Colombian children's experiences of structural and direct violence shift from premobilization to demobilization. Marks and colleagues (Chapter 4) elucidate how adverse experiences associated with migration vary across time, including the experience of premigration stressors and postmigration experiences of xenophobia.

Second, numerous chapters highlight the importance of capturing intersecting forms of direct, structural, and cultural violence—not as anecdotal information about the larger social context, but rather as central to ways in which VAC is exerted upon and experienced by children. Wessells and colleagues (Chapter 10), for example, present qualitative data that demonstrates the ways in which patriarchal norms intersect with direct forms of exploitation and sexual violence of young girls. Bernard and colleagues (Chapter 6) document how systemic racism in the United States pervades the social ecologies of Black youth, underscoring the critical importance of incorporating the evaluation of youths' experiences of racism into culturally informed assessments of adverse childhood experiences (Bernard et al., 2020). Together, these chapters suggest that psychologists should consider comprehensive assessments of VAC that (a) reflect developmental and time-varying changes in adversity, (b) include diverse forms of violence (i.e., direct, structural, cultural), and (c) include assessments of violence across multiple social-ecological systems. Since no one study can assess all of these constructs in depth, and because there is meaningful cross-context variation in the manifestations of violence, researchers should carefully consider their selection of assessments. Here, polyvictimization and intersectional frameworks are useful guides (Cho et al., 2013; Hamby & Grych, 2013), and the integration of community-based participatory methods may provide additional insight into intersections and forms of violence relative to specific research questions and local contexts.

Community-Based Participatory Methods and Mixed-Methods Analysis

Research in the field of peace studies has recently shifted to explore the "local turn." In contrast to liberal peace frameworks, which emphasize the role of international norms and institutions, the local turn has had an increased emphasis on peacebuilding not as a top-down endeavor, but rather as a bottom-up effort that is driven by authentic engagement with local voices. According to Mac Ginty and Richmond (2013),

> The local turn effectively allows for the reconstruction of emancipation, via the everyday, in an empathetic frame (solidarity), in which subjects have agency (meaning we are all subjects). Structural obstacles to peace can be better redressed, although this may demand radical solutions. (Mac Ginty & Richmond, 2013, p. 770)

This volume affirms the importance of attending to individual knowledge and experiences and highlights mixed-method research as a particularly fruitful approach for capturing more nuanced information. Moreover, the local turn—applied in the context of psychological research—suggests that contextually grounded and integrated modes of inquiry should build children's and families' feedback into the research design at every phase.

Townsend and colleagues (Chapter 15), for example, describe how the integration of youth and family feedback in intervention development was critical in developing appropriate content that effectively engaged youth. They also note, however, that there was disagreement and contention—a reminder that community-based and reciprocal forms of engagement are not a panacea or a simple solution, but that researchers and practitioners still must contend with the substantial within-context variability between persons. Boothby and colleagues' mixed-methods work on accelerated educational programs (Chapter 12) illuminates the critical value of qualitative data in the accurate interpretation of quantitative data. For example, parent and child interviews demonstrated that absenteeism from school was driven by structural violence that necessitated children's absence (e.g., needing to be home from school on food distribution days to support their families) and, further, that parents and teachers often went "above and beyond" to support student engagement around absenteeism given the high value placed on education. Without question, this integrated and multimethod data brings to light information that would have been lost or easily misconstrued if the research examined rates of absenteeism alone as predictors of educational engagement. Thus, the work in this volume affirms that robust mixed-methods work, and particularly the meaningful integration of well-done qualitative work, does not represent a "supplemental" mode of analysis that produces interesting but anecdotal information for the "more rigorous" quantitative data. Rather, this volume asserts that serious, integrated, multimodal, and participatory forms of inquiry should be the norm for rigorous psychological science (Hartmann et al., 2020).

Longitudinal Research That Addresses Multisystemic Risk and Resilience

Several of the works in this volume have indicated the importance of longitudinal research. Cummings and colleagues' (Chapter 2) work highlights how constructs such as intergroup bias shift across development, demonstrating direct implications for clinical work by examining how intergroup contact affects children's trajectories of bias over time (Merrilees et al., 2017). Such longitudinal work, Cummings and colleagues argue, forms the necessary foundation for robust, translational work on program development because it gives unique insights into potential causal processes that underlie the relationship between adversity and adaptive and maladaptive outcomes.

Although much research and clinical work focuses on the remediation of maladaptive outcomes, many of the authors in this volume also note the importance of strengths-based approaches that recognize and support children's resilience (Howell et al., Chapter 8; Marks et al., Chapter 4; Theron et al., Chapter 5). Consistent with the framing of this volume, contemporary resilience theory posits that resilience unfolds as a transactional process across social-ecological systems, operating dynamically across multiple scales (Ungar, 2021). Individual-level resilience is understood to include both manifested adapted outcomes and generative processes that reflect individuals' mounted responses to adversity (e.g., coping, resistance; Miller-Graff, 2022). In line with this perspective, the authors in this volume consider ways in which broader social structures thwart youths' access to needed resources and supports, making a compelling case for the argument that resilience, absent a broader justice-focused lens, would lead to an impoverished— and problematic—understanding of and response to adversity and intervention in the context of ongoing violence (Theron et al., Chapter 5).

Despite the importance of resilience and protective factors discussed throughout this volume, it is important to note that research on resilience interventions lags behind the research on psychological interventions for specific forms of psychopathology. This is in part driven by diversity in how resilience has been studied and defined, resulting in a gap in how resilience is often measured in intervention research as compared to how it is assessed in contemporary conceptualizations of the concept (Liu et al., 2021). Specifically, resilience interventions often include assessments that focus on coping and trait-based factors (e.g., hardiness, ego resilience) and rarely consider the multidimensional and multisystemic nature of resilience (Miller-Graff, 2022; Ungar, 2021), making it difficult to identify how basic and applied research in this domain are interrelated (Liu et al., 2021). As research and measurement on resilience in psychology continue to coalesce, there is new opportunity for advancing robust, theory-driven translational work that is guided by longitudinal, process-oriented research (e.g., Höltge et al., 2021).

CROSS-CUTTING THEMES AND FUTURE DIRECTIONS: PRACTICE

Multisystem and Developmentally Attuned Care

In addition to providing a synthesis of research evidence, each chapter of this volume takes up questions regarding the translation of research into practice. As all of our authors note, children's exposure to violence is associated with significant psychological distress, and access to high-quality, effective, and affordable care is critically important. Several models of individual support of children have been studied. Kinnish and colleagues (Chapter 7), for example, review the evidence for Trauma-Focused Cognitive Behavioral Therapy for survivors of child trafficking. This program has demonstrated wide utility, acceptability, and effectiveness in a large number of cultural contexts (Thomas et al., 2020). Not all children who have experienced violence, however, experience clinical levels of psychological distress, and not all who experience significant psychological distress experience posttraumatic stress, so other evidence-based interventions should be available to address a diverse range of experiences. In line with this, many of the authors in this volume also note the importance of strengths-based interventions that promote positive adaptation and flourishing (Marks et al., Chapter 4). Research on resilience- and strengths-based approaches to care for children exposed to violence should continue to be prioritized in research to further advance practice in this area.

Quite salient across the chapters is the importance of care that is well attuned to children's specific developmental needs and is meaningfully integrated with key social-ecological systems that support their protection. In Townsend and colleagues' chapter (Chapter 15), focused on digital mental health supports for Syrian refugee adolescents, one facilitator poignantly comments that the failure to incorporate parents into their children's care would be "like clapping with one hand." Chapter 13, by Puffer and colleagues, underscores the importance of familial involvement in care—documenting evidence for family-based interventions in a variety of low-income contexts. Chapter 11, by Hecker and colleagues, takes up how school-based interventions can be leveraged to prevent teacher violence, making this critical social system a safer and more secure one for children.

Violence Prevention

Consistent across many of the chapters is a focus on prevention. Although it is certainly necessary to support children who have experienced violence, preventing VAC in the first place is well within the purview of applied psychological research and should be a priority (e.g., Hecker et al., Chapter 11; Kinnish et al., Chapter 7; Puffer et al., Chapter 13). This includes recognizing that children who have experienced violence are vulnerable to additional violence, including retrafficking, engagement in armed groups, and sexual exploitation (Kinnish et al., Chapter 7; Velez et al., Chapter 2; Wessells et al., Chapter 10). In their multilevel analysis of systemic racism and its impact on Black youth in the United States, Bernard and colleagues (Chapter 6) point to ways in which responding to the adverse effects of racism on youth requires a system-wide approach that addresses the etiology of violence.

Research on violence prevention programs, however, has been challenged by limited effectiveness and difficulty with replication, with some studies even documenting backlash and iatrogenic effects of prevention programming (i.e., negative responses by the group receiving the program; Banyard & Hamby, 2022). Peace studies frameworks and the work in this volume provide valuable insights for prevention science. Prevention programs have most typically focused on the alleviation of direct violence (e.g., child maltreatment) or the attitudinal antecedents to direct violence (e.g., developmentally inappropriate expectations of child behavior) and do not fully incorporate an understanding of the structural and cultural violence that peace studies frameworks advance (e.g., reflexive relationship with direct violence; Christie, 2006; Lederach, 2015; Wessells & Kostelny, 2021). Psychological frameworks may greatly benefit from reconceptualizing large-scale prevention with conflict transformation frameworks while considering how to address both direct violence against children and the societal substrates that give rise to and enable them (e.g., racism, xenophobia). Emery and colleagues (Chapter 14), for example, review preliminary evidence for the effectiveness of restorative justice programs to prevent family violence.

Multisectoral Partnerships to Address Structural Violence

Authors of the chapters in this volume recognize that mental health supports are likely to be further strengthened by multisectoral partnerships that provide co-occurring interventions aimed at redressing structural violence. This approach is highly resonant with strategic peacebuilding, which asserts that multisectoral, integrated partnerships are necessary to achieve a just and sustainable peace (Lederach & Appleby, 2010; Shirch, 2008). Lederach and Appleby (2010) describe this process as follows,

> Peacebuilding that is strategic draws intentionally and shrewdly on the overlapping, imperfectly coordinated presences, activities, and resources of various international, transnational, national, regional, and local institutions, agencies, and movements that influence the causes, expressions, and outcomes of conflict. Strategic peacebuilders take advantage of emerging and established patterns of collaboration and interdependence for the purposes of reducing violence and alleviating the root causes of deadly conflict. (p. 22)

Although practicing psychologists are often trained in systems-focused case conceptualization, less common is an explicit consideration of integrated care that addresses multiple forms of violence and injustice. The works in this volume, however, suggest the promise of this approach. Puffer and colleagues (Chapter 13), for example, review promising pilot work on integrated parenting and poverty alleviation interventions. Velez and colleagues (Chapter 2) conclude that the integration of educational and vocational supports—in addition to psychosocial care—is an important aspect of holistic care for demobilizing youth in Colombia. Kinnish and colleagues (Chapter 7) discuss the importance of comprehensive care models that are designed not only to meet the complex psychosocial ramifications of child trafficking but also to prevent retrafficking. While psychologists are of course not trained or prepared to deliver all forms of care, the chapters in this volume speak to the importance of psychologists understanding the network of community resources and relationships that can be utilized to better support children's needs.

CROSS-CUTTING THEMES AND FUTURE DIRECTIONS: POLICY

Complex social problems cannot be fully understood by a single disciplinary perspective; rather, individuals with a range of training and experience contribute meaningful and diverse forms of knowledge. Psychologists rarely receive formal training in public policy, but insights from psychologists and from psychological research offer valuable contributions for policymaking. McKnight and colleagues (2005) outline several domains of potential contributions of psychological research to public policy, such as articulating theoretical models for intervention that describe mechanisms of change, conducting translational research that establishes the link between basic and applied research, and generating and synthesizing knowledge to inform evidence-based decision-making. Cummings and colleagues' (Chapter 2) four-tiered model of research is therefore a useful model for researchers examining all types of VAC, as it documents the progression of basic psychological research to theoretically driven, process-oriented intervention. The distinction between formal and informal social controls for violence (Emery & Abdullah, Chapter 14) also suggests that violence prevention efforts may be strengthened by multisystem coordination, through both formal policy supports and the development of informal channels for violence prevention via social and community relationships.

The chapters in this volume represent a synthesis of a great deal of research on VAC around the world; as such, this volume itself represents a valuable source of information for policymakers. As a volume focused on understanding, redressing, and preventing VAC, this resource is a particularly useful synthesis of information for working to end violence against children (Sustainable Development Goal [SDG] 16.2, "End abuse, exploitation, trafficking, and all forms of violence against and torture of children," United Nations, n.d.). Yet, what this edited volume emphasizes is that work on ending VAC must also engage other aspects of policy, such as poverty and inequality (SDGs 1 and 10). For example, the combined work of Theron and colleagues (Chapter 5), Bernard and colleagues (Chapter 6), and Puffer and colleagues (Chapter 13) offers important insights for how historic, cultural, and structural factors converge to perpetuate social exclusion and inequality. For those interested in education (SDG 5), the work by Velez and colleagues (Chapter 2) and Boothby and colleagues (Chapter 12) examines how high-quality education supports children who have experienced violence. Hecker and colleagues (Chapter 11) provide insights into how to further protect children from harm in school environments. The integration of insights across domains of psychological research and across sectors is already in progress, such as through the INSPIRE framework for child protection (World Health Organization, 2016), which is a seven-point framework that carefully draws together global research on child protection to suggest comprehensive and multisystem efforts at violence prevention (Wessells & Kostelny, 2021).

CONCLUSIONS

Violence against children is a complex social problem that has significant short- and long-term ramifications for children's well-being and health. Research, practice, and policy aiming to prevent VAC and support children affected by VAC should focus on integrating sources of information across social-ecological levels. Such work will continue to advance understanding of the processes that underlie trajectories of risk and resilience and the mechanisms at play within effective interventions. Researchers, practitioners, and policymakers should also engage in multisectoral efforts that are characterized by reflexive cross-sector learning and the incorporation of diverse perspectives. As evidenced by this volume, psychologists have much to contribute to the dialogue on how best to support children's flourishing and uphold their right to have lives free from violence in all its forms. In partnership with others, this work can continue to advance a vision of sustainable and just peace for children that stands to contribute to intergenerational flourishing.

REFERENCES

Banyard, V., & Hamby, S. (2022). *Strengths-based prevention: Reducing violence and other public health problems.* American Psychological Association. https://doi.org/10.1037/0000267-000

Bernard, D. L., Calhoun, C. D., Banks, D. E., Halliday, C. A., Hughes-Halbert, C., & Danielson, C. K. (2020). Making the "C-ACE" for a culturally-informed adverse childhood experiences framework to understand the pervasive mental health impact of racism on Black youth. *Journal of Child & Adolescent Trauma, 14.* https://doi.org/10.1007/s40653-020-00319-9

Cho, S., Crenshaw, K. W., & McCall, L. (2013). Toward a field of intersectionality studies: Theory, applications, and praxis. *Signs: Journal of Women in Culture and Society, 38*(4), 785–810. https://doi.org/10.1086/669608

Christie, D. J. (2006). What is peace psychology the psychology of? *Journal of Social Issues, 62*(1), 1–17. https://doi.org/10.1111/j.1540-4560.2006.00436.x

Hamby, S., & Grych, J. H. (2013). *The web of violence: Exploring connections among different forms of interpersonal violence and abuse.* Springer.

Hartmann, W. E., Gone, J. P., & Saint Arnault, D. M. (2020). Reconsidering rigor in psychological science: Lessons from a brief clinical ethnography. *Qualitative Psychology, 7*(2), 169.

Höltge, J., Theron, L., & Ungar, M. (2021). A multisystemic perspective on the temporal interplay between adolescent depression and resilience-supporting individual and social resources. *Journal of Affective Disorders, 297.* https://doi.org/10.1016/j.jad.2021.10.030

Lederach, J. (2015). *Little book of conflict transformation: Clear articulation of the guiding principles by a pioneer in the field.* Simon and Schuster.

Lederach, J. P., & Appleby, R. S. (2010). Strategic peacebuilding: An overview. In Daniel Philpott & Gerard F. Powers (Eds.), *Strategies of peace: Transforming conflict in a violent world* (pp. 19–44). Oxford University Press.

Liu, J. J. W., Ein, N., Gervasio, J., Battaion, M., & Fung, K. (2021). The pursuit of resilience: A meta-analysis and systematic review of resilience-promoting interventions. *Journal of Happiness Studies, 23,* 1–21. https://doi.org/10.1007/s10902-021-00452-8

Mac Ginty, R., & Richmond, O. P. (2013). The local turn in peace building: A critical agenda for peace. *Third World Quarterly, 34*(5), 763–783. https://doi.org/10.1080/01436597.2013.800750

McKnight, K. M., Sechrest, L., & McKnight, P. E. (2005). Psychology, psychologists, and public policy. *Annual Review of Clinical Psychology, 1,* 557–576. https://doi.org/10.1146/annurev.clinpsy.1.102803.144130

Merrilees, C. E., Taylor, L. K., Baird, R., Goeke-Morey, M. C., Shirlow, P., & Cummings, E. M. (2017). Neighborhood effects of intergroup contact on change in youth intergroup bias. *Journal of Youth and Adolescence, 47,* 77–87. https://doi.org/10.1007/s10964-017-0684-6

Miller-Graff, L. E. (2022). The multidimensional taxonomy of individual resilience. *Trauma, Violence, & Abuse, 23*(2), 660–675. https://doi.org/10.1177/1524838020967329

Schirch, L. (2008). *Strategic peacebuilding: State of the field.* Women in Security Conflict Management and Peace.

Thomas, F. C., Puente-Duran, S., Mutschler, C., & Monson, C. M. (2020). Trauma-focused cognitive behavioral therapy for children and youth in low and middle-income countries: A systematic review. *Child and Adolescent Mental Health, 27*(2). https://doi.org/10.1111/camh.12435

Ungar, M. (2021). *Multisystemic resilience: Adaptation and transformation in contexts of change.* Oxford University Press.

United Nations. (n.d.). *SDG indicators: Metadata repository.* https://unstats.un.org/sdgs/metadata/?Text=&Goal=16&Target=16.2

World Health Organization. (2016). *INSPIRE: Seven strategies for ending violence against children.*

Wessells, M. G., & Kostelny, K. (2021). Understanding and ending violence against children: A holistic approach. *Peace and Conflict: Journal of Peace Psychology, 27*(1), 3. https://doi.org/10.1037/pac0000475

For the benefit of digital users, indexed terms that span two pages (e.g., 52–53) may, on occasion, appear on only one of those pages.

Tables and figures are indicated by an italic *t* and *f* following the page/paragraph number.